CLINICAL APPLICATIONS OF

Evidence-Based Family Interventions

JACQUELINE CORCORAN

Clinical Applications of Evidence-Based Family Interventions

OXFORD
UNIVERSITY PRESS

2003

OXFORD

UNIVERSITY PRESS

Oxford   New York
Auckland   Bangkok   Buenos Aires   Cape Town   Chennai
Dar es Salaam   Delhi   Hong Kong   Istanbul   Karachi   Kolkata
Kuala Lumpur   Madrid   Melbourne   Mexico City   Mumbai   Nairobi
São Paulo   Shanghai   Taipei   Tokyo   Toronto

Copyright © 2003 by Oxford University Press, Inc.

Published by Oxford University Press, Inc.
198 Madison Avenue, New York, New York 10016

www.oup.com

Oxford is a registered trademark of Oxford University Press

Library of Congress Cataloging-in-Publication Data
Corcoran, Jacqueline.
Clinical applications of evidence-based family interventions : / by
Jacqueline Corcoran.
    p. cm.
Includes bibliographical references and index
ISBN: 978-0-19-514952-4
1. Family social work.   2. Family psychotherapy.   I. Title.
HV697 .C67 2003
362.82'86—dc21   2002006008

Printed in the United States of America
on acid-free paper

To Mark

I want to call the reader's attention to this excellent book, which systematically presents evidence-based practices for complex clinical disorders, while applying numerous clinical case scenarios in each chapter. The central role of evidence-based practice guidelines in facilitating family treatment has emerged during the past decade. This book is the first to bring together the interdisciplinary practice research on family treatment and apply it to complex externalizing problems and mental disorders prevalent throughout the life span. *Clinical Applications of Evidence-Based Family Interventions* has been designed to serve two purposes:

1. To examine the most effective family intervention practices based on the outcome studies and other reliable empirical evidence.
2. To provide detailed applications of the evidence-based interventions through case illustrations.

Dr. Jacqueline Corcoran, with the valuable assistance of Dr. Joseph Walsh and Dr. Patricia Gleason-Wynn, has completed a masterful and well-written text. I applaud the originality, conceptual rigor, and integration of bridging theory with evidence-based practice. I anticipate that this critically important clinical handbook will be treasured by clinicians, researchers, and graduate students for years to come.

This volume focuses on family approaches (i.e., behavioral parent training, multisystemic family treatment, structural family therapy, and cognitive-behavioral intervention) with attention deficit/hyperactivity disorder (ADHD), oppositional defiance disorder, conduct disorder, juvenile offenders, substance abuse, adolescent pregnancy, adolescent physical abuse, and mothers of sexual abuse victims. It also examines psychoeducational groups with ADHD, parents of persons with schizophrenia, and caregivers of older adults.

In conclusion, this valuable book will increase all social workers' and counselors' understanding of evidence-based family treatment strategies and guidelines. I highly recommend this original and timely book to graduate students and to beginning and seasoned practitioners.

Albert R. Roberts, Ph.D.
Professor of Social Work and Criminal Justice
Faculty of Arts and Sciences
Rutgers, the State University of New Jersey

ACKNOWLEDGMENTS

To those who read and reviewed chapters—Melissa Abell, Kristin Garell, Elizabeth Hutchinson, Mo-Yee Lee, Holly Matto, Mary Katherine O'Connor, Jane Hanvey Phillips, and Joseph Walsh—I appreciate your comments, ideas, and suggestions. Special gratitude to Albert Roberts for recruiting me as an Oxford author and for useful editorial suggestions. For preparation of the genograms, I am grateful to Rich Klein. To my contributors, Joseph Walsh and Pat Gleason-Wynn, thank you for all your hard work. Further appreciation to Joseph Walsh for his help in researching the family treatment of bipolar disorder.

CONTENTS

PATRICIA GLEASON-WYNN, LMSW-ACP, has a Ph.D. in social work from the University of Texas at Arlington. Her primary area of interest is gerontology with a particular focus on nursing home social work practice. For the past 19 years, she has worked with older people living in the community and in nursing homes. Currently, she teaches part time in the School of Social Work at UT, Arlington, and provides social work services to two nursing homes in the Fort Worth area. She was the director of the Bachelor of Social Work Program until January 2000 and was formerly an assistant professor at Southwest Texas State University in San Marcos, where she taught from 1995.

Dr. Gleason-Wynn coauthored the book *Social Work Practice in the Nursing Home Setting* (with K. Fonville, 1996). As the director of Elder Care Specialists, her consulting company, she is involved in assessing the needs of community-based frail older adults, planning care management services, presenting community seminars on aging-related topics, and providing litigation consultation in aging-related cases, including will contests and guardianship hearings.

JOSEPH WALSH, Ph.D., LCSW, is an associate professor of social work at Virginia Commonwealth University. He received his academic degrees from Ohio State University. Dr. Walsh has been a direct services practitioner in the field of mental health since 1974, first in a psychiatric hospital and later in community mental health center settings. He has provided services to older adult and general outpatient populations but specializes in services to persons with serious mental illnesses and their families. His writing focuses on clinical social work and serious mental illness. He is the author of *Clinical Case Management with Persons Having Mental Illness: A Relationship-Based Perspective* (2000) and coauthor (with Kia Bentley) of *The Social Worker and Psychotropic Medications* (2001).

CLINICAL APPLICATIONS OF

Evidence-Based Family Interventions

Introduction

While many excellent books cover family therapy theory, none has a unique emphasis on the evidence that supports such theories nor on how to apply these theories. And yet the emphasis on evidence-based practice is becoming increasingly important with the push of managed care to require accountability in mental health and other health care services (Gibelman, 2002). Practitioners have a responsibility to the families that seek services to intervene with the most effective theoretical methods possible, methods that have been tested and that have proven clinical utility.

But what busy practitioner has time to search through numerous databases, retrieve, and then sift through all the research to locate the studies that can inform practice? And what agency has the resources to commit to such a task? A further problem is, if such information is finally gathered, what does one do with it? How does this information translate into practice?

Clinical Applications of Evidence-Based Family Interventions was developed to answer these questions, to familiarize the practitioner with evidence-based approaches for common problems for which families seek treatment, and then to illustrate, in detail with clinical vignettes, how to apply these theories in practice.

■ Definition of Evidence-Based Practice

"Evidence-based" involves a process of locating research findings through electronic searches in a particular problem area to decide the intervention that has the best available support. In order to promote confidence in one approach over another for a defined problem, priority is given to studies using experimental designs (randomization to treatment condition[s] and a control group, pretest/posttest/follow-up, data collection with standardized measures), followed by comparison-group studies with randomization to treatment conditions, then comparison group designs with non-randomization, and finally pretest/posttest designs. This book focuses on portraying the family approaches that have emerged for treating certain problems after critical evaluation of the available outcome research. In the following section, the selection process is further detailed. (For discussion on evidence-based practice, please see Chambless & Hollon, 1998; Cournoyer & Powers, 2002; Gambrill, 1999; Sackett, Robinson, Rosenberg, & Haynes, 1997; Thyer, 2002.)

■ Problem Areas Chosen

Clinical Applications of Evidence-Based Family Interventions is organized by problem area. For a problem to be included, sufficient research must have demonstrated that a particular family approach is helpful. The reader will note that, for child and adolescent problems, the emphasis is on *externalizing* disorders, such as attention deficit/hyperactivity disorder (ADHD), oppositional defiant disorder, conduct disorder, and substance abuse, rather than *internalizing* problems, such as depression and eating disorders. This reflects the current state of the research, which may be explained by several different factors. First, externalizing problems tend to create more problems for others than they do for clients themselves, requiring the involvement of family members. Second, conduct problems are the foremost reason for child referrals to treatment (American Psychiatric Association [APA], 2000; Kazdin, 1995). In comparison to the enormous body of work conducted on family approaches to externalizing disorders, the family treatment of internalizing disorders is very small. For instance, only one study was located on a family systems approach to adolescent depression, and this study found that individual cognitive-behavioral treatment was more effective than either family systems treatment or individual supportive therapy (Brent et al., 1997).

In the area of eating disorders, the family treatment studies are characterized by methodological limitations (see Corcoran, 2000). In addition, studies were conducted in the 1980s with little recent research on family approaches. Taken as a whole, the research fails to provide the practitioner with clear direction on the theoretical approach to take and the role that family treatment plays, although family and marital components are seen as important aspects of treatment (see Foreyt, Poston, Winebarger, & McGavin, 1998). For these reasons, the treatment of eating disorders is excluded from this volume.

Bipolar disorder is another disorder for which a psychoeducational family component to treatment has been recommended (e.g., Miklowitz & Goldstein, 1997). Little research has been published on its efficacy up to this point with the exception of Glick, Clarkin, Haas, Spencer, and Chen (1991) and Miklowitz et al. (2000). Studies indicate much promise for family treatment in terms of delaying relapse. However, until more research has been published on the studies currently under way (e.g., George, Friedman, & Miklowitz, 2000), the decision was made to exclude the treatment from this volume.

Finally, an area of controversy in the family therapy literature involves the couples treatment of domestic violence. Foremost are concerns for victim safety and the responsibility that is implicitly placed on the victim in couples treatment (see Corcoran, 2000, for a review). In examining the research on couples treatment with family violence, studies tend to be marked by methodological limitations. A relatively recent and rigorous study reported that men who were court mandated to attend treatment performed better in the couples groups when alcohol was being treated with Antabuse (Brannen & Rubin, 1996). This program maintained many safeguards for the protection of women, however, which seemed to demand resources that many agencies would be unable to supply. Given the controversies and the lack of strong and consistent support for the efficacy of a couples approach, this volume offers the prevailing practice conclusion that couples treatment of family violence should follow individual or group treatment of the violent partner. For this reason, the couples treatment of family violence is not included in this volume.

Given the criteria for selection, the problems chosen for focus here include attention deficit/hyperactivity disorder, oppositional defiant disorder, physical abuse, sexual abuse, adolescent conduct disorder, adolescent substance abuse, juvenile offending, adolescent pregnancy prevention, adult substance abuse, depression, schizophrenia, and caregiving for older persons.

Problem areas are presented in the order they may appear developmentally and are further divided into clinical disorders and social problems. Clinical disorders are defined by the American Psychiatric Association's *Diagnostic and Statistical Manual of Mental Disorders* (2000) criteria (attention deficit/hyperactivity disorder, oppositional defiant disorder, substance abuse, depression, schizophrenia). Social problems are seen as those that arise out of the environmental context (physical abuse, sexual abuse, juvenile offending, teen pregnancy, caregiving for older persons). The overlap between clinical disorders and social problems, however, is recognized. For instance, the majority of adolescents who are in the law enforcement system for juvenile offending can be diagnosed with conduct disorder or oppositional defiant disorder. In addition, the *Diagnostic and Statistical Manual* has been criticized for its emphasis on individual pathology rather than viewing disorders as arising, at least in part, from an environmental context (Kutchins & Kirk, 1997). It is acknowledged that the division between clinical and social disorders is somewhat artificial, but it has been employed as a way to organize chapters around the problems with which families may present across the lifespan.

Following this framework, first the childhood clinical disorders are covered (attention deficit/hyperactivity disorder and oppositional defiant disorder). Then, social problems that often begin in childhood are discussed (physical abuse and sexual abuse). Adolescent conduct disorder and substance abuse are the clinical disorders followed by the social problems that may present in adolescence, which include juvenile offending and teen pregnancy (the overlap between clinical and social problems is represented in chapter 7, on multisystemic treatment of juvenile offending, substance abuse, and teen pregnancy). Adult clinical disorders include substance abuse, depression, and schizophrenia. A social problem involving older adulthood involves caregiving for elder persons.

Family Theories

In the early days of family therapy, theorists presumed that family therapy could cure all nature of ills, such as diabetes (e.g., Minuchin et al., 1975), eating disorders (e.g., Minuchin, Rosman, & Baker, 1978), and schizophrenia (Bateson, Jackson, Haley, & Weakland, 1956). At present, much greater understanding of the complexity of disorders has emerged with the biopsychosocial framework. Biological and genetic vulnerabilities, a certain cognitive psychological style operating in the individual, as well as coercive interactions or escalating feedback loops in families may all play roles, among other contributing factors. In recognition of the complexity of disorders and problems, many of the models that have gained empirical support, such as multisystemic family therapy, psychoeducational approaches, and functional family therapy,[1] are integrative models, which combine different approaches.

Problem areas described in each chapter intersect with the theories for which there is research support (psychoeducation, behavioral parent training, solution-focused therapy, cognitive-behavioral treatment, structural family therapy, and multisystemic treatment). The main emphasis is the application of the theory, illustrating how the techniques and the particular perspective can be employed with a case study family.

Some definitions of *evidence-based* have included empirical examination of individual families' progress in treatment, as well as knowledge of the research in a particular problem area (see Cournoyer & Powers, 2002, for a review). Discussion of measurement instruments and their use with case study families is not an emphasis here because of space considerations. However, the interested reader is referred to Corcoran (2000) for recommended measurement instruments for use with the different problem areas.

The limitations of applying the criteria of evidence-based practice must also be acknowledged. A certain selection process occurs as theories are chosen for empirical study. The reader will notice, for example, that many chapters discuss behavioral and cognitive-behavioral approaches. This content reflects the state of the research. Cognitive-behavioral approaches arose out of a research paradigm and, to some degree, are easier to test than other models since they rely on educational materials, skills training, and observable phenomena. To illustrate the bias in the research, in 1990, Kazdin, Bass, Ayers, and Rodgers

1. While functional family therapy (Alexander & Parsons, 1982) is empirically supported for the treatment of juvenile offending, a chapter on this model is not included since adolescent conduct disorder and juvenile offending, adolescent substance abuse, and teen pregnancy are covered in other chapters.

conducted a review of two decades of the child and adolescent therapy outcome literature. They found that behavioral and cognitive-behavioral methods accounted for half of the studies. Other practice orientations and methods, including family therapy, psychodynamic therapy, relationship-centered therapy, play therapy, and art therapy, each comprised less than 5% of studies (Kazdin et al., 1990). The state of the research appears to have changed little since then although it is hoped that in response to the current environment, proponents of other theoretical approaches will add their perspective to the research.

Format

The reader will find that chapters will only briefly summarize key points of theory since, as mentioned, many other family therapy books have as their emphasis theory (see, for example, Franklin & Jordan, 1999; Goldenberg & Goldenberg, 2000; Nichols & Schwartz, 2001). Boxes delineating theory and additional resources the reader can consult will be provided in each chapter. The empirical support for the particular theory will only be briefly described; for further details of the research studies supporting each theory by problem area, the reader is referred to Corcoran (2000).

The bulk of each chapter will be devoted to the application of the theory through the case study. A visual diagram will be provided for each family so that the reader can follow the relationships involved.[2] Sessions are detailed, highlighted by dialogue, with subsequent sessions summarized for the reader. Each chapter essentially provides detailed treatment plans with step-by-step illustrations of how these perspectives can be applied. *Clinical Applications of Evidence-Based Family Interventions* serves to provide both practitioners and students with the practical knowledge to apply both theory and evidence-based practice.

One objective of the case study is to relay the complexities and realities of family treatment through the example. For instance, chapters 1 and 2 cover the same case, a child who has been diagnosed with oppositional defiant disorder and ADHD. These two diagnoses often

2. Diagrammatic notation was drawn from McGoldrick and Gerson's (1985) excellent book on genograms. However, the symbols of family dynamics and intergenerational patterns were avoided due to their theoretical association with Bowenian family therapy.

co-occur and in clinical settings might represent 90% of children who seek treatment for ADHD (Abikoff & Klein, 1992).

Discussion of how to overcome barriers and how to help families progress is a focus of the chapters with the main theme of using a collaborative approach with families. The reader will note that while some of the theoretical frameworks are skills or educationally based, services are still administered in a style that is collaborative and process-based in nature.

Cases presented are those that reflect the current practice environment. The author either personally worked with these families, they are families from cases that she supervised, or they are composites based on her practice experience (the information in all cases has been de-identified). Because the author's expertise is mainly in the areas of child, couple, and family services, two other authors, Joseph Walsh, currently associate professor at the Virginia Commonwealth University School of Social Work, and Patricia Gleason-Wynn, director of Elder Care Specialists and adjunct instructor at the University of Texas at Arlington School of Social Work, were called upon to contribute their expertise in the family treatment of schizophrenia and of caregivers of the elderly, respectively. With their contributions, *Clinical Applications of Evidence-Based Family Interventions* conveys effective family treatment approaches to problems that families may experience throughout the lifespan.

■■■■ Audience

The audience for this book includes students and practitioners, who are most often interested in the question: What do you actually do with a real-life family when using a particular theory? The book also attempts to respond to the pressures that students and practitioners feel to demonstrate the validity of their approaches. Hence, *Clinical Applications of Evidence-Based Family Interventions* provides a unique, integrated perspective; here, problem area, theory, research, and application of techniques come together.

The audience for this book is not limited to any particular mental health or helping professions field even though the author's background is social work. Therefore, potential audiences include individuals from the social work, counseling, clinical psychology, marriage and family therapy, nursing, and psychiatric fields. The reason for this breadth is that the various helping professions are all operating under the same pressures and environmental demands for evidence for their services. In addition, agencies that serve particular populations or problems often employ individuals who have been trained across different disciplines. It is the author's hope that, no matter the background of the reader, *Clinical Applications of Evidence-Based Family Interventions* will help the reader understand the application of both theory and evidence-based practice to families that seek help for their suffering.

PART I

Childhood

CLINICAL DISORDERS

SOCIAL PROBLEMS

1 Psychoeducation with Attention Deficit/Hyperactivity Disorder

▬▬ Presenting Problem

Mrs. Patsy Abell, a Caucasian woman, age 32, brought her son, Andy Stevens, an 8-year-old third-grader, who was school-referred, to an outpatient mental health clinic. Mrs. Abell complained that Andy's problems were not confined to the school; they also happened at home. For example, when she asked him to do his chores or his homework, he argued or flat-out refused. Similarly, her requests that he *not* do something (blowing a whistle, banging a stick in the house) met with his continued persistence in doing the activity, almost as if he derived pleasure from annoying family members.

His teacher reported the same behaviors (arguing about teacher commands, refusing to do schoolwork) and that he blamed others (e.g., the student sitting next to him) for his disruptive behavior. Andy's conduct grades, ever since kindergarten, were poor. He barely eked by each grade, and his math and science grades were currently at failing levels.

When asked about Andy's ability to attend to tasks, Mrs. Abell reported his distractibility (looking out the window at home or at school when he's supposed to do his work). She added, "He doesn't listen at all when you tell him something," but Mrs. Abell attributed this tendency to pure spite. "And he's always losing things. I tell him he'd lose his head if it wasn't attached to his neck." He misplaced his math book; he forgot to bring his homework home. "Pretty convenient, huh?" Mrs. Abell said, implying that he does these things to get out of work. When asked about activities he enjoyed, she said Andy loves helping out at the fish and tackle shop (the business she helps her husband run). Her husband said Andy seems like a different kid there.

Mrs. Abell reported that she was married to her former husband for 9 years, and he was physically abusive to her but not to their children, Nikki (now age 10) and Andy. Mrs. Abell's ex-husband hung around with a motorcycle gang and used to have a problem with drugs (speed) during their early marriage, but now only drank heavily. He left her 2 years ago to be with his current girlfriend. Mrs. Abell relayed that the children have regular visitation with their father. The children said they like his girlfriend and that he is not drunk when they are over there, although he sometimes drinks beer.

One measure Mrs. Abell had taken to protect the children against her ex-husband's drinking was to drop the children off and pick them up from visitation so there was less risk when he drinks. She informed the children to call her if he had been drinking to the point where they felt uncomfortable. Mrs. Abell feared no further violence now that she was remarried.

"What's Andy's behavior like when he's at his father's?" the practitioner asked.

"His daddy can yell pretty good. Andy always did obey him more than me."

Mrs. Abell was able to see that Andy might have felt threatened by his father's violence, which included shoving, pushing, and restraining Mrs. Abell if she tried to leave. Mrs. Abell said this occurred on average once a month when her husband drank whiskey instead of his usual beer. The police were never involved.

After assessing the level and frequency of the violence, the practitioner asked Mrs. Abell how the children reacted during these episodes. She said that Andy and his sister would usually hide in the closet and cry. (See figure 1.1 for the genogram of this family.)

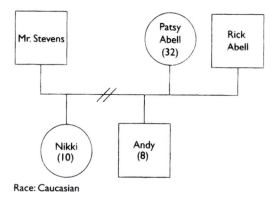

Figure 1.1. Psychoeducation Case Study: Andy Stevens's Family

◼◼ Diagnostic Information

The school initiated testing due to Andy's school failure and poor conduct grades. As part of testing, Mrs. Abell and his teacher were interviewed, and each completed standardized behavior rating scales. Andy also completed intelligence and achievement tests. Mrs. Abell produced the results of these tests, which revealed no cognitive deficit or learning disability as the source of his poor school performance. However, he did meet American Psychiatric Association (2000) criteria for attention deficit/hyperactivity disorder (ADHD) (more specifically predominantly inattentive type) and oppositional defiant disorder (ODD). The school psychologist recommended that Mrs. Abell take the school testing information to a medical doctor for evaluation. Meanwhile, Andy was referred to a self-control skills training group at the school due to his symptoms.

◼◼ Differential Diagnosis

Although the school recognized Andy's symptoms of ADHD and ODD, Andy's history must also be taken into account. Andy witnessed ongoing violence for years, which could result in posttraumatic stress disorder (PTSD) symptoms. Some of the symptoms of PTSD, such as "acting or feeling as if the traumatic event were recurring," "problems concentrating," and "avoiding stimuli associated with trauma," can be confused with symptoms of inattention (Weinstein, Staffelbach, & Biaggio, 2000, p. 368). Other symptoms of trauma might include "inability to appropriately inhibit response due to hypervigilance" and "physiological reactivity when exposed to cues symbolizing an aspect of the trauma," which resemble symptoms of hyperactivity or impulsivity (Weinstein et al., 2000, p. 368). As a result, it was possible that his symptoms were derived from PTSD rather than ADHD. A careful assessment, relying on multiple sources of data (child interview, parent interview, standardized measures), was made to determine whether PTSD plays a role in Andy's symptoms.

The practitioner asked his mother if Andy showed symptoms, such as nightmares, hypervigilance, or repetitive play themes of violence. Mrs. Abell denied that her children showed any of these effects or that they had been physically or sexually abused.

The practitioner conducted an individual assessment of Andy to see if posttraumatic stress were playing a role in his symptoms. In the first part of the individual assessment of Andy, he didn't talk at all, not even making eye contact. He looked around the office, ignoring the practitioner as various attempts were made to establish rapport, and would not even draw or play with the office toys.

The second time Andy came in, he had been prompted by his mother to cooperate with the practitioner. He started by drawing a picture of his family. While he drew, he answered some questions, saying his father hit his mother but "it didn't really hurt."

By his account, Andy seemed to enjoy visits with his father and liked his father's girlfriend. His father drank beer "but not that much." Andy also liked Rick, his stepfather of one year, although he "yells a lot." Andy denied any nightmares. He was able to complete the Trauma Symptom Checklist for Children (Briere, 1996) by the practitioner reading the questions. Scoring did not reveal posttraumatic stress.

Therefore, the symptoms of ADHD and ODD still seemed to account for Andy's presentation. The comorbid diagnoses of both ADHD and ODD are exceedingly common in clinical settings and may be as high as 90% (Abikoff & Klein, 1992). Indeed, between 30 and 50% of children with ADHD develop conduct or oppositional defiant disorder by the ages of 8 to 12. The psychoeducational model described in this chapter will target ADHD and its concomitant disorders.

▬▬ Overview of Psychoeducation

Psychoeducational approaches began with the treatment of schizophrenia (see chapter 10 for discussion of this literature) after research revealed the association between *expressed emotion* in the family (hostility, criticism, and overinvolvement) and higher relapse rates in the individual with schizophrenia (Brown, Monck, Carstairs, & Wing, 1962). In contrast to family systems models (e.g., Bateson, Jackson, Haley, & Weakland, 1956), psychoeducational models do not see the family as the source of the illness; rather, illness is largely determined by genetic vulnerabilities. From the psychoeducational perspective, the family's role is to create an atmosphere conducive to continued remission and adequate functioning at considerably less stress to family members. This approach contrasts with the early family systems view that altering family interaction patterns could result in cure of the identified patient (Anderson, Reiss, & Hogarty, 1986). (See also box 1.1 for a brief summary of the psychoeducational framework and resources for the reader.)

Box 1.1

Key Points of Psychoeducational Framework and Additional Resources

Key Points

- Psychoeducational approaches began in the field of schizophrenia (see Anderson, Reiss, & Hogarty, 1986) and have been extended to the family treatment of other disorders viewed as largely genetically determined, such as ADHD.
- Through psychoeducation, the family's role is to create an atmosphere conducive to adequate functioning of the individual with the disorder at considerably less stress to family members.
- Parents are educated about the disorder and available treatment. They are also taught strategies for managing their children with ADHD and coping strategies for themselves to help manage the stress involved.
- Psychoeducation allows for cognitive-behavioral interventions integrated within the model, as a shared assumption is that information and knowledge mediates distress.

Additional Resources

C. M. Anderson, D. J. Reiss, & G. E. Hogarty. (1986). *Schizophrenia and the family: A practitioner's guide to psychoeducation and management.* New York: Guilford.

R. A. Barkley. (2000). *Taking charge of ADHD* (Revised ed.). New York: Guilford.

▆▆▆ Psychoeducation and ADHD

Psychoeducation is appropriate to ADHD because it is believed to have a biological and, specifically, a genetic basis (Barkley, 1998). Second, the diagnosis of ADHD in a child brings significant challenges to family functioning in terms of increased parenting stress, conflict with siblings, depression in mothers, abuse of substances, marital conflict, and an increased likelihood of separation and divorce of the parents (Barkley, 1998; Pelham, Wheeler, & Chronis, 1998). A psychoeducational approach may reduce the level of strain on family members through education of parents on helpful strategies for managing a child with the disorder. The focus on education rather than therapy reflects the psychoeducational assumption that families are healthy and functional and as such may contribute to the management of a member's disorder (Franklin & Jordan, 1999).

In the ADHD treatment field, the psychoeducational approach has dominated as a way to work with families, although it is generally not named as such in the literature, with the exception of Shelton, et al. (2000). However, the combination of strategies—sharing information about the disorder and medication treatment, teaching parents behavioral management strategies with their children, and using cognitive strategies to manage parental frustrations—essentially translates into a psychoeducational approach.

Most studies on family treatment of ADHD are instead theoretically associated with behavioral or cognitive-behavioral schools (e.g., Anastopoulos, Shelton, DuPaul, & Guevremont, 1993; Basu & Aniruddha, 1996; Frankel, Myatt, Cantwell, & Feinberg, 1997). The cognitive-behavioral orientation is compatible with a psychoeducational approach they share an assumption that providing information can mediate distress (Nichols & Schwartz, 2001). Indeed, theories that help family members manage the disorder, such as training them in behavioral management strategies, can be integrated within the psychoeducaitonal approach. (See chapter 2 for an application of behavioral parent training for the treatment of Andy's oppositional and defiant symptoms.)

The treatment needs of children with ADHD and their families are complex and intense, with multimodal approaches, including medication, psychosocial interventions for both child and parent, and school-based approaches, necessary to produce adequate outcome (MTA Cooperative Group, 1999; Satterfield, Satterfield, & Schell, 1987). Psycho-education can help parents organize the many and varied treatment needs of their children. Education about the disorder helps family members revise their often too-high expectations for the child and re-place these with clear and reasonable goals. Education also aids the family in creating the type of environment that is most conducive for optimal functioning.

Case Application

In this chapter, the case application will be used to illustrate the main components of a psychoeducational approach. The application will first involve *joining* with Mrs. Abell to help her recognize her stress and cope with it. Education about ADHD follows, which involves a de-scription of the disorder, its prevalence, and a discussion of its causes. A rationale for the importance of including all caregivers is provided, as well as methods to encourage their participation. Education about medication and interfacing with the medical system is followed by in-formation on risk factors for the disorder and strategies to ameliorate risk. Methods to reinforce children's social skills are taught to parents, as are strategies for interfacing with the school system. Finally, edu-cation about ODD is provided. Chapter 2 will continue with the psy-choeducational approach for Andy with a focus on strategies for be-havioral management of his ODD symptoms.

Joining

When parents bring their child into a clinic setting for disruptive dis-orders, they tend to expect the practitioner to work alone with the child (Morrissey-Kane & Prinz, 1999). For example, Mrs. Abell began by say-ing, "I just want you to talk to Andy, find out why he's doing those things." However, McMahon (1994) suggests that only when children succeed at externally controlled programs should parent training and classroom management programs segue into those that are more inter-nally based, such as cognitive-behavioral programs.

The practitioner started by explaining that she first wanted to work with Mrs. Abell rather than dividing the session between parent and child. Once there was some environmental structure for Andy, the practitioner could work with Andy on controlling his behaviors and communicating appropriately. She could also process with him his reactions to the family violence, his parents' divorce, and his mother's recent marriage.

The practitioner offered several other reasons to convince Mrs. Abell to act as the initial focus of the intervention. "First, you are the most important person to your child, more than I ever will be. If I work with you on some things, you can be much more effective than I could ever hope to be in my hour a week." Like most parents, Mrs. Abell was pleased to admit that she played a dominant role in her child's life. A second reason involved the lack of feasibility associated with seeing both parent and child during the same session as that left Andy and his sister alone in the waiting room for some time. The office manager had already complained about their unruly behavior. A third reason involved children's cognitive limitations. "Young children have a difficult time learning a new behavior in one place, such as my office, and then generalizing that skill to another context. For example, if I teach your son some techniques for the classroom, it will be hard for him to remember when he is actually in the classroom. That's why it's good that he's in the social skills training group at school, so it's right there in the environment with the other kids he sees. And if you can learn what I will be teaching him, you can prompt him for these behaviors at home and then reinforce him for doing them."

Mrs. Abell was interested to hear that working with the parent to change the child's environment was a way to make treatment move along more quickly. "Work with children tends to go slowly. Even with a child who is able to listen and follow directions, attention can only be focused on one subject, especially if it is uncomfortable or unfamiliar, for only so long. You describe Andy as having some difficulties with paying attention and complying, so that would make the work even more challenging."

A final way to engage Mrs. Abell was to describe the benefits to her. The next session would cover the stress to parents of having a child diagnosed with ADHD, as one of the goals of a psychoeducational approach is to reduce the burden associated with caregiving.

◼︎ Dealing with Maternal Stress

The stress experienced by a parent with a child with ADHD is at least as severe as that experienced by parents of children with autism, a developmental disorder that is far more serious and pervasive. "The excessive, demanding, intrusive, and generally high-intensity behavior of children with ADHD as well as their clear impairment in self-control, naturally elicit greater efforts at direction, help, supervision, and monitoring by parents" (Barkley, 2000, p. 113). The impact on parents includes low self-esteem, depression, self-blame, and social isolation (Barkley, 2000).

Mrs. Abell identified with this information and shared some of her caregiving difficulties, which began, she said, as soon as Andy was born. "He was different from Nikki from the start. He cried a lot, fussed, wouldn't get on schedule." The practitioner normalized Mrs. Abell's experience. Many children who have ADHD are irritable, hard to soothe, and have difficulty with regulation from birth (Barkley, 2000).

After empathizing with some of Mrs. Abell's parenting challenges, the practitioner discussed with Mrs. Abell the coping strategies she used. Mrs. Abell said the situation was much better since she married her husband. When she was a single parent, she worked at a convenience store and didn't have as much time to spend with the children. The family's finances improved dramatically with the addition of Mr. Abell's income, and she now had his help with parenting. They also enjoyed time together as a couple: "His brother and wife will take the kids every once in a while, so we can get something to eat, or go see a movie." Clearly, Mrs. Abell's relationship with her new husband was important to her.

The practitioner then inquired about sources of social support other than Mrs. Abell's husband since social support has been consistently associated with reduced stress (e.g., Cohen & Wills, 1985; Lincoln, 2000). "Well, now I have Rick's family. Before that, I didn't really have anyone."

"How about friends with children or extended family?"

"My sister and I don't talk much. She thought I was an idiot to stay with my ex-husband. I know she meant well, but he was my husband, so I didn't feel much support from her. Now we're just out of the habit of talking. The kids see my mother occasionally, but it's a

2-hour drive to get there, and my mom's too old to be driving down here. My dad died about 15 years ago now."

"Any other relatives?"

"Just my brother, but he's in the army, always being stationed somewhere else, divorced."

When the practitioner mentioned friends, Mrs. Abell gave an ironic laugh. "My ex-husband was so jealous, he always thought I was with some guy, so it just became easier to stay home. And then he's the one who ran off with someone else."

Since Mrs. Abell did not seem linked to many informal supports, the practitioner suggested a support group for mothers with children with ADHD.

Mrs. Abell looked dubious. "I don't know. It was hard enough to come here. This is okay, but I can't imagine talking about this stuff in front of a room full of strangers." Despite the practitioner's attempt at reassurance ("They would all be going through the same kind of experiences you are"), Mrs. Abell was still not convinced.

To further assist in the alleviation of stress, the practitioner inquired about what Mrs. Abell did for herself that was pleasurable. She identified watching TV and reading women's magazines and further said that she enjoyed these activities daily. After joining with Mrs. Abell and attending to aspects of her stress, the practitioner moved into providing education on ADHD.

▬▬▬ Education on ADHD

Information on ADHD included its description, prevalence, and the etiology of the disorder.[1] Further, risk factors for the disorder were discussed. All information was imparted *collaboratively*, which means that efforts were made to personalize material to the family's situation and to allow time for processing reactions and experiences to the educational material (Webster-Stratton & Herbert, 1993). Part of a collaborative approach also means bringing to light concerns parents have about new material (Webster-Stratton & Herbert, 1993). In this way,

---

1. As a source for further information, the practitioner recommended R. A. Barkley's revised edition (2000) of *Taking Charge of ADHD: The Complete, Authoritative Guide for Parents*, which also lists many other helpful resources (organizations, books, and videotapes).

information can be clarified or strategies can be made more relevant for a particular family's situation. Collaboration further involves valuing the expertise parents may bring after years of coping with a child who has a disorder (Franklin & Jordan, 1999).

Description of ADHD

The practitioner began the discussion of ADHD by first eliciting from Mrs. Abell what she already knew. Like many people, Mrs. Abell had "heard a lot" about ADHD through the media. Her impression was that ADHD was overdiagnosed. The practitioner gave her some surprising news: "Actually, a recent study by the National Institute of Mental Health on ADHD found that underdiagnosis and undertreatment are the big problems. Only about 50% are diagnosed, and less than one half of these are appropriately treated with medication" (see Barkley, 2000).

According to the American Psychiatric Association, 5% of males and 1% of the female population are diagnosed (APA, 2000). School-age children represent about 2 million cases of ADHD (Barkley, 2000). "We see a lot of cases of ADHD here at our clinic," the practitioner said. "Like most outpatient mental health clinic settings, about 50% of our cases involve ADHD" (Cantwell, 1996). Mrs. Abell reacted with surprise to these statistics, but this information began to normalize her situation; her family was certainly not the only one affected by ADHD.

When Mrs. Abell was asked to describe ADHD, she said, "Kids can't sit still. They're always jumping around. That's not really like Andy."

"Yes, hyperactivity is part of the picture." The practitioner pulled out a fact sheet on ADHD and handed it to Mrs. Abell to keep as a reference. "ADHD stands for 'attention deficit/hyperactivity disorder' so you're mainly referring to the hyperactivity side. See the list of symptoms." She pointed to them on the sheet. "Fidgeting and squirming, difficulties engaging in quiet activities and staying in one place. Then there's impulsivity—can't wait for his turn, blurts out things."

"He does have a hard time staying with one thing," Mrs. Abell remarked.

"There's also the 'attention deficit' side. Kids usually have either the hyperactivity or the attention deficit type. Some kids have both, and that's called the 'combined type.' From what you're telling me and what the records show, Andy seems to have the inattention type."

When they examined the criteria further, Andy's behavior appeared to fit many of the symptoms of inattention: "appearing not to listen when being told something," "disliking or avoiding tasks that involve sustained mental effort," "losing materials needed for activities" (math book), "easily distracted by external stimuli" (watching out windows), and "being forgetful" (APA, 2000).

"But when he wants to pay attention, he can," said Mrs. Abell. "He watches TV all the time. He gets in this kind of trance. And the same with video games. And he loves working at the shop with my husband. He's lifting things there and moving supplies around, and he's fine."

"Actually, that's not uncommon either," the practitioner responded. "Kids with ADHD seem able to perform activities that require physical effort. And the TV watching is common, too. Kids with ADHD like things with a lot of color, movement, and stimulation, like TV and video games" (Barkley, 1998).

To familiarize Mrs. Abell with the symptoms of ADHD, the practitioner provided information verbally and in written form. She applied it to the family's case, allowing Mrs. Abell to make connections between the list of criteria and Andy's symptoms. In this way, Mrs. Abell was engaged in a more active way with the information; it was no longer abstract knowledge but was personalized to her own situation.

Causes and Course

Mrs. Abell inquired as to the cause of ADHD and was told that biological and, more specifically, genetic factors appear to be the basis for the disorder. "However, researchers still haven't figured out how this happens precisely and what gene or constellation of genes is responsible. Isn't that strange," remarked the practitioner, "as much as you hear about it, we still don't know what really causes ADHD? But it's believed to be a disorder in brain development or functioning in the frontal regions of the brain that involves inhibition, attention, and self-control" (Barkley, 1998; Barkley, 2000; Cantwell, 1996).

"You mean he inherited it from someone?"

"If a parent has ADHD, then a child has an increased risk of also having it. In twin studies, heredity seems to account for between 55 and 97% of symptoms. Environmental factors—diet, lead poisoning, pregnancy or birth complications—in contrast, account for between 1 and 10%" (Barkley, 2000).

"I sometimes wonder if my ex-husband has ADHD." Mrs. Abell cataloged some of her husband's characteristics—his substance abuse, his inability to hold a job, the fact that he never finished high school, his irritability, impatience, and lack of impulse control. The practitioner stated that while she, of course, could not make a thirdhand diagnosis, these are certainly some of the symptoms. She added that in about 40% of child cases, at least one parent also has the diagnosis (Barkley, 2000).

When they started to talk about the course of the disorder, Mrs. Abell asked hopefully, "Isn't there a chance Andy could just outgrow it?"

"Some kids do outgrow it, but about half to 80% of kids continue to have ADHD in adolescence" (Barkley, Fischer, Edelbrock, & Smallish, 1990; Klein & Mannuzza, 1991; Sheridan, Dee, Morgan, McCormick, & Walker, 1996). "Between 30 and 65% will continue to have ADHD into adulthood, about 2 to 3% of the adult population" (Barkley, 2000).

Education About Medication as Treatment

Mrs. Abell was already aware that psychostimulant medications and, more specifically, Ritalin (methylphenidate), are the dominant treatment choice for ADHD, consistent with the disorder's biological causation. The practitioner explained that Ritalin stimulates the part of the brain related to inhibition, attention, and self-control, which is underactive in the child with ADHD, and it works on the neurons dopamine and norepinephrine. The practitioner used the analogy posed by Barkley (2000) that taking stimulants for ADHD is like the use of insulin for diabetes: "Similar to insulin, the effect of stimulants are temporary, which means some people think the problem is being masked rather than treated. However, stimulants are the sole treatment to normalize the inattentive and impulsive symptoms of children with ADHD" (Barkley, 2000).

The practitioner also shared information from a recent study of 579 children from the National Institute of Mental Health in which medication alone was very effective (MTA Cooperative Group, 1999). Psychostimulants produce a positive effect for the majority of children with ADHD (about 70–80%) who take them. "There's better attention span, more impulse control, and reduced restlessness, motor activity, and aggression. They are more likely to listen and obey commands. Because they're able to attend better and show persistence, they improve in their school performance."

"The school said all that. They want him on medication. That's why they sent me here—because I wouldn't do it. I don't want him to learn that a pill can help him feel better."

The practitioner provided some information from the research to address Mrs. Abell's concerns. In general, the practitioner explained that boys with ADHD have what's called a "self-enhancing bias." When they succeed, they believe it's because they have the ability or that they have tried hard. When they fail, they believe it's because of how hard the task is, not because of their lack of ability or effort (Hoza, Waschbusch, Pelham, Molina, & Milich, 2000). Taking medication doesn't change this tendency one way or the other for younger children (Johnston et al., 2000).

"Are you saying these kids blame other things when they fail and take credit when they do good?" asked Mrs. Abell. "That sounds like Andy."

"And taking Ritalin doesn't seem to make a difference in this tendency for kids of Andy's age," the practitioner stressed again.

Mrs. Abell feared various other side effects, however, and, of most concern, had heard that children had died from medication. The practitioner then proceeded to educate Mrs. Abell on various side effects, validating some of her concerns: "For about 25% of children, Ritalin doesn't work." Possible side effects include insomnia, loss of appetite, irritability, nausea, vomiting, mood alterations, and an increase in heart rate or blood pressure (Ervin, Bankert, & DuPaul, 1996; Jacobvitz, Sroufe, Stewart, & Leffert, 1990; Simeon & Wiggins, 1993). "However, many of these effects are related to dosage or type of psychostimulant and can be controlled" (Simeon & Wiggins, 1993). "That is why regular monitoring of medication through a doctor is essential." The practitioner provided Mrs. Abell with a handout on these medications for her reference. (See box 1.2.)

Specifically, to address Mrs. Abell's concern about stunted growth, the practitioner explained that this used to be a widely held belief and that medication was often limited to school hours in the past. "However, recent evidence," she said, "shows that the effects on growth of

Box 1.2

Psychopharmacological Treatment of ADHD

Stimulants

- Are effective for children over 5
- Produce effects on behavior within 30–45 minutes
- Peak in effects in 2–4 hours
- For 70–80% of children, enhance attention span, impulse control, academic productivity, social relationships, and compliance with authority figure commands, but do not affect long-term achievement
- Ritalin most commonly prescribed; Adderall most recently approved; little published research as of yet

Types

Methylphenidate (Ritalin; Concerta [time release version])

D-Amphetamine (Dexedrine)

Pemoline (Cyclert)

Amphetamine (Adderall)

Tricyclic Antidepressants

- Have arisen from
  a. occasional negative publicity about stimulants
  b. a need in cases where stimulants have been contraindicated or not effective
  c. a need in cases where mood disturbance is present
- Longer acting than stimulants
- Low doses may produce increased vigilance and sustained attention with decreased impulsivity
- Produce elevation in mood
- Possible problems:
  a. treatment effects may diminish over time
  b. possible cardiac problems (tachycardia or arrhythmia)

Types

Imipramine

Desipramine

Antihypertensives

- Not FDA approved for treatment of ADHD
- Limited research; not as effective as stimulants in decreasing inattention and improving school productivity though equal to stimulants in decreasing hyperactivity and moodiness; helpful for sleep problems
- Should *not* be combined with stimulants since fatalities have occurred

Type

Clonidine (Catepres)

Note: From Barkley, 1998; Bentley & Walsh, 2001.

Ritalin are only temporary, and there is no reason to limit the usage of medication to school hours or the school year" (Barkley, 2000).

The practitioner further explained that perhaps Mrs. Abell's concern about child deaths was linked to one of the types of medication to treat ADHD, the antihypertensive Clonidine. Research on the effects of this medication is limited, yet doctors sometimes prescribe it (Barkley, 1998). When used in conjunction with Ritalin, child deaths have occurred.

Mrs. Abell shuddered and said she still was not convinced that the benefits of taking medication outweighed the potential costs. She recently read in a women's magazine of an herb for ADHD symptoms and wanted to try that first. Unfamiliar with the herb, the practitioner stressed that monitoring by a doctor is still essential. Herbal remedies have not gone through Federal Drug Administration requirements, and therefore dosage and effects are uncontrolled.

In order to establish a good working relationship and to reduce noncompliance, the practitioner must avoid getting into a position with parents of telling them what they "must do." To avoid getting polarized into an argument about a course of action, the practitioner supported Mrs. Abell's plan of trying an herbal remedy; however, she still wanted to ensure that this course of action remained linked to the traditional medical care system.

Further, discussion about treatment of ADHD had to involve the availability of and the family's access to the health system since treatment is inexorably bound with this system. The practitioner needed to provide a list of referrals to child psychiatrists, Medicaid, and government-funded mental health and mental retardation services.

With her husband's income, Mrs. Abell explained, she was no longer eligible for the Medicaid benefits she received as a single parent. She planned to use the government-funded community health clinic if a medical need arose as the family didn't have insurance. Mrs. Abell was unaware of the state mental health/mental retardation department where mental health services were delivered at free and sliding scale schedules. She was urged to call and make an appointment since there was a long waiting list. She could cancel the appointment if she decided not to pursue medication; in the meantime, however, it allowed for treatment options to remain open.

Education About Risk Factors

Several factors have been identified as placing the child with ADHD at risk of worsened outcomes. The first is the co-occurrence of conduct problems and aggression (Barkley, 1998), which sometimes result in poor adult outcomes, including substance abuse, unemployment, marital problems and divorce, and car accidents (Kazdin, 1985, 1987; Reid, 1993). Another risk factor is the presence of parental psychopathology, such as parental antisocial behavior and substance abuse (Barkley, 1998). Although a potential strength exists in that Andy at least has an ongoing relationship with his natural father, he is at risk for adopting his father's violence and substance abuse patterns as these have been modeled for him throughout the years. The importance of modeling is central to social learning theory, which represents an effort to integrate principles of learning and reinforcement with an understanding of the environmental conditions under which learning occurs (Bandura & Walters, 1963). The premise is that people are capable of learning vicariously, by observing reinforcement resulting from the behavior of others and then imitating that behavior.

The practitioner commended Mrs. Abell on the precautions she had taken to protect her children from the harmful effects of their father's drinking (driving the children to and from visits, urging them to call if his drinking became a problem). Other options included renegotiating visitation through the court system and involving the children in an additional support system (Ala-Teen) to help combat the influence of their father's substance abuse.

One way to counteract the possible negative influence of Andy's father was to involve him in the counseling process. After explaining her rationale, the practitioner asked, "How do you think your ex-husband would respond if you invited him to be part of the counseling—separate from you, of course—but for the benefit of Andy?"

Mrs. Abell laughed skeptically. "People have been trying to get him to go to counseling for years."

"Who's tried to get him to counseling?"

"Well, me, for one. So he could deal with his temper and his drinking. Even when he got a DWI, they offered him counseling as an alternative, but then he never would show up. So he had to do time instead."

"Does he know you're bringing Andy in for counseling?"

"Yes, he says it's a waste of money. I can ask him, but he won't go."

"Even if it's for Andy and not himself?"

"He won't see it that way," Mrs. Abell said but agreed to ask him.

The practitioner also discussed with Mrs. Abell some of the protective factors that could lead to improved outcomes for Andy. Mrs. Abell was commended for seeking treatment, as delivery of services is associated with a better prognosis (MTA Cooperative Group, 1999; Satterfield et al., 1987). The practitioner further discussed the presence of Andy's stepfather as a potential protective factor and requested that Mrs. Abell also include him in sessions. "The reason I'm asking is because Andy does seem to have a positive bond with his stepfather," the practitioner explained. "Your husband's doing some important role modeling for Andy, teaching him how to work and have responsibility at the shop. And when both parents act as a team and do the same things to manage his behavior, the child will learn that much faster. That's why I'd like your husband to be here, too. I think he would have a lot to offer."

"He actually has an easier time than me handling Andy. He doesn't think I'm strict enough with Andy."

"What does he do that is so effective?"

"Well, he's really tall and big, and he has a deep voice, so when he raises his voice, Andy just listens to that more."

"Do you think Andy's scared of him?"

"No, Andy doesn't have any reason to be scared. Rick would never hit Andy, but when he yells, you don't want to question it."

"Actually, what you're describing is typical. Children with ADHD behave better for fathers than mothers" (Barkley, 2000). "We don't exactly know why. Maybe it's just because mothers have more responsibility for taking care of children. All that time spent together means a greater potential for conflict. Perhaps it's the difference in parenting styles between men and women. Mothers rely more on praise and reasoning than fathers, who typically enforce punishment quickly when commands are not obeyed. And what you're suggesting, too, the sheer physical size of men may be more intimidating for children and lead to their swifter obedience."

Another reason for including Mr. Abell in the psychoeducational process stemmed from the practitioner's sense that Mrs. Abell was anxious about her new marriage working out. From Mrs. Abell's perspective, Mr. Abell possessed many of the qualities her ex-husband lacked.

The practitioner not only wanted to assess the impact of Mr. Abell's parenting on Andy, she also wanted to help Mrs. Abell and her husband work together as a team as they were still making the transition into a blended family. If parenting strategies were negotiated between Mr. and Mrs. Abell, the relationship would operate more smoothly, and the family's functioning would be optimized.

Ideally, all adults living in a child's household (mother's partners, other relatives) and all other adults who have responsibility for the care of the child (for example, a grandmother who cares for him every day after school or who has primary responsibility for the child on the weekends) should be included in the treatment process.

Follow-Up on Homework Assignments

The practitioner is advised to check in at the beginning of the session about the results of homework. This attention to it each week stresses its importance (Webster-Stratton & Herbert, 1993). As Mrs. Abell had predicted, neither her husband nor her ex-husband were interested in attending counseling. Mrs. Abell said she had shared the handouts with her husband, however, and agreed to keep him informed about the strategies discussed. At this point, the practitioner obtained Mrs. Abell's permission to call her ex-husband directly to invite him to participate in treatment.

Regarding the herbal remedy, Mrs. Abell said she couldn't find the magazine article on the alternative remedies and seemed at a loss about where to go from there. Various strategies were discussed: waiting until the medical appointment to find out more information on herbal treatments of ADHD; asking the librarian at the public library to help her search for resources; and going to a health food store and talking to the manager about recommendations. Out of the various options, Mrs. Abell committed to consulting a health food store manager.

The next week, Mrs. Abell set an appointment at the mental health/mental retardation department and also researched the herbal remedy at the health food store. She now felt less enthusiastic about this option, which turned out to be much more costly than anticipated. Another drawback involved the amount of time the herbal remedy would take to affect Andy's system—3 weeks.

Rather than giving advice at this point on what Mrs. Abell "should do," the collaborative approach described by Webster-Stratton and Herbert (1993) suggested asking the parent to delineate the advantages and disadvantages of a particular course of action. In this way, parents discover for themselves the gains and costs associated with behaviors and make conclusions for themselves on what action they should take.

In response to this exercise, Mrs. Abell produced the following disadvantages:

1. He might attribute his behavior to the "power of a pill."
2. He might see substances as a way to solve his problems and be prone to future substance abuse.
3. He might suffer side effects.

The practitioner's job was to reduce some of the disadvantages that accompany change. For example, the practitioner educated Mrs. Abell on the effects of medications and the different types of medication and allayed some of her fears about the potential deleterious side effects.

The advantages of pursuing medication named by Mrs. Abell were:

1. Better attention at school and completion of tasks with more accuracy
2. Improved conduct and grades
3. A chance of passing the third grade
4. More likely to remember things

Mrs. Abell could see the many potential benefits of trying medication. Most important to her, Mrs. Abell only had to pay a minimal fee for his appointments, and the medication would be at no cost through the state department of mental health and mental retardation. She agreed to accompany Andy to the appointment and give the medication a chance. Meanwhile, the practitioner turned to another aspect of treatment for children with ADHD with which parents can be involved: the development of children's social skills.

Social Skills Training

Well documented are the problems children with ADHD and other disruptive behavior problems display with their social interactions and peer groups. A review by Barkley (2000) indicated that at least half demonstrate significant problems in their peer relationships with their inattentive, disruptive, off-task, immature, and provocative behaviors. Further, children with disruptive behavior problems display a style of cognitive processing in which they are likely to make hostile attributions regarding neutral events (Bienert & Schneider, 1995). This hostile attributional bias impedes their ability to effectively problem solve in social situations, which contributes to aggressive behavior (Dodge, Price, Bachorowski, & Newman, 1990). Mrs. Abell described Andy's neighborhood friends as younger than him. At school, Andy and a couple of the other "trouble makers" consort, hence, his referral to the social skills training group at school. Social skills training is a behavioral approach that focuses on improving social adjustment with peers. Treatment goals include enhancing personal interaction skills, managing group entry and rejection, handling confrontations, and decreasing aggression. Since school is the setting in which Andy interacts with other students, generalizability might be improved from his social skills training group. However, the issue of generalizability has prompted some studies that concentrate on training parents on how to prompt and reinforce their children's social skills (Frankel et al., 1997; Pfiffner & McBurnett, 1997). In these studies, children's social skills and problem behaviors showed improvement, according to parent reports, although teachers did not always notice the same results. These mixed results might again be indicative of the lack of generalizability between settings. If parents train their children in social skills in the home, these behaviors may not be replicated at the school and vice versa.

Mrs. Abell was to encourage prosocial friendships by letting Andy invite over peers who could act as positive role models. She was taught how to structure and monitor activities while other children were over, changing the focus of play if it became too disruptive (Barkley, 2000). Extracurricular activities were also encouraged so that Andy could interact with prosocial peers in a structured way. These activities would also have the advantage of providing Andy with alternate avenues for mastery. He became interested in karate lessons, which also helped develop his focus and concentration.

The practitioner arranged with Mrs. Abell that, when Andy performed successfully in social situations, she would send a letter, congratulating him on his success. A study by McCormick (2000) indicated that a personal letter mailed by the practitioner when children achieved goals in this area encouraged them to improve even further.

Working with the School System

In cases involving ADHD and ODD, it is essential that the practitioner work with the parent on how to coordinate efforts with the school system. The school setting is one in which the child with ADHD is at high risk for failure and conduct problems. Between 30 and 50% of children with ADHD fail at least one grade (Barkley, 2000).

Classroom management is one crucial aspect of a multimodal approach to the treatment of ADHD (Barkley, 1998; MTA Cooperative Group, 1999). Another aspect of working with the school might be advocating for appropriate services, which may be provided under the Individuals with Disabilities Education Act (Public Law 105–17). Advocacy might mean providing the teacher with written materials on the special needs of ADHD children, or requesting a child study so that the child will be evaluated and served according to his or her needs. However, a balance needs to be struck. If parents consistently take the child's position over the school's, the child learns there are no consequences from parents for school misbehavior, and the teacher's authority is undermined.

Parents often feel defensive, however, when interacting with the school because of the frequent negative reports about their children or because parents feel accused by the school of poor parenting. Mrs. Abell said she got a call from Andy's teacher that he had been particularly disruptive and noncompliant in the classroom. His teacher requested that Mrs. Abell come in for another conference.

In this case, Mrs. Abell felt defensive about the tone the teacher took with her on the phone, especially when Andy's teacher asked about whether medication had been initiated. However, Mrs. Abell could honestly say that the appointment had been made at the state mental health/mental retardation department. Mrs. Abell refrained from mentioning that she still felt ambivalent about the use of medication for Andy.

The practitioner advised Mrs. Abell to take a team approach when she went in to talk to the teacher, rather than getting locked into a discussion about medication. The practitioner reminded Mrs. Abell that she and the teacher held common goals: for Andy's behavior to improve and for his grades to rise. The practitioner suggested that Mrs. Abell be proactive and request daily communication from his teacher so that the school and Mrs. Abell could coordinate their efforts. (See the next chapter for the behavioral system devised with the school.) Many teachers will be amenable to providing such communication when parents offer to be actively involved.

The practitioner offered another recommendation for school involvement. The Multimodal Treatment for ADHD Cooperative Study found that teachers were the best source of information on the efficacy of medication while parents were better at reporting child side effects (Swanson, Lerner, March, & Gresham, 1999). If Andy were placed on medication, Mrs. Abell could sign a release for the doctor to gather information from his teacher.

■■■■■ Conclusion

In this chapter, a psychoeducational approach was applied to the treatment of ADHD, covering aspects of parental stress, education about ADHD and treatment, helping parents reinforce their children's social skills, and working with the school system. For education about and management of Andy's oppositional and defiant behaviors, the next chapter will more specifically address the behavioral training techniques that were integrated within the psychoeducational model.

2 Behavioral Parent Training with Oppositional Defiant Disorder

■■■■■ Presenting Problem

The case for this chapter continues from the previous chapter with Andy Stevens, age 8, who has been diagnosed with both ODD and ADHD. As part of the psychoeducational framework introduced in chapter 1, Mrs. Abell will be taught behavioral management strategies to handle Andy's oppositional and defiant symptoms. This chapter will first illustrate with the case example how information about ODD can be covered. Then the behavioral theory basis of the parent management techniques will be discussed, followed by empirical support for this approach. The application of training Mrs. Abell in techniques will follow.

■■■■■ Education About Oppositional Defiant Disorder

The practitioner introduced the topic of oppositional defiant disorder, usually known by its initials, ODD, which is characterized by a range of behaviors, including a pattern of negative, hostile, and defiant actions toward authority figures lasting at least 6 months and starting before the age of 8 (APA, 2000). ODD is the most common child behavior disorder, with a prevalence rate of between 2 and 16% in the general population (APA, 2000).

The practitioner handed Mrs. Abell a sheet with the diagnostic criteria of ODD outlined. The practitioner went through each criterion, with Mrs. Abell making applications to Andy's behavior:

1. Refusal to carry out rules or requests by adults (refusing to do schoolwork)
2. Blaming others (blaming other students for misbehavior at school)
3. Arguing with adults ("All the time," said Mrs. Abell, "and I think his teachers would agree with me.")
4. Deliberately doing things to annoy others (e.g., banging a stick in the house)

Regarding the interplay between inattention/hyperactivity and oppositional/defiant characteristics, the practitioner advised Mrs. Abell that both sets of symptoms should be targeted simultaneously: medication for the inattention and parenting strategies and skill building for the oppositional qualities. It was crucial to address the ODD behaviors before they became entrenched. If left untreated, they could evolve into the more severe behaviors characterized by a diagnosis of conduct disorder (CD) (Barkley, 1998). The next section will describe parent training and how it can be applied for the amelioration of conduct symptoms.

Description of Behavioral Parent Training

The theoretical basis of parent training is operant behavioral theory. (See box 2.1 for an overview of operant behavioral theory and additional resources for the reader to pursue.) The following components of parent training will be illustrated in the case application (Miller & Prinz, 1990):

1. To behaviorally specify goals for change
2. To track target behaviors
3. To positively reinforce prosocial conduct through the use of attention, praise, point systems, and other tangible reinforcers
4. To employ alternative discipline methods, such as differential attention, natural and logical consequences, time out from reinforcement, response cost, and the removal of privileges

Key Points of Operant Behavioral Theory and Additional Resources

Key Points

The consequences of a behavior determine its frequency.
* *Positive reinforcement:* increasing a response by the presentation of an event
* *Negative reinforcement:* the action taken to remove a negative event is reinforced when the behavior results in termination of the event
* *Punishment:* the presentation of negative events or the removal of positive events, which decrease the occurrence of a response

Stimulus conditions (those already in place) also influence the occurrence of behavior.

Methods to train individuals in applying conducive stimulus and reinforcement patterns include lecture, discussion, *modeling* by the practitioner, and *behavioral rehearsal* by the individual with *coaching* and *feedback* by the practitioner.

Parent training is the application of operant behavioral theory techniques to parents with children with behavior problems.
* *Reinforcement systems* by parents include the use of *high-probability behaviors, social reinforcement,* and *token economies.*
* *Extinction* involves no longer reinforcing a behavior, which results in a decrease in the behavior or its possible eradication.
* *Punishment* involves time out from reinforcement, overcorrection, and the taking away of privileges.

Additional Resources

A. Kazdin. (2000). *Behavior modification in applied settings* (6th ed.). Pacific Grove, CA: Brooks/Cole.

G. R. Patterson, J. B. Reid, & T. J. Dishion. (1997). *Antisocial boys: A social interactional approach* (vol. 4). Eugene, OR: Castalia.

Material is generally presented through a variety of formats, including didactic instruction, interactive discussion, modeling, role play, and feedback (Miller & Prinz, 1990).

Treatment can be conducted in mental health clinics, community centers, or in the home. Employed in group (e.g., MTA Group, 1999; Weinberg, 1999), individual (e.g., Barkley, Edwards, Laneri, Fletcher, & Metevia, 2001), and family settings (e.g., Sonuga-Barke, Daley, Thompson, Laver-Bradbury, & Weeks, 2001), parent training is usually a brief treatment model (9 to 12 sessions). However, it must be stressed to parents that techniques will have to be applied consistently over time, long after treatment is completed (Barkley, 1998).

Due to developmental considerations, interventions for school-age children need to be extended beyond home reinforcement programs (McMahon, 1994; Reid, 1993). Specifically, children at this stage require reinforcement systems at school so that behavioral and academic competencies can be built and relationship problems with peers can be addressed.

▰▰ Empirical Evidence for Parent Training

A meta-analysis of 26 studies of the effect of parent training on antisocial behaviors in children found impressive results for parent training (Serketich & Dumas, 1996). According to parents, teachers, and the children themselves, child behaviors significantly improved by at least 77 to 81% for those whose parents received parent training over those who had undergone an alternative intervention or a control condition. Parents also reported better adjustment—more than 67% better than the comparison or control group. More recently, Brestan and Eyberg (1998) examined 82 well-controlled outcome studies for children and teenagers with conduct problems. Parent training and its variants were represented among approaches with strong empirical support.

For ADHD specifically, parent training programs reduce parenting stress and increase parents' sense of competence over control-comparison groups (Anastopoulos et al., 1993; Odom, 1996; Weinberg, 1999). When compared to medication, parent training does not appear to affect child attentional and hyperactivity symptoms (Firestone, Crowe, Goodman, & McGrath, 1986), although it seems effective for child oppositional conduct problems (McNeil, Eyberg, Eisenstadt, Newcomb, & Funderburk, 1991). As discussed in the previous chapter, a multimodal approach, including medication management and behavioral treatment with parent, school, and child components, shows the most positive benefits (MTA Cooperative Group, 1999).

▰▰ Case Application

This section will cover the application of the following techniques: behavioral goal setting, reinforcement, command giving, using natural and logical consequences, extinction, and time out. The importance of practicing the techniques is emphasized, along with how to use role plays in session to increase the generalizability of skills.

Behavioral Goal Setting

The components of successful goal setting are:

1. Parents select a priority goal around the child's behavior.
2. Goals are broken down into smaller, observable components called *tasks*.
3. Goals and tasks should involve the presence of positive behaviors rather than the absence of negative behaviors.
4. A baseline is determined.
5. A target goal is established.

The practitioner began the session by saying, "Mrs. Abell, I know you mentioned several things that bothered you about Andy's behavior, but if you wanted to center on one thing, what would help the most?"

"There's so many things I'd like to change."

"I know, but we'll be better off if we take things one at a time, have a little success, and then move on to other things. I want you to think of one behavior you'd like to start with."

Although Mrs. Abell desires many changes from Andy, centering on more than one at once might overwhelm and frustrate her as she learns to respond to Andy differently. A sense of failure may cause her to feel worse about her parenting competence or to blame the approach; in either case, Andy's behavior would be left unchanged, and she might quit treatment before seeing results.

As is typical, the goal Mrs. Abell selected—"Andy completing his homework"—involved a complex set of behaviors. Therefore, the goal needed to be broken down further into *tasks*, defined as a number of small, trainable, and highly concrete behaviors (Kazdin, 2000). As much as possible, goals and tasks should be stated as the presence of positive behaviors (e.g., following through with commands, completing homework) rather than as the absence of negative behaviors (e.g., not hitting, not talking back). Although negative behaviors can be reduced, it is advisable to work simultaneously on increasing behaviors that are incompatible with the negative actions (Kazdin, 2000). For instance, if a parent names the goal as "not hitting siblings," incompatible behaviors may involve talking in a normal voice tone with siblings, sharing toys, and negotiating.

Along with attention to the consequences of behaviors for children with ADHD, Barkley (1998) urges consideration of stimulus (preceding) conditions, such as reducing the complexity of tasks, repeating instructions frequently, using a lot of stimulation when presenting information (using color, allowing the child to move around), remaining on one topic for only a brief time, presenting material quickly, providing frequent breaks, and representing time limits in concrete ways, such as the use of a timer on the child's desk. The practitioner provided Mrs. Abell with this information and explored the setting characteristics. Mrs. Abell admitted that Andy does not have his own space (for instance, a desk in a quiet place of the house) to do his work. Until this is established for Andy, Mrs. Abell says he can use the kitchen table after he has had a snack in the afternoon.

The tasks are broken down as follows:

1. Get pencil and notebook paper, open book, find correct page.
2. Read directions.
3. Do assigned problems.
4. Check work.
5. Ask mom for approval.

The practitioner gave Mrs. Abell the list and explained that lists can be helpful for children with ADHD because they have difficulty with " 'working memory' or the ability to keep in mind information necessary to complete a task" (Barkley, 2000, p. 149).

In order to determine a reasonable target for the desired behavior, the *baseline*, the current occurrence of the behavior, must be determined. Occurrence can be measured in different ways—through its frequency (Mrs. Abell says that Andy never does his homework so his baseline would be zero) or its duration (Mrs. Abell says that Andy shows "appropriate homework behaviors" for only 2 minutes at a time).

The next step was for the practitioner to help Mrs. Abell set a reasonable target for the goal of Andy completing his homework. "He should finish all of it," Mrs. Abell insisted.

Since Andy currently completed no homework, however, expecting him to finish all of it seemed unrealistic. One option was to divide each homework assignment into smaller units. For instance, if Andy were assigned ten math problems, then he would have to complete five before he was rewarded. Andy would be much more motivated to work toward an attainable goal, the practitioner explained.

Reinforcement Systems

The main premise of behavioral theory involves the role of reinforcement in increasing positive behaviors. Reinforcement systems include the use of high-probability behaviors, social reinforcement, and token economies. The practitioner began this topic by discovering how Andy's behavior is being reinforced. After last semester, when he received a failing grade, Mrs. Abell related that she had imposed the consequence on Andy of not being allowed to play outside after school for the rest of the semester.

In reality, she says, when he sees his sister (10-year-old Nikki) playing with the other kids in the neighborhood, Andy begs, whines, and gets on Mrs. Abell's nerves so much that she eventually ends up letting him go outside. Since she has allowed him to do this so many times, the consequence has become meaningless.

The practitioner asked, "What do you think Andy has learned from all this?"

Mrs. Abell smiled ruefully, "I guess that he doesn't have to do his homework."

At this point, Mrs. Abell recognized that her consequences (giving in to whining so he could go outside without his homework completed) had not reinforced homework behavior; rather, Mrs. Abell had inadvertently caused him to learn that whining is an effective way to get out of doing things he didn't enjoy. *Negative reinforcement* is exemplified through this process. Andy has learned that begging and whining (the behavior that is being reinforced) lets him escape from an aversive task (doing his homework).

The original consequence for Andy to go all semester without playing outside because he failed math was, in fact, punishment rather than reinforcement. *Punishment* involves the presentation of negative events (e.g., physical discipline, harsh words, criticism) or the removal of positive events (e.g., privileges) in order to decrease the occurrence of a response (Kazdin, 2000). This stands in contrast to reinforcement, which involves increasing a response by the presentation of an event. Positive reinforcement, the practitioner emphasized, is more effective than punishment, and she urged Mrs. Abell to begin a regime of positive reinforcement before resorting to punishment. Barkley (2000) suggests that only after a new behavior has been reinforced for a week should punishment for the opposite, undesired behavior be initiated. Even then, positive reinforcement should outweigh punishment by about 3:1 (Barkley, 2000).

The practitioner explained that with the cognitive abilities of young children, immediate consequences are more effective because children cannot easily consider consequences that may occur in the future. Therefore, the punishment of "not being able to play outside all semester" would, in all likelihood, fail to mobilize Andy's compliance.

Another aspect to consider, the practitioner explained, was setting a consequence that the mother could maintain. Ensuring that Andy stayed indoors all semester would cause her a great deal of effort. "You want to make it as easy on yourself as possible," the practitioner said. She explained that they would discuss in session three different types of reinforcement systems, which could be applied concurrently: high-probability behaviors, social reinforcers, and token economies.

High-Probability Behaviors

High-probability behaviors are defined as those behaviors in which children frequently engage, such as playing outside, talking on the phone, using the Internet, playing video games, and watching TV. The practitioner suggested that Andy be allowed to engage in high-probability behaviors only as positive reinforcement for completing an agreed-upon segment of his homework. For Andy, playing outside in the afternoon was tremendously reinforcing. At night, he enjoyed watching TV with the rest of the family.

"So, maybe a little bit of homework, and then some TV?" Mrs. Abell said, catching on. The practitioner and the parent worked out the details of the plan. Mrs. Abell was to select manageable portions of homework that Andy could reasonably complete in one sitting. Homework finished after dinner could be traded in for a half hour of either playtime or TV watching.

Social Reinforcers

Although Barkley (2000) believes that children with ADHD may find concrete reinforcers more powerful, social reinforcement (praise, hugs, pats on the head or shoulder, an arm around the child, a smile, a wink, a thumbs-up sign) is important to discuss. "Right now, because of his annoying behaviors, adults tend to pay more attention to Andy then," said the practitioner. "Believe it or not, that has been very reinforcing for him."

"He likes making people mad, I'm telling you."

"You're right. Attention, no matter what kind, is reinforcing for children, and they'll try to get it however they can. So we'll have to work on reversing that, directing your attention to times when he is doing well."

The practitioner gave Mrs. Abell another handout, this one on the topic of praise. They went down a list of "do's" and "don'ts" (Webster-Stratton, 2001), with Mrs. Abell demonstrating how she could enact each of the principles of praise with Andy. The "do" list included:

1. Labeling praise (describing specifically what a child does to deserve praise)
2. Coupling verbal praise with eye contact, a smile, or physical affection
3. Praising effort and progress rather than just achievement
4. Praising immediately after the behavior is performed

The list of "don'ts" included:

1. Using unlabeled praise (global statements about the child, e.g., "What a good boy!")
2. Coupling praise and criticism ("You did a good job washing the dishes, but why can't you dry them right?")
3. Waiting too long after the behavior to praise
4. Taking feelings of awkwardness as a sign to stop praising

Mrs. Abell said, "It's not like I don't want to praise him. He just does so little that deserves praise."

The practitioner validated her experience. "I know. In the beginning you're going to have to be quite vigilant—catching him those few seconds perhaps—for when he is doing what he's supposed to."

"The problem with Andy," Mrs. Abell countered, "is that when you praise him, he starts acting bad again."

"Then what happens?"

"I end up scolding him."

"I suspect," said the practitioner, "that he is returning to behavior he knows has worked for him in the past to get the kind of attention he is used to. Don't take this as a sign to stop the praise. Keep doing it and ignore his attempts to get you off track until the new behavior becomes more routine for the both of you."

Token Economies

Another type of reinforcement system to use with children involves *token economies* in which points or tokens are given for desirable behaviors and are then traded in for an agreed-upon reward (Barkley, 2000). Barkley (1998) suggests the use of token economies, with the rationale that children with ADHD appear to have deficits with internally representing motivation. Therefore, they may require more concrete, external sources of motivation as represented by tokens. Token economies can be very effective although there are some challenges to their implementation. (See chapter 4 for the use of token economies in a home in which physical abuse has occurred.)

One way in which token economies can be employed in the home is to use them to reinforce appropriate behaviors at school. A reinforcement system carried over from the school to the home would help Andy bridge the cognitive gap he had between the two settings and would enforce a message that his parents and his teachers were aligned in their expectations. Forehand and Wierson (1993) advise that only in the third grade can children begin to cognitively broach the time frame between school and home. However, the connection between the two can be strengthened by discussing Andy's school behavior as soon as he returns home.

Some teachers already implement behavioral systems in their classrooms: Children receive reinforcement in the way of points or symbols (smiley faces, traffic lights, colors, and so on) to indicate their progress. Since Mrs. Abell insisted that Andy's school had no such program, the practitioner suggested that Mrs. Abell ask for an overall teacher rating for Andy each day—perhaps a 5-point rating or other type of scale.

Mrs. Abell could work with the teacher on formulating a baseline for Andy's conduct and on-task behavior and a reasonable target for him to work toward. For example, if Andy's baseline indicated unsatisfactory progress every day of the week, then a goal of 5 satisfactory days would be out of his reach. Perhaps an achievable beginning goal instead might be 2 satisfactory days. The target would be adjusted over time so that more was expected of Andy as he met initial goals.

Rewards for meeting his goals would be chosen with Andy's input. The practitioner reassured Mrs. Abell that many rewards are free. For instance, if Andy enjoyed spending time with his stepfather, then even 15 minutes playing Nintendo or catch in the yard might serve as reinforcing properties.

Command Giving

One way to reduce the coercive interchanges that are so common with ODD is to make command giving more effective. The practitioner introduced a handout on command giving, which included the following points (Webster-Stratton, 1989):

1. Only use commands that are necessary rather than giving too many commands, which may stifle a child, lead to negative interactions, and parental commands being ignored.
2. Issue only one command at a time.
3. Issue clear and specific commands ("Look both ways before you cross the street") rather than vague warnings ("Be careful," "Watch out").
4. Issue statements ("Please clean up your toys and put them in the box") rather than questions ("Why don't you pick up your toys?") or "let's" commands ("Let's clean up the toys"), unless the parent plans on being part of the effort.
5. Phrase commands as to what the child should do ("Please play in the kitchen rather than in the living room") rather than on what the child should not do ("Don't play in the living room").
6. Keep commands brief rather than lecturing.
7. Praise compliance to a command.

To make this didactic material come alive for Mrs. Abell, she was asked how each of these principles could be demonstrated with Andy. Mrs. Abell role played how she would make commands while the practitioner wrote down her responses so she could take them home as a written reminder.

Natural and Logical Consequences

Although the practitioner had emphasized the use of positive reinforcement over punishment, the issue of the lost math book could not go unrecognized. The practitioner explained the concept of natural and logical consequences (Dinkmeyer, McKay, & Dinkmeyer, 1990). Naturally occurring consequences arise out of the original misbehavior. For example, if a toy is left out on the street and then the toy gets run over by a car, the natural consequence is that the child no longer owns that toy, and it should not be replaced. Because natural consequences do not always occur or they are inappropriate and unsafe (e.g., the child runs into the street and is hit by a car), logical consequences, those that are rationally connected to the misbehavior, should be put in place instead.

Mrs. Abell was quick to pick up on this concept. "I get it. He now has to pay for the math book. But it'll take him forever to earn back the money. He only gets $3 a week. It'll take him months to pay back the money, and I thought you said things should be immediate in time."

"I'm really glad that you're able to remember all these concepts. We've talked about a lot here already. But each week, or whenever you give him his allowance, he'll have to remember it again. And I would suggest that he still receive a portion of his allowance—say $1.50— otherwise he might just give up. Another option is that he can earn certain amounts for doing extra chores. Does your garage need cleaning? He can help you with that. Or is there some other big task that you've been putting off?"

"There's no shortage of those," said Mrs. Abell, laughing.

Results of Homework: Implementing
Behavioral Techniques

Behavioral parent training relies heavily on homework with parents practicing their new skills with their children each week. The practitioner is advised to check in at the beginning of the session about the results of homework. This attention to it each week stresses its importance (Webster-Stratton & Herbert, 1993). (Also see chapter 4 for more discussion of homework with parents.)

Mrs. Abell announced dramatically at the beginning of the following session, "Andy is impossible. Nothing works with him!" With little prompting from the practitioner, she described that the first day she told Andy he would have to do his math homework before he went out to play, he just laughed. Mrs. Abell proceeded to lecture him about who was boss, that he was just the child, and that he *would* do his homework. He said, "I'm not going to do my stupid homework," and kicked his chair repeatedly.

As Mrs. Abell paused for breath, the practitioner asked, "What do you think happened here?"

Mrs. Abell answered that she was just trying to lay down the law like the practitioner and her husband had told her. She would no longer let herself be pushed around by an 8-year-old.

"Maybe I gave the wrong impression last week," the practitioner said, "and, if so, I apologize. I don't think any of these strategies have to be done in a punitive or heavy-handed way. A choice is simply given to the child. If he wants to play, then he must do his homework. If he wants to watch TV, he must do his homework. There's no need for arguing, lecture, or debate. That's simply the way it will be."

Mrs. Abell didn't seem to take in this information, saying, "Let me tell you what happened next. The kicking of the chair really started to bother me, so I told him to stop that minute. Of course, he didn't. Then he started bargaining with me, 'I'll stop if you let me go outside. Please, mom! Please!' He kept begging and pleading until finally, I'd had it and said, 'By the way, if you think you're getting an allowance again, you better think twice because you're paying for that math book, Mister.' He threw himself down on the floor in a tantrum like he hasn't done since he was a little kid. I couldn't believe it."

"What happened then?"

"I told him to stop acting like such a baby, get off the floor that minute, and do his homework if he ever wanted to go outside again. He screamed even louder after this." Mrs. Abell then grabbed his arm and tried to pull him toward the kitchen, saying, "You are going to do your homework!" She said he was crying and screaming so much, she thought he was going to hyperventilate.

Then she started to feel sorry for him and felt like maybe she had been a little harsh. Just to make him stop, she finally said, "All right then, you can go outside." He told her he didn't want to play now, but eventually his sobs subsided, and he went out. When she looked out the window later, she saw him laughing and calling to the other children, with no sign of his earlier upset.

Mrs. Abell concluded from this encounter that the practitioner had no real understanding of how difficult Andy was. The usual pattern was then allowed to resume in which Andy didn't do his homework for the rest of the week.

The interaction pattern Mrs. Abell described typifies the kind of coercive exchange common between a child who is ODD and his parent. Mother and child have trained each other in these coercive cycles (Patterson, 1982, 1986). In behavioral terms, the cycle begins with the application of what the child experiences as an aversive stimulus (Mrs. Abell says, "Do your homework"). Mrs. Abell's command is then followed by Andy's coercive response—noncompliance, whining, yelling, crying. Parents usually display one of two response patterns to the child's reaction. The parent may remove the aversive stimulus (Mrs. Abell drops the homework issue). Alternatively, the parent may reapply the aversive stimulus (raising her voice to repeat the command or using threats of physical aggression to encourage compliance).

The child, in turn, responds in two different ways: he may comply, reinforcing the parent's aversive behavior, or he may escalate, reinforcing the parent's withdrawal of commands. As both family members train each other to become increasingly averse in their interactions, coerciveness is generated and maintained. This negative reinforcement for antisocial behavior along with the modeling of the coercive responses by the parent serves to teach the child a behavior pattern that is increasingly expanded to other social environments, such as the school environment (e.g., Conduct Problems Prevention Research Group, 1992).

Role Playing

Because Mrs. Abell was still so caught up in her emotions about the exchange, she wasn't able to cognitively process information. Therefore, the practitioner moved into the experiential piece of behavioral parent training, which involves role playing. Role playing starts with modeling, in which the practitioner enacts the behavior: "You be Andy at his most annoying, whining self, and I'll be the mother." The second component of role playing involves behavior rehearsal, in which the parent practices the new behavior with the practitioner providing feedback: "Then we can switch roles, and you can play yourself, and I'll be Andy."

Mrs. Abell looked skeptical but went along. Mrs. Abell began by asking in a whiney voice if she (as Andy) could go out and play. The practitioner demonstrated a "when-then" statement ("When you finish your math homework, then you can go out to play") in a calm tone of voice. "Mrs. Abell" then refused to respond to any subsequent attempts by "Andy" to change her mind, including saying he'll be good for the rest of his life, that she probably doesn't care about him anyway and no one does, that he'll be sure to do all his homework after dinner, if she'd just let him go out to play now.

Playing Andy's part first seemed to discharge some of Mrs. Abell's frustrations and introduced a note of playfulness into the session. Mrs. Abell had lost her discomfort with the role-playing situation by the time it was her turn to rehearse the new parenting skill. By this time, she had also learned from the practitioner's modeling of the situation and was able to show appropriate parenting responses. In behavioral terms, practicing the skills in the office setting increases the probability that the parent will be able to generalize the skills used to the home environment.

Extinction

The definition of *extinction* involves no longer reinforcing a behavior, resulting in a decrease in the behavior or its possible eradication (Kazdin, 2000). Andy's begging and whining had previously been negatively reinforced in that he was allowed to get out of doing his homework. Therefore, ignoring his behavior will break this connection (begging and whining = getting out of doing onerous tasks). Kazdin (2000) instructs that before undertaking extinction, it is important to know the reinforcer maintaining the behavior and if it can be controlled. In this case, Mrs. Abell theoretically has control over Andy going out to play.

The practitioner explained that Mrs. Abell would have to completely ignore his attempts to get to her: "Don't talk to him. Don't even look at him. Don't even make eye contact. Leave the room if you have to."

"He'll follow me."

"Just keep ignoring him, and he can follow you all he wants to. If you don't ignore him, what will happen?"

"I'll get mad, and then probably end up giving in, and he won't do his math homework."

The practitioner told her that the process was gradual. "Don't expect him to give up right away or after the first time. He will keep trying for a while because it has worked so well for him." The practitioner normalized that it would be difficult initially. Not only was this unfamiliar behavior for Mrs. Abell, she could also expect an *ex-*

tinction burst, in which trying to get the reinforcement he was used to, Andy would redouble his efforts to obtain it. His behavior might become extremely obnoxious, the practitioner warned, to the point where he might tantrum again. "Hearing him scream and cry might feel intolerable to you, but it is actually a sign that what you're doing is working." Mrs. Abell was also told that ignoring should be accompanied by positive reinforcement for appropriate behaviors (Kazdin, 2000). Therefore, any sign of Andy doing his homework should be positively reinforced with praise, no matter how negatively Mrs. Abell felt toward Andy. In the next section, another aspect of the exchange Mrs. Abell discussed, the administration of punishment, will be examined, including how ignoring can be used as part of this technique.

Enforcing Consequences

In the "disastrous" exchange Mrs. Abell had reported to the practitioner, Mrs. Abell had inadvertently introduced punishment with the consequence of the math book. The practitioner questioned Mrs. Abell's timing of the delivery of punishment. Mrs. Abell readily identified that she had been very angry and was surprised to learn that punishment should be avoided when parents are in this state.

"What other kind of mood would you be in?" asked Mrs. Abell.

As much as possible, the practitioner explained, a calm and neutral demeanor was desired, although admittedly difficult to achieve.

Mrs. Abell then confessed that she'd given Andy his allowance anyway. Later during the week, the family was at the store, where Nikki bought some candy. Andy asked for his allowance, so he could buy some, too. Mrs. Abell gave in to him because she didn't want a scene at the store.

"Let's try another role play," said the practitioner. They followed the usual format in which Mrs. Abell first played Andy at his most difficult and demanding in the candy store situation. Then she rehearsed the practitioner's modeling, calmly walking out of the store and ignoring Andy as he started to cry about not getting money to buy candy. She demonstrated herself driving home, still not attending to his crying and whining and his attempts to get her in an argument by calling her "mean" and accusing her of not loving him. Following the role play, Mrs. Abell committed to trying out the techniques once more.

Reapplication of Behavioral Techniques

At the next session, Mrs. Abell came in with an air of grim satisfaction. She described that the week began with 3 days of Andy temper tantruming when his attempts to get his way to go out and play were unsuccessful. During the tantrum on the third day, Mrs. Abell became immersed in vacuuming to block out the noise. After what seemed like hours but was, in actuality, only 15 minutes, Andy quieted down and went to his own room. Mrs. Abell didn't see him again until dinnertime.

After dinner, Andy strolled into the living room to settle in for his nightly TV watching. Mrs. Abell and her husband informed him he would have to complete at least half of his math homework in order to watch a half hour of TV. He begged and whined, saying he'd do his homework as he watched TV and would be sure to finish all of it. Mrs. Abell repeated the command in a calm tone of voice: "When you finish six math problems, then you can watch TV." Andy cried, saying she couldn't make him. Her husband started to admonish Andy, but Mrs. Abell touched his arm and shook her head. With great effort, Mr. Abell managed to ignore Andy as he left the room, wailing. Mrs. Abell reminded her husband of Andy's ploy, which was to have his parents argue with him about some rule. Mr. Abell grumbled about "letting Andy get away with that kind of thing," saying she was "too soft on him." But she told him she was going to stick to her plan and that wasn't being soft.

Since the central premise of behavioral theory is that reinforcing a behavior increases its likelihood, the practitioner also utilizes this principle with the parent. If the practitioner reinforces her with praise, Mrs. Abell will be more likely to continue the new parenting behaviors she has learned.

"Wow, I'm really impressed," said the practitioner. "Andy attempted to get one over on you, and you were able to communicate effectively with your husband to be sure you were acting as a team. And you knew to have the discussion when you were alone so the children wouldn't hear your conflicting views."

Mrs. Abell, pleased, went on to describe that Andy slipped out occasionally from his room to try to watch TV, but that they stopped him, asking him for his homework first. He would retreat to his room, shrieking how "unfair and mean everyone was." Finally, he fell asleep without doing any of his homework. At that point, Mrs. Abell was about to quit therapy, thinking that nothing would work.

The next afternoon, Andy wanted to go out and play. He could see from the window that his sister and two younger neighborhood boys were playing hide and seek, a game he really enjoyed. He begged, whined, and cried, to no avail. Finally, he sat down and did a math problem. When Mrs. Abell praised him for concentrating so well on his work, he went to the window and tried to yell at the kids outside. They asked him to join them, but Nikki told them he couldn't until he had finished his homework. "You're supposed to ignore him until he does it," Nikki told the other children. The practitioner and Mrs. Abell shared a laugh at her daughter's precociousness.

Mrs. Abell concluded from her experience with praise that it only made him lose focus. "That might happen initially because he is so unused to praise," the practitioner reminded her.

"It's not like I don't want to praise him," Mrs. Abell said defensively. "It's just that he does so few things right."

"That will start to change as he realizes he will receive no attention or he will be disciplined for negative behaviors. Just stick with it."

The game of hide and seek outside motivated Andy to complete three problems. He struggled with the fourth and asked his mother for help. However, her assistance only seemed to give him license to go to the window again, waving and calling to the other children. Mrs. Abell reminded him with a simple command, "As soon as you finish these two other problems, then you can go outside and join them. It sure looks like they're having a lot of fun out there today."

He muttered that she was "mean" but returned to his chair. She suppressed a smile since his attempts to provoke her now seemed a little more transparent. She walked him through the next problem, then instructed that the next one he had to do on his own. He said this was "unfair" but then settled down to do it. After she checked the problems over, she started to praise him, but he interrupted, saying, "Can I play now?" Moments later, he was running around outside.

Andy continued to test these new rules a little bit each day by trying to watch TV after having done no homework, crying, sulking, complaining, arguing, expressing disgust, outright tantruming, doing homework sloppily or incorrectly so it would have to be done over, and so on. The practitioner praised the mother, asking her how she was able to stick to the plan when Andy kept testing the limits. Mrs.

Abell said that, in some ways, she was doing it to prove the practitioner wrong at first, that she could do everything she was supposed to with Andy, and it still wouldn't help. But, to her surprise (and her husband's), she admitted, Andy was actually doing at least some of his homework by the end of the week, a minor miracle since he had essentially not finished an assignment during the whole school year.

The simple act of getting Andy to complete even a portion of his homework involved a complex system of new behaviors for both Mrs. Abell and Andy. Parents might get bogged down at an early point and give up. Time in session should be focused around anticipated obstacles. Once the behavior is attempted, other stumbling blocks are dismantled until techniques are implemented effectively.

Time Out

Along with the natural and logical consequences that have already been discussed, potential punishments include extra chores and time outs. Like many parents, Mrs. Abell claimed she had tried everything, including time out. When parents make the announcement that they "have tried everything," the practitioner must then ask about what has been specifically tried and how it was applied. When Mrs. Abell was asked about her use of time out, she said that Andy was usually sent to his room for an unspecified time period. She admitted that he had plenty of toys in the room; sometimes, he would nap. By the time he emerged from the room, everyone had forgotten why he had been sent in there.

To provide a contrast, the place for time out should be free from reinforcement, meaning there should be no activities available, and the child is to do nothing. Mrs. Abell said she could move a stool to the front hallway for a time out, although he could see the other family members in the living room from there and would probably call out to them. She was instructed that his attempts to engage family members in annoying behaviors should be ignored. If he escalated into complete disruption, the time-out period would only resume after he got his behavior under control.

The time out should be structured around a specific time frame with the general guideline of a minute per year of the child's age. Eight minutes seemed awfully short to Mrs. Abell but is a long time, the practitioner explained, for a child to go without reinforcement (doing nothing and not getting any attention). After the time out is over, the child must recount the reason for the punishment and what he or she has learned to do differently next time.

Conclusion

Over time, through implementation of parent training techniques, Andy's behavior became more manageable. Once he started taking Ritalin, combined with Mrs. Abell's new strategies and her working with the school system, his behavior and task focus at school improved. However, he had performed so poorly for most of the year, he still had to take summer school classes in order to proceed into the fourth grade.

This case application demonstrates that while the parent training approach is a teaching model, the practitioner must use process-based skills so that parents are able to take in new information and apply it to their family situation. The application also shows the necessity of using behavioral methods, such as modeling by the practitioner and behavioral rehearsal by parents through the use of role plays, so that the new skills learned can be generalized to the problem situation.

The treatment of both ADHD and ODD requires a multimodal approach with interventions aimed at multiple settings. However, parents' involvement is a crucial aspect of intervention since they control many aspects of their children's environment and are responsible, to a great degree, for coordinating aspects of the child's care.

3   Solution-Focused Therapy with Oppositional Defiant Disorder

▆▆ Presenting Problem

Rubin Cruz, age 11, was referred by the school system because of difficulty with his teacher, who reported that he often refused to follow directions and complete his school work. He provoked other students into talking with him and by playing class clown. He instigated arguments with the teacher and was in detention at least twice a week for these infractions.

Rubin lived with his parents, Phillip and Anna Cruz, and his 14-year-old brother, Joey. His mother, Anna Cruz, says that Rubin shows similar behaviors at home. He argues about doing chores and "everything else" and won't follow his mother's directions. (See figure 3.1 for the genogram of this family.)

▆▆ Introduction

While solution-focused therapy shares with other family therapy models a focus on the contextual nature of behavior, its unique focus is on exceptions, times when the problem is not a problem (de Shazer et al.,

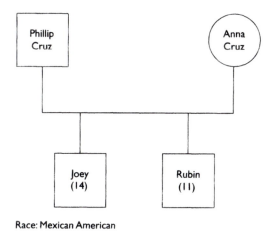

Race: Mexican American

Figure 3.1. Solution-Focused Therapy Case Study: Rubin Cruz's Family

1986). The practitioner helps the family to identify resources used during exceptions and then how to amplify strengths and apply them to problem situations. With solution-focused interventions, people are led to imagine the future without the problem and then develop concrete steps toward that view.

In this chapter, the beginning empirical evidence for solution-focused therapy will be discussed, followed by a delineation of the assumptions of the model, illustrated with the case study. The body of the chapter will describe and apply solution-focused techniques to the work with the Cruz family.

▆▆▆▆ Empirical Evidence

Empirical evidence for solution-focused therapy is developing although it lags far behind the anecdotal discussions of its effectiveness (Lee, 1997; Wheeler, 1995). Specific to child behavior problems, solution-focused therapy treatment outcome research has been conducted on an individual (Franklin, Biever, Moore, Clemons, & Scamardo, 2001; Littrell, Malia, & Vanderwood, 1995; Thompson & Litrell, 1998), group (LaFountain & Garner, 1996; Zimmerman, Jacobsen, MacIntyre, & Watson, 1996), and family basis (Corcoran, 2002; Corcoran & Stephenson, 2000).

As the focus of this book is on family approaches, the studies reviewed will be those with parental involvement, however, an assumption of solution-focused therapy is that a change in one individual can alter the family since change reverberates throughout the system. Zimmerman et al. (1996) examined group treatment with 42 parents reporting conflict with their teens. At 6 weeks posttest, randomly assigned solution-focused therapy participants revealed significant improvements on certain subscales of the Parenting Skills Inventory, including role image, communication, limit setting, and rapport, compared to a wait-listed control group.

Corcoran (2002) compared solution-focused therapy to a "treatment-as-usual" condition primarily comprising cognitive-behavioral therapy. Although there were no statistically significant differences between groups on outcome measures, the solution-focused therapy condition produced higher treatment engagement. For the solution-focused therapy group, significant improvements between pre- and posttest scores were found on the following parent ratings of child behaviors: conduct problems, learning problems, psychosomatic problems, impulsivity-hyperactivity, and the hyperactivity index (Corcoran & Stephenson, 2000). Currently, many other studies on solution-focused therapy are being conducted, so we will soon have more information on its effectiveness.

Assumptions of Solution-Focused Therapy

In solution-focused therapy, clients are given credit for deciding their own goals and having the necessary strengths and capacities to achieve their own goals (Berg, 1994; Cade & O'Hanlon, 1993; deJong & Berg, 2001; O'Hanlon & Weiner-Davis, 1989). Applying these concepts to the case study, Rubin Cruz's goal is to stop getting into trouble. His mother's goal is for Rubin to "do what he's told," which she further elaborates as completing his chores and his schoolwork without arguing. In order to reach these goals, the work does not center on presumed deficits in terms of Mrs. Cruz's parenting skills or Rubin's self-control or problem-solving skills. Rather, the practitioner works to elicit times when Rubin's behavior is more aligned with compliance and completion of chores and schoolwork.

Given the lack of emphasis on problems, history taking about the causes and manifestation of symptoms is not detailed. According to solution-focused therapy, understanding the problem does little in the way of solving the problem (deJong & Berg, 2001). In general, the past is deemphasized other than at the times when exceptions to problems occur. In applying these assumptions with the Cruzes, asking questions about the problem is not emphasized (e.g., When did Rubin start acting this way? For how long? How many times a day does the problem behavior occur?). In solution-focused therapy, the construction of solutions from exceptions is seen as easier and ultimately more successful than stopping or changing existing problem behavior. Once exceptions are identified, resources are enlarged upon through the use of questions that presuppose that positive change will occur: "When you are following directions, what *will* you be doing differently?" as contrasted to "If you were following directions, what *would* you be doing differently?" This illustrates the solution-focused assumption that the way the practitioner uses language will influence clients on how to view their problems and the solutions to these problems (Bertolino & O'Hanlon, 2002; Cade & O'Hanlon, 1993).

As well as changes in perception, change in behavior is also implicated in solution-focused therapy. People are empowered through making small behavioral changes to view themselves as charged with the necessary strengths and resources. Simultaneously, small changes may affect the context of the behavior, which will, in turn, affect the behavior further. This phenomenon has also resulted in the onset and maintenance of child behavior problems. By the time a family with such a child comes to treatment, a negative pattern has developed: the child "acts out"; the parent views the child negatively; the parent communicates this negative view to the child, who then acts in a manner consistent with this view; and the spiral continues. In solution-focused treatment, the aim is to reverse this pattern, so that a positive spiral instead results: specific behaviors the parent wants to see are elicited; the child's positive behavior is attended to and reinforced; the parent views the child more favorably; the child acts more consistently with this view; and the upward spiral continues. One example involves Rubin's school behavior. If he begins to respond with more compliance to his teacher, she may act differently toward him, which may in turn create a context more supportive of compliance. The view is that change in specific areas can "snowball" into bigger changes due to the systems orientation assumed to be present: Change in one part of the system can lead to change in other parts of the system (O'Hanlon &

Weiner-Davis, 1989). Therefore, treatment may need only to be brief in duration as the small, specific changes can encourage larger and continued changes.

Along with this systemic view, in solution-focused therapy, the context of a particular behavior is viewed as more influential than innate individual characteristics. Therefore, Rubin is not viewed as his "oppositional defiant disorder." The emphasis instead is on situational aspects, the who, what, where, when, and how of a particular behavior (deJong & Berg, 2001).

Solution-focused therapy also assumes that change can occur at any point in the system and will reverberate from there. Time is not spent in sessions, for instance, on the reasons that Rubin's father does not attend, nor is energy put into trying to engage him in treatment. The solution-focused assumption is that the small changes Rubin and his mother enact in treatment will spiral into other parts of the family system. (See box 3.1 for a brief overview of the key assumptions of solution-focused therapy and other resources for the interested reader.)

■■■■ Application of Techniques

This application will be organized according to the following techniques: engagement, identifying resources through exceptions, the miracle question, scaling questions, and termination. The case study will be used to illustrate the application of techniques.

Engagement

Joining, the first part of the engagement process, involves building a foundation for collaborative work (Berg, 1994). Joining begins with the simple act of making small talk with the client, which may revolve around a particular situation that the practitioner and the family share, such as finding the office location and locating a parking spot (Berg, 1994; O'Hanlon & Weiner-Davis, 1989). Small talk with Mrs. Cruz revolved around her difficulties getting to the appointment on time because of traffic and the endless construction at a nearby intersection. Eleven-year-old Rubin was asked about his grade in school (sixth), favorite subjects (in general, he said he hated school, but math was least despised), and what he likes to do (play basketball, hang around his friends and his 14-year-old brother, Joey, watch TV, go to amuse-

Box 3.1

**Key Assumptions of Solution-Focused
Therapy and Additional Resources**

Key Assumptions

- Client strengths, abilities, and resources are emphasized.
- Attention, rather than being focused on the past and a history of the problem, orients on a future without the problem to build vision, hope, and motivation for the client.
- Change occurs in a systematic way. Small change is all that is necessary as a "spiral effect" takes place: The client takes a step in the right direction; others in the context respond differently; the client feels more empowered and is encouraged toward further change.
- Since no one holds the objective truth, individuals' ways of solving problems are unique and valued, and individuals have the right to determine their own goals.
- Interventions to enact these assumptions include the use of language by the practitioner to imply that change will occur, *exception finding*, the *miracle question*, and *scaling questions*.

Additional Resources

P. deJong & I. K. Berg. (2001). *Interviewing for solutions* (2nd ed.). Pacific Grove, CA.: Brooks/Cole.

B. Bertolino & B. O'Hanlon. (2002). *Collaborative, competency-based counseling and therapy*. Boston: Allyn & Bacon.

M. Selekman. (1997). *Solution-focused therapy with children*. New York: Guilford.

ment parks) (Selekman, 1993, 1997). Part of engagement involves taking into account the relationship of the client to the helping process and using various strategies for the different client relationships.

In solution-focused therapy, three main types of client relationships present in treatment: the customer (the voluntary client wanting to make changes), the complainant (who is more interested in change for another), and the visitor (the involuntary client who has been mandated to attend) (deJong & Berg, 2001). When parents bring their child to treatment for behavior problems, two types of client relationships are typically present. Parents are the complainant type; they see their children as the problem and want change to come from them. Children with behavior problems are usually engaged in the visitor relationship (Selekman, 1993, 1997). Generally less concerned about their behaviors than others (their parents, the school system, the courts), their main goal is to terminate treatment. Strategies to engage the visitor and the complainant relationship will be detailed below.

Visitor Relationship

Engagement strategies with the visitor relationship include:

- Creating goals around the referral source requirements
- Allowing clients to take responsibility for their own change
- Asking relationship questions

Orienting Toward Goals

The child with a behavior problem is engaged in the goal of terminating treatment as quickly as possible with the opening questions: "Whose idea was it that you came here? What do they need to see to know you don't have to come here any more?" (Selekman, 1993, 1997). In this way, young clients see that the practitioner is not invested in a long-term relationship and will work with her on results to end treatment.

Rubin answered this line of questioning in the following way:

PRACTITIONER: Whose idea was it that you come here?

RUBIN: My teacher, I guess. [glances at his mother with a smile] And maybe my mom, too.

PRACTITIONER: What do they need to see to know you don't have to come here any more?

[Rubin seems a little taken aback by this question and is silent for a moment.]

RUBIN: I don't know.

PRACTITIONER: Come on, I know you don't want to keep coming here. What do you need to do so that they'll be satisfied, and you don't need to come any more?

RUBIN: To be good.

PRACTITIONER: What does being good look like?

RUBIN: Not fighting.

PRACTITIONER: What will you be doing instead of fighting?

RUBIN: Being good.

PRACTITIONER: If I was seeing you through a video camera [mimes this action], what would I see you doing?

[Rubin laughs at the idea but it gets him to think for a moment.]

RUBIN: Well, in school, I won't tell the teacher, "No!"

PRACTITIONER: What will you do instead when she asks you to do something?

RUBIN: I'll just do it. I'll sit there and just do my work.

In this example, the practitioner gets the client to identify how to end treatment as quickly as possibly, a goal in which he is invested, by seeking the specific behaviors that are required.

Allowing the Client to Do the Work

Along with the solution-focused therapy view that clients are the experts on their own lives, clients are also allowed to come up with their own answers and solutions rather than having the practitioner lecture them on what they "must do." However, Rubin, like many youngsters, used the default response of "I don't know" to many practitioner questions. Several different strategies may be used at this point. The first is to allow silence (Berg, 1994). The child may then become uncomfortable and will talk to fill the silence. (Parents should be blocked from filling the silence themselves.) The silence should not go on too long since power struggles might result, and these inhibit rapport building. The second way to handle an "I don't know" response is to rephrase the question (Berg, 1994), so the client understands that the practitioner will persist until the question is answered. A third way to handle an "I don't know" response is to use a relationship question, which will be described and illustrated in the next section.

Relationship Questions

Relationship questions ask clients to view themselves from the perspective of another (deJong & Berg, 2001), a process that enables clients to understand the influence of their behavior on others and to view themselves from a more objective position. Rubin was asked, "What do you think your mom (or teacher) would say needs to happen so you don't have to come here any more?" He still said he didn't know, so his mother was asked, "He doesn't seem to know, Mom. What can you tell him about what he needs to be doing so he doesn't need to keep coming back here?" After Mrs. Cruz gave her perspective on what should happen, Rubin was asked to repeat what he heard his mother say to make sure expectations were clarified into specific and concrete behaviors. Relationship questions are particularly helpful with non-voluntary clients, who perhaps because they are not interested in change for itself, do not know how it is they can change. However, they are often aware of what others would like them to do. This perspective is tapped with solution-focused therapy in the question of what goals need to be achieved so that treatment is no longer necessary.

Joining with the Complainant Relationship

Joining with the complainant involves asking coping questions, normalizing, reframing, asking questions about the desired outcome rather than the problem, and eliciting details from clients about the context, including how the individual plays a role in the solution (Berg, 1994; O'Hanlon & Weiner-Davis, 1989). The following engagement strategies with the complainant relationship will be described below:

- Aligning with the client's goals
- Coping questions around "problem talk"
- Discovering previous solution-finding attempts
- Reframing
- Normalizing
- Eliciting details about the context
- Rephrasing complaints as positive behaviors enacted in the present

Aligning with Client Goals

Parents who bring in their children for behavior problems can usually be engaged in a treatment approach that is explained as working with the child and family's inherent strengths and that is time limited in nature. The solution-focused practitioner also works to align with client goals. She sides with Rubin on how they will collaborate to get his parents and the school "off his back" so he will no longer have to come for treatment. At the same time, the practitioner shares the parent's view that the focus should be on the child's behavior problems rather than on parenting skills.

Coping Questions

Coping questions are one way to join with parents who complain about their children's behavior problems. If complainants' struggles are not validated, they will not readily engage in "solution talk." The main purpose of coping questions, however, is to elicit from parents the skills, abilities, and resources they have used to manage difficulties with a child and other adversity (Berg & Kelly, 2000; deJong & Berg, 2001). For example, Mrs. Cruz was asked how she managed with the multiple stressors that afflicted her: a son that required frequent meetings with the school, full-time receptionist work at a state agency, and the unemployment of her husband from the construction industry due to injury. In answer to coping questions ("How do you manage?" "How do you cope?" "How do you find the strength to keep going?"), Mrs. Cruz said that she was grateful for her family and loved her two boys and her husband, no matter what the problems. The practitioner learned from this conversation that Mrs. Cruz's caring and gratitude for her family is a strength she draws on to cope with adversity.

Solution-Finding Attempts

In the solution-focused model, clients are considered the experts on their own lives and are asked about what has and has not worked for them (Bertolino & O'Hanlon, 2002). If they participated in previous treatment, these experiences are explored. The Cruzes were asked, "What was helpful about working with that counselor? What didn't work so well for you?" Clients are given credit for knowing what is best for them (Berg, 1994): "I want to make sure that we don't try something that already hasn't worked for you. And if something's worked, we don't need to reinvent the wheel." Mrs. Cruz said that the only treatment Rubin had received was occasional visits to the school counselor. Rubin said his talks with Ms. Gonzales made him "feel in a better mood" and "not so mad" at his teachers. When asked what Ms. Gonzales did that he found helpful, Rubin said, "She would just ask me what happened, and I would tell her. She wouldn't lecture me or nothing." "So you find your mood gets better when you're not lectured," the practitioner reflected back to him. Here, she began to find a way into exception finding, discovering the details of what is different when the problem is either not present or is lessened to some degree.

Mrs. Cruz identified that past problem-solving attempts included her husband spanking Rubin when he was younger, but she said, "He's too big for that now." Taking away privileges is a discipline method she and her husband currently use, but she says, "It gets to the point where Rubin will have everything taken away from him—the TV, the phone, trips to the local amusement park—there's nothing left to take away, and he's arguing all the time because he's bored." She alluded to the counseling, "That's why we have to come here, to find out other things we can do."

The practitioner said she would hold off on making suggestions and telling the family what they must do because, first of all, "they must have already heard all that." Mrs. Cruz said that Rubin's new school counselor, Mrs. Crawley, had told her that Rubin should have consequences for his actions, though taking away privileges had seemingly escalated the situation. The practitioner explained that the solution-focused approach would work with the strengths and resources of the family members rather than telling them what they should do. In solution-focused therapy, making clients feel worse about their abilities is not considered helpful since a disempowered view of themselves leads clients to feel more discouraged and less hopeful about the future. Instead, the opposite is emphasized. Clients are empowered by focusing on their strengths, successes, and a future without the problem. This view then encourages them to take small steps to solve their problems.

Reframing

Reframing is the process by which the client is given credit for positive aspects of behavior previously seen as negative (Berg, 1994), with the recognition that every problem behavior contains within it an inherent strength (O'Hanlon & Weiner-Davis, 1989). In Rubin's case, the practitioner laughed off Rubin's constant attempts at arguing. When she responded in this way, he would laugh as well, and she reframed these behaviors as his having a "sense of humor." As his attempts at arguing were taken less seriously in session, his mother began to stop engaging in debates with him about his responsibilities. This new response pattern had the effect of reversing the negative cycle of arguing, which Rubin and his mother had previously shared.

The practitioner was also able to reframe Rubin's arguing in another way. She said, "Rubin can always find the angle. He would really make a good lawyer. Have you thought about that, Rubin, becoming a lawyer?" Rubin said he had, especially when he saw the lawyer shows on TV. Then the conversation turned to what he needed to accomplish in school now in the sixth grade to be prepared for a potential career as a lawyer.

Normalizing

Normalizing is a solution-focused technique to depathologize people's concerns and present them instead as normal life difficulties (Bertolino & O'Hanlon, 2002; O'Hanlon & Weiner-Davis, 1989). With children, sometimes parents have expectations beyond their developmental stage, and they become frustrated when they are not met. When a parent is frustrated and places pressure on a child, some children will be even less likely to perform new behaviors. Normalizing might involve educating parents on what children at certain levels can do.

For parents of preteens, normalizing can be around aspects of the adolescent's developmental stage. Mrs. Cruz complained about her son's choice of clothing. He would then become more defiant, insisting on the clothes; they would argue, and she would feel even less positively toward him. Although the practitioner could join with Mrs. Cruz that his clothing style might seem distasteful to adults, she normalized that experimentation with nonmainstream clothing as part of a transitional phase appropriate to adolescence.

With children and teenagers, normalizing can be done around "what a drag it is to do homework and chores" or how people (other kids, teachers, parents) don't act as the client wants. The practitioner can use self-disclosure, which is suggested as a way to demonstrate that everyone, including the practitioner, suffers from these same life difficulties (O'Hanlon & Weiner-Davis, 1989). For example, since Rubin found washing dishes so onerous, the practitioner joined with him in stating that she, too, found washing dishes to be "a drag." The practitioner explained that "it was worth it though because otherwise you would find that suddenly you had no more dishes to eat from. Does that ever happen at your house?" Rubin enjoyed the joke, which distracted him from his previous tirade about having to do dishes each night, again lessening the seriousness of his behavior.

Discussing the Context

Solution-focused therapy concerns itself with the context of the problem, and the parent's behavior is part of this context. Inquiry about the impact of the child's behavior can be determined by asking the question, "How is this a problem for you?" (O'Hanlon & Weiner-Davis, 1989). When Mrs. Cruz was asked, "How is his wearing those clothes a problem for you?" the parent replied that the clothing style made her son look like he belonged to a gang: "The first step, he looks the part, the next step he's playing it." She was asked if other youth in her neighborhood wore those kind of clothes and were not in gangs and performed well in school. Indeed, she had to admit, "All the kids wear that style these days, even the 'good kids.' "

The question "How is this a problem for you?" sometimes changes a parent's perspective about the problem and focuses her on the specific behaviors she would like to see changed rather than aspects of the problem that have seemingly taken on a life of their own. A purpose of solution-focused therapy is to reverse this snowballing effect so that, instead, small changes in a positive direction lead to larger changes, which reverbate throughout the system (O'Hanlon & Weiner-Davis, 1989).

Rephrasing Complaints as Positive Behaviors

Parents who bring in their children for behavior problems will usually catalog their children's negative behaviors. Similarly, Mrs. Cruz talked about Rubin's noncompliance at school, the frequent parent-teacher conferences, his lack of follow-through with rules at home, and his defiance. A key question then becomes "What do you want to see instead?" with the practitioner working to identify the presence of positive behaviors. For example, rather than "not talking back," the goal becomes "to follow directions"; rather than "not fighting," the goal becomes "to get along with classmates."

Parents generally have some difficulty orienting toward the behaviors they desire in their children. Typically, they have been used to viewing their children through a "problem frame" and have lost sight of positive behaviors that may not fit this frame. In addition, parents often hold the expectation that in a help-seeking setting they are supposed to talk about problems and the negatives. These tendencies necessitate persistence from the practitioner in helping parents produce behaviors they do want rather than the absence of behaviors they do not want.

Once parents have recognized these behaviors, the practitioner endeavors to enlist family corroboration about what they are working toward. Specifically, Rubin was asked, "What do you hear your mom saying she wants you to do?" Rubin said, "I don't remember," after he was asked this question. In many instances, parents talk so long or in such a general manner that the gist of the message is lost, and the child is unable to reflect back their parents' expectations. In these cases, parents are asked to repeat themselves. Through this process, parents learn to be brief and specific in making their requests.

When agreement has been reached about desired outcomes, the practitioner can move to eliciting from the family members "exceptions," times when the desired performance has already been manifest.

Engagement Process as Intervention

As can be seen from the engagement strategies described, the practitioner intervenes from the beginning of the helping process. Goals start to be negotiated and the work is oriented toward meeting these goals by focusing on client resources and amplifying these. The next section will explore in-depth how this is achieved.

Exceptions

One of the main interventions for solution-focused therapy is identifying *exceptions*, times when the problem is not a problem (Bertolino & O'Hanlon, 2002; de Shazer et al., 1986; Selekman, 1993). Once the parent or the child identifies the desired behaviors, family members are asked about times when those behaviors have already occurred. Exception finding can be discovered through the following format:

1. Identify the presence of positive behaviors.
2. Conduct investigative interviewing around the context of the exception.
3. Be alert for exceptions during the session.
4. Compliment the strengths and resources used.
5. Have children draw pictures of their exceptions.
6. Role play with children on how they can apply exceptions to the future.
7. Find a way to have clients give themselves credit for exceptions.
8. Use externalizing to further generate exceptions.
9. Use the first-session formula for homework.

Identify the Presence of Positive Behaviors

To begin the process of exception finding, clients can be asked, "Tell me about a time when the [solution] occurred." Usually, people have become so immersed in their problems and in their expectation that counseling involves discussion of these (O'Hanlon & Weiner-Davis, 1989), they are taken aback by questions about nonproblem times and are sometimes initially unable to answer. Practitioners must allow space (time and silence) for family members to identify exceptions, with perhaps additional probing questions if they are still unable to answer.

For example, Mrs. Cruz was asked to consider a time when Rubin washed the dishes (his nightly chore) without an argument. She said, "No, he always argues." When Rubin was asked if he could think of an instance, he said, "I do the dishes all the time. It's Joey [his brother] who doesn't do them."

"He doesn't complain like you do," Mrs. Cruz retorted. "You complain and argue about doing anything I want you to do."

When, despite the attempts of the practitioner, people still struggle with finding exceptions, questions can be asked about when the problem was less intense, frequent, or severe (O'Hanlon & Weiner-Davis, 1989). The practitioner said, "I know Rubin seems to do a lot of arguing. I wonder when he argued just a little bit or only made one comment and then did what he was supposed to do."

In answer to this question, Rubin produced an instance from that week in which he said he didn't want to do the dishes, he had hardly eaten anything compared to all the other people in the family, so why should he have to clean up? Despite his grumblings and attempts to get out of the chore, he went ahead and did them.

Explore the Context of the Exception

Once an exception has been identified, the practitioner probes for what was different about the contextual details of the situation: who was there, when it happened, what was happening, how it happened (deJong & Berg, 2001). In this instance, Mrs. Cruz said she had just ignored him; his argument was so "lame" that it was not worth responding to, and she went on talking to her husband, who also ignored Rubin. The practitioner paraphrased back to her, "So when you didn't pay attention to his argument, he just went ahead and did the chore? What does that tell you about what you can do?" Mrs. Cruz was able to see that she could ignore some of her son's attempts to engage her in debates.

If people still struggle, sometimes examples of behavior in the session can be used. One time, Mrs. Cruz talked at length about a report from the teacher about Rubin's noncompliance. Growing bored, Rubin started playing with an alarm clock in the office until it was finally in pieces. Realizing what he had done, Mrs. Cruz shouted at him to put it back together again. After a pleased look at his handiwork, he began to replace the parts. The practitioner noted to Mrs. Cruz that he had followed her direction the first time. Mrs. Cruz downplayed his compliance in this instance, saying, "It's only because you're here." The practitioner reassured Mrs. Cruz that her very presence did not necessarily command obedience and could give many examples of children disobeying in session.

Another example of exception finding involved Rubin's intermittent tendency to get into fights at school. This illustration will also show that clients often attribute their exceptions to entities outside of themselves. Rather than accepting this view, the practitioner works with the client to take credit for what is different about the exception.

PRACTITIONER: Tell me about a time when you avoided getting into a fight.

RUBIN: I don't know. At school, I guess.

PRACTITIONER: Oh, okay, at school. Where were you at school?

RUBIN: At math class.

PRACTITIONER: Who was there?

RUBIN: This jerk.

PRACTITIONER: What was happening?

RUBIN: He was trying to poke me with a pencil.

PRACTITIONER: Then what did you do?

RUBIN: I told him to stop messing with me.

PRACTITIONER: What were you thinking about when you told him that?

RUBIN: That the teacher was watching and that we would get in trouble if I did something back.

PRACTITIONER: Then what did you do?

RUBIN: I turned around and looked at the teacher.

PRACTITIONER: What did "the jerk" do then?

RUBIN [laughing at the practitioner's use of the term "jerk"]: He was still saying stuff.

PRACTITIONER: What were you doing then?

RUBIN: I just stayed turned around.

PRACTITIONER: What were you telling yourself then?

RUBIN: The teacher was still looking, I wasn't going to do nothing.

As in this example, some children and adolescents give credit to people or entities outside of themselves. The practitioner must work to empower clients and help them take credit for the success. "Good, so you knew that the teacher saw you, so you wouldn't let yourself fight." "But if the teacher wasn't there, I would have knocked the jerk's face in." "I'm sure you would have," said the practitioner easily. "So what does that say about what you can do to avoid fights?" Rubin was eventually led to the response that he could make sure a teacher saw him when a provocative situation developed, which would prevent him from responding in a way that got him in trouble.

Another central aspect of the context of children's behavior includes the parent's role in the interaction (O'Hanlon & Weiner-Davis, 1989): "What are you doing when your child is behaving?" Parents may realize, for instance, that they have given their children special attention or remained calm. In solution-focused therapy, the context of a behavior is seen as crucial. Problems do not reside so much in the individual as in the behavior patterns, which influence others to act a certain way. With child behavior problems, parents play a large role in this context. In the previous example that Mrs. Cruz had identified, she had just ignored Rubin rather than arguing back with him. That kept him on-task, and he did the dishes with a minimum of grumbling.

Complimenting

Solution-focused writers pay a great deal of attention to complimenting clients and being vigilant for opportunities to praise (deJong & Berg, 2001). For example, in the example in which Rubin took apart the clock in session, the practitioner praised him for his "mechanical abilities" and for following his mother's direction to put the clock back together.

As a general guideline, indirect rather than direct complimenting should be used whenever possible and can be directed toward either parent or child. A direct compliment is when the practitioner praises the client: "You did a good job" or "I liked the way you said that." An indirect compliment implies something positive about the client, but pushes the client to figure out the resources used to achieve success (deJong & Berg, 2001): "How were you able to do that?" "How did you know that was the right thing to do/say?" Compliments are more powerful when clients generate them for themselves. When clients realize their own resources, change begins to occur.

For instance, Rubin was asked about his chores, "How did you manage to do the dishes when you find it such a drag?" Rubin answered, "I just did them." He was then asked, "But how did you get yourself to do them when you didn't want to?" He answered, "There was a TV show I wanted to watch, and I knew my dad wouldn't let me go in there until I finished the dishes." The practitioner, ever vigilant for exceptions, seized on this strategy as well, bringing it to the attention of Mrs. Cruz. "How did you come up with that idea, that he doesn't get to watch TV until he's done the dishes? That's a great idea!" Mrs. Cruz admitted that her husband tended to resort to this measure more than she did, but they didn't use it as often as they could. This tactic, giving Rubin privileges when he did behave, seemed to work much better than taking them away when he didn't obey. In an attempt to enlarge upon the exception, the practitioner asked, "How could you do more of that?" Although not allowing Rubin privileges until he had completed chores seemed an obvious solution, until the practitioner focused her attention on it, Mrs. Cruz had not taken advantage of this strategy.

The practitioner also works to evoke more compliments from the parent to the child since a solution-focused premise is to change the viewing as well as "the doing" (de Shazer, 1988). Rubin was asked, "What does your mom tell you when you're doing a good job or are doing what she wants you to do?" When Rubin had some difficulty with this question, Mrs. Cruz saw she did not often give Rubin credit for his positive behaviors.

When parents do praise their children in session, youth are asked to repeat what they have heard their parents say. In this way, the positive message is reinforced, and parents begin to realize the powerful effect their words have on their children. When parents have a more positive view of their children and communicate this, children tend to increase their positive behaviors, and the relationship between parent and child becomes strengthened.

Techniques to Make Exceptions Concrete

Young children have difficulty cognitively going into the past to retrieve exceptions (Selekman, 1997). While parents can help them with this process, other techniques are needed to bring the material into more concrete and present focus. One way to do this is through the use of drawings to make exceptions more concrete (Selekman, 1997). Rubin enjoyed drawing a picture of himself in the classroom, sitting quietly doing his work and following his teacher's directions. At the practitioner's request, he displayed, in comic-strip bubble fashion, what would be said aloud and what he would be telling himself. He wrote the teacher as saying, "Rubin, do this, do that," and he was saying, "Yes, Mrs. Wymann." In a bubble above his head he wrote, "This work is boring, but I'm so smart I can finish it fast and then I can draw cartoons."

Another way to help children apply the exceptions they have identified is to role play situations to make concrete their strategies. A playful atmosphere is generated in session when children are asked to assign roles to the therapist and to their parents. This sense of playfulness
lightens up the negativity that surrounds problems and introduces new
possibilities for behavior. Role playing also forces members to take on
new perspectives, which helps introduce new possibilities for behavior.
Rubin conducted a role play for a situation in which a classmate had
tried to provoke him into a fight by calling him "Mexican." He had
previously handled the situation by hitting the classmate and a physical fight ensued, for which both he and the other boy were suspended.
Earlier, the practitioner had helped Rubin identify that humor was one
way he could handle difficult situations. Rubin came up with a response in session (but said he would try to think of something better
in the meantime): "That's right, I'm Mexican, and proud of it," while
smiling.

He enjoyed having both the practitioner and his mother play him
in turn, with him acting as difficult as possible as the other boy. The
practitioner complimented Rubin on making the role play so challenging, mentioning that a lot of children just tell her that they would "walk
away" from provocation without thinking through how difficult this
will be and without rehearsal. Then, when they are faced with a tense
situation, they do not know how to enact the solutions they have identified. She then had Rubin play himself with her being the instigator.
By this time, Rubin was quite amused and had no trouble laughing a
lot as he said his "lines."

Externalizing

Exceptions can further be identified through a narrative intervention
formulated by Michael White called "externalizing the problem"
(White & Epston, 1990), which has been adopted by some solution-
focused writers (e.g., Berg, 1994; Bertolino & O'Hanlon, 2002). Externalizing the problem involves a linguistic separation of the presenting problem from the person. Instead of the problem being one of
personal dynamics and an inherent quality, it is seen as an external
entity.

For young children, drawings can make externalizing explicit.
For example, if a child is being seen for anger problems, he can be
asked, "What do you want to call the anger?" Common responses

are "the volcano" and "the tornado." Children are then asked to either draw this externalized entity or to draw themselves taking control over it. Questions are asked about times when they have control over the volcano and when it has control over them to discover the strategies they enact to gain influence over their behaviors (White & Epston, 1990).

School-age children still may enjoy playful names for the externalized objects. Rubin was asked, "What do you call all that stuff you do at school?" He answered, "The crap," and thoroughly enjoyed his practitioner and his mother referring to "the crap" in the ensuing conversation and in subsequent sessions. The sense of playfulness generated by the constant references to "the crap" decreased the seriousness of the problem and seemed to reduce his need to engage in these behaviors. Both the client and his mother reported that school referrals over "the crap" had reduced dramatically. Externalization enables clients to take a less serious approach to their problems, freeing them to come up with options and, thus, empowering them to fight against their external oppressors (White & Epston, 1990).

Typical externalizing questions of parents who come into treatment for their children's behavior problems involve how they can resist their children's invitation to debate or argue with them. This question was asked of Mrs. Cruz, who continuously said how clever Rubin was at "pushing her buttons" and engaging her and her husband in senseless arguments about chores, homework, compliance at school, and other tasks Rubin found distasteful. To this externalizing question, Mrs. Cruz said she would just laugh off his complaints or ignore him and make him do the task anyway.

Homework on Exceptions

A common task for the first session prescribes that family members take note of "all the things that are happening that you want to have continue to happen" (e.g., deJong & Berg, 2001; O'Hanlon & Weiner-Davis, 1989). Through this assignment, parents and children are directed to further focus their attention on nonproblem times and the resources and abilities they draw upon.

In subsequent sessions, practitioners can start by asking the client to "Tell me what is better" (Berg, 1994; O'Hanlon & Weiner-Davis, 1989). Despite the positive orientation of this question, sometimes parents still try to catalog their children's transgressions from the prior week. Rather than allowing the session to be taken over by "problem talk," the family can be reoriented by asking, "How could the situation have been handled instead?" This discussion could also be followed by a role play so that new behavior choices are made more concrete. This process is much more productive than spending time with a family going over in detail problems that have already occurred.

■ The Miracle Question

People who have experienced a negative and stressful past may easily project this past into the future and assume their lives will always be the same. The *miracle question* is one way that clients can begin to envision a blueprint for a more hopeful future (Cade & O'Hanlon, 1993). In the miracle question, clients are asked to conjure a detailed view of a future without the problem. The miracle question is: "Let's say that while you're sleeping, a miracle occurs, and the problem you came here with is solved. What will let you know the next morning that a miracle happened?" (de Shazer, 1988). Specifics are elicited about this no-problem experience so that clients may develop a vision of a more hopeful and satisfying future (deJong & Berg, 2001). Rubin and his mother responded in the following way to the miracle question:

RUBIN: I will want to get up in the morning.
PRACTITIONER: What will you be doing to show you want to get up?
RUBIN: I will jump out of bed.
MRS. CRUZ: Instead of me telling him over and over again that he has to get up now.
PRACTITIONER: So what will your mom notice about you, Rubin?
RUBIN: She would be really surprised if I just came into the kitchen already dressed. She would turn around to yell at me, and there I would be—right behind her. It would scare her.
PRACTITIONER: What's the next thing you would notice?
MRS. CRUZ: There wouldn't be this big hunt for his homework. He would already have it together, and we would be ready to leave on time.
PRACTITIONER: What would you notice, Rubin?
RUBIN: My mom wouldn't be all stressed out. She would be laughing and joking around with me.

The practitioner continued to elicit specific behavioral sequences for Rubin as he went to school in the morning, continuing to ask the question, "What will your mom/teacher notice you are doing? What is different about you?" to help him see the perspective of others and to demonstrate the influence of contextual factors.

Sometimes, asking clients to envision a brighter future may help them to be clearer on what they want or to see a path to problem solving. By discussing the future in a positive light, hope can be generated, and change can be enacted in the present by the recognition of both strengths to cope with obstacles and signs of possibilities for change (Cade & O'Hanlon, 1993).

▄▄▄▄ Scaling Questions

A more specific way to address future goals is through the *scaling question* intervention. Scaling questions involve ranking progress toward goals on a 10-point scale (deJong & Berg, 2001). Although scaling questions are primarily used for goal setting, multiple interventions can follow this technique, including relationship questions, exception finding, complimenting, and task setting.

Scaling questions for child behavior problems involve the following format:

1. Have the family identify the priority goal.
2. Draw a scale from 1 to 10 that will be kept in the case file.
3. Limit the goal to one setting (i.e., home or school) and identify at least three concrete indicators to anchor a rating of 10.
4. Anchor a rating of 1 simply as "the day you decided to call for the appointment."
5. Ask children to rank themselves on the scale.
6. Compliment the client on progress already made.
7. Have the child identify the exceptions that were used to account for the current ranking.
8. Ask the child relationship questions about where others affected by his behavior problems would rank him.
9. Have parents, in session, rank the child and discuss disparities.
10. Set tasks by asking, "What needs to happen between now and next time, so you move one number up on the scale?"

11. Continue to monitor progress over subsequent sessions on the same scale.

Scaling questions begin when family members are asked to identify the priority goal. Complainant-driven goals dictate that child behaviors are the focus. The goal should be achievable (rather than perfection), limited to one setting (i.e., home or school), and involve the presence of concrete positive behaviors rather than the absence of negative behaviors.

Mrs. Cruz selected Rubin's school behaviors as a priority since that was the reason for the referral. Both Mrs. Cruz and Rubin were involved in developing the concrete indicators, and these included "completing work without arguing," "being respectful to the teacher," which was defined even further as accepting her directions by nodding and smiling, and "leaving the other kids alone."

After the concrete indicators were formulated, Rubin was asked to rank his current functioning on the scale, with 10 defined as the behaviors formulated above and 1 as "the day you called for the appointment." Rubin ranked himself as a 7 and said that he did a lot of the positive behaviors already. He was complimented for having made so much progress already ("Wow, you're almost home free!") and asked how he was able to achieve this level of success. After some discussion of exceptions, Rubin was asked a relationship question about where his mother would place him. He said a 6 and was shocked when his mother ranked him at a 2. Rubin was asked about his stunned reaction and to account for the disparity between how his mother and he had ranked him. He said he couldn't account for it; his mother was his biggest support. Asked to elaborate, Rubin said his mother was always behind him when no one else was and always encouraged him. The practitioner asked Mrs. Cruz, "Mom, did you realize he saw you this way?" "No, I'm really surprised." Mrs. Cruz then explained her ranking, "Rubin, you've been in detention at school twice a week practically all semester, and you've been suspended twice. I call that a 2, not a 7." This seemed to get across to Rubin, as nothing else had, apparently, that he needed to make improvements in his behaviors.

At this point, he was also asked relationship questions about other people affected by his behavior, namely, his father and his teacher. He ranked his father as a 5, which Mrs. Cruz agreed was a realistic appraisal as she was the one who handled the calls from the school and the parent-child conferences.

Chastened by his mother's ranking, Rubin ranked himself at a 2 from his teacher's perspective. Opportunities for exceptions can even develop from low rankings: "A 2! You've already taken some steps. What have you been doing?" If clients give a 1 as a ranking, then the client can be asked, "What are you doing to make sure it's not getting any worse?" In this way, clients can still be given credit for the actions they are taking to overcome their problems.

Task setting follows from the scale by asking children, "What needs to happen so that you can move one number up on the scale before the next time we meet?" Even young children grasp the ordinal nature of the scale and often find moving up on the numbers quite reinforcing in itself. Children often proudly come into subsequent sessions, announcing how they have advanced on the scale. Progress is tracked over time so the scale serves as a measure of goal achievement. Scales make goals and the steps necessary to attain the goals concrete and specific.

Summary of Subsequent Sessions and Termination

Mrs. Cruz and Rubin attended five sessions total. Because Rubin improved steadily on his school behaviors, according to both Mrs. Cruz and his teacher, another solution-focused scale was developed for Rubin's home behaviors. Part of his home behavior involved getting along with his 14-year-old brother, who was included in the fourth and fifth sessions. Although a sixth session was scheduled, the Cruzes didn't return for their appointment. When the practitioner called Mrs. Cruz, she said that the family didn't need to come back because Rubin's behavior was much better.

Although the Cruz family did not terminate formally, in solution-focused therapy, termination in general orients clients toward maintaining the momentum so further change will occur (Selekman, 1993). To prepare the client for difficulties that may arise, possibility rather than definitive phrasing is used. For example, "What *would* be the first thing you'd notice *if* you started to find things slipping back?" "What *could* you do to prevent things from getting any worse?" "*If* you have the urge to fool around in class, what *could* you do to make sure this didn't go any further?" might be typical inquiries to elicit strategies to use if there is a return to old behaviors.

Termination involves building on the changes that have occurred, with optimism that they will continue into the future. Selekman (1993, 1997) has proposed a number of such questions, including, "With all the changes you are making, what would I see if I were a fly on your wall 6 months from now? What will you be telling me if I run into you at the convenience store 6 months from now?" (Selekman, 1997). Questions are phrased to set up the expectation that change will continue to happen.

Conclusion

This case application demonstrates the solution-focused model with child behavior problems. The emphasis of techniques is on identifying and elaborating the strengths of clients and families rather than focusing on their deficits. In this way, the positive aspects of children's behavior are highlighted, and the successful strategies they use are applied toward problem areas.

4 Cognitive-Behavioral Intervention with Physical Abuse

▬▬ Case Presentation

Deanna Williams, a 21-year-old African American woman, came to the attention of Child Protective Services because she had whipped her 5-year-old, Janice, with a belt to the point of leaving welts. Ms. Williams reports that Janice is not only disobedient, she lies and hits her other children (Yolanda, age 4, and Freddy, age 2). Ms. Williams lives in Section 8 housing, is supported by public assistance, and has never been married. Ms. Williams dropped out of high school to give birth to Janice. Ms. Williams is not involved with the children's fathers, except Freddy's father, who sometimes comes by with diapers and groceries. Janice's father is presently in jail for lack of payment of child support. Ms. Williams has one, slightly older sister who lives locally with four children of her own. Ms. Williams's mother also lives in the neighborhood. Ms. Williams describes her as critical although she helps with the kids sometimes.

Janice's teacher says that Janice shouts out of turn in her kindergarten classroom and occasionally hits other children. She says Janice sometimes lies to get out of trouble. The school's primary concern,

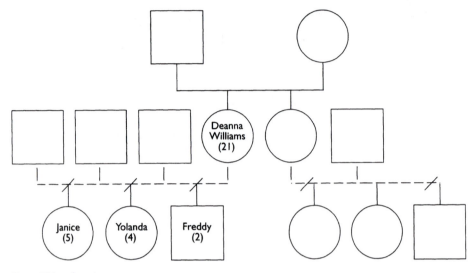

Race: African American

Figure 4.1. Cognitive-Behavioral Therapy Case Study: Deanna Williams's Family

however, is with the amount of time Janice attends school, which is usually only two to three times a week.

Janice's sister, Yolanda, attends Head Start. According to the Head Start teacher, Yolanda seems to have some problems paying attention, staying in her seat, and following directions, although she enjoys attending. The Head Start teacher is also concerned about the number of days Yolanda has missed. She said that Ms. Williams has not responded to any attempts by Head Start personnel to become involved with program services. (See figure 4.1 for the genogram of this family.)

▇▇▇ Introduction

This chapter will take a cognitive-behavioral approach to intervention. First, a description of the theoretical basis for a cognitive-behavioral parent approach with child physical abuse will be explored, followed by the empirical evidence for such an approach. A rationale will also be provided for the training of caseworkers as the application will demonstrate the Child Protective Services (CPS) worker delivering services in the home. The majority of the chapter will demonstrate how the cognitive-behavioral intervention can be applied to the case study.

**Key Points of Cognitive-Behavioral
Theory and Additional Resources**

Key Points

Cognitions, or thoughts, are assumed to mediate behavior and feeling states.
People's cognitions are altered in two ways:
- *cognitively*, by teaching clients how to identify and change their distorted thinking
  through interventions such as cognitive restructuring and positive self-talk; and
- *behaviorally*, by helping clients learn new skills, such as problem solving, relaxation,
  and communication skills.

Additional Resources

J. Beck. (1995). *Cognitive therapy: Basics and beyond.* New York: Guilford.
A. Ellis & C. McLaren. (1998). *Rational emotive behavior therapy: A therapist's guide*
(Vol. 2). Atascadero, CA: Impact.
M. McKay, M. Davis, & P. Fanning. (1997). *Thoughts and feelings: Taking control of your
moods and your life.* Oakland, CA: New Harbinger.
D. Meichenbaum. (1999). *Cognitive-behavior modification: An integrative approach.*
Cambridge, MA: Perseus.

Cognitive-Behavioral Intervention

First, behavioral parent training will be discussed, along with its empirical validation. (See box 2.1 for the key points of operant behavioral
theory and additional resources.) Then, other cognitive-behavioral approaches, including problem solving, self-talk, and cognitive restructuring, will be presented, along with the empirical support for their
use with this population. (See box 4.1 for an overview of cognitive-
behavioral theory and additional resources for the interested reader.)

Theoretical Basis for Parent Training

The reader will find the description in this section similar to the theoretical approach for oppositional defiant disorder in chapter 2. Indeed,
behavior problems in children and physical abuse often co-occur (Gelardo & Sanford, 1987; Wolfe, Jaffe, Wilson, & Zak, 1985), and both can
be explained by the theoretical framework of operant behavioral theory. The framework will be described here briefly using as illustration
the circumstances of the referral of the Williams family to Child Pro-

tective Services. The reader is referred back to chapter 2 for a more detailed discussion of the model developed by Patterson and associates (Patterson, 1986; Patterson, Dishion, & Reid, 1998; Patterson & Reid, 2002) to explain how interactions between parent and child serve to maintain harsh parenting behaviors and child misbehavior.

The cycle begins with the application of an aversive stimulus. A typical aversive stimulus involves the parent issuing a command to the child (Ms. Williams tells Janice it is time for bed). The command is then followed by a coercive response by the child, such as noncompliance, whining, yelling, or crying. Janice cries and screams, saying she doesn't want to go to bed. She wants to stay up and watch TV. Two typical patterns may ensue. One possibility is that the parent removes the aversive stimulus by withdrawing the command. Ms. Williams, for instance, sometimes lets Janice watch TV for a while longer. This response has the effect of teaching Janice that her aversive behavior will sometimes get her what she wants. Negative reinforcement is at play as Janice's behavior (crying and screaming) leads to the removal of a negative event (the maternal command is withdrawn), which leads to an increase in the aversive behavior (Janice crying and screaming in the face of her mother's commands).

Another alternative in the face of child noncompliance is for the parent to reapply the aversive stimulus (raising her voice to repeat the command, using physical aggression to encourage compliance). Ms. Williams often shouts at Janice that she "better get her little butt to bed right now." This, in turn, might lead to several different responses by the child. If Janice complies, which Ms. Williams said is "not often," the parent's aversive behavior (yelling) is reinforced. More frequently, Janice still refuses to go to bed and escalates further, crying and screaming louder. Ms. Williams sometimes gives up at this point, but this has the unfortunate effect of training Janice to escalate her behavior in order to get her mother to withdraw her command. Ms. Williams's most common response, however, is to become even more aversive, at first threatening punishment, "You're going to get a whipping on your butt if you don't get to bed right now!" and then actually hitting Janice.

After an episode in which Janice obeyed and went to bed, Ms. Williams concluded that physical punishment "worked." Negative reinforcement is again at play as Ms. Williams's behavior (hitting Janice) leads to the removal of a negative event (Janice's misbehavior), which, in turn, reinforces the aversive behavior (mother's spanking).

Ms. Williams described a similar pattern in the morning although

Ms. Williams admitted she often slept in to avoid the hassles of getting her children ready. When she did wake up in time, family members were often tired from lack of sleep and upset from the negative interactions of the night before. Janice either kept resisting her mother's commands, and her mother eventually gave up, or her mother escalated into physical punishment. Unfortunately, negative reinforcement and modeling of aggression together serve to teach the child a behavior pattern increasingly expanded to other social environments, such as the school system (Conduct Problems Prevention Research Group, 1992; Forehand & Long, 1988; Patterson, 1986). Indeed, Janice now hits her siblings and classmates and shouts out in the classroom.

The purpose of parent training is to intervene in these interactional processes. Parents are trained in goal setting, effective command setting, positive reinforcement (praise, token economies, privileges), extinction, and punishment (taking away privileges, time out).

Empirical Evidence for Parent Training

As discussed in chapter 2, the effective treatment of behavior problems through parent training has been well documented for preschool (e.g., Webster-Stratton, Hollinsworth, & Kolpacoff, 1989; Webster-Stratton, Kolpacoff, & Hollinsworth, 1988) and school-age children (e.g., Kazdin, Hayes, Henry, Schacht, & Strupp, 1992; Sayger, Horne, Walter, & Passmore, 1988; Serketich & Dumas, 1996). In comparison to the conduct disorder literature, which has developed over two decades of research, only four studies examined parent training with child physical abuse. This difference is striking when one considers the wide overlap between conduct problems and physical abuse in the home, which can be traced to the coercive cycles occurring between parents and children (Azar, Barnes, & Twentyman, 1988; Gelardo & Sanford, 1987; Wolfe et al., 1985).

Treatment described in the four studies is generally brief in nature, ranging from 8 (Wolfe, Edwards, Manion, & Koverola, 1988) to 12 (Brunk, Henggeler, & Whelan, 1987) to 24 sessions (Nicol et al., 1988), although behavioral training was carried out for 9 months in Szykula and Fleishman (1985). Services have been delivered in the office (Brunk et al., 1987; Wolfe et al., 1988) and in the home (Nicol et al., 1988; Szykula & Fleishman, 1985), and in individual (Nicol et al., 1988; Szykula & Fleishman, 1985; Wolfe et al., 1988) and group formats (Brunk et al., 1987).

Brunk et al. (1987) found that both parent training and multisystemic therapy (which will be the focus of chapter 7 on substance-related offenses and teen pregnancy) were effective in improving parental adjustment and reducing psychiatric symptoms in parents, parental stress, and individual and family problems. Positive results for parent training were also found by Wolfe et al. (1988). At 3-month follow-up, both the treatment and the comparison group (the latter only received information on parenting skills) showed improvement in the quality of the child-rearing environment and in child developmental skills. The treatment group, however, showed more improvements in child adjustment and greater reductions in the frequency and intensity of child behavior problems, according to parental reports. According to caseworkers, there was also a lessened risk of maltreatment in the treatment group.

In a study conducted in England, Nicol et al. (1988) compared a behavioral family approach in the home to individual child play therapy sessions in the clinic. On a family interaction assessment, statistically, though not clinically, significant improvements were made for the behavioral approach. Finally, in Szykula and Fleishman (1985), caseworkers produced effective results with behavioral methods in terms of preventing out-of-home placement. The Szykula and Fleishman (1985) findings will serve as the basis for caseworker delivery of services as described in this application.

Besides the theoretical and empirical evidence, there are several other reasons that behavioral parent training with physically abusive parents is supported (Azar & Wolfe, 1998; Kaufman & Rudy, 1991). Behavioral techniques focused on parenting skills may seem more relevant to parents than approaches targeting psychological functioning. In addition, insight-based treatment oriented toward feelings and motivations originating in childhood require a certain level of cognitive and verbal functioning, whereas maltreating parents often perform at a concrete cognitive level (Azar & Wolfe, 1998). While behavioral approaches may be effective with this population, more cognitive and skills-based techniques might also need to be implemented to address certain distortions and deficits that may be present.

Description of Other Cognitive-Behavioral Methods

Cognitive interventions emphasize the beliefs, attitudes, appraisals, perceptions, and expectations of the parent as factors mediating behavior (Azar et al., 1988). Parents who physically maltreat their children display certain cognitive distortions. First, maltreating parents hold expectations for their children that are higher than children's developmental capacities allow (Azar et al., 1988). For instance, Ms. Williams believed that Janice should be able to get herself ready in the morning and even help out with the other children. Second, physically abusive parents attribute negative intentions to their child's behavior (Morrissey-Kane & Prinz, 1999). They may believe, for instance, that their children purposefully act in a provocative or antagonizing manner. For instance, Ms. Williams says Janice "should know better than to fuss, she knows she's making me mad," and "she wants me to look bad" in front of others (e.g., the school).

Third, abusive parents and parents of children with behavior problems often attribute dispositional qualities (i.e., laziness) for their children's misbehavior rather than transient states (i.e., hunger, fatigue) or external circumstances (i.e., task difficulty) (Morrisey-Kane & Prinz, 1999). Ms. Williams says that Janice is turning out "bad, just like her daddy." Along with this attribution comes a mind-set for parents that they are little able to affect their children's behavior (Morrisey-Kane & Prinz, 1999).

Physically abusive parents also often lack problem-solving skills. For instance, Ms. Williams's way to problem solve around getting the family ready in the morning involved either counting on chance to wake her up since there was no alarm clock in the home or avoiding the whole process.

These faulty processes enacted together result in frustration for the parent and may result in physical abuse (Hansen, Pallotta, Tishelman, Conaway, & MacMillan, 1989) and impaired caregiving (Azar et al., 1988). These deficits also cause problems for the parents in other relationships and in the management of their stress. Ms. Williams describes that she and her mother often argue, and she seems to lack supportive friendships. Ms. Williams also reports multiple stressors: poverty, lack of transportation, single-parenthood. Lack of social support and high stress, in turn, represent significant predictors of child abuse (Azar et al., 1988). Cognitive-behavioral treatment targets the following skills (Kolko & Swenson, 2002): communication skills (Acton & During, 1992; Schinke et al., 1986); problem solving to help parents find more effective ways to respond to their child's behavior (Acton & During, 1992; Whiteman, Fanshel, & Grundy, 1987); education about child development and realistic expectations for behavior (Kolko, 1996); empathy building (Acton & During, 1992); altering affirmations of negative intentionality through cognitive restructuring (Acton & During, 1992; Kolko, 1996; Whiteman et al., 1987); self-control methods to handle anger (Kolko, 1996; Schinke et al., 1986); and relaxation training to reduce the level of physiological arousal associated with anger (Whiteman et al., 1987). The next section will briefly review the studies that have been conducted in this area.

Empirical Evidence of Other Cognitive-Behavioral Methods

Cognitive-behavioral treatment has been delivered in groups (Acton & During, 1992; Schinke et al., 1986) and home visits (Kolko, 1996; Whiteman et al., 1987). Treatment is brief in nature, ranging from 6 sessions (Whiteman et al., 1987) to 13 weeks (Acton & During, 1992; Schinke et al., 1986) to 19 weeks (Kolko, 1996). Improvements were noted in the following outcomes: parenting attitudes (Acton & During, 1992; Schinke et al., 1986; Kolko, 1996), parenting stress (Acton & During, 1992), child abuse potential (Acton & During, 1992), coping skills (Schinke et al., 1986; Kolko, 1996), child discipline (Schinke et al., 1986; Kolko, 1996), anger toward children (Acton & During, 1992; Kolko, 1996; Schinke et al., 1986; Whiteman et al., 1987), child management skills (Whiteman et al., 1987), and physical abuse rates (Kolko, 1996). Although follow-up was often lacking in studies, Schinke et al. (1986) found that gains were maintained at 6-month follow-up. In addition, cognitive-behavioral treatment involving both parent and child may be more effective than family therapy (Kolko, 1996). Further, a combination of methods (cognitive restructuring, relaxation training, problem solving) is more effective than a single component alone (Whiteman et al., 1987). In the next section, a rationale will be presented for training caseworkers in these methods so that they will be better able to assist their clients to improve their parenting skills.

Rationale for Caseworker Delivery of Services

The caseworker from the Child Protective Services (CPS) system was responsible for delivery of in-home services. In addition to case management functions, such as accessing resources, linking the client with these resources, and monitoring the safety of children, the caseworker was also trained to deliver cognitive-behavioral treatment. There are several reasons to support such training. The Szykula and Fleishman (1985) study suggests that CPS caseworkers can effectively deliver this treatment in the home. The family preservation movement in child welfare has also resulted in more in-home service workers, and some of these approaches have been described in a general way as cognitive-behavioral in nature (Barth, 1990; Nelson & Landsman, 1992; Wells, 1994).

Second, regular CPS visits are mandated, which often means that the caseworker spends more time with the family than any other professional. It is hoped that the amount of time spent also translates into rapport with the client and a supportive relationship, which means that a foundation for intervention can be built.

Third, follow-up to therapy in CPS clients tends to be low. For example, in one study, only 21% of 91 clients referred for substance abuse treatment complied (Famularo, Kinscherff, Bunshaft, Spivak, & Fenton, 1989). Another study found that only one third of parents who had physically abused their young children (under 2 years old) participated in mandated treatment (Rivara, 1985).

Like many CPS families, Ms. Williams lacked reliable transportation. Taking three young children on the bus across town to arrive on time for a treatment appointment presented a substantial barrier. Since Ms. Williams's child care options were limited, sessions in the office might become centered on keeping three young children occupied rather than on working with Ms. Williams on skills.

Providing services in the home avoids these problems. The caseworker can work in the present moment on parenting behaviors in the natural environment as they occur. Barriers to effective parenting techniques can also be identified by working with parents in their homes, and caseworkers can help parents problem solve around these barriers. Further, opportunities are provided during in-home supervision visits for the practice of new techniques, which increases their generalizability. If other potential caregivers, such as Ms. Williams's mother or sister, are present when the caseworker pays home visits, these people can be incorporated into the session, accessing their cooperation and creating continuity in discipline methods among caregivers.

Another advantage to the delivery of services by caseworkers is that they have substantial control over potential reinforcers. Obviously, resources for basic needs for food, shelter, safety, transportation, and medical care should not be restricted, but some nonessentials to which caseworkers have access—new furniture, movie tickets, toys, fast food coupons—can be earned with follow-through of new parenting strategies and child compliance (Azar & Wolfe, 1998).

Now that a rationale has been provided, let us turn to how a cognitive-behavioral intervention was implemented with Deanna Williams, who was court mandated to receive in-home supervision from the local CPS agency.

Application to the Williams Family

A cognitive-behavioral approach, combining parent training and strategies that work on creating more positive parental attributions for child behavior, as well as building problem-solving and self-control skills, will be applied to the case of the Williams family. In order to enhance the effectiveness of cognitive-behavioral treatment with clients in the child welfare system, several adaptations may be necessary, including:

- Using a collaborative approach
- More frequent and shorter meetings
- Using reinforcement strategies with parents, including contingency contracts
- Avoiding technical explanations
- Using a videotaped training course
- Setting a minimum number of goals
- Selecting goals with client input
- Using physical, concrete prompts
- Employing frequent modeling and behavioral rehearsal
- Problem solving barriers to missed appointments and noncompliance with parenting skills

Some elaboration of this bulleted information will follow. The remainder will be discussed in the next section, which involves techniques and how they can be applied to the case study.

Using a Collaborative Approach

A collaborative approach is taken in that the caseworker avoids lectures but rather processes information to ensure that it is being conveyed and is attentive to client signals about the level of comprehension and engagement (Webster-Stratton & Herbert, 1993). Carroll (1998) discusses several specific ways the caseworker can achieve this:

- Ask clients to provide concrete examples from their own experiences on how material can be applied. ("Can you think of a time last week when your children did that?")
- Elicit clients' views on how they might use particular skills. ("Now that we've talked about praising, when-then strategies, and token economies, what do you think would work best for you? Which of these techniques have you used in the past? Is there any other way you've tried to teach your children how to mind?")
- Elicit clients' reactions to the material. ("Does this seem like it's an important issue for us to be working on right now, or do you have something else in mind?")
- Ask parents to describe the skill in their own words. ("We've talked a lot about having the kids take a time out when they're misbehaving. Just to make sure you're confident about what you want to do, can you tell me what you plan to do when they are fighting with each other and won't stop?")
- Pay attention to clients' verbal and nonverbal cues (e.g., lack of eye contact, one-word responses, yawning). ("I notice that you keep looking out the window and I was wondering what your thoughts are on what we're talking about today.")

A collaborative approach allows clients to bring up concerns they have with the implementation of techniques. Humor is used to put parents at ease and to reduce anxiety (Webster-Stratton & Herbert, 1993). A collaborative approach further makes use of self-disclosure, when appropriate. If caseworkers are parents themselves, bringing up some of their own parenting challenges and solutions will help parents feel that the caseworker understands their present circumstances. If caseworkers are not parents, they may consider talking about their experiences with their relatives' children in their role of aunt or uncle, or discuss how other parents with whom they have worked have coped with challenges.

More Frequent and Shorter Meetings

The caseworker met with Ms. Williams on a frequent basis (twice a week) and limited sessions to 45 minutes to an hour since Ms. Williams seemed to lose focus and expressed "boredom" if sessions were any longer.

Using Reinforcement

Another way to encourage Ms. Williams's participation in intervention was to use the principle of reinforcement, which is central to behavioral theory, and apply it to Ms. Williams's learning of new parenting skills. Just as parents will be taught skills to reinforce their children's appropriate behaviors, they can also be reinforced with praise and rewards as they learn skills. Practitioners should try to shape parents' behavior by praising attendance, participation, and even small attempts at working on assignments.

Contingency contracting was also used with Ms. Williams in order to invoke compliance through rewards. A *contingency contract* is a written agreement that specifies the relationship between behaviors and their consequences (Kazdin, 1989). In a contingency contract, the target behavior is specified in explicit, unambiguous terms. *Participation* was defined as being at home during scheduled appointments, engaging in discussions and role plays, and practicing the skills with her children. In a contingency contract, the consequences for performing the target behavior are clearly stated. It was negotiated with Ms. Williams that after six sessions of her participation, the caseworker would reward the family with a meal at McDonald's. A benefit of contingency contracting is that it clarifies expectations (Kazdin, 1989). Signing a contract also tends to encourage more active and committed participation in treatment. As contractual obligations are met and parents receive the rewards associated with them, the contracts can be continually renewed.

Avoiding the Use of Technical Explanations

Another way to increase compliance and cooperation is to avoid the use of technical explanations. The words *learning* or *rewards*, for instance, can be used instead of *reinforcement, contingencies,* and *stimulus conditions* to make information more understandable to parents.

Using a Modeling Course

Another way to make material more salient when teaching skills for parents in the child welfare system is to use a videotape training course. Webster-Stratton and colleagues (1989) have developed a parent training curriculum for parents of young children (ages 3 to 8) with behavior problems. In this training program, behavioral techniques are modeled through brief vignettes on videotape. After presentation of each vignette, the facilitator emphasizes key points in the implementation of certain techniques and involves parents in problem solving, role playing, and rehearsal. Webster-Stratton and colleagues have completed a series of well-designed studies showing the efficacy of their course in terms of reduced behavior problems, parental physical abuse, and parenting stress (Webster-Stratton et al., 1989; Webster-Stratton et al., 1988).

If a family does not possess a TV or VCR, one can be brought into the home so that a videotape training series can be shown, with certain parenting skills covered during each home visit. Discussion with the parents on how techniques can be used with their children will then follow. Whether or not such a course is implemented, it is crucial that information on parenting skills not only be discussed, but also modeled and rehearsed so that material is made as concrete as possible.

Formulating a Minimum Number of Goals

A problem with the way many CPS cases are handled is that the client is given too many goals at once to achieve, an approach that is doomed to failure (Azar & Wolfe, 1998). Clients who are already overwhelmed by multiple life stressors will not be able to successfully tackle many objectives, which often requires them to seek services from different agencies in the community at once. Obtaining a G.E.D. and receiving job training were clearly important aspects of the intervention for Ms. Williams so that she could eventually work to support her family. However, tackling these objectives and parenting strategies initially were seen as an overload by the caseworker and her supervisor. Therefore, the caseworker concentrated on only parenting skills at the start.

Selecting Goals with Client Input

As much as possible, goals should be developed with client input. Unfortunately, some Child Protective Services agencies now assign goals to clients, even to the point where they are computer-generated for certain types of problems—physical abuse, sexual abuse, neglect, substance abuse, and so on. However, if a goal is not personally important to clients, they will not be motivated to pursue it. Goals should be related as much as possible to what clients see as the problem. Clients who have physically abused their children will usually see their child's behavior as the problem. When formulating goals, this viewpoint should be exploited. In Ms. Williams's case, she saw the problem as Janice's misbehavior. Therefore, the goals formulated were around child compliance, and the caseworker explained that the way to achieve compliance from young children was for Ms. Williams to structure the environment in a way that trained Janice to obey her mother's directions.

▮▮▮ Behavioral Techniques

The following behavioral techniques will be discussed: behavioral assessment, goal construction, collaboratively discussing physical punishment, token economies, extinction, distraction, effective command giving, and praise. Integrated in each section is a discussion of how to work collaboratively with parents to encourage attendance and compliance.

Behavioral Assessment

Parent training seeks to determine the operational aspects of behaviors and its reinforcement schedule. The practitioner, rather than accepting Ms. Williams's global description of Janice as "bad" and "hardheaded," began by asking Ms. Williams to describe Janice's behavior in observable ways: "What is Janice doing when she's 'bad?" "What is going on?" The context of the troublesome behavior is then examined, which includes its setting (in behavioral terms, the stimulus) and the consequences that follow: "Where does this happen?" "What happens?" "When does it happen?" "How often?" "What happens after she doesn't follow your direction?" "What do you do?" "What does she do?" "What happens next?"

Although the focus is on child behavior, each episode of physical abuse also warrants a functional analysis of its own. For each episode, the practitioner should explore what happened before, when the parent was first aware of the urge to hit the child, the feelings experienced, how and where the abuse occurred, and what happened afterward.

Out of an understanding of the stimulus and contingency conditions arise goal formulation.

Goal Construction

When asked to identify a goal, Ms. Williams said the children should "mind" her. When asked to be more specific, she said, "They should do what I say." When parents make statements that their children should "just obey" or follow directions, the practitioner should work with them on more specifically identifying their expectations regarding chores, completion of homework, getting along with others, cleaning up after themselves, and so on. Clearly delineating expectations for children will act to limit the number of commands issued; otherwise, young children may become overwhelmed and fail to understand which commands take priority. If expectations are clearly specified (and strategies for making these concrete for very young children will be covered in the section on token economies), then parents should not be embroiled in constant command giving. Another advantage of clarifying expectations is that the caseworker may learn that some exceed the developmental stage of the child. If this occurs, the practitioner can educate the parent on the reasonable achievements for a child of that age.

As part of developing goals and tasks, a baseline of the desired behaviors must be established first so that the frequency of the target goal can be determined. Ms. Williams reported, with the school's confirmation, that Janice and Yolanda had only been attending two to three days a week. Therefore, a reasonable target goal might involve the children's school attendance four times a week.

Because bedtime and morning routines proved the most difficult regarding child compliance and also related to the children's lack of school attendance, the caseworker had to help Ms. Williams break down the goal (being ready by 7:45 A.M.) into tasks, defined as a number of small, trainable, and highly concrete behaviors (Kazdin, 1989). Since the goal involved a certain time by which a complex set of behaviors needed accomplishing, the component tasks involved the specific child behaviors and their time frames.

To achieve a departure time of 7:45, the caseworker helped Ms. Williams trace back the behaviors involved, and they discovered that the family would have to wake by 6:15. So this time was no longer left to chance, the caseworker provided the mother with an alarm clock and showed her how to use it. Other tasks were broken down as follows: dressed by 6:30, breakfast by 7:15, teeth brushed by 7:20, hair fixed by mother by 7:35, backpack and supplies together by 7:40, and at the door and ready to leave by 7:45.

After the tasks were delineated, Janice and Yolanda were asked to draw pictures of the actions they needed to perform in the morning: "Draw a picture of what it looks like when you first get up in the morning like your mother wants you to." "Show me the next thing you need to do." "Show me brushing your teeth."

Although Yolanda's pictures were merely scribbles, Janice could recount and draw, with prompting, the necessary processes. In a collaborative approach, children are involved as much as possible so they will have ownership over the behaviors they are expected to enact. The drawings were then pasted onto the refrigerator as visual prompts. Ms. Williams was shown how they could be used in the morning. For instance, if the children began to dawdle over breakfast, she could point to the next picture of Janice brushing her teeth.

Rehearsal followed in which first the caseworker modeled the "getting ready in the morning" behaviors as "Momma," and "Momma" played one of the children with the children as viewers. Then Janice and Yolanda, in turn, played "Momma," and they assigned the caseworker and Ms. Williams to child roles.

Although an essential guideline involves keeping goals and tasks few in number, the caseworker decided that the nighttime routine played into the family's morning experience. Exploration about the sequences of behavior at night revealed that Ms. Williams bathed her children right after dinner. In a collaborative approach, the caseworker seeks opportunities to congratulate parents on their successes. The caseworker, in this instance, complimented Ms. Williams on getting the bathing of the children completed early rather than waiting until the end of the evening.

Continuing to identify specific behavioral sequences, the caseworker discovered no set bedtime in the Williams household. Ms. Williams described that it was determined by her own fatigue level and the schedule of TV programs, and that she and the children went to bed at the same time. The caseworker suggested that a specific bedtime be determined for the children so that the hour would cease to become negotiable. Janice couldn't as easily wrangle her mother into staying up "just a few minutes more" if there were a set time. Ms. Williams's objection to a set plan involved the possible interruption of a show she was watching. The caseworker reiterated that if Ms. Williams allowed the children to stay up past their bedtime, then the specific time would have little meaning, and bedtime would continue to be a struggle. The quicker she established a regular routine for the children, the fewer disruptions she would find.

Ms. Williams initially considered a bedtime of 10 o'clock, but the caseworker educated her that as early as 7:30 was not unreasonable, especially for a child of Freddy's age. Indeed, getting Freddy ready for bed could cue the girls that their own bedtime approached. Ms. Williams especially looked forward to having time in the evening for herself.

To begin the process, the caseworker gave Ms. Williams an inexpensive clock to hang on the wall so she could use it as a prompt for bedtime: "In 5 minutes, the big hand will be on the 8, and then I'm going to turn off the TV." The children were involved again in the rehearsal of the appropriate bedtime routine by drawing pictures of what they were supposed to do and then engaging in role plays. Rather than yelling or cajoling, in the future Ms. Williams could show the children these pictures as prompts for their appropriate behavior.

However, before they begin to consider other options for discipline, parents who have physically abused their children must come to believe that such an approach is worth trying. In the following section, an approach to such a discussion is described.

Collaborative Discussions About Physical Punishment

A collaborative discussion centers on parents' beliefs and feelings about physical punishment, their perceptions of risks and benefits, and the effects on the family. The caseworker must be sensitive to cultural beliefs about the appropriateness of physical punishment. In a discussion of parent training with families of different cultural backgrounds, Forehand and Kotchick (1996) state that, for various historical reasons, African American parents socialize their children for obedience to authority, which is often achieved through physical punishment. Cultural beliefs about the necessity of physical punishment seem to operate for Ms. Williams. For example, she says she was physically punished as a child, and all of her relatives and neighbors in her community use physical punishment.

The following questions devised by Webster-Stratton and Herbert

(1993) explore belief systems in a sensitive fashion. In the illustration, the reader will see how the caseworker responded to Ms. Williams, educating her along the way about the disadvantages of physical punishment without resorting to lectures.

"Tell Me How Spanking Works for You"

Ms. Williams responded that spanking was the only type of discipline that worked to change her children's behavior because it scared them into knowing "who's boss." The caseworker then asked, "How much do you want your children's behavior to be based on fear?" How willing will children be to discuss their questions and concerns if they have fear for their mother? Ms. Williams then revised her goal to compliance based on respect rather than fear, but was unable to see other alternatives for cultivating respect.

The caseworker joined with Ms. Williams on the goal of authoritative parenting, which has repeatedly been associated with positive outcomes in low-income children and adolescents (Steinberg, 2000). *Authority* was defined as having clear and consistent rules and monitoring children's whereabouts and activities. The caseworker suggested, however, that there were ways other than physical punishment to achieve authoritative parenting and that she would work with Ms. Williams on some of these strategies.

"How Often Do You Use It?"

"Only when they won't mind any other way," Ms. Williams responded. In simple terms, the caseworker explained that if parents resort to physical punishment "only when they have to," they train their children to disobey until physical punishment is threatened or actually used. In behavioral terms, the principle involved is negative reinforcement; the removal of a coercive event (child misbehavior) through parent behavior (physical punishment) reinforces the behavior (physical abuse) responsible for removing the coercive event (Kazdin, 1989).

"How Do You Feel Afterward?"

Ms. Williams described a reduction in tension after striking out at her children and getting them to obey. Kazdin (1989) reported that while the original purpose of punishment is to reduce noncompliance and teach appropriate behavior, in actuality, negative reinforcement, the satisfaction parents get from "teaching the child a lesson," the reduction of parental frustration, and the exacting of "revenge" on the child play larger roles.

"How Does Your Child Feel About Physical Punishment?"

Ms. Williams claimed her children were "mostly" unaffected. Probing by the caseworker revealed that Janice is sometimes angry and Freddy clings to his mother more after an episode.

"Do You Ever Feel You Lose Control When You Spank?"

Ms. Williams admitted that physical punishment always followed a "loss of control" when she has "had it." She further admitted that sometimes the loss of control concerns her; she doesn't want to react to events so violently.

"What Do You See as Its Advantages?"

The main advantage of physical punishment was that it invoked child compliance, although Ms. Williams admitted that the effect was not long lasting. Questioning by the caseworker further revealed Ms. Williams's belief that increasing the intensity of the punishment (the amount of force or number of strikes used) affected a child's misbehavior to an even greater degree. The caseworker educated her on the fact that intensity of punishment does not translate into increased results (Kazdin, 1989).

When asked if spanking seemed to increase compliance in other settings where physical punishment was not used (e.g., the school, the Head Start program), Ms. Williams could see that Janice was not afraid of her teachers, therefore, she did not obey. Ms. Williams admitted this was a problem as it was important for Janice to do well in school in order to succeed in life.

"Are There any Disadvantages?"

The most salient disadvantage for Ms. Williams was her involvement with the CPS system. She would have agency involvement in her life for at least 6 months and had to prove before a judge that she had improved in her parenting skills. The other disadvantage was that she sometimes lost control and bruised her children or marked them in some other way. However, she also saw her children as provoking her to that point.

These discussion questions allowed Mrs. Williams to consider her perceptions about the effectiveness of physical punishment and the impact of its use. Ms. Williams was also educated on the other possible negative consequences of punishment (Kazdin, 1989):

1. Children may feel negatively toward the person enacting the punishment and the behaviors for which they are being punished. For instance, if Janice is physically punished for not treating her younger brother and sister well, then she might have negative feelings toward her siblings.
2. Children may avoid the consequences of punishment by lying about behaviors (one of Ms. Williams's complaints about Janice).
3. It teaches children aggression by modeling aggression (another complaint against Janice is her aggressiveness toward her siblings and other children at kindergarten).
4. Punishment may teach children what they shouldn't do, but not what they should do.

The caseworker went on to provide Ms. Williams with the consequences of physical punishment that have been identified through empirical study. Short-term consequences include cognitive deficits in terms of language and IQ, social impairment in terms of increased risk of aggression toward other children and reduced empathy and concern for peers (Azar et al., 1988; Conaway & Hansen, 1989; Graziano & Mills, 1992; Malinosky-Rummell & Hansen, 1993; Mueller & Silverman, 1989), problem-solving deficits, lack of self-control and poor impulse control, academic and behavior problems in school (Graziano & Mills, 1992), and depression and low self-esteem (Toth, Manly, & Cicchetti, 1992). Research has also indicated that adolescents physically abused as children exhibit more externalizing behaviors and violent criminal offending compared to their non–physically abused counterparts (Malinosky-Rummell & Hansen, 1993). Longer-term consequences for adults include increased rates of violence, including criminal offenses (Malinosky-Rummell & Hansen, 1993); and for women, internalizing problems, such as self-abuse, suicidality, dissociation, somatization, depression, and anxiety (Malinosky-Rummell & Hansen, 1993).

The case study demonstrates that educational material is only provided after parents are given the opportunity to discuss and explore their belief systems. Through this discussion, Ms. Williams began to question how well physical punishment worked and became more amenable to learning new skills that would be less dependent on spanking. Many of the new skills are grouped under the general category of reinforcement programs, which can be implemented to encourage children's positive behavior.

Token Economy

Different kinds of reinforcement systems are possible: praise and other social reinforcers, token economies, and high-probability behaviors. The caseworker focused initially on only one method of reinforcement, a *token economy*, so as not to overwhelm Ms. Williams before she became comfortable with the new skills. A token economy involves the use of tangible reinforcers, such as chips, coins, tickets, stars, points, stickers, or check marks, for desirable behaviors, which are then traded in for an agreed-upon reward (Barkley, 2000).

This method of reinforcement was chosen for several different reasons. First, Ms. Williams expressed that praising her children didn't seem to have much value. "They know what they're supposed to do, so why praise them?" The caseworker would work with these belief systems but, in the meantime, she wanted to start on a program of tangible reinforcement as quickly as possible to increase the safety of the children.

Ms. Williams correctly assumed that Janice's behavior would be more difficult to control once physical punishment was no longer used. Therefore, a token economy system, implemented quickly, could help the parent gain control over the child's behavior (Kazdin, 1989). An advantage of token economies is that they can initially procure high levels of performance from children. Another advantage of token economies is that tokens bridge the gap between the desired behavior and the reward (Kazdin, 1989). Points can further be attached to different tasks that may comprise a desired goal when the behavior involved is complex. For instance, "getting to school on time" comprises several behavioral sequences, therefore, each sequence can be reinforced rather than waiting until the whole behavior is performed. Further, tokens can be quickly and easily administered without interrupting the desired behavior. In addition, tokens are less prone to satiation. When the rewards chosen lose their reinforcing value, they can simply be exchanged for other rewards (Kazdin, 1989).

Although token economies can be very effective, one drawback is that parents have to be organized about implementing them consistently. Families that are already overwhelmed by multiple stressors may have some difficulty following through with the necessary structure. Some adaptations may be useful so that parents experience a greater likelihood of success. First, the target behaviors identified on a token economy chart should come directly from the tasks that have already developed from the priority goals. Second, the number of target behaviors is kept low. Third, the target behaviors should be the same for all children in a household in which there are multiple children. Fourth, the chart should be placed in a physical position that the children can reach. In this way, children can place the stars or stickers themselves, although parents are responsible for assigning points and doling out tokens. Children find the process of placing tokens on the chart reinforcing in itself; in this way, they take more ownership over their behavior.

The caseworker then explained the role of rewards in the reinforcement program in that stars are accumulated to earn rewards. Ms. Williams immediately replied she had no money for such things. Quickly, the caseworker explained that rewards need not cost money. Indeed, she suggested that rewards should involve relationship rather than material reinforcers (Hepworth, Rooney, & Larsen, 2002). Possible examples included a trip to the park with their mother, playing a game with her, a story at bedtime, checking out books from the library. In keeping with the Webster-Stratton and Herbert (1993) model of collaboration, Ms. Williams was treated as the expert about her children and was assigned the task of establishing the appropriate rewards. Ms. Williams decided the reward would involve selecting a video to rent, which the family would then watch together.

In order to improve parents' success with new skills, it is important to elicit from them the potential barriers for implementing techniques (Webster-Stratton & Herbert, 1993). These discussions allow for parents to ask questions, express concerns, and problem solve around barriers. Parents should be active participants in this process and have the opportunity to change or develop the task with the caseworker and plan how the skill will be put into practice. The goal of this discussion should be the parents' expressed commitment to complete the exercise (Carroll, 1998).

Ms. Williams had a number of questions and concerns about the use of the token economy. First, Ms. Williams said, "Well, what if Yolanda gets to have a reward, but Janice doesn't make it? How am I supposed to take one kid to the park without the other ones? I can't leave them alone in the house. I'd get in trouble for that, too. And if I read a story to one, then I'll have another fit on my hands because the other one would want a story, too." When multiple children are involved, it is admittedly harder to administer social rewards. Special outings for one child and not another would require childcare for the other children. Allowing a child to play with her mother might involve another one "throwing a fit," but there would be other strategies offered (ignoring or extinction) for dealing with those kinds of child behaviors.

Another concern Ms. Williams shared was that "checking off all those behaviors" would take a lot of work in the morning. The caseworker offered a reframe, saying that it sounded as if Ms. Williams had a real appreciation for the many behavioral sequences involved in getting her children to bed and ready in the morning. The caseworker agreed with her that while it would initially take more work to follow through with the token economy, she wouldn't always have to put stars down "for every little thing." As the children's behaviors took hold, over time the tokens could be phased out. The term in behavioral theory, *shaping*, means to reinforce successive approximations of a behavior to eventually meet a goal that is initially out of reach (i.e., getting ready by 7:45 A.M.) (Kazdin, 1989).

Ms. Williams's final concern with the token economy was that it seemed "fake." She said the world didn't work like that. The caseworker agreed that tokens often didn't exert control over other settings where tokens were not used. However, the caseworker learned from conversations with the children's teachers that behavioral management systems were used in both Janice's kindergarten classroom and Yolanda's Head Start program. If used in both the home and the school, the children would quickly catch on to how such a system operated.

The caseworker further explained that if considered more broadly, reinforcement and reward systems did operate in everyday life. For example, she asked about Ms. Williams's last paying position, which Ms. Williams said was at a fast-food establishment. Ms. Williams admitted she wouldn't have gone to this job if a paycheck hadn't been forthcoming on a regular basis. The caseworker explained that the paycheck operated as a reward. She further asked if Ms. Williams has been praised by her supervisor. Ms. Williams described her supervisor as so "mean" that she had to quit. By using this example from Ms. Williams's experience, the caseworker helped build Ms. Williams's perspective-taking for her children and to understand that people require reinforcement and rewards to perform certain behaviors.

After mother and caseworker spent a lot of time discussing the reinforcement system, in the caseworker's presence, the mother explained the use of the token economy to her children. She described it as a way to get "you all to mind me." She placed the chart on the refrigerator along with the children's pictures and showed them how they would get the stars the caseworker had supplied.

At the end of the session, Ms. Williams was asked to repeat her commitments for the following week. She agreed to figure out rewards for the children and to implement the token economy. The caseworker actively sought a commitment from the client so that the client understood the importance of the task and its usefulness (Carroll, 1998).

Encouraging Compliance

Behavioral parent training relies heavily on the implementation of homework tasks for its success. In order to stress its importance, the caseworker is advised to check in at the beginning of each session about the results of homework (Webster-Stratton & Herbert, 1993). Carroll (1998) warns against merely asking clients whether they completed the task or accepting a one-word (yes or no) response without further probing, but to explore for at least 5 minutes what the client has learned from the assignment.

When the caseworker returned for another home session 3 days later, Ms. Williams had not implemented the token economy system, and Janice and Yolanda had attended only 1 day at school. Webster-Stratton and Herbert (1993) suggest that if a parent fails to complete an assignment, this matter should receive immediate attention. The following questions can be explored with the client:

1. What makes it hard for you to do the assignment?
2. How have you overcome this problem in the past?
3. What advice would you give to someone else who has this problem?
4. What can you do to make it easier for you to complete the assignment this week?
5. Do you think there's another assignment that might be more useful for you?
6. What thoughts come to mind when you think about this assignment?
7. What makes it hard to do?
8. Does this seem relevant to your life?
9. How could we make this more helpful?

Ms. Williams still wasn't convinced that a token economy would be helpful, and it would take so much more time in the morning when she was already so tired, she said. To the caseworker's question of what would make the token economy more helpful, Ms. Williams didn't have any ideas other than just to sleep in and avoid it all. Ms. Williams was asked about the advantages of this plan. She could only name one: that she didn't have to deal with the children in the morning. The caseworker asked about some of the disadvantages. Ms. Williams could see that continued lack of attendance at school was a problem, that it wasn't a good start to the girls' education. It also might gain her continued CPS involvement.

Ms. Williams expressed frustration and helplessness about not being able to use physical punishment. However, she said, "If that's what you people want, that's what I'll do." The caseworker validated her feelings of anger and helplessness about people "telling her what to do," rather than allowing her to make decisions about how to rear her children. The caseworker then complimented Ms. Williams on the obvious importance of her children to her since she was willing to have the caseworker come into her home and work with her. Ms. Williams said that, without her children, her life would have no meaning, and she was willing to do whatever she could for them.

The caseworker then asked again if there were another way Ms. Williams could handle the bedtime and morning routines that would have more relevance for her. Ms. Williams, sighing, said, "I guess I'll just go ahead and do it." The caseworker offered to come by the following morning and walk through the routine with her. Ms. Williams seemed pleased and agreed this would be helpful.

This conversation illustrates the necessity of exploring the reasons that parents might have difficulty with assignments. Otherwise, parents will conclude that the practitioner is either not committed to the usefulness of the homework tasks or that she fails to understand the family's particular situation (Webster-Stratton & Herbert, 1993). Most important, without actual implementation of skills, parent training methods will not work.

As discussed earlier, compliance with treatment is also often low for CPS clients. Although home visits are a way to increase participation, parents are sometimes not present for their scheduled sessions. Missed sessions warrant the same type of attention that lack of compliance with homework receives. The problem-solving process, which is detailed in a following section, can be applied when there are missed sessions. The problem behind the absenteeism can be defined, solutions can be brainstormed, and then the caseworker can plan with the client how attendance during sessions can be assured.

Follow-Up on Token Economies

After the caseworker had come for her morning appointment, Ms. Williams started to implement the token economy. In a follow-up session, Ms. Williams described that Janice became very frustrated with her lack of stickers because she so desperately wanted to win the reward for the week, which was to go to a video rental store and pick out a video the family would watch. The caseworker said, "The good news is that Janice seems to be very motivated by the reinforcement system. She wants to earn enough points to get a reward. You want her to experience success with the system initially so that she will continue to be motivated by it, instead of feeling hopeless and just wanting to give up." The caseworker and Ms. Williams then examined more specific aspects of her implementation.

One issue was that while Ms. Williams wanted Janice to have responsibility for dressing herself, she didn't like the clothes Janice picked—they didn't match, they were inappropriate, and so on. Then she and her child would battle over these choices, which infringed on the rest of the time needed to get ready and also precluded Janice from receiving stickers.

The caseworker reminded Ms. Williams that she wanted foremost to instill in her daughter autonomy and self-reliance. Therefore, Janice's efforts toward dressing herself should be reinforced rather than become a topic for argument. Ms. Williams said she didn't want Janice's teacher to think Ms. Williams had not dressed her properly, nor did she want the other children to tease Janice for wearing mismatched clothes. The caseworker assured Ms. Williams that the teacher would be much happier if Janice attended school in clothes that did not match as opposed to her not coming to school at all. In addition, as much as possible, Janice should be allowed to experience the consequences for her actions. For instance, if she insisted on wearing mismatched clothes to school and then children teased her for it, in order to avoid teasing in the future, Janice might be more prone to choose matching clothes. The caseworker also seized on information Ms. Williams had provided, that Janice enjoyed her mother fixing her hair before school and took pride in the way her hair looked. If Ms. Williams could spend more time on these positive aspects, the relationship would improve, and mornings would be more pleasant for everyone. The caseworker further suggested that although Janice may not always do exactly what Ms. Williams wanted, efforts in the right direction, at least initially, should be reinforced through stickers. Over time, Ms. Williams could become more exacting about requirements as her children's behavior was shaped. In the beginning, criteria for dressing could be low in order to obtain reinforcement. Over time, the criteria are gradually increased before reinforcement is earned.

Another issue brought up by Ms. Williams was her desire for Janice to do what she's asked without complaining, "fussing," and "giving attitude." The caseworker explained that trying to change too many behaviors at once sets up failure rather than success. The priority behaviors at the moment were the children going to bed and getting ready in the morning. After these were established, then the system could change to accommodate compliance without "attitude" with reinforcement only occurring if Janice followed through on her mother's commands politely. In the meantime, Ms. Williams needed to be taught to ignore Janice's complaining since that might eradicate the undesirable behaviors in itself and to model polite command giving to her children.

Ms. Williams said that she always seemed to run out of time for the children to eat breakfast, and Janice's teacher had spoken to Ms. Williams about Janice complaining she was hungry. The caseworker asked Ms. Williams to consider her options. Ms. Williams said she couldn't possibly get up any earlier, but she could at least give them some graham crackers or a breakfast bar to eat on the way to school. In addition, one morning, Ms. Williams admitted she may have turned off the alarm and simply returned to sleep. The caseworker suggested putting the alarm clock on the other side of the room so that she was forced to get up in order to turn it off.

As for bedtime, Ms. Williams said she hadn't paid attention to an exact bedtime, but when she decided they should go to bed, she would give them a 15-minute warning and then turn the TV off. Janice would beg, cry, and eventually throw a tantrum. Ms. Williams would raise her voice to her and threaten her, saying, "You better get your butt into your bed right now before I give you a whipping." She admitted she had spanked Janice to get into bed, but it had worked, she was quick to add. She also said that she was careful to just use her hand rather than an extension cord or a paddle so that she didn't lose control of the force. The caseworker complimented her for changing the way she administered the spanking but suggested that reinforcement and extinction would probably be quite effective without resorting to punishment.

Extinction and Distraction

Extinction (also called *ignoring*, the term used with Ms. Williams) is the cessation of reinforcement for a behavior, which results in the eventual decline in the frequency of the behavior or its eradication (Kazdin, 1989). When applying extinction to a particular behavior, one must first examine the function of the behavior. Ms. Williams could see that the tantrums prolonged bedtime. She also thought that Janice enjoyed "getting to her" and "making her mad." The latter explanation was reframed by noticing that, like all children, Janice liked attention. Tantrums, complaints, and so on were very effective in getting her mother to pay attention to her. Extinction was a way to reverse this behavior. Janice would find that these behaviors no longer gained for her the attention and prolonged bedtime she was seeking.

Since the procedures for extinction have been detailed in chapter 2, only certain characteristics of extinction are explained here. Ms. Williams was told about the importance of being consistent, ignoring the complaints *every* time they occurred. She was also asked to practice in the session after watching the caseworker model appropriate techniques, such as looking away, maintaining a neutral facial expression, and avoiding any verbal or physical contact.

It was essential that Ms. Williams rehearse the ignoring behaviors, first with the caseworker and then with her children "pretending" to throw a tantrum. Role playing with her children also provided an opportunity for Ms. Williams to explain to the children and demonstrate with them how she would handle certain kinds of misbehavior in the future (Hembree-Kigin & McNeil, 1995).

Crucially important, parents have to be warned that they will experience an initial increase in the undesirable behavior when they first begin employing extinction techniques. Ms. Williams was told to take the inevitable *extinction burst* as a sign that the technique was working. She was assured that Janice's behavior would improve and the gains would last if Ms. Williams consistently ignored any recurrence of the undesirable behaviors.

After the information had been imparted and the role plays conducted, Ms. Williams was encouraged to think of the problems that might come up with this technique or other barriers that would prevent her from enacting the extinction. Ms. Williams worried that ignoring "bad" behavior seemed to implicitly encourage it. The caseworker emphasized that looking at the function of the behavior was important. If the purpose was to get out of doing something or to get what she wanted, refusing to give in to the behaviors would help Janice learn over time that they had no effect. If reinforcement of desirable behaviors and ignoring undesirable behaviors didn't stamp out the problems, then they would consider punishment.

Ms. Williams wondered if she could use it with Freddy because he was so young. The caseworker explained that he could be taught through ignoring that tantrums and "fussing" would no longer gain him what he wanted. Of course, with a 2-year-old, safety had to be a prime consideration; she had to be mindful that he didn't place himself in a dangerous situation when he was ignored.

Webster-Stratton (1989) also suggests the technique of distraction paired with ignoring for young children. For instance, if Freddy cries because he wants to play with the remote control, rather than shouting at him, Ms. Williams could take the remote control away and divert his attention to a brightly colored ball: "Here's something else you can play with. See if you can catch it!" Distraction could also be used with Yolanda and Janice, particularly to avoid an argument about a command (Webster-Stratton, 1989).

Effective Command Giving

Before providing information, in the usual spirit of collaboration, the caseworker first asked Ms. Williams about how she typically went about getting her children to obey her. Ms. Williams said she "hollered" and threatened to "whip their butts." Ms. Williams was convinced of the effectiveness of these methods, especially since she was brought up with the same pattern of discipline. In order to develop Ms. Williams's empathy for the impact of shouting at her children and threatening them with physical harm, the caseworker asked again about the job Ms. Williams had held at the fast-food restaurant, asking her to describe how her "mean" supervisor had handled the employees. Ms. Williams said that the supervisor hadn't treated them with "respect."

Ms. Williams had initial difficulty defining "respect" behaviorally but, with the caseworker's help, was able to view respect as treating people as if they had worth and dignity, speaking to them in a normal tone of voice rather than "hollering," making requests of people politely rather than demanding things of them, and telling them when they had done well. Ms. Williams said she had quit because her supervisor had been so disrespectful.

The caseworker then asked Ms. Williams to consider how her children could be treated with respect. Mrs. Williams said, "With kids, it's different." "How is it different?" the caseworker asked, but Ms. Williams was not able to come up with an explanation other than "Kids need to know their place." The caseworker agreed that children needed to understand their place in terms of following rules that had been set for them and to act with respect toward those in authority, but that yelling only taught them how to be disrespectful toward others.

Since Ms. Williams didn't seem very convinced, the caseworker asked about her relationship with her own mother. Although Ms. Williams relied on her mother for childcare and some financial resources, she said, "I don't like being around her. She's always talking me down." Ms. Williams described that, from when she was young, she could never do anything right, according to her mother, who would call her "dumb-ass" and "stupid" on a regular basis. Ms. Williams could see that this hadn't helped her feel very good about herself; as for her own children, she wanted to instill in them a sense of their own worth without spoiling them.

The caseworker encouraged Ms. Williams to talk more about the meaning of *spoiling*. Together, they defined spoiling as giving children too many material goods, particularly when they had done nothing to earn them, to hold low expectations for school attendance and performance, and to allow them to overrun authority. After this discussion, Ms. Williams seemed reassured that the caseworker's parenting techniques were not oriented toward the spoiling of her children. This reassurance made her more amenable to hearing information about effective command giving and praise. The reader is referred to chapter 2 as space precludes detailing the effective components of command giving here. However, before parents can accept didactic material, material must be made relevant to parents' experiences as this example illustrates.

Praise

Since Ms. Williams's initial reaction to praise was that it might spoil her children and give them "big heads," the caseworker used the collaborative technique of having her list all of the disadvantages and advantages of praising her children (Webster-Stratton & Herbert, 1993). As well as possibly spoiling her children, Ms. Williams named other disadvantages: Ms. Williams would have to get used to praising when she "didn't talk like that," and if she praised her children, "they would go back to being bad." As advantages, Ms. Williams was only able to name one: Praise might help her children have more respect for themselves. The caseworker educated her on other benefits in addition to raising the self-esteem of her children: Praise was free and plentiful, and it provided a reward that could be internalized by the child. The caseworker also pointed out times she had praised Ms. Williams, asking how it had felt to be the recipient. Ms. Williams admitted that the praise and compliments had motivated her. This conversation caused Ms. Williams to see some value in praise. As space precludes detailing the components of successful praise, the reader is referred to chapter 2 for more specific information.

Summary of Subsequent Parent Training Sessions

The emphasis here has been on positive reinforcement because, with physically abusive parents, punishment has been overused. In addition, parent training experts recommend that positive reinforcement should be applied at a rate of three times the number of punishments (Barkley, 2000). For more discussion on alternative discipline methods, please see chapter 2 for discussion of natural and logical consequences and time outs. Effort-based consequences, such as chore completion, might be a type of punishment Ms. Williams will adopt as Janice grows older, since in a single-parent household with three children, there will be many chores to perform.

Work on parent training revealed that some of the barriers to effective implementation involved certain deficits in terms of stress management and problem solving and the negative attributions Ms. Williams held toward her children's behavior.

Cognitive-Behavioral Interventions

Cognitive-behavioral interventions used with Ms. Williams involved relaxation training, problem-solving skills training, self-reinforcement and self-instructional training, and cognitive restructuring. Work began with stress management techniques, specifically how to identify and decrease the physiological arousal associated with anger. Ms. Williams related that when she got mad, she felt "hot all over," her head started to hurt, and her jaw clenched. Because Ms. Williams showed some awareness of these physical cues, the caseworker began to describe progressive muscle relaxation in which successive muscles in the body are tensed and relaxed, in order to reduce arousal. However, Ms. Williams was not amenable to using this technique. Working collaboratively, the caseworker said, "Okay, let's find out what will work better for you." In order to figure out alternative ways to manage stress, the caseworker taught Ms. Williams the problem-solving method, which will be detailed in the next section.

Problem-Solving

Briefly, the caseworker described the problem-solving model as comprising the following steps (D'Zurilla & Nezu, 2001): identify the problem, generate alternatives to solving the problem, examine the pros and cons of each alternative, select the best alternative, implement the alternative, and evaluate the alternative.

Identify the Problem

The problem was defined as "How does Ms. Williams calm down her body when stress starts to arise?"

Generate Alternatives to Solving the Problem

The caseworker explained that at this stage, Ms. Williams was to brainstorm possible alternatives, censoring herself as little as possible; the aim was to produce as many options as possible.

Since Ms. Williams couldn't think of anything initially, the caseworker used some self-disclosure. She said that when she felt stressed out, she liked to work out, followed by a hot bath. Ms. Williams said she wasn't going to go to "no aerobics class" but that a walk to the store, which took about 5 minutes, might at least get her out of the house and give her a chance to calm down. Ms. Williams said, "The problem is, it's the kids stressing me, and I can't leave them alone to go to the store, otherwise you people will come back saying I don't take care of my kids right."

The caseworker explained that at this stage of the problem-solving process, it was important to generate as many options as possible without making judgments. If Ms. Williams started to critique herself at this point, she might shut down the flow of ideas. "What other ways could you help yourself calm down?" the caseworker asked. "Raising three small children by yourself is very stressful. What can you do to help your stress level?"

Ms. Williams said she liked talking on the phone to her sister or her friend Tricia. "Who else could you call?" asked the caseworker.

"That's about it. They're the only ones."

"I know it feels better to talk to people who know you very well, but in case they're not around one day when you need them, how about calling me or a parenting hotline?"

"I guess so," said Ms. Williams with a notable lack of enthusiasm.

The caseworker added these to the list and said, "Remember, right now, we're just trying to get as many options as possible. Later on, you can decide which ones fit you."

Ms. Williams seemed stuck again after the caseworker wrote these ideas down, so the caseworker prompted her by saying, "What are some other ways that might involve relaxation for the body?"

Ms. Williams said she liked doing her nails. When they were painted, she felt better about herself, and the process of doing her nails meant she had to focus and block out distractions. Ms. Williams found the same sense of relaxation when she did her hair. Sometimes her sister would come over, and they would trade off doing each other's hair. In the same vein, Ms. Williams found applying body lotion to her skin to be relaxing.

When Ms. Williams got stuck again, the caseworker suggested, "How about taking the kids out somewhere, just so there's a change of scene, and you can get out of the house?" Ms. Williams said she occasionally went to the housing project playground, although some of the teenage boys and older men sold drugs there.

"What about other parks in the area?" the caseworker asked.

Ms. Williams said that if her car was working, she could maybe drive them to a safer park.

The caseworker then gave her some other ideas: counting to 10 or backward from 10, visualization of a peaceful place, taking deep breaths, drinking a cold glass of water, journaling, self-talk. Ms. Williams added, "Going to the mall."

The caseworker read her the list they had generated: going to the mall; self-talk; deep breathing; counting to 10; calling her sister; calling her friend; calling the caseworker; calling a parenting hotline; applying body lotion; doing her nails; doing her hair; going to the store for a 5-minute break from the kids and picking herself up a treat, an orange Fanta, for instance; taking the children to the housing project playground; taking her children to another playground.

Examine the Pros and Cons of Each Alternative

The caseworker went through each item on the list with Ms. Williams, figuring out how to make them viable. For instance, Ms. Williams was praised for realizing that she could not leave her children unattended for the 5 minutes it took to go to the store and back. "So what ideas do you have about that?" the caseworker asked. "How can you take a short break away from them without leaving them alone?" With a great deal of probing, Ms. Williams said she could ask the teenage girl who lived next door to watch them for 5 minutes; she could call her mother to come over; or she could call her friend Tricia, who lived in the same project.

Some of the other strategies didn't have many disadvantages attached to them other than that they couldn't always be used. For instance, sometimes Ms. Williams's nails or hair were already done. However, body lotion could be applied at least once a day and had the additional advantage that her children would then want some for themselves. Rubbing lotion on their skin might also nurture and calm them.

Ms. Williams admitted that the playground was free of drug traffic most of the day until the late afternoon when the teenagers came home from school. Ms. Williams liked the idea of meeting Tricia out there with her children not only for the support and companionship but also so that parents and their children could reclaim the playground area for themselves.

Some of the other options, such as taking deep breaths and self-talk, required training and role playing to make the most effective use of these techniques.

Select the Best Alternative

The next part of the problem-solving process involves selecting the best alternative. As mentioned, many viable alternatives were presented during this problem-solving session. Indeed, the caseworker and Ms. Williams decided that the list of options could be tacked onto the refrigerator, so when Ms. Williams felt herself "losing her cool," she could select one of the alternatives. A visual reminder is helpful since when one starts to get stressed out, the caseworker explained, it is difficult to generate options and think clearly. If the first alternative selected didn't act to calm her down, Ms. Williams could then work through some of the other ideas.

Implement the Alternative

Ms. Williams committed to trying a couple of the options and reporting back to the caseworker her results, so that they could enact the final stage of the problem-solving process, which is to evaluate the implementation of the alternative selected.

In addition to problem solving, another strategy for Ms. Williams involved self-talk, which includes self-reinforcement and self-instructional training.

Self-Reinforcement and Self-Instructional Training

The caseworker grouped self-reinforcement and self-instructional training together as *self-talk*. Self-instructional training was developed by Meichenbaum (1999) to give people an internal cognitive framework to instruct themselves in how to cope effectively with difficult situations. Self-reinforcement involves giving "yourself pats on the back, telling yourself that you're doing a good job," the caseworker explained to Ms. Williams. After providing information about self-talk, the caseworker modeled using self-instruction and reinforcement together to demonstrate how Ms. Williams could cope with getting the children ready in the morning:

> It's 6:30 already. I can do this. Once I get moving, it won't be so bad. First, I better get the girls up. They're hard to wake up but I'll be gentle with them, nothing worse than being woken up abruptly. I'll tell them that once they get out of bed without me telling them again, they can earn a sticker. Okay, Yolanda is up,

good. I praise her for getting up right away. I'm doing a good job. Oh, praising her has made Janice want to get up, too. That works real well to pay attention to what's going well with one child, then sometimes the other one will want to do the same. I remember learning about that. I'm doing a good job learning about how to manage the kids' behavior. It's tough with three of them, but I'm doing fine. Okay, now I'm going to choose something for Yolanda to wear. She likes red, so I'll choose this little red outfit. Janice is interested in what she's going to wear. I start dressing Yolanda, but then she wants to do it herself. Good, I praise her for being able to dress herself. Janice shows me that she wants to wear black and blue together. I don't think it matches, but I want her to learn how to do things for herself . . .

After the caseworker models the skill of self-talk, the parent performs the task under the direction of the caseworker. The caseworker then models the task while whispering the above instructions and has the parent do the same. The final step is for the caseworker to model the behaviors covertly (saying the directions internally) and then the parent performs the task through internalized instructions.

Self-reinforcement and self-instructional training were implemented to bolster Ms. Williams's repertoire of cognitive strategies. The skill described in the next section, cognitive restructuring, works on altering existing negative and irrational thinking, which impede logical and functional behaviors.

Cognitive Restructuring

A brief explanation of the premise behind cognitive restructuring was provided to Ms. Williams. She was told that often, unknown to ourselves, we have automatic thoughts that are reflexive and habitual in nature and that give way to the emotions we feel (Beck, 1995). Cognitive restructuring works by identifying the thoughts that are negative or irrational and replacing them with more hopeful, positive, and realistic appraisals of situations.

Cognitive restructuring works a great deal with abstractions in that one is required to think about one's thoughts. Ms. Williams, however, operates on a concrete level of thinking, therefore, techniques will have to be made concrete through the following measures: providing only brief explanations, using visualization to make situations more immediate, writing thoughts and their alternatives down, and keeping expectations for homework minimal.

These adaptations will be made clear by detailing the application of the following steps for cognitive restructuring: identify a situation that elicits negative emotions, identify the uncomfortable feeling and rate its intensity, identify the thinking behind the negative emotions, examine the validity of the thoughts and replace them with more realistic appraisals, and rerate the feelings.

Identify a Situation That Elicits Negative Emotions

Ms. Williams, tired of talking about morning and bedtime routines, came up with a recent situation in which she had taken the children to McDonald's. Janice had wanted to play on the playground, but Ms. Williams would not allow her to do so until she ate. Ms. Williams said Janice refused to eat and just cried louder and louder until everyone was looking.

Identify the Uncomfortable Feeling and Rate Its Intensity

The practitioner asked Ms. Williams to recount what she felt at the time. Ms. Williams identified "embarrassment." The practitioner drew a 10-point scale on a sheet of paper with "embarrassment" at 10. Ms. Williams said she was at an 8.

Identify the Thoughts Underlying the Negative Feelings

The practitioner asked Ms. Williams her thoughts during this time. Ms. Williams repeated that she felt embarrassed. The caseworker educated her that embarrassment was a feeling rather than a thought. The caseworker then used visualization to help Ms. Williams uncover her automatic thoughts. The caseworker asked her to relax, close her eyes with her feet on the ground and her arms uncrossed, take a deep breath, imagine the distressing situation ("You are now in McDonald's. Your child is crying. You feel hot and embarrassed"), and discuss in detail the thoughts surrounding the event. Ms. Williams responded, "Everyone is staring at me. They all think my child is spoiled and that I can't control her." The caseworker commended her for identifying these thoughts and wrote them down as she asked, "What are you thinking about your child?"

"She's doing this on purpose to get me mad," said Ms. Williams.

The practitioner also wrote this response down. "That was good, you were able to pinpoint the thoughts. Were you aware of this running commentary through your mind?"

"No, not really."

"Many people are not, so you've just made a big step there in making that connection."

Examine the Validity of the Thoughts

Examining the validity of the thoughts involves looking at the evidence to support the thoughts, viewing the situation from the perspective of others, figuring out how to cope in a "worst case" scenario, and getting education about child development, which may affect perception. The following dialogue illustrates how the caseworker, through questioning, got Ms. Williams to examine the validity of her thoughts.

"Let's look in more detail at these thoughts," the caseworker said. "Let's take the first one, 'Everyone is staring at me. They all think my child is spoiled and that I can't control my child.' "

"I don't want people thinking that."

"What makes you believe people were thinking that?"

"I know they were."

"How do you know?"

"Because they were looking at me. Everyone was staring."

"*Everyone* in the whole McDonald's was staring at you? No one was eating or trying to take care of their own kids?"

Ms. Williams laughed at the exaggeration. "I guess some people was minding their business."

"Okay, so not everyone was staring. If you had to guess, how many were—" The practitioner pantomimed an exaggerated staring expression.

Ms. Williams laughed again. "No one looked like that. They would just look and then look away, look again."

"Okay, so people weren't really staring. They were glancing at you from time to time."

"Yeah, I guess that's what they were doing."

"And was *everyone* doing that?"

"Yeah, everybody in the playground."

"How many were in the play area? Just make a guess."

"Maybe five grown-ups and their kids."

"Okay, so 10 to 12 people were glancing at you from time to time."

The caseworker continued to ask questions so that Ms. Williams had the opportunity to dispute her own negative appraisals. One way of doing this was to inquire about how Ms. Williams might view a parent in a similar situation and then apply this reaction to herself.

"But they was thinking I couldn't control my child," Ms. Williams insisted.

"How do you know they were thinking that?"

"I just know."

The practitioner asked jokingly, "Is there something you haven't told me about before, that you can read minds?"

Ms. Williams laughed but said she knew because that's how she would think about a parent in a similar situation.

"Do you *always* think that when you see a child tantruming and a parent is unable to make them stop?"

When Ms. Williams said she did, the caseworker referred Ms. Williams to her friend Tricia. "Let's say you and Tricia took your kids to McDonald's, and the same thing happened to her, and she felt really embarrassed. What would you tell her to make her feel better?"

"Maybe I'd say, 'That's how kids are. They act bad sometimes.' "

"Okay, so you'd empathize with her that she was in a tough situation and that it was difficult raising kids sometimes?"

Ms. Williams nodded her agreement.

"Have you heard that term before, 'empathy'?" the caseworker asked. When Ms. Williams said she hadn't, the caseworker explained that it meant to "put yourself in the situation of another person and imagine how that person feels." "I wonder if any of those parents at the McDonald's have been in that same situation with their own children and felt empathy for you."

"I don't want nobody feeling sorry for me," said Ms. Williams.

"Empathy is not really pity—it's more like understanding: 'Oh, yeah, I've been there, too.' Do you see the difference?"

"Kind of."

"So do you think anyone in the McDonald's had that kind of understanding for you?"

"Yeah, maybe, because they all had kids."

In the above dialogue, the caseworker had Ms. Williams take the perspective of others, to begin to question her belief that "everyone thought she was a bad mother." The next strategy the caseworker used was to exaggerate Ms. Williams's worst fears about what people were thinking and then discuss how she would cope with that. The caseworker said, "Okay, assuming that you are right, and they were thinking you didn't have any control over your child, what could you tell yourself to make you feel better?"

"They don't have no right to judge me."

The caseworker reframed this statement: "Is it that we all go through some of the same things, so if other people think that, they don't have the right because they've probably been in a similar situation themselves?"

"Yeah."

To tackle Ms. Williams's negative attributions about Janice's intention—that she was acting purposefully to spite her mother—Ms. Williams was asked to consider other possibilities for Janice's behavior.

"She wanted to play on that slide. She loves that slide."

"Right, children love to play. Sometimes they would rather play than eat."

"But we don't get to go to McDonald's too often. I bought her a Happy Meal, and she didn't even appreciate it."

The caseworker validated her disappointment. "So this was a special occasion for your family. You had saved up the money to eat at McDonald's. You wanted your family to have a good time, and by playing instead of eating, she wasn't showing appreciation."

The caseworker asked if there were another way to view "appreciation," but Ms. Williams couldn't see any other options. Therefore, the practitioner provided her with a possible viewpoint: "It sounds like she really appreciated being taken to McDonald's. She wanted to play on all the playground equipment."

Ms. Williams looked like she was considering this alternative viewpoint but didn't say anything. The caseworker continued, "Were there a lot of other children playing, too?" Ms. Williams nodded affirmatively.

"That's why McDonald's builds those playscapes. They know it's not just the food that will bring the kids in."

The caseworker then checked in with Ms. Williams and asked, "How much do you think your daughter was purposefully trying to make you mad and look bad in front of those people versus just wanting to play on all that fun, brightly colored equipment?" Ms. Williams could see that McDonald's purposefully made their franchises enticing to children and that Janice's response was therefore fairly normal. In this example, the reason for Janice's misbehavior was attributed instead to her developmental level.

Rerating the Feelings

The caseworker asked Ms. Williams to review the different possibilities they had now generated: not everyone was staring; maybe some people understood Ms. Williams; if some people thought she was a bad mother, she could cope with it; McDonald's purposefully built their franchises to appeal to children. She was then asked to rerate her embarrassment. Ms. Williams ranked herself now at a 5, three points lower than before.

Summary of Cognitive Restructuring

The main purpose of cognitive restructuring with physically abusive parents is to reduce their hostile attributional bias toward other people, particularly their children, and to help manage their stress so that arousal does not result in physical punishment. The caseworker continued to target negative parenting appraisals when they presented a barrier to the implementation of safe and effective parenting practices. She then worked with Ms. Williams on helping her replace these thoughts with more realistic and neutral appraisals of her children's and other people's motivations.

Conclusion

The caseworker's efforts centered on cognitive-behavioral work for the first 6 months that Ms. Williams's case was under ongoing supervision with the CPS agency. The caseworker then moved into a focus on Ms. Williams completing her high school education with a graduate equivalence diploma (G.E.D.) and job training skills. After a year of CPS involvement, further monitoring was no longer seen as necessary.

This case was used to demonstrate how a caseworker working in the home with a parent can systematically implement a cognitive-behavioral intervention to affect the problem of physical abuse. The case application showed how techniques can be made concrete so that parents who are plagued by numerous life stressors can improve their ability to parent effectively without resorting to physical abuse of their children.

5 Cognitive-Behavioral Group Treatment with Mothers of Sexual Abuse Victims

▌ Case Studies

Case #1

Mexican American Octavia, a nursing home aid, discovered that her father had sexually abused her 3-year-old, Maria. Octavia had lived with her parents since Maria's father had divorced her. Her father also sexually abused Octavia when she was young, up until she was 12. She says she has three sisters, two older, one younger, and a younger brother. Octavia reports that her father sexually abused all of her sisters, but they still defended him, asking how she could send him to jail. (See figure 5.1 for a genogram of this family.)

Case #2

Demetria, an African American woman, has a 5-year-old daughter, Samantha, and a 3-year-old son, Darren, who were sexually abused by Demetria's live-in partner. Initially, Demetria didn't believe it, but her boyfriend agreed to stay with his mother while the investigation

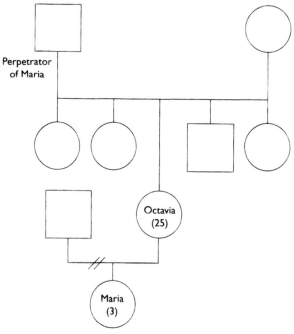

Race: Mexican American

Figure 5.1. Cognitive-Behavioral Group Therapy Case Study #1: Octavia's Family

pended. Subsequently charged with the sexual assaults, he spent some time in jail. When he got out on bond, Demetria took the children and moved in with her sister, who has four children of her own. The household was too crowded, so she is now staying in women's transitional housing. (See figure 5.2 for a genogram of this family.)

Case #3

Miranda is a Caucasian, 32-year-old mother of Wendy, a 10-year-old girl from a previous marriage, and Summer, her 4-year-old daughter from her current marriage. The girls have described abuse from Miranda's husband. Wendy and Summer now live with Miranda's mother since Miranda sided with her husband's denials. Miranda doesn't work outside the home, and worries about how she'd manage on her own with two children. (See figure 5.3 for a genogram of this family.)

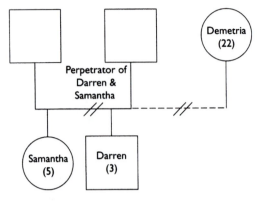

Race: African American

Figure 5.2. Cognitive-Behavioral Group Therapy Case Study #2: Demetria's Family

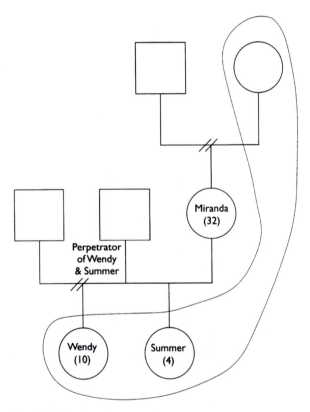

Race: Caucasian

Figure 5.3. Cognitive-Behavioral Group Therapy Case Study #3: Miranda's Family

Introduction

This chapter will illustrate the use of cognitive-behavior group treatment with non-offending parents whose children have been sexually abused. The three case studies will be interwoven into an explication and application of a group curriculum. Before delineating the group format and the curriculum topics, the empirical evidence for cognitive-behavioral treatment with sexual abuse victims and their families will be described.

Empirical Evidence

Testing of cognitive-behavioral treatment with sexual abuse victims and their families has been pursued by Deblinger and colleagues (Deblinger, McLeer, & Henry, 1990; Deblinger, Lippman, & Steer, 1996; Deblinger, Stauffer, & Steer, 2001; Stauffer & Deblinger, 1996) and Cohen and Mannarino (Cohen & Mannarino, 1996a, 1996b, 1997, 1998). A recent addition to this literature has also come from King et al. (2000). The approaches to cognitive-behavioral treatment hold many common elements. (See table 5.1.) Deblinger and colleagues, however, focus on posttraumatic stress in which gradual exposure techniques play a large role. (See box 5.1.) Cohen and Mannarino's (1993) particular focus is preschool children given that one third of children who are sexually abused are under the age of 6.

Deblinger and colleagues have carried out three separate studies. In a pretest-posttest design, Deblinger et al. (1990) studied school-age children and their non-offending parents and found that PTSD symptoms, anxiety, and depression in children decreased after the intervention. Stauffer and Deblinger (1996) then used a quasi-experimental design to evaluate group treatment of preschool children and their parents. Child externalizing, internalizing, sexual behaviors, and PTSD symptoms were reduced as the result of treatment over a wait-listed control group. It seemed that parent involvement in treatment produced important benefits for children.

Deblinger et al. (1996) and King et al. (2000) are the only studies to examine the differential effects of parent and child treatment with randomization to groups. When parents only were involved in treatment, depression levels and PTSD decreased. These positive results

Table 5.1	
Cognitive-Behavioral Treatments for Child and Non-Offending Parent	
Child	Parent
Deblinger & Colleagues	
1. Gradual exposure to abuse-related memories	1. Training in gradual exposure techniques to assist in reducing their children's anxiety toward abuse-related stimuli
2. Coping skills (relaxation training, emotional expression, and cognitive restructuring)	2. Emotional expression and management
3. Education on sexuality, sexual abuse, and sexual abuse prevention	3. Sexual abuse education
	4. Communicating about sexual abuse to children
	5. Training in behavior management skills
Cohen & Mannarino	
1. Sexual abuse prevention	1. Increasing parental supportiveness
2. Assertiveness training	2. Addressing ambivalence toward the abuser
3. Attribution training	3. Attribution training
4. Addressing aggressive and sexual acting-out behaviors	4. Addressing history of abuse in the parent's background, if applicable
5. Coping with fear and anxiety	5. Education about legal issues
	6. Training in skills to manage children's anxieties and inappropriate sexual behaviors

were maintained at 2-year follow-up (Deblinger et al., 1999). King et al. (2000) also found that child treatment was necessary to reduce PTSD in children. It seems necessary, therefore, that both parent and child should receive treatment so that both child internalizing and externalizing symptoms can be addressed, along with parents' skill at managing their children.

The most recent study located involved preschool sexual abuse victims and their parents (Deblinger et al., 2001). Forty-four children and their caretakers were randomized to either eight sessions of cognitive-behavioral or supportive group treatment. Improvements for both conditions were reported with superior outcomes for the

How Does PTSD Develop from Sexual Abuse?

Deblinger, McLeer, and Henry (1990) discuss a behavioral conceptualization of post-traumatic stress disorder (PTSD) involving both classical and operant conditioning. In classical conditioning, an initially neutral stimulus becomes paired with an uncondi-tioned stimulus. In cases of sexual abuse, certain places, people, and sensory experi-ences, such as smells or hearing certain words or phrases, may become associated with the trauma. The neutral stimulus then becomes a conditioned stimulus, capable of evoking anxiety. Operant conditioning comes into play as the child avoids such anxiety-provoking stimulus. The relief associated with the avoidance of anxiety is negatively reinforced and increases the frequency of avoidance behavior in the fu-ture.

Treatment involves gradual exposure to abuse-related memories in order to dis-connect the respondently conditioned stimuli. Gradual exposure combines pro-longed exposure and systematic desensitization, so that children are encouraged to confront feared stimuli (thoughts and memories of abuse) in a graduated fashion. While parents are trained on gradual exposure techniques to use with their chil-dren, the therapist also works directly with the child.

cognitive-behavioral group in terms of reducing parental negative emo-tional reactions.

Cohen and Mannarino (1996a, 1996b) conducted one study, a quasi-experimental design with preschool children and their caretakers. Child internalizing, externalizing, and sexual acting-out behaviors im-proved in the cognitive-behavioral treatment over attention control. Predictors of success from the cognitive-behavior protocol were the cognitive abilities of the children (children with more advanced cog-nitive capacity showed increased benefits from treatment), maternal adjustment at posttest, and social support of parents at 6- and 12-month follow-up (Cohen & Mannarino, 1996b). At follow-up, gains made by cognitive-behavioral treatment were maintained.

Illustration of Group Treatment

The cognitive-behavioral group treatment offered for mothers of sexual abuse victims will use elements common to both the Deblinger and associates and Cohen and Mannarino protocols: emotional expression, coping mechanisms, increasing maternal supportiveness, information on sexual abuse dynamics, handling symptoms of child sexual abuse, cognitive coping through cognitive restructuring, sex education for children, talking to children about sexual abuse, and sexual abuse prevention. (For an overview of cognitive-behavioral theory, see box 5.2.)

Deblinger and Heflin (1996) have published a guide to their treatment for PTSD arising from sexual abuse, therefore, many aspects of their protocol will be used. However, the focus of this group treatment will be on the array of effects that sexually abused children may show since PTSD, while a common result of sexual abuse, is not the only symptom pattern. Indeed, PTSD, demonstrated in approximately one third of child sexual abuse samples, is no more common than some of the other symptom patterns, such as sexual acting out, lowered self-esteem, and behavior problems (Kendall-Tackett, Williams, & Finkelhor, 1993).

Children's treatment is offered concurrently with the parents' treatment, but will not be detailed here due to space considerations (see Cohen & Mannarino, 1993; Deblinger & Heflin, 1996, for explications of child cognitive-behavioral treatments). Conjoint sessions, with both

---

Box 5.2

Key Assumptions of Cognitive-Behavioral Theory and Additional Resources

Key Assumptions

Cognitions, or thoughts, are assumed to mediate behavior and feeling states. People's cognitions are altered in two ways:

- *cognitively*, by teaching clients how to identify and change their distorted thinking through interventions such as cognitive restructuring and positive self-talk. With sexual abuse, education is provided to parents about sexual abuse dynamics and children's reactions, so that parents can correct their distorted thinking around the abuse, feel better, and provide more appropriate responses to the sexually abused child and to the perpetrator of the abuse.
- *behaviorally*, by helping clients learn coping skills, such as appropriate emotional expression, problem solving, relaxation, and communication skills.

Additional Resources

J. A. Cohen & A. P. Mannarino. (1993). A treatment model for sexually abused pre-schoolers. *Journal of Interpersonal Violence, 8*, 115–131.

E. Deblinger & A. H. Heflin. (1996). *Treating sexually abused children and their non-offending parents: A cognitive-behavioral approach.* Thousand Oaks, CA: Sage.

---

parent and child present, are typically held after parent and child have progressed sufficiently in their individual formats. Conjoint therapy will be briefly summarized at the end of the chapter.

Group Format

The group treatment can be conducted as either an open- or closed-ended group, depending on agency and client needs and an assessment of the advantages and disadvantages of each type of group. (See box 5.3 for whether to choose an open or closed group.) If treatment is delivered in an open-ended format, sessions will rotate, and members will repeat cycles. If treatment is offered as a closed-ended format, then after each 6-week period, the group will be reopened to admit new members. As in the open-ended group, mothers keep cycling through treatment as long as necessary.

Many of the women attending group will be court ordered for services, but women from the community can also participate. In order to successfully recruit and maintain members, it is necessary for practitioners to work with the local CPS agencies and family court judges.

Curriculum Topics

Curriculum topics include introductions, emotional expression for mothers, coping mechanisms, belief and support, information on sexual abuse dynamics, symptoms of sexual abuse and management of symptoms, cognitive coping, and communication skills training. These topics will be detailed below.

Introducing Parents to Treatment

Introducing parents to group includes the use of icebreakers to build rapport among members and providing an explanation of group rules and the purpose of the group.

Icebreakers

Icebreaker exercises are a way to develop rapport among members and leaders. (See box 5.4 for some suggestions.)

Advantages and Disadvantages of Open Versus Closed Groups

Advantages of an Open Group

1. Membership can be maintained or expanded so the group does not get too small.
2. Many different perspectives are offered by people at different stages.
3. Support is offered to those in immediate need as there is no waiting list.
4. The presence of members who have spent more time in the group can offer hope for members who are in severe crisis about the disclosure.
5. New members can handle being challenged about nonsupportiveness more easily from people who have shared some of their same experiences than from the group leader.

Potential Disadvantages of an Open Group

1. Membership in the group might become so large that group members lack opportunities for individualized attention.
2. There is the possibility of less cohesion.
3. Changing membership and the lack of stability may discourage members from developing trust and a sense of safety in the group to openly confide in group members.
4. Individual members can withdraw and take a nonparticipatory role.
5. There is the potential of fragmentation into subgroups.
6. It may be more difficult for a facilitator to manage.

Advantages of a Closed Group

1. Trust, cohesion, and cooperation can develop among members.
2. Topics can proceed in sequence with subsequent material building on earlier discussions.

Disadvantages of a Closed Group

1. Dropout may lead to too few members being maintained.
2. There is a risk of losing clients as they are assigned to a waiting list.

Note: From Toseland & Rivas, 2001.

Group Rules

Rules for the group should be covered, including the necessity for regular attendance, punctuality, participation, confidentiality, access of information to caseworkers and other professionals, sharing group time, and showing respect for others while they are talking.

Icebreakers

Exercise #1

Supplies needed: large ball and sufficient space
Directions: One person starts off by throwing the ball and saying her name. The person who catches the ball then has to say the name of the person who has thrown the ball and then her own. The next person to whom the ball is thrown has to say the name of each person who has come before her, and so on. This icebreaker not only builds rapport, it is very effective for helping people learn the names of group members quickly.

Exercise #2

Supplies needed: large bag of candy
Directions: A bag of candy is passed around. Each woman is invited to take as many candies as she wants. Then each woman in turn has to reveal one thing about herself for each candy she has taken.

Exercise #3

Supplies needed: paper and pens, a few prepared interview questions (hobbies, number of children, where they are from, and so on)
Directions: Group members break into dyads, interview each other, and then introduce the partner who has been interviewed to the group.

Purpose of Group

A discussion of the purpose of the group begins with the facilitator eliciting from parents their perceptions of why they are in treatment. Once verbalized, expectations can be clarified. Responses such as the following may be typical:

- "My caseworker says I have to."
- "The judge ordered it if I want my girls to live with me again."
- "My lawyer said it would look good."
- "I don't have anyone else to talk to."
- "My child's therapist suggested it."
- "Because I'm a basket case right now."
- "Because we're role models for our children."
- "Because we have to learn how to deal with our children's sexual abuse."

The facilitator elaborates that the disclosure of sexual abuse thrusts a mother into crisis. Other than the victim, no one suffers like the non-offending parent, and part of the group's purpose is to help mothers with their distress. If mothers feel better as a result of coming to group, benefits will be reaped for their children as maternal adjustment has been linked to child recovery from sexual abuse (Cohen & Mannarino, 1996b; Deblinger, Taub, Maedel, Lippman, & Stauffer, 1997; Deblinger, Steer, & Lippman, 1999; Newberger, Gremy, Waternaux, & Newberger, 1993).

The facilitator outlines the goals of the group (Deblinger & Heflin, 1996):

1. To educate mothers on sexual abuse dynamics, possible effects, and the recovery process
2. To help mothers demonstrate support to their children and to help in the children's recovery process
3. To help mothers develop more successful coping skills to deal with the crisis of disclosure
4. To provide appropriate role modeling for their children

To begin to help mothers cope with the crisis, work in group centers on helping parents identify and express their distressing emotions.

▮▮▮▮ Emotional Expression

Deblinger and Heflin (1996) describe emotional expression as an initial component of therapy for both parents and children. Feeling identification is important so that mothers will more effectively manage their emotional reactions. Mothers will later be taught cognitive restructuring as a cognitive coping strategy. Learning to identify feelings will be the first step in tracking back feeling states to their thought origins.

The facilitator begins the discussion by asking mothers to name the feelings they first had when they learned about their child's sexual abuse. Feelings named usually included shock and denial/disbelief ("This isn't happening. This can't be happening," "This isn't real," "She can't be saying the truth"); anger (at the perpetrator, at the child, at themselves); sadness for what has been lost and at the hurt that has been done to the child; disgusted/sick; betrayal; and fear (of losing their children, their partners, their homes, their freedoms). The mixed feelings inherent to intrafamilial sexual abuse are also discussed.

The facilitator avoids confronting individuals when they express disbelief that the abuse occurred. However, she will not stop group members from challenging unsupportive mothers. It is especially helpful if these group members have moved on from an initial period of disbelief themselves.

Group facilitators ask mothers, given their strong feelings during the crisis of disclosure, how they protected their children from hearing about their feelings and their difficulties. Members say that they don't talk to their children about these matters, knowing it isn't appropriate. Some admit, however, to talking to other adults in their children's presence, believing their children too busy playing or watching TV to hear. The facilitator stresses that children will sense the emotions of others around them, but because they are egocentric, they will tend to explain the upset in relation to themselves ("It's my fault").

When the facilitator asks how a child may interpret a parent's strong emotional reactions, group members are able to see that a child might be frightened and that the child's sense of stability might be threatened, especially when this occurs in the midst of all the other changes that disclosure of sexual abuse brings. The facilitator adds that witnessing strong emotions in a parent may inadvertently pressure the child to share the parent's viewpoint of the offender. Instead, children should be encouraged to have their own attitudes and feelings toward the perpetrator.

Octavia defends her recent phone arguments with her sisters, which were held in her daughter's presence, by saying, "I don't want sexual abuse to be a secret any more. I want to make sure she knows about all this stuff. I didn't talk about it, and look what happened to me, and now her." The facilitator agrees that open communication is important and that a subsequent topic in group will be how to talk to your child about sexual abuse. These conversations are better held, however, after mothers have the opportunity to process their own reactions and to develop appropriate ways of expressing these emotions. Ways to help mothers cope with difficult and painful feelings and reactions will be covered in the next section.

Coping Mechanisms

The crisis of disclosure may overwhelm many parents' normal coping mechanisms. Crisis theory, however, assumes that during a crisis an individual is amenable to learning new mechanisms (Parad & Caplan, 1960). A central way to cope is through a social support network (e.g., Lazarus & Folkman, 1984). Specific to sexual abuse, Cohen and Mannarino (1998) discovered that at 1-year follow-up, maternal social support predicted children's overall adjustment.

Many women whose children have been sexually abused, however, have suffered disruptions to their network. Partners, relatives, or friends might have actually perpetrated the abuse, or other family members might have aligned behind the offending member. Some families have to move their households because of risk to the child. Moving from one community to another further disrupts support networks.

Because of these possible problems, the group can become a major source of support. The group may provide a venue where mothers can speak openly about the sexual abuse with other people who have undergone similar experiences. For additional support, some women also participate in individual therapy. This may be encouraged, especially for those who have their own sexual abuse history, as group time will not allow in-depth explorations of these issues.

Aside from social support, women talk about their other coping mechanisms, which may include journaling, exercise, and other self-care activities. Some name "keeping busy," which isn't difficult in the aftermath of disclosure when so many aspects of these families' lives change.

When group members bring up maladaptive responses and activities, such as substance use, excessive TV watching, binge eating, oversleeping, or dysfunctional cognitive coping strategies, such as minimization of the abuse, the facilitator engages the group members in a process by which they address the advantages and disadvantages of a particular problematic coping strategy. In this way, clients can examine for themselves how a particular coping strategy benefits them and can learn from the group alternative methods.

Other coping methods, such as relaxation training and visualization, are taught (see McKay, Davis, & Fanning, 1997, for example). The facilitator reads a script for progressive muscle relaxation, and members practice the relaxation exercise. Mothers are given a copy of the script to take home and are urged to use it when facing a stressful situation, when they feel their stress levels rising, or if they have difficulties sleeping.

Thus far, the content of the group focuses on the mother's experience. This is an important component due to the crisis reactions that non-offending mothers often experience and the effect this distress has on their children. The curriculum now turns more directly to how mothers can support their children's recovery and adjustment.

Belief and Support

The facilitator introduces the session on support of children by asking group members to define the two components of support: belief and protective action. *Belief* involves validation of the child's account, placing the responsibility on the adult rather than on the child, and conveying an attitude of concern (Corcoran, 1998). *Protective action* involves behaviors that protect the child from further abuse and aid in recovery, such as cooperating with Child Protective Services and criminal justice agencies, removing the child from perpetrator access, and seeking counseling (Corcoran, 1998).

"There's more involved than I thought," commented Demetria.

"But it makes me realize I'm doing all that now," said another member. "We're here—that means we're in counseling. I am being protective. I don't know why my caseworker keeps telling me I'm not."

"Let's look at this a little more closely," said the facilitator, "because it's not like support is an either/or concept."

To illustrate, the facilitator made a visual aid by drawing, on a chalkboard or flip chart, a scale from 1 to 10. One is anchored as "no support," and 10 is total support. Women were asked to rank where they were on the scale at first disclosure, and where they would rank themselves currently. Usually, mothers will have made some progress on the scale. They are then asked to account for their change in belief over time.

The facilitator then worked with the group members on how belief of their child could be conveyed to the child and how supportiveness can be put into action.

Octavia said, "Maria knows I believe her."

The practitioner pushed a bit further. "How do you know she knows?"

"I told her when we went to the advocacy center. I said I believed her, and I was glad she told, and that she did a good job of telling the lady there." The practitioner complimented Octavia and stressed to the group that this message bears repeating to their children.

Group members admitted, however, when the facilitator brought up the practice, to questioning their children about the details of the abuse, which conveys an attitude. But as Demetria said, "Sexual abuse is a serious charge. You have to figure it out for yourself. It can't just be all these strangers talking to your child. No one knows your child better than you do."

Miranda said her 4-year-old's story wasn't clear. "It keeps changing."

"I was getting stuck on that, in the beginning," said Octavia. "But my caseworker said that isn't uncommon for the real little ones because they're thinking of different incidents each time. And they can't tell you how many times it happened."

The facilitator elaborated further on young children's limited cognitive development. "The abstract quality of time is beyond most young children's capabilities. When preschoolers are questioned about abuse, the interviewer is trained to break time down into some very basic categories so the child can more easily understand ('Before or after your birthday/Christmas/summer?' 'Did it happen one time, a few times, or lots of times?')." Parents are urged to stay with the gist of the information that has been gathered from multiple interviews by professionals: a child has conveyed sexual contact with an adult and has provided enough details to suggest its veracity. Given the sheer quantity of interviews from professionals from varying sources (law enforcement, victim services, district attorney's office, Child Protective Services, and so on), parents should further avoid interviewing their children.

Turning now to protective action, the facilitator stressed that treatment for children is an important component of protective action. To gather group members' perceptions about counseling, women were asked, "What are some of the reasons a mother might not want her child to receive treatment for the sexual abuse?" Responses to this question will tend to gravitate to the following (James, 1989):

"I don't want her to keep dwelling on it."
"She had to talk to all these people already. I don't want her to
    have to keep talking about it."
"His behavior is worse after he goes to therapy."
"There doesn't seem like much therapy is going on. She plays
    with sand and puppets and draws."
"How much therapy can you do with a 3-year-old?"

"I want to get on with our lives. I just want her to forget about it."

"It's too expensive. The sliding scale fee is still a lot for me to pay."

"Transportation. It takes all day to get there on the bus."

"There doesn't seem to be anything wrong with her. She acts like a normal 3-year-old." (See box 5.5 for apparently asymptomatic children.)

Parents may not as easily mention the guilt they feel for failing to protect their children (James, 1989). Another reason for parents' discomfort with children's therapy involves the possibility that some mothers have been sexually abused themselves. High rates of sexual abuse have been found in mothers whose children are sexually abused, with estimates ranging from 23% to 65% of samples (Deblinger, Stauffer, & Landsberg, 1994; DeJong, 1988; Faller, 1989; Goodwin, McCarthy, & DiVasto, 1981; Myer, 1985; Peterson, Basta, & Dykstra, 1993; Tufts New England Medical Center, 1984). The sexual abuse of their children may raise mothers' own issues, which may feel overwhelming to the parent, particularly in the midst of also handling the crisis of the child's sexual abuse.

At the close of this discussion, the practitioner emphasized the purpose of therapy, so that sexually abused children are able to (Deblinger & Heflin, 1996; James, 1989)

- talk about the abuse without shame to the appropriate people,
- process the feelings associated with the abuse, and
- correct any misperceptions that have arisen as a result of the abuse.

Box 5.5

Apparently Asymptomatic Children

Possible reasons why one third of children do not display ill effects:
- Some children may be relatively unaffected.
- Measures used may not have captured the effects of the sexual abuse.
- The symptoms may be delayed. The children may be suppressing their symptoms or may have not yet processed the abuse.

Note: From Kendall-Tackett, Williams, and Finkelhor, 1993.

■ Information on Sexual Abuse Dynamics

Information about sexual abuse dynamics is important to provide to non-offending parents as this will help mediate mothers' emotional distress and assist them in gaining more empathy for their children (Deblinger & Heflin, 1996). Two aspects of sexual abuse dynamics will be covered here: the reasons why many children do not reveal the abuse immediately and how perpetrators involve children.

Reasons for Not Disclosing

Since many mothers are angry at their children for not disclosing the abuse to them first, the group facilitator asked the mothers to come up with a list of reasons to explain why children do not tell their mothers. Parents tend to produce the following reasons (Deblinger & Heflin, 1996):

1. Fear for the child's safety ("He told her he would kill her if she told anyone.")
2. Children don't want to get the offender in trouble ("He said he would go to jail if she told.")
3. Fear of blame and punishment ("She thought she would get in trouble," "She thought I'd be mad.")
4. Loyalty to the perpetrator ("He said no one else would understand how much he loved her.")
5. Fear for the effect on the family ("If he had to go to jail, there would be no more money for the family.") Many young children are aware that their parents will be hurt and angry at hearing of the abuse and that it will lead to family disruption.
6. Shame and embarrassment ("He said people would think there was something wrong with her.")
7. Confusion/helplessness ("They like the special attention, but don't like and can't stop what's happening.")

The practitioner further addressed the length of time before disclosure. "Does anyone want to guess how long the research tells us it takes before a child will disclose sexual abuse?" asked the facilitator.

"Sometimes not until they're adults," said Octavia. "I didn't tell anyone that I was sexually abused by my father until all this came out."

"Sometimes people don't talk about it until they are all grown up. Fortunately, there is now more attention to sexual abuse, so hopefully people won't wait as long. Despite all the awareness, though, children still delay telling an average of 1.5 years. If the offender is a family member, it is even longer: 2.6 years" (Wolfe, 1998). This information teaches parents that delayed disclosure in children is very common.

How Perpetrators Involve Children in Sexual Abuse

Another question with which parents struggle is how the child has "allowed" the perpetrator to molest them. The term *grooming* is introduced, defined as "the offenders' deliberate efforts to shape and reinforce specific sexual behaviors" (Deblinger & Heflin, 1996).

"Offenders take steps to get children to trust them," the facilitator explained. "First, they may just start out being the kid's friend, taking them for treats, giving them attention. Then, when they've gained the child's trust, and the kid is enjoying all the goodies she's getting, the offender will do a little touching, maybe so subtle the kid even questions that it happened. Abuse rarely starts out with intercourse or oral sex. It starts subtly with touching, sitting on laps, etc. Over time, the offender knows how much further he can extend the touching so the child goes along."

The facilitator asked mothers to think of some of the other strategies perpetrators use to engage children in sexual activity (Deblinger & Heflin, 1996):

1. "The offender took advantage of my child's curiosity about sexuality."
2. "He called it a game."
3. "He gave her a lot of attention/things."
4. "He told her that was how people who loved each other showed it."
5. "The offender took advantage of my child's eagerness to please an adult."
6. "The offender took advantage of my child's natural responsiveness to authority."
7. "My child was taught to obey adults."

Information on the grooming process helps mothers understand the methods by which offenders get children to go along with the sexual abuse and why children have such difficulty in telling.

Miranda said she was still confused because her husband keeps denying the sexual abuse. The facilitator asked the group why some offenders might lie about the sexual abuse. Group members easily volunteered that offenders have a lot to lose if they admit their responsibility: arrest, possible prison time, probation, mandated treatment, loss of the family. In fact, a majority of offenders deny the abuse, at least initially (Sirles & Franke, 1989), the practitioner informed the group.

Indicators of Sexual Abuse

To build awareness and to prevent against revictimization of the child, the facilitator asked parents to think back to signs they now realize indicated sexual abuse.

"He would go into her room at night, 'to check on her,' " Demetria said. "I thought it was a little weird, but I didn't question it. I was sleeping too hard."

"But are you supposed to question everything?" Miranda asked. "I mean, you can't go around seeing sexual abuse everywhere. So what if he bathed her? Don't dads bathe their kids?"

"You're right. If you're in a relationship with somebody, then there's supposed to be trust," Demetria said. "You can't be suspicious all the time."

"But that's what the caseworker said to me," Miranda said. " 'You should have known.' "

"He would want to take her places by himself," Octavia remembered. "I didn't mind because I was so tired from working all the time."

The signs of sexual abuse vary from subtle behaviors by the perpetrator, which do not typically arouse suspicion, to flagrant acts. By engaging in this discussion and experiencing other group members' reactions, the women were made aware of the behaviors that may indicate sexual abuse.

Symptoms of Sexual Abuse

A related subject to indicators of abuse is the potential symptoms children might display. Although a range of symptoms may exist (see Kendall-Tackett et al., 1993, for a review), providing group members with an exhaustive list might lead to parents' believing their children are irrevocably damaged. Instead, only common symptoms are covered and then in the context of what parents can do to help children.

The group facilitator presented some of the common symptoms: impaired self-esteem (35%), behavior problems (37%), and PTSD (35%). She explained further that PTSD is actually a constellation of symptoms, including guilt, fear, autonomic arousal, nightmares, somatic problems, and dissociation. Rather than demonstrating full-blown PTSD, children may show any of these individual reactions (Kendall-Tackett et al., 1993). Other internalizing symptoms include depression and withdrawal. Up to 41% also display sexual problems, in terms of hyperarousal (excessive flirtatiousness, inappropriate touching), exposing, and victimizing.

The following discussion covers briefly how parents can manage some of the common child symptoms, including sexual acting out, behavior problems, nightmares/traumatic play, and low self-esteem.

Sexual Acting Out

To help identify sexual acting-out symptoms, normal and abnormal aspects of child sexuality are first covered. Normal sexual behaviors may include shyness with men, walking around at home in underwear or in the nude, undressing in front of other people, and touching one's own private parts at home. These types of behaviors are exhibited by 40% of nonabused children, according to a review by Wolfe (1998). Behaviors that seem to be specific to children that have been sexually abused include French (tongue) kissing, touching another person's private parts, simulating intercourse, engaging in oral sexual behavior, or inserting objects in the vagina or anus.

Overall, parents are urged to remain calm when faced with these behaviors. A shocked or angry reaction may actually reinforce the charge for the child (James, 1989). Parents are taught to transmit to their children that sexual feelings and urges are bodily functions, such as passing gas or nose picking, which are best done in private. Children are told matter-of-factly when their erotic behaviors are not acceptable, and they are shown more appropriate ways to act (e.g., sitting still in a parent's lap, keeping their hands to themselves, respecting others' private space). They are then praised once they demonstrate these behaviors (James, 1989).

Behavior Problems

Parent training skills are offered in group: reinforcement (praise, privileges, tokens exchanged for rewards), extinction (ignoring), and punishment. (See chapters 2 and 4 for a detailing of these techniques.)

Traumatic Play and Nightmares

Children demonstrate *traumatic play* when they get caught up in repetitious play themes that involve danger (for example, a family of dolls that is blown up over and over again) or helplessness (dolls, puppets, stuffed animals are trapped or at the mercy of powerful others who hurt them). To handle such themes, parents are told to empower their children to find a new course of action for the play (James, 1989). Parents are instructed to ask questions, such as "Who can we get to help the doll from this?" "How can we make sure that she saves herself from this?" "Who do you want me to play and how can I help this character?" In this way, the child can gain mastery from the play experience rather than keep reenacting traumatic play themes.

A similar strategy is used for nightmares. Parents are instructed to empower their children by having them retell the dream so that it ends on a note in which the child is victorious (James, 1989). Children can be told to use either their internal qualities (strength, wit, sense of humor) to solve the dilemma presented in the dream, or they can call on human or superhuman powers for assistance.

Low Self-Esteem

Parents are instructed in the use of praise (see chapter 2) and to help their children explore activities that will provide them with a sense of self-competence. It is stressed once again to parents that their modeling of coping is important to their children, so that their children will learn appropriate skills from them. At this point, the group topic turns to cognitive coping strategies for mothers.

Cognitive Coping Strategies

Cognitive coping strategies include cognitive restructuring and problem-solving skills training.

Cognitive Restructuring

Along with providing information about sexual abuse dynamics, another way to address parents' distressing thoughts is to work with them on identifying and altering their inaccurate thinking (Deblinger

& Heflin, 1996).[1] To introduce the topic, the practitioner outlined a triangle on the board with "feelings," "thoughts," and "behaviors" at each of the legs and stressed the interconnection of all three. "It is difficult to control our feelings," the facilitator said. "But we have more control over our thoughts and behaviors, and by working with these, we can affect our feelings."

She provided the example of a woman who gets a flat tire on the way to the work. Her thoughts are "Nothing ever works out for me. The whole day is ruined. I'm going to be late for work now, and I'll probably get fired. I don't know what I'm going to do. I can't stand this."

When the facilitator asked, "How would you feel if you had these thoughts?" group members were able to see that this pattern of thinking could lead to negative feelings, such as depression, helplessness, and anxiety.

The facilitator contrasted the same situation with the flat tire but with a different set of thinking patterns: "Well, this is inconvenient getting a flat tire, but it happens to everyone once in a while. It's lucky I'm only five blocks away from a garage. I can walk there and get help. I can also call work to tell them what happened. I'll be late. I don't like that this happened, but I'll be able to take care of it." Group members saw that the alternative response was more likely to lead to problem-solving attempts and coping rather than hopelessness, dejection, and stress.

The facilitator reviewed the process of cognitive restructuring, which involves the following steps:

1. Identify the feeling
2. Identify the underlying thoughts
3. Challenge the inaccuracies
4. Construct alternative thoughts
5. Reassess the feeling

Using this outline, the practitioner demonstrated the technique with Miranda, who had volunteered for this purpose. Miranda said she misses her daughters and wants them back, but doesn't know how to make it without her husband. Miranda was asked to identify her

1. Deblinger and Heflin's (1996) terminology is *inaccurate thinking*, although other models have referred to these thoughts as *irrational* or *negative*.

thoughts. She said, "I was a single parent for a little while—6 months—and it was the worst time of my life. I had a hard time finding work because all I had was a G.E.D. I ended up at a fast-food restaurant, which was totally humiliating with all these kids working there. I was always struggling and couldn't pay my bills. We lived in this crappy apartment, and I could never get the landlord to fix anything. Now we live in a house, and my husband makes good money as a plumber. What am I going to do if I'm alone again? And this time I'd have two kids to take care of, not just one. I want my daughters back with me, but without him I don't think I can make it."

The facilitator asked the group to help Miranda name her inaccurate thoughts, providing the hint that words such as "never" "always," and other absolutist language usually signal inaccurate thinking. Some group members had difficulty differentiating thoughts and feelings; some confused facts ("I was a single parent for 6 months") with inaccurate thoughts. Group members started to catch on though as the inaccurate thoughts were named correctly and listed on the flip chart: "What am I going to do if I'm alone again?" "Without him, I don't think I can make it." "I could never get the landlord to fix anything."

Miranda defended her thoughts, insisting, "But they are all true." The facilitator responded that, while thoughts can seem very convincing, that doesn't mean they're true. If they're producing negative emotions (helplessness, confusion) and behaviors (staying with her husband and allowing her children to live outside of the home), then they need to be questioned.

Miranda couldn't come up with any alternative thoughts that would help her feel more empowered, therefore, group members were asked to offer their suggestions. It is generally easier for others to address an individual's negative thought patterns, see them as irrational, and produce alternative, more productive thinking patterns. In going through this process for others, however, they gain practice in doing it for themselves.

The group challenged Miranda's belief that she wouldn't be able to make it without her partner since many of the members were struggling on their own. Octavia said, "Me and my little girl had to move out of my parents' house, and that was hard, because the reason I moved in with them is because I didn't have any money. My ex left me with all these debts. I still have his debts to pay, and we're just staying with a cousin of mine right now. It's hard, but it's better than my little girl getting abused."

"I just don't think I could do what you're going through," Miranda replied.

"It's worth it. Because I know what I'm doing is right," Octavia said. "No one has ever stood up to my dad before. All my life he did whatever he wanted to all of us, and my mother let him. Finally, I'm standing up to that, and it feels real good."

Demetria said she is staying in a transitional living program for homeless women because her family members are worse off than she is. She said it was hard living among a bunch of women "who can't control their kids" and sharing space with people who "don't know how to act." But she also said that the program has a lot to offer in the way of job training, vocational guidance, and assistance with housing.

After the group provided Miranda with some possible alternatives, the facilitator asked Miranda to reassess her feelings. Miranda admitted to feeling a bit better, as if her situation were not as hopeless. The facilitator instructed that, by continuing to target and challenge inaccurate thoughts and beliefs, distressing emotions can be ameliorated and changed into more positive feelings.

Problem-Solving Skills

The material on cognitive restructuring segues to problem solving, because sometimes in order to debunk negative thinking, a mother might have to come up with alternatives she hasn't yet tried. Problem-solving skills are taught so that when mothers encounter an unfamiliar situation, instead of resorting to hopeless thinking ("I can't do anything about this," "I'm powerless"), they will work to generate alternatives.

The other rationale for material on problem solving involves the tendency of groups to jump into problem-solving mode (Toseland & Rivas, 2001). This group tendency can be channeled into a productive process, and members can learn there should be a specific method for handling problems.

The problem-solving process involves the following steps (D'Zurilla, 1986; Spivack, Platt, & Shure, 1976): define the problem, brainstorm options, weigh the pros and cons of various options, select the best alternative and implement, and evaluate the implementation. Miranda's situation will be used to illustrate the problem-solving process. (Also see chapter 4 for more discussion on problem solving.)

1. The facilitator asked the group to define the problem, and the women decided that the problem is that Miranda doesn't know how she will support herself without her husband's income.
2. The facilitator asked the group to brainstorm options to solve the problem. Some options: Miranda could choose to stay with him; she could struggle on public assistance for a while until she got on her feet; Miranda could get a low-skill-level job; Miranda could go back to school or attend a training program: or Miranda could seek a lawyer's help to get child support payments in the event of divorce.
3. The group then named the advantages and disadvantages of the various courses of action. Options were then weighed.
4. Miranda chose an option. She continued to choose to live with her husband, but said that she would consider the other alternatives presented and that she had found the process of examining decisions helpful.

The advantage of groups is that they can offer many different perspectives and insights to different situations. This tendency can be productively channeled, so that problem solving can be taught as a process that group members can learn to do for themselves.

Communication Skills Building

The facilitator began the session on communication skills building with a rationale for the importance of such skills, so that mothers can perform the following behaviors:

1. Initiate new relationships
2. Build on or maintain existing relationships
3. Experience closeness with others
4. Talk with their children about the sexual abuse and other important topics
5. State feelings and reactions to influence other people's behavior
6. Cope with feelings by sharing them with others

The facilitator explained that she will address the communication skills of reflective listening and assertiveness. To introduce the topic of reflective listening, the facilitator asked the group, "How do people show they're listening to you?" Group members are usually attuned to body language (leaning forward with an open posture, eye contact, a focus on the person "without looking around for someone better to talk to"). Demetria described a good listener as someone "who just does that—listen. They're not trying to put you down for thinking something or telling you what to do like you don't know anything."

The facilitator complimented the group members for their knowledge of these elements and then explained how to convey skillful listening through *reflective listening*, which means paraphrasing back to the speaker the gist of his or her message with the following format: "What I hear you saying is . . ." or "You feel (feeling word)."

Group members were then asked to pair together in dyads. Each person in the dyad talked for a few moments on any topic while the listener reflected back the message. The facilitator strolled around to assist those who struggled with the new communication pattern. When mothers rehearse reflective listening, they find it more challenging than they assumed from merely hearing the facilitator present the information. However, members commented after the exercise how helpful and satisfying it was to have their messages heard.

The facilitator then went through the benefits of using reflective listening with children. Not only does it help them to feel understood by and close to their parents, it also gives them the words to express their own feelings and thoughts. When this communication is internalized, the child is more self-aware and has more self-control (Deblinger & Heflin, 1996).

Specific to statements the child may make about sexual abuse, a parent's use of reflective listening conveys acceptance of the child's concerns. Parents often feel anxious that they do not know how to respond to their child's remarks about sexual abuse. However, the facilitator stressed that the parents need not always have the answers; the skill of reflective listening will help their children feel validated (Deblinger & Heflin, 1996).

The next skill taught was *assertive communication* (stating feelings and needs without infringing on the rights of others), which was contrasted with passivity (avoidance of stating one's needs) and aggression (stating feelings and needs at the expense of others). Group members were taught that assertive communication comprises three essential parts: *I feel* (their reactions) in response to *what happened* (a specific activating event), and I *need* (request for desired behavior change).

To illustrate, the facilitator contrasted three different ways to handle a situation with a store clerk who doesn't return a sufficient amount of change. Passivity involves not speaking up at all. Aggressive communication involves accusations, name calling, and blame of the other person: "You were trying to rip me off." The third way uses the "I" position: "I have counted my change, and I don't think it's right." The group members discussed the possible reactions of the clerk to the different messages. Although some group members felt justified in speaking harshly if they felt the clerk purposefully duped them, they could see that such an exchange might invoke defensiveness, which could dissolve into an unproductive argument. In contrast, if they asked politely and without accusation, a clerk might be more prone to consider whether a mistake were made.

To practice the skill further, group members were asked to come up with a situation in which they needed to communicate a negative feeling and ask for a behavior change from another person. In "round robin" style (Toseland & Rivas, 2001), group members, without going into the details of their situation, were asked to recite an "I feel . . . when you. . . . I need . . ." format response. These were written down by the facilitator so statements could be examined more closely. Some needed to be revised as they were nothing more than disguised "you" statements ("I feel that you lied," rather than "I feel disappointed that you didn't tell me the truth"). Group members gained practice in the skill by helping other members construct appropriate statements.

Then the facilitator brought up the more challenging assertiveness topic of how to respond to a common situation these mothers may face, in which the offender tries to talk the woman into siding with him. Women were asked to list all of the arguments that offenders might use, and the facilitator wrote them on a flip chart. Part of the rationale for this exercise is not only to improve communication skills but also to expose in the supportive atmosphere of the group the persuasive statements a perpetrator might make to deny or minimize the abuse.

After a list was generated, women were taught "the broken record" technique in which they only have to repeat a stock line, such as "I'm sorry, I have to protect my child" or "I'm not supposed to be talking to you about this." Group members were relieved to discover that when someone is trying to persuade them, they could simply restate their own position, without getting embroiled in an argument.

After group members engaged in role plays of the new communication skills, they were urged to practice the new techniques during the coming week and to report back to the group on their progress.

Communication About Sexual Abuse

The rationale presented to parents about talking to their children about the sexual abuse is that they, unlike therapists, spend the most time with their children. Therefore, if they are trained in appropriate responses, they can help their children handle the abuse experience as it presents over time. Despite the rationale given, parents may demonstrate some resistance about talking to the child about sexual abuse. In table 5.2, the various reasons named by parents are presented along with some responses to reassure them.

For talking to girls about sexual abuse, Deblinger and Heflin (1996) recommend *I Can't Talk About It* (Sanford, 1986) and, for boys, *Some-*

Table 5.2

Addressing Parents' Concerns About Talking to Their Children About Sexual Abuse

Parent's Concerns	Possible Responses
1. Parents worry that they (parents) will get upset.	a. Process the abuse experience in group or individual therapy first. b. If parents do become emotionally upset: • reassure the child that she is not to blame for feelings • identify feelings for the child • reassure the child that the parent has other adults she can turn to for support
2. Parents worry that their child will become upset.	a. See this as a positive sign that the child is expressing her feelings about the abuse. b. Reinforce the child for sharing feelings with parent ("I'm glad you told me about this"). c. Provide reflective listening for the child and comfort.
3. Parents won't know how to respond to children's questions or concerns.	a. Reflectively listen to children's concerns. b. Admit that aspects of the abuse or the disclosure process are difficult to understand. c. Tell the child that the parent will seek guidance from the group facilitator or individual therapist.
4. Children start to talk about the abuse or other serious subjects when parents are busy.	a. Take time out to listen to the child's concerns, if possible. b. If not possible, assure the child that the parent will come back to the topic later and set a specific time.

thing Must Be Wrong with Me (Sanford, 1993). Another book, *No More Secrets for Me* (Wachter, 1983), presents a series of short vignettes on different sexual abuse scenarios. Parts of these books may be read in group aloud so that parents can familiarize themselves with the content, express their reactions, and anticipate how their children will respond. Talking to children about how to prevent future abuse is also covered as part of the conversations about sexual abuse. This information is important as sexually abused children suffer from high rates of revictimization (see Wolfe, 1998).

Communication About Healthy Sexual Development

When the topic of talking to children about healthy sexual development is brought up, often parents will claim that their preschool children are too young for such information. Unfortunately, the child has already been prematurely exposed to sexuality. Sex education from parents is therefore important for the following reasons (Deblinger & Heflin, 1996):

1. To correct inaccurate information and misperceptions children may have received as a result of the abuse
2. To prevent further abuse
3. To reduce the risk of early sexual activity later on
4. To model for children how discussions about sex can take place without embarrassment

In a session with parents on sex education, the facilitator brought in books written for children's level of understanding. Deblinger and Heflin (1996) suggest *Where Did I Come From* (Mayle, 1990) for information on conception and birth for young children. For preteens, *Asking About Sex and Growing Up* (Cole, 1988) comprehensively covers sexuality and topics of interest to preteens, including puberty, conception, masturbation, contraceptive methods, and homosexuality. To guide parents, Deblinger and Heflin (1996) recommend a Planned Parenthood publication called *How to Talk with Your Child About Sexuality* (1986).

Sections of the books are read aloud in group so that parents can not only learn how to impart information to their children, but also so that any of their own reactions, such as discomfort and embarrassment, can be expressed and processed. Parents also anticipate in group how their children might respond. Parents are coached in how to answer children's questions. This information prepares them for the parent-child conjoint sessions where part of the work will be devoted to parents and children discussing healthy sexuality.

Conjoint Sessions

The group session cycle described in this chapter is repeated as many times as necessary. Meanwhile, children are also seen in an individual or a group setting. The parent is ready for conjoint mother-child sessions when several criteria are met. First, the parent must actively support the child. Second, the parent's anxieties and concerns have been sufficiently reduced so she can attend to her child's reactions. Third, the parent must be able to discuss the abuse without excessive emotional reaction. The aims of the conjoint sessions are the following (Deblinger & Heflin, 1996):

1. To establish open communication regarding the abuse, sex education, and personal safety skills
2. To serve as role models for coping for their children
3. To be trained to continue the therapeutic work at home

Summary

This chapter has covered a cognitive-behavioral approach to group treatment of non-offending parents whose children have been sexually abused. A cognitive-behavioral approach focuses on information and education about sexual abuse dynamics to allay parents' distress and teaches them skills to cope more effectively and to facilitate their children's recovery.

The group context of the cognitive-behavioral curriculum offers benefits for non-offending mothers beyond the cost-effective delivery of services. Group treatment reduces the isolation of the non-offending parents and helps them build a social support network. Parents in group often learn from others' experiences and assist each other in modeling and practicing the new skills. Parents who are initially disbelieving of their children can particularly be helped by other group members to gain a higher level of support for their children, which, in turn, results in improved child recovery from the sexual abuse.

PART II

Adolescence

CLINICAL DISORDERS

SOCIAL PROBLEMS

6 Structural Family Therapy with Adolescent Conduct Disorder

■■■■■ **Presenting Problem**

Jamie Saunders, a Caucasian 15-year-old, has been mandated to attend counseling by his probation officer due to shoplifting charges and assaulting his younger brother (he broke his brother's arm). Services will be delivered in the home where Jamie lives with his mother, Sandra Witt, age 42; his brother, Samuel, age 11; his maternal grandmother, Betty Clayborne, age 65; and his maternal uncle, Howard Witt, age 38. Divorced from the children's father for 5 years, Sandra says that even though she feels like giving up on Jamie at times, she won't send Jamie to her ex-husband since he was physically abusive to Jamie in the past when the children went to visit him. The children now haven't seen their father for 2 years. Sandra says she has been depressed for most of her adult life but that it has worsened in the last 2 years. She currently is prescribed Prozac.

Sandra and her children moved from the state they had been living in a year ago to move in with Sandra's mother, Betty Clayborne, who is long-divorced from her third husband. Sandra and Howard Witt are the children from Betty's first marriage. Sandra explains that the reason for the move to her mother's house was financial; Sandra is unable to work because of a disability (carpal tunnel syndrome) and is waiting to find out her eligibility for government benefits. Howard Witt lives in the household due to financial problems after a divorce but has recently started a sales position. (See figure 6.1 for the genogram of this family and box 6.1 for APA diagnostic information on this case.)

This chapter will begin with a brief overview of structural family therapy and then follow with an empirical rationale for the use of structural family therapy with adolescent conduct problems. Following will be the application of structural family therapy to the Saunders/Witt/Clayborne family. The first session with this family will be detailed with commentary on how the structural family therapy approach is enacted. The chapter will conclude with a discussion on the direction of future sessions.

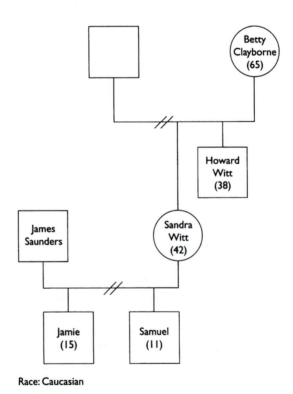

Race: Caucasian

Figure 6.1. Structural Family Therapy Case Study: Jamie Saunders's Family

Box 6.1

APA Diagnostic Information on the Case Study

Jamie Saunders meets the minimal criteria for conduct disorder, a pattern of behavior marked by violations of rules and societal norms or by harm to others (APA, 2000). At least three symptoms of the following four categories of behaviors are present: (1) aggression to people and animals (Jamie has broken his brother's arm, bullies and threatens his brother, and initiates fights with him), (2) destruction of property, (3) deceitfulness or theft (shoplifting), and (4) serious violations of rules.

Jamie also meets the criteria for oppositional defiant disorder (ODD) in that he often loses his temper, argues with adults, actively defies or refuses to comply with adults' requests or rules, deliberately annoys people, often blames others for his mistakes or misbehavior, is touchy or easily annoyed by others, is angry and resentful, and is often spiteful and vindictive (APA, 2000). (For more information on ODD, see chapter 2.) When criteria are met for ODD and conduct disorder, the more serious disorder, which is conduct disorder, is diagnosed.

■■■■ Overview of Structural Family Therapy

Developed by Salvador Minuchin (Minuchin, 1974; Minuchin & Fishman, 1981; Minuchin, Montalvo, Guerney, Rosman, & Schumer, 1967; Minuchin & Nichols, 1993; Minuchin, Rosman, & Baker, 1978), structural family therapy has played an influential role in the practice of family work for the last 30 years. As a family systems approach, structural family therapy is bound by certain concepts. A primary concept involves *circular causality* in that symptoms are not viewed as stemming from linear causes (i.e., by one person's problems); instead, they emerge from family interaction patterns (Aponte, 2002; Minuchin, 1974). Like any system, families operate under the principle of *homeostasis* (Minuchin & Nichols, 1993; Nichols & Schwartz, 2001). That is, symptoms arise and resistance to change occurs because of the nature of systems to remain in a status quo position.

The main assumption of the structural approach is that families present to treatment with symptoms because of a problematic structure (Minuchin, 1974). While every family experiences problems and stresses, the normal family manages stressors because the structure of the family is sufficiently flexible and adaptive to change while still remaining hierarchical. A hierarchical structure means that interaction patterns are such that the family is organized so that parents lead the family.

A healthy structure also means there are distinct subsystems in the family with clear boundaries surrounding them. The term *subsystem* is used to describe the way in which certain family members join together to enact various functions (Minuchin, 1974). The function of the *parental subsystem* is to care for, protect, and discipline children. Parents have more responsibilities than their children and, along with these, more rights. Parents are also joined together in the *couple subsystem*, where they interact not as parents but spend time being a couple, enacting such functions as giving and receiving affection and handling conflict.

Another key subsystem in families is the *sibling subsystem* where children have their first experience of being part of a peer group; they learn how to cooperate, resolve conflict, and negotiate differences. If a parent tries to solve problems for siblings ("Who started it?"), then children do not learn these critical functions. Hierarchical principles still operate within the sibling subsystem. Older siblings enjoy more rights than do their younger siblings; increased responsibility also accompanies these rights.

Subsystems are separated by *boundaries*, invisible demarcation lines that regulate hierarchy and proximity. Boundaries are problematic either by being diffuse (weak and blurred) or rigid (impenetrable), which lead to enmeshment or disengagement respectively (Minuchin et al., 1967). *Enmeshment* is defined as family members' overinvolvement with each other to the detriment of either individual growth and autonomy or to appropriate subsystem functioning. *Disengagement*, on the other hand, is a situation in which individual members are distant and disconnected from other family members and function in isolation from each other.

A maladaptive hierarchy in which there are no clear boundaries between parent and sibling subsystems may produce problems as a by-product. Unfortunately, children often bear the symptoms of a malfunctioning hierarchy. Families are also vulnerable when negotiating a particular life stage or when stressors pile up and the family is unable to manage (Minuchin et al., 1967; Minuchin et al., 1978). In such cases, the family is not flexibly able to adapt its interaction patterns to changed circumstances, and symptoms may result.

The central goal of structural family therapy, therefore, is to create a well-functioning structure, which is hierarchically organized with clear boundaries around subsystems. The by-product of a healthy structure is the amelioration of presenting symptoms. These goals are

**Key Assumptions of Structural Family
Therapy and Additional Resources**

Key Assumptions

• The central goal of structural family therapy is to create a well-functioning hierarchical pattern in which parents have clear authority over children.
• Subsystems in families (the parent and child subsystems, namely) should have
  clear boundaries (invisible demarcation lines that regulate hierarchy and proximity) around them so that the functions of the family appropriate to the developmental stage are carried out.
• The practitioner works with family interactions in session through the use of *enactments*, so that new patterns are developed in which parents are placed in
  charge of children, and subsystems carry out their functions.

Additional Resources

S. Minuchin. (1974). *Families and family therapy.* Cambridge, MA: Harvard University
  Press.
S. Minuchin & M. P. Nichols. (1993). *Family healing: Tales of hope and renewal from
  family therapy.* New York: Free Press.

achieved through *enactments*, working with interactions in the session,
so that new patterns are formed (Aponte, 2002; Minuchin, 1974). (See
box 6.2 for a brief summary of structural family therapy and a list of
additional resources for the interested reader to pursue.)

Empirical Evidence

In general, research with well-established methodologies has not been
a focus of structural family therapy. However, some evidence for the
effectiveness of the approach has been established in the treatment of
child and adolescent conduct problems. (For an expanded review of
the empirical evidence for structural family therapy, see Corcoran,
2000.) Structural family therapy has provided some symptom relief for
the conflict between adolescents diagnosed with attention deficit/hy-
peractivity disorder and their families (Barkley, Guevremont, Anastopoulos, & Fletcher, 1992). In addition, Szapocznik et al. (1988) worked
with family structure in order to more effectively engage teenagers
with drug abuse problems and their families in treatment. They found
that the joining and restructuring approach not only helped to get fam-

ilies into treatment, but also led to a higher level of satisfactory outcomes than the usual empathy and support given to engage families.

Szapocznik and colleagues (1989) also used a structural approach with school-age boys with conduct problems. While child individual functioning improved for the structural family therapy condition as well as the individual psychodynamic therapy condition, family functioning only improved when the child had taken part in family counseling; when the child attended only individual counseling, family functioning worsened.

As well as being an approach on its own, structural family therapy is the cornerstone of other family systems models. Family systems approaches have successfully reduced drug use (Friedman, Tomko, & Utada, 1991; Joanning, Thomas, Quinn, & Mullen, 1992; Lewis, Piercy, Sprenkle, & Trepper, 1990, 1991) and improved family functioning (Friedman et al., 1991) in teens with substance abuse. For juvenile offending problems, both functional family therapy (Barton, Alexander, Waldron, Turner, & Warburton, 1985; Gordon, Arbuthnot, Gustafson, & McGreen, 1988; Gordon, Graves, & Arbuthnot, 1995) and multisystemic treatment (e.g., Borduin, et al., 1995; Henggeler, Cunningham, Pickrel, Schoenwald, & Brondino, 1996; Scherer, Brondino, Henggeler, Melton, & Hanley, 1994) have had empirical validation. Both are integrative approaches in which different models are combined. For instance, functional family therapy possesses elements of structural and strategic family systems approaches, as well as behavioral family therapy, with a particular emphasis on the functions of symptoms (hence, the name) (Alexander & Parsons, 1982). Multisystemic therapy relies heavily on structural and strategic techniques but also includes behavioral parent training strategies and other interventions targeted at the different system levels in which the adolescent is embedded (e.g., Henggeler, 1989; Henggeler & Borduin, 1990). At the core of both the functional and multisystemic approaches are structural ideas and techniques, as well as strategic concepts. (See chapter 7 for an application of multisystemic treatment.)

▮ Structural Family Therapy Application

Assumptions of the structural family approach will be explored through a detailed illustration of the first session with the Saunders/

Witt/Clayborne family. In-session work with the family will be described with periodic discussion of how structural family concepts and techniques are applied to this family. Techniques of joining will first be discussed followed by the central strategy of structural family therapy, which is intervening with the family through the use of enactments.

Joining

Like most therapeutic interventions, beginning work with structural family therapy involves *joining*, defined as rapport building and helping family members feel accepted and understood. Specific techniques of joining involve *reframing* (attributing a positive intention to behavior), *tracking* (using language idiosyncratic to the family), and *mimesis* (matching the family's style and tone). Joining is particularly important for the structural family therapist, who will have to exert considerable influence on families in order to change entrenched interaction patterns (Minuchin, 1974). This is due to homeostasis, the tendency of family systems to remain in a steady state and to resist change. The therapist has first to become a part of the family system to enact this level of influence. However, even during the joining stage, techniques to bolster parental authority are used, such as addressing parents first and referring to them more formally than to their children. In addition, while the practitioner works on joining with the family, hypotheses are constructed about the structure of the family, and the practitioner may begin to intervene with family interaction patterns.

The site of the first session is Betty Clayborne's (Grandmother) house, a two-story rental property located in a quiet neighborhood. The practitioner's previous contact with the family involved a telephone conversation with Sandra Witt, Jamie's mother, to set up the appointment. She said that she was willing to participate and had received counseling in the past for her depression, but that no one else in the family wanted to be part of the family counseling. She said her mother flatly refused to take part. At the time, Ms. Witt said, "She [her mother] is the one who really needs it." Although Ms. Witt stated her willingness to participate, she also expressed her sense of hopelessness about the situation.

The practitioner is therefore surprised when she is ushered into the home by Ms. Witt and introduced to her mother. Mrs. Clayborne is nicely dressed and made up, as opposed to Ms. Witt, who is slightly overweight, with a flat, exhausted expression. Sandra next introduces her brother, Howard, who is tall, balding, and looks a little older than his age.

GRANDMOTHER [to her daughter]: Where are the boys?
MOM: I told them to come down here.
GRANDMOTHER: They need to be ready. We're keeping the counselor waiting.
MOM: I know, Mother. [bellows up the stairs] Jamie, Samuel, come down here!

As they wait for the boys to respond, the practitioner compliments Ms. Witt and Mrs. Clayborne on the way the home is decorated. Mrs. Clayborne seems pleased.

Suddenly, a thundering of footsteps is heard, and Jamie, a tall, gangly youth jumps down the last six stairs and stumbles to his feet. Samuel, blond and attractive, follows behind, giggling.

MOM [wearily]: How many times have I told you not to do that? Jamie, this is—
[But he is off, moving to the dining room.]
JAMIE [drawing his grandmother along with him]: Okay, Grandma, you sit here.
[His grandmother sits in the seat he has chosen for her.]
JAMIE: Uncle Howard, you're over there.
[Howard doesn't move. He looks annoyed.]
JAMIE: Mom, sit here and—[to practitioner]—I guess there's no room for you.
MOM: Jamie, you're not in charge of where everyone sits.
JAMIE: Yes, I am.
MOM: Don't be rude.
JAMIE [to practitioner]: Okay, we'll find you another chair.
[He starts to pull a heavy armchair from the living room.]
MOM: Don't be dragging that over here.
JAMIE: But we don't have enough seats.
[Samuel sits on the floor, leaning up against the wall.]
MOM: Why don't you sit down there on the floor next to your brother?
JAMIE [bitterly]: Oh, I know, he's always perfect.
MOM: I didn't say that.

JAMIE [to his mother with a defiant giggle]: Why don't you sit on the floor?

HOWARD [starting to get mad]: Don't talk to your mother that way!

JAMIE: Uncle Howard, you sit there. I'll bring in a chair from the porch.

HOWARD: Jamie, those chairs are chained down. And stop telling everyone where to sit.

Much can be learned from the initial seating arrangements. For instance, Jamie's grandmother seems to do what he wants; Jamie's mother and Uncle Howard resist his commands but remain ineffectual. At this point, the interaction about seating has bogged down into a power struggle. A structural family therapist might have to lend his influence to unfreeze the family from this "stuck" position, by siding with the person who should be the authority over the children.

Note that in the following exchange, Ms. Witt is referred to as "Mom." Parents and other adults involved in caretaking should be referred to by their role, "Mom," "Grandmother," "Uncle," or by their formal title (Ms., Mrs., Mr.) so that their authority is reinforced. Calling a grown-up by her first name in front of children tends to put adult and child on the same level.

PRACTITIONER: Mom, where would you like me to sit?

[The maneuver succeeds, at least partly. Without Mom having to say anything, Jamie gives up his chair and hops to the floor, where he starts to tussle with his younger brother.]

GRANDMOTHER [to her daughter]: You haven't even offered the counselor anything to drink. [addressing practitioner] Would you like something to drink? I have some coffee made.

[After a slight hesitation, the practitioner agrees to coffee. Mrs. Clayborne seems to enjoy fussing over its preparation and brings out the coffee in a cup and saucer.]

A dilemma underlies the practitioner's hesitation: If she takes Grandmother's offering, this might be seen as acceptance of Grandmother's implicit reprimand of her daughter. On the other hand, this is Grandmother's first involvement in counseling, and she was a reluctant participant, according to Mom. Joining with Grandmother is very important since she plays a key role in the family.

In the joining stage, each family member shares his or her perspective on the family's functioning and what needs changing. In keeping with the structural emphasis, the practitioner asks Mom first, to reinforce her parental authority, although Jamie jumps in before Mom can begin talking.

JAMIE: I think counseling's stupid.

MOM: Don't talk like that, son.

JAMIE: It is stupid. [puts his head in his arms so his voice is muffled] And boring, too.

MOM: That's an example right there. He has no respect for adults. He doesn't listen to anything I say, and it doesn't help when she [indicates her mother] is always taking up for him. I don't know if you've noticed, but she isn't even speaking to me, hasn't been for 3 days. Do you know what she did? She went out and bought Jamie a new CD player. Does she get Samuel anything? No! Does she even acknowledge that he just got straight As on his last report card? No! While this one [jabs a finger at Jamie] is not even passing!

JAMIE: I hate that stupid school! It's full of preps.

MOM: Samuel's never here. And I don't blame him. He doesn't want to be around this. He's always off with his friends. And then there's Jamie—he has no friends.

JAMIE [hotly]: I do, too, have friends!

MOM: Who?

JAMIE: Paul!

MOM: Paul? [dismissively] He lives in an apartment complex. I don't have very much money right now, but it's very important that my kids don't live in an apartment complex. Paul just comes and goes as he pleases, and his mother doesn't even care.

JAMIE: You don't know what you've talking about.

Reframing, attributing a positive intention to behavior, forestalls the argument brewing between Mom and Jamie:

PRACTITIONER: It sounds like you really care about your son and want the best for him. You feel it's important for him to have a good home, and you are doing something about it—even though it's difficult sometimes.

MOM [visibly pleased]: I do care about Jamie, even though he's always saying I'm mean. I could just ship him to his father, but I wouldn't do that to him. His father was physically abusive to me, and he was abusive to the boys, too. I'm not going to let them go back to that.

Now it's Grandmother's turn:

GRANDMOTHER: I just know from my work in sales you've got to build people up, if you want them to do things well. You've got to build a boy up, rather than tearing him down all the time.

MOM [explosively]: I do encourage him, but when he does something wrong, you don't give him a CD player. And when I set up a punishment, you don't go behind my back and undo it by giving him gifts and special treatment.

JAMIE [to his mother]: Don't you even try to take that CD player away from me.

HOWARD [to Jamie]: Shut up, Jamie. [to his mother] It's true, Mom. Jamie thinks he can get away with murder the way you go about getting him everything he wants.

PRACTITIONER: Let's give Grandmother a chance to finish, and then we'll go around the table until everyone has had a chance to talk.

MOM [to her mother]: All my life you've downplayed what I've done! You've always totally discounted me, and you reverse everything I do with Jamie, until he knows he doesn't have to follow rules.

PRACTITIONER [to Grandmother]: Okay, so Mrs. Clayborne, you want there to be more positive reinforcement for what Jamie does right, rather than punishment for what he does wrong? You're right, that can be very effective.

The practitioner responds to Grandmother's statement, rather than Mom's, for a couple of reasons. The practitioner's responsibility is to provide direction in the session, to make new patterns happen, rather than allowing the family interaction to move in its usual course. The practitioner also has to join with each individual in the family and furthers joining by giving Grandmother the opportunity to speak and offering a reframe. Grandmother states her fear that all the negative attention Jamie receives from Mom will "tear him down," and so she wants to "build him up." The phrase, "building a boy up, not tearing him down" will now be tracked across sessions. *Tracking*, which is noting unique and idiosyncratic phrases the family uses and incorporating them into the practitioner's repertoire, is another part of the joining process so that the practitioner will feel familiar to the family members (Minuchin, 1974).

Now, it's time for Uncle Howard:

HOWARD: I've never known how to be a dad. Me and my ex-wife didn't have children. I've never been a parent, but I do know that boy is totally out of control. He doesn't listen to anyone, until I get in his face. He doesn't do anything around here. He's failing in school and just got out of jail last week.

JAMIE: It wasn't jail—it was juvenile.

HOWARD: You see how he interrupts and tries to argue? You know why he was locked up? Because he broke his brother's arm. The kid is dangerous, and his mother can't control him.

MOM: How can I control him when I don't have anyone backing me up?

HOWARD: I back you up. I'm the only one Jamie listens to around here.

MOM: That's because he's scared of you.

HOWARD: Look who's talking—you get pretty scary yourself sometimes. [to practitioner] I'm the one who spends time with him— all buddy-buddy—fixing up the stereo, fixing that old car back there. I don't know why I'm even here at this counseling. I've got my own stuff to deal with. I've just gotten a divorce, financial problems—

MOM: That's what counseling is supposed to help you with. I don't know how many times you've come crying to me about your ex. You could use some help dealing with that.

The practitioner interjects before the focus can get off-track with a summary of Howard's statement so he knows he's been heard.

PRACTITIONER: So you are trying to be involved in these kids' lives in a positive way—you fix up old cars with them—

MOM: With Jamie, not Samuel.

PRACTITIONER: —and help with enforcing the rules.

HOWARD: Yeah, but I don't know anything about being a dad.

PRACTITIONER: Who says you have to be?

HOWARD: I don't know. I know they don't have much of one, and they need a positive male influence.

PRACTITIONER: You don't have to be their dad. You can't be. All you can be is their uncle. And that means not having to set rules, just backing up Mom's authority as the parent.

Enactments

In structural family therapy, most of the work involves altering family interactions in the session through *enactments*. Enactments involve allowing family patterns to emerge, but with the practitioner pushing for a different outcome in which parental hierarchy is bolstered. Different techniques are used during the enactment. Habitual patterns are blocked, and the parent is impelled to take command over children. Changing these patterns may require the practitioner to use *intensity* in applying techniques and to occasionally employ *unbalancing*, siding with one family member over another to shift a stuck position in the system. This focus on enactments reflects the assumption that a change in behavior leads to a change in cognitive understanding.

However, to a lesser extent, it is assumed that change can also happen from cognitive understanding delivered through information and reframing. In this case example, Howard's obvious sense of pressure and confusion about fulfilling a father's role is quickly dispelled with a little information about the healthy structure of families, information that the other members also hear.

PRACTITIONER: Okay, Jamie, your turn.

[Jamie feigns snoring.]

[The practitioner realizes that she has succumbed to the family rule that Samuel is ignored by its members.]

PRACTITIONER: Let's go to Samuel then.

[Mom decides to get into a power struggle with Jamie instead.]

MOM: Jamie, answer her when she's talking to you.

JAMIE: This is so boring. Why do we have to be here?

HOWARD: You've been wanting to talk, Jamie. Now it's your turn. So go.

JAMIE: Aren't we done yet? You've been talking the whole time.

HOWARD: We're not the one who broke his brother's arm. You're the one that needs help.

JAMIE [playfully drumming on Samuel's head]: But he forgives me now, don't you?

MOM: Jamie, let go of him.

PRACTITIONER: Actually, I would like to hear from Samuel.

[Unfortunately, Samuel can't lift his head for the pummeling he is receiving.]

HOWARD: Jamie, I'm fixing to come over there and do the same thing to your head. Now let Samuel talk.

JAMIE: Counseling's boring is all. I've been to counselors ever since I first got put on Ritalin. That's 5 years of counseling. No, wait—[counts on fingers]—4. That's too long.

PRACTITIONER: This is counseling for the family. What about your family?

JAMIE: Well, everybody's always fighting.

HOWARD: It's mainly about you.

JAMIE: That is not so. You've been fighting about the same shit ever since you were my age.

[Howard and Sandra subsequently get lost in a battle about Jamie using a swear word.]

Family members usually ascribe causation in a linear fashion (i.e., one person is to blame for the problems). However, from a family systems standpoint, systems are involved in circular causality: interaction patterns maintain the faulty structure. In this view, Jamie's behavior is symptomatic of the family's patterns rather than Jamie causing the family's problems. Finally, it's Samuel's turn.

SAMUEL [ducking his head]: Everyone's always fighting. I just want everyone to get along.

[Jamie starts pounding Samuel's head again.]

MOM: Jamie, after what you did to him, I don't want you touching him at all.

JAMIE: Not even like this?

[Jamie provocatively goes back to his pummeling.]

HOWARD: Jamie, stop that right now.

[Jamie acts like he hasn't heard.]

HOWARD: Do you want me to come over there and stop you myself? [starts to get up]

JAMIE: No, no, I'll stop!

PRACTITIONER: Mom, what was your reaction to Uncle Howard stopping Jamie?

MOM: Thank you, Howard, but sometimes you're damn scary. I hope you're happy—Jamie's scared of you.

HOWARD: At least he listens to me.

PRACTITIONER: I wonder, how can you two work together as a team? [They look dubious. The practitioner decides on a bold move.]

PRACTITIONER: Samuel, Jamie, why don't you leave for right now? I think I'll just work with the grown-ups.

JAMIE: We can go?

MOM: But he's the one that needs counseling.

PRACTITIONER: First, we have to get all the adults working together.

MOM: I don't want them going off together unsupervised. Jamie's just out of juvenile for breaking his brother's arm.

The practitioner's decision to begin work with the parental subsystem stemmed from the inability of the adult members to work together as a team with Ms. Witt at the helm. Forming clear boundaries around a parental subsystem is more challenging in an intergenerational family than in the classic two-parent household because of the simultaneous roles people embody. Howard and Sandra are both the children of Betty Clayborne, but Sandra Witt is also a mother to two children. In addition, both Howard and Sandra have moved back with their mother because of financial problems and are now dependent on their mother for support. It might be difficult for Mom to assume parental control (and for others to let her) when she is in such a dependent role with her own mother. However, the rule in structural family therapy is that parents should be in control of their own children with other adult relatives and authority figures enforcing parental rules.

Ms. Witt complains about her mother and brother not backing her up, but when her brother successfully enforces her command, Ms. Witt complains about her brother's "scary" behavior. Understandably, she doesn't want her son to react out of fear, but she also tends to use punishment in order to get Jamie into line.

Ms. Witt is also concerned that, without Jamie in the session, problems won't be solved. However, one of the assumptions of structural family therapy is that problems are not caused by an individual in the family; rather, problems stem from the family system interaction patterns. In structural family therapy, the structure of the family system is seen as problematic, which, in turn, has resulted in Jamie being symptomatic. In addition, the structure of the family is challenged by multiple stressors: divorce, single-parenthood, financial problems, recent moves, and disability. The family also faces stress from the many developmental changes that its members are simultaneously experiencing. There is the socialization of children (11-year-old Samuel), adolescence with Jamie, retirement/growing older (65-year-old Grandmother), and divorce (Uncle Howard).

As for Ms. Witt's concern that Jamie will hurt Samuel if he is left alone with him, the assumption of structural family therapy is that the family subsystems should be strengthened, which includes both the parent and the sibling subsystems. The two boys being unable to resolve conflict without adult intervention is indicative of the problematic sibling subsystem functioning. If Mom continues to intervene between the brothers, without allowing them to work out their own problems, then paradoxically, Jamie may be more likely to lose control with his brother in the future.

MOM: You ask, how can we work together as a team? How can we work together when whatever I decide with Jamie, she'll [indicates her mother] reverse what I've said? A CD player? He didn't even pass this 6 weeks. I told him he wouldn't get to go to Six Flags if he didn't pass. And she gives him a CD player.

GRANDMOTHER: It's not just for him. It's here in the living room where everyone can use it.

MOM: You never said anyone else could use it. Jamie thinks it's his.

HOWARD: Mom, it is Jamie's. You gave it to him.

GRANDMOTHER: It is Jamie's, but he knows he's supposed to let everyone use it.

MOM: But he hasn't let anyone else use it. And what was the point in giving him a CD player? Just so I could look bad? So I can be the bad guy? He doesn't deserve a CD player. He's got to know if he starts doing something good, then he gets rewards. Why should he work if he gets his rewards anyway?

GRANDMOTHER: A boy doesn't start to act good unless he feels good about himself.

MOM: And a CD player is going to make him feel good about himself when he's done nothing to deserve it?

HOWARD [to Mom]: Why can't you just tell her thank you for buying your son a present? You can't afford to get them anything.

MOM: You're in the same position I am—what are you talking about? You wouldn't be here either if you had any money of your own. That's why we're all here. If I could work, you think I'd be here?

HOWARD: You could work if you wanted to.

MOM: Oh, sure, with these hands? [holds her hands up helplessly]

HOWARD: There's some things you could do.

MOM: Like what?

HOWARD: You could take tickets in a theater. You could answer phones. You could work in a 7-11.

MOM [to Howard]: After owning my own business, do you really think I'm going to do anything like that? You haven't heard one word I've told you all summer. I've listened to you for hours about your ex-wife and all about her affair, and you haven't understood one thing I've said.

GRANDMOTHER: Some people have an anger control problem. And you can't figure out why Jamie has problems with his anger?

MOM: So you finally admit Jamie has an anger control problem. I thought he was perfect.

GRANDMOTHER: Of course he's got problems. Who wouldn't have problems if someone kept telling him that he was no good?

MOM: You can't just reward him when he's bad, Mother. [appeals to practitioner] You know that!

HOWARD: But you can be kind of harsh sometimes.

MOM: [to her brother]: You're the one he's scared of.

GRANDMOTHER: [to Mom]: Well, you can be pretty scary, too, when you lay into him.

PRACTITIONER: I'd like you to think of a way to have both things operating—a mix between letting Jamie face his consequences and also building up his self-esteem—because both those things need to happen.

MOM: No one else will punish him if I don't. He's already out of control.

PRACTITIONER: Can you plan how gift giving might fit into some agreed-upon rules and consequences?

MOM: My mother would never do anything like that. She does all of this completely behind my back.

PRACTITIONER: Well, pick one thing you would like everyone to be on the same page on.

MOM: The CD player. I think it's ridiculous that Jamie now has one downstairs, although supposedly his younger brother can use it, when he's already got one upstairs that she [jabs at Grandmother] gave him only 6 months ago.

GRANDMOTHER: Don't be silly, Sandra. That was for his birthday.

MOM: She asked us how we were going to be on the same page. I chose the CD player. I want that CD player to be returned and the boys to share the one in their room.

GRANDMOTHER: They have never had to share a CD player. That one in the room is for Jamie. It was for his birthday. Samuel has a little portable one. Both the boys use their headphones.

MOM: No, they don't. That's why I'm always screaming at Jamie to turn it down.

GRANDMOTHER: Like you need an excuse to scream?

MOM: Are you telling me the way he blasts that thing, we're just going to sit down here and be completely drowned out by his bass?

HOWARD: Mom, it is loud—that rap music. [smiles at practitioner] I'm more of an oldies rock person myself.

GRANDMOTHER: I can't take the CD player back now.

MOM: Why not? It's been less than 30 days.

GRANDMOTHER: He'd be heartbroken.

MOM: He didn't deserve it in the first place.

HOWARD: See how hard you can be? I think you'd enjoy taking it away from him.

PRACTITIONER: Well, let's find out where every one is at. Mom, we already know what you want. How about the rest of you?

HOWARD: I don't even care. I don't want any part of it. I just don't want any more fighting.

MOM: If you say you give up, you can't argue with me later about it.

HOWARD: When do I ever do that?

MOM: Your ex even said you did that—passive-aggressive, she called it. It is very passive-aggressive, Howard.

PRACTITIONER: So, Howard, you're saying you don't really care about who has rights and access to which CD player?

[He is red now though and probably hasn't heard the practitioner's last question. Brother and sister are off, exchanging insults in an escalating fashion.]

The reader may feel that the practitioner did not step in as often as needed. However, Minuchin (1974) has suggested that with disengaged relationships, in which there is little communication and warmth, as in the case with Ms. Witt and her mother, it is necessary to have conflict occur first.

In the subsequent interaction, the practitioner begins to redirect the sequence of communication. It will be necessary for her to blast through the family's homeostasis by using the technique of *intensity*, a redirection of the family interaction through the practitioner's repetition of instructions, her use of a loud and emphatic voice tone, or requiring that an interaction endure longer than families are comfortable (Minuchin & Fishman, 1981). Using a loud tone of voice may be quite acceptable in a family such as this one in which members frequently use raised voices. This also involves mimesis, part of the joining process, in which the practitioner purposely mimics the family's affect or style of communication, so that families feel comfortable with the practitioner as part of their system (Minuchin, 1974).

In the session, the practitioner subsequently tries to block the escalating interaction between Sandra and Howard Witt. She repeats herself, louder each time, to break up the argument, and nonverbally uses her arm to block the stream of interaction. But it is not until she has challenged their assumptions by making the comment "It seems like the adults in this family have just as hard a time listening as the kids" that they finally subside into silence. Although neither Mom nor Uncle Howard respond verbally to this provocative remark, a change in perspective seemed to result as the interactions between them thereafter become more contained.

The rest of the session is spent discussing why certain sound systems have been given to one child and not another, on what occasions they were given, the state of repair of the systems, the rules about when they could be played and who could play them, and so on. The discussion about compact disc players and stereos grinds along so endlessly that at times the practitioner feels compelled to solve the problem for the family. However, a structural family therapist must attend to *process*, the sequence of interactions, rather than *content*, the subject matter that is being discussed. If the structural family therapist solves the problem for the family, the family does not find a new process for handling its problems. A family is defined as healthy not by the absence of problems, but by its ability to handle the problems that inevitably come. Problem solving is assumed to occur as a by-product of improved structure (Minuchin & Nichols, 1993).

▬▬ Assessment of First Session

By the end of the first session, much has been learned. From a structural family therapy viewpoint, Jamie's acting out has arisen from a faulty structure in the family. Jamie and his mother bicker like equals; his mother's attempts to establish control are challenged by Jamie until she loses her own temper, and they are both out of control. These behaviors are all indicators of an enmeshed relationship. That Jamie takes Ritalin signals the presence of hyperactivity, which Nichols and Schwartz (2001) suggest as further evidence of the enmeshed relationship between Jamie and his mother. Mom is unable to take charge of his behavior.

Ms. Witt's difficulties with managing her son are aggravated by her own mother's usurpation of her rules. Grandmother and Jamie have established an *intergenerational coalition* in which she and Jamie are joined against Ms. Witt. *Coalitions* involve alignments of power in a family in which certain members join together (Minuchin et al., 1978). The coalition between Grandmother and Jamie gives Jamie an inappropriate level of power in the family hierarchy. This is seen in his behavior in the session (bossing around the adult members of his family and dominating the session discussion) and in his mother's and uncle's ineffective efforts to establish control.

Evidence of circular causality is present with the interactions of Grandmother and Mom in regard to Jamie. Grandmother is concerned about the boy's self-esteem, "building a boy up." However, the more she treats Jamie with favoritism, the angrier Ms. Witt becomes and the harder she is on Jamie. When Ms. Witt comes down on Jamie, then Mrs. Clayborne wants to do nice things for him so he'll feel better. Further, Ms. Witt and Mrs. Clayborne show evidence of a disengaged relationship in that they go for periods of time without speaking to each other and fail to negotiate between them how to handle the children. Each person has a different way of handling the functions of caring for and disciplining the children. They *detour* a lot of their conflict with each other onto Jamie, and Jamie is only too willing to become embroiled in their arguments.

Howard's role is that he fluctuates between playing the parent, thus undermining Mom's role, or playing the friend, increasing Jamie's power in the family. Howard's alternating alignment with his mother and his sister further illustrates the confused boundaries between family subsystems and each member's role in the household, and how these alternating interactions maintain the balance or the homeostasis of the family. Homeostasis is further displayed by the *complementarity* of roles of the two boys (Goldenberg & Goldenberg, 2000): Samuel (good son)–Jamie (bad son). The assumption is that if transaction patterns are modified in session through enactments, these new interactions can organize the family in a more functional state of balance in which boundaries between parent and sibling subsystems are more clearly drawn.

Summary of Second Session

In the second session, the parental hierarchy continued to be charged with the task of deciding on how they would "build both boys up," as well as give them consequences. Intensity, in the form of repeating instructions to talk over what needed to be done about a particular misbehavior of Jamie's, continued to be necessary to prevent members from becoming divided over "building up" and "tearing down."

The technique of *unbalancing* (Minuchin & Fishman, 1981) became necessary when Mrs. Clayborne and Ms. Witt were stuck in arguments. In this technique, the practitioner sides with one family member in order to unblock the stuck interaction, being careful to take turns with different family members so that one person doesn't feel "ganged up on." Another technique was to promote healthy complementarity in the family. When Ms. Witt began to report that Jamie seemed less argumentative, she was asked what she was doing to account for his improved behavior. The assumption of circularity is inherent in this question.

To block Uncle Howard from continuing to maintain family balance by alternately siding with first his mother and then his sister, he was challenged as to why he was putting himself in the middle of their arguments. He said he always had felt responsible for helping them get along with each other. When asked how successful his "help" has been, he admitted "not at all." Similar to his relief at being told that he could not be Jamie's father, Howard was noticeably unburdened to find he held no responsibility for his mother and sister's relationship, and his role in maintaining the family status quo was lessened.

Summary of Third Session

By the third session, a tremendous breakthrough occurred. The adults shared with the practitioner a plan they had formulated. It was much more complex a plan than the practitioner could have ever assigned. Each of the adults was to contribute money proportionate to her or his income to a fund for each child, who would receive certain amounts for reaching agreed-upon academic and behavioral standards in school at the end of each grade. Jamie and Samuel could choose to use the money they received in any way they wished. The adults reported this plan with a great deal of enthusiasm, with each person finishing another's sentences. This manner of interaction was in marked contrast to the bitterness apparent in the first session.

As was appropriate to the parental hierarchy, Mom was selected to report the plan to the children. However, the boys reacted in a fairly low-key way, to the adults' disappointment. The practitioner stressed the importance of the adults working together to come up with a plan. The practitioner also explained the concept of homeostasis, that family members may resist change to maintain the status quo. She suggested that the children might have felt uncomfortable with the adults' united front and may have been trying to provoke them into "changing back." The adults were warned to be on the alert for the boys' resistance and to regard even negative signs as further evidence of the positive changes that were occurring in the family system.

This session marked a turning point, and soon after, the family members decided they had gotten what they needed from the counseling. Somehow, the sound system issue was resolved, although the practitioner could never track the details of the solution. Ms. Witt began to show more warmth toward Jamie, as well as to Samuel, who even displayed some normal infractions of rules at times. Mom was surprised to discover that although she spent less time refereeing the boys' fights and monitoring Jamie, the boys seemed better able to manage their own problems. On an individual basis, Jamie's behavior, although by no means perfect, seemed generally more compliant. Ms. Witt's affect was altered in the process. Her tired, hopeless air had lifted, and she even considered working toward a mental health degree if she got her disability insurance. She said she wanted to help others as the practitioner had helped her family.

Conclusion

This illustration with the Saunders/Witt/Clayborne family demonstrates the use of structural family therapy with intergenerational families when adolescent behavior problems are the presenting symptom. Although the same general principles (interaction patterns should be such that the family is organized along clear hierarchical lines) are used with any family, complexity is added when there are more adult caretakers since adult members play more than one family role. At the same time, strengths are added with intergenerational families. Financial and emotional resources are potentially more available, and more adult caretakers can lend support to the parent subsystem. As was seen with this family, in order to make such intergenerational systems functional, enactments during sessions should center on creating clear boundaries around the parent subsystem and dismantling any intergenerational alignments that have formed.

7   Multisystemic Treatment with Juvenile Offending, Substance Abuse, and Prevention of Adolescent Pregnancy

▰▰▰ Case Study

Olivia Ramirez, age 15, biracial (Hispanic on her father's side, Caucasian on her mother's side), is on probation for possession of marijuana, assaults against other female classmates, and riding in a stolen car. She lives with her mother, Pearl Cottrell, and her 11-year-old brother, Kevin, in a two-bedroom apartment. Her parents' divorce 2 years ago was initiated by Ms. Cottrell. During their marriage, her husband, Joe Ramirez, abused alcohol and marijuana on a regular basis and was sometimes violent to her.

Although Mr. Ramirez's child support payments are inconsistent, Olivia maintains regular visitation with him every other weekend in the home where he lives with his brother and wife. He is sporadically employed as a house painter. Olivia's mother works as a bookkeeper for a small business. (See figure 7.1 for the genogram of this family.)

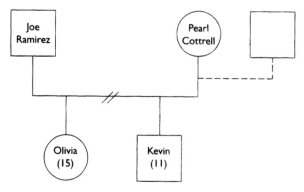

Race: Biracial (Caucasian and Hispanic)

Figure 7.1. Multisystemic Treatment Case Study: Olivia Ramirez's Family

▇▇▇▇ Description of Multisystemic Treatment

Drawing on family systems theory (Bateson, 1972; Bateson, Jackson, Haley, & Weakland, 1956) and Brofenbrenner's (1979) ecological model as the theoretical basis, in multisystemic treatment, the juvenile offender is viewed as embedded within the context of multiple inter-related systems (Henggeler, Schoenwald, Borduin, Rowland, & Cunningham, 1998). Systems that both affect and are affected by delinquent behavior include the child's own intrapersonal system (i.e., cognitive ability, social skills), the parent-child system, the parental system, peers, the school system, and the neighborhood system (Henggeler, 1991; Henggeler et al., 1986). The model extends beyond family therapy in that "the recursive sequences of family interaction that sustain a particular problem are often viewed as part of a longer, more complex chain of interactions among participants within and outside the family that sustain problem behaviors" (Henggeler et al., 1998, p. 77).

As well as systems theories, multisystemic therapy draws on several other models. Multisystemic therapy shares with family preservation the central aim of retaining adolescents in the home, rather than institutionalizing or incarcerating them. Along with this goal, enhancing generalization is key, therefore, treatment is usually delivered in the home or a community setting. Also similar to family preservation, multisystemic therapy combines treatment modalities and venues in an individualized approach to take into account the individual's strengths and limitations. In contrast to family preservation, multisystemic therapy, however, is theoretically based and systematically applied (treatment is manualized).

While multisystemic therapy includes family systems interventions (structural and strategic family therapy), it also focuses on nonsystemic interventions, specifically, those stemming from cognitive-behavioral therapy, such as parent training, social skills training, problem solving, and multicomponent behavior therapy (Henggeler & Borduin, 1990; Henggeler, Cunningham, Pickrel, Schoenwald, & Brondino, 1996); Henggeler et al., 1998). Interventions are delivered in a collaborative manner. (See chapters 1, 2, and 4 for further discussion of collaborative approaches.) Other characteristics of multisystemic therapy include a focus on specific behavioral goals, such as following curfew, completing chores, and separating from antisocial peers (Henggeler & Borduin, 1990; Henggeler et al., 1996). Goals should be realistic and time-limited. As well as addressing needs and problems, assessment also orients individuals and families toward their strengths. (For a brief overview of multisystemic therapy and additional resources for the interested reader, see box 7.1.)

Box 7.1

Key Assumptions of Multisystemic Therapy and Additional Resources

Key Assumptions

- Youth are embedded within the context of multiple interrelated systems, including the intrapersonal system, the parent-child system, the family system, the school system, peers, and the neighborhood system; assessment and intervention occur at all of these levels.
- Services are delivered in the home to the adolescent and the family with the goal of retaining the child in the home.
- Depending on the needs of the family, different theories are drawn upon, including family systems therapies (structural and strategic) and cognitive-behavioral therapy.

Additional Resources

S. W. Henggeler, S. K. Schoenwald, C. Borduin, M. Rowland, & P. B. Cunningham. (1998). *Multisystemic treatment of antisocial behavior in children and adolescents*. New York: Guilford.

MST Services Inc., www.mstservices.com

This chapter will present the empirical evidence to support multisystemic treatment. The different system levels involved with juvenile offending will then be discussed, along with illustrations from the case study. Following the assessment at the different system levels, goals and interventions will be discussed, using the case study as a basis.

Empirical Evidence

Multisystemic therapy has been extensively studied; approximately 800 families have participated in treatment (Henggeler, Schoenwald, Rowland, & Cunningham, 2002). Several prominent national organizations, including the National Institute of Mental Health, the National Institute on Drug Abuse, the Center for Substance Abuse Prevention, and the Office of Juvenile Justice and Delinquency Prevention, promote multisystemic therapy as a model community program due to its strong empirical support (Henggeler et al., 2002). Table 7.1 reviews studies that play a role in juvenile offending by system-level outcomes. Of note is that the success of the multisystemic model seems to depend on fidelity to the treatment. Therefore, community agencies that adopt multisystemic treatment receive training and supervision by MST Services Inc. (See the website listed in the resources section of box 7.1.)

Systems Involved with Juvenile Offending

The multisystemic model conceptualizes systems as interrelated and interactional. For example, in examining parental discipline strategies, the parents' behavior is not only crucial, but the practitioner must also take into account the youth's behavior and how this shapes and influences the parents' behavior. Further, the practitioner must assess how the parent-child interactions are influenced by the parents' relationships and the child's peer and school functioning (Henggeler et al., 1998). With recognition of these interrelationships, assessment of the different systems often involved with juvenile offending will be delineated separately, along with their case illustrations. Assessment also orients individuals and families toward their strengths, which can be drawn upon to design individualized interventions.

Table 7.1

Key Findings from Studies on Multisystemic Treatment

System Level	Key Findings
Individual Adolescent	• High engagement in treatment with substance abusers (Henggeler, Pickrel, Brondino, & Couch, 1996)
	• Lower self-reported drug use (Henggeler et al., 1997; Henggeler, Pickrel, & Brondino, 1999)
	• Reduced behavior problems (Borduin et al., 1995; Henggeler et al., 1986; Henggeler et al., 1997; Scherer et al., 1994)
	• Decreased psychiatric symptomatology (withdrawal, anxiety, and aggression) (Borduin et al., 1995; Henggeler et al., 1986; Scherer et al., 1994)
Parent	• Decreased psychiatric symptomology (Borduin et al., 1995; Scherer et al., 1994)
Family	• Positive effects on family conflict and supportiveness (Borduin et al., 1995; Henggeler et al., 1986)
	• Increased cohesion and adaptability (Borduin et al., 1995; Henggeler, Melton, & Smith, 1992)
School	• At 6-month follow-up, school attendance improved with juvenile offenders with substance abuse problems (Brown, Henggeler, Schoenwald, Brondino, & Pickrel, 1999)
Peers	• Decreased peer aggression (Henggeler, Melton, & Smith, 1992); decreased socialized aggression observed by parents in some cases (Henggeler et al., 1986; Scherer et al., 1994)
Criminal Justice	• 25–70% reductions in rates of rearrest
	• 47–64% reductions in days of out-of-home placements (Henggeler et al., 2002)
Cost Savings	• Cost per client of multisystemic treatment was $2,800 compared to average cost of local institutional placement of $16,300 (Henggeler, Melton, & Smith, 1992)
	• Cost per client of multisystemic treatment was $4,000, with an estimated savings of $7,440 for each youth (Henggeler et al., 1997)
	• Washington State Institute for Public Policy estimated average net gain per youth of $61,068 in criminal justice system costs, placement costs, and crime victim benefits (Henggeler et al., 2002)

The Individual System

Individual functioning may include cognitions, behavior, social capabilities, and psychological adjustment. Antisocial children are characterized by a style of cognitive processing that impedes their ability to effectively problem solve in social situations (Dodge, Price, Bachorowski, & Newman, 1990). Given the tendency to make hostile attributions regarding neutral events, they may be quick to react with aggression (Dodge et al., 1990; Bienert & Schneider, 1995), particularly when impulse control is low.

Olivia's physical fights with classmates start, she claims, because they stare at her in a way that challenges her to fight. She is convinced they are making derogatory remarks about her. In one instance, Olivia said, "What are you looking at?" The other girl responded in kind, and the argument escalated into a physical altercation. In order to stop her from responding aggressively to cues in the environment, a goal will therefore be to train Olivia to interpret events in her environment in a more neutral fashion through attributional retraining.

At the individual level, Henggeler et al. (1998) discuss the following potential strengths youth may display:

1. Competencies and abilities (e.g., social skills and academic skills)
2. Attractiveness
3. Intelligence
4. Hobbies and interests
5. Hygiene
6. Motivation
7. Temperament

Olivia demonstrates a number of strengths. She is able to reflect on her actions and demonstrate insight into some of her motivations. For example, she quickly showed awareness about her high-risk behaviors, realizing that they were attached to the crowd she hung around with. She also demonstrated remorse for treating her mother badly at times (yelling at her and ignoring rules). She has a future goal—to become a model—even though she might not have a realistic appraisal of the probability of success in such a field. She is motivated to stop her substance abuse for the sake of her brother. She expresses a great deal of concern about being a poor role model for her younger brother and doesn't want him to begin smoking marijuana. Olivia also has some coping mechanisms in place. She likes physical activity, such as jogging and working out at the gym with her mother. These activities, she claims, help reduce feelings of frustration and stress and make her lose the urge to smoke.

Parent-Child System

The parent-child relationship is often a focus of intervention due to several factors empirically shown to characterize families of offenders.[1] These factors include poor parental monitoring, inconsistent discipline, and a lack of clear rules in the household (Loeber, Farrington, Stouthamer-Loeber, & Van Kammen, 1998; Patterson, 1986), along with impaired communication between parents and adolescents (Henggeler, 1989).

Olivia says she gets along well with her mother even though she is sometimes mean to her mother, yelling at her when she gets mad or frustrated. Olivia says that she "pretty much gets to do what she wants," and her mother can't do anything to stop her. Olivia says that her mother even allows Olivia's boyfriend, Gilbert, to spend the night sometimes.

Olivia visits her father every other weekend; he lives with his brother and his family. She says that, during this time, he is often working and that she gets bored. She says she knows where he hides his marijuana, and when he is gone, she sometimes smokes, "just for something to do."

Goals at the parent-child system level will include increased structure of the environment and supervision for Olivia. In order to impose the level of rules and structure necessary, Ms. Cottrell will be trained in parenting, assertiveness, and communication building, and efforts will be made to increase her level of support.

As well as addressing limitations, Henggeler et al. (1998) name the following potential strengths at the level of the parent-child system:

1. Financial resources (e.g., money, property, welfare benefits, employment income)
2. Basic needs are met (e.g., housing, food)
3. Child care is provided

---

1. Space precludes discussion of how to possibly involve Olivia's father in the treatment process. However, Henggeler et al. (1998) seem to center efforts on working with the custodial parent of the child.

4. Available transportation
5. Strong affective and instrumental relations among spouses, parents, and children
6. Number and variety of social supports (e.g., extended family, friends, neighbors, coworkers, and church members)
7. Characteristics of the extended family

For Olivia and her mother, strengths in the parent-child system include the warmth shared between mother and daughter, their ability to laugh together, and their affection for each other. In addition, they enjoy some activities together (i.e., going to the gym to work out). Another strength is that Olivia's father maintains regular visitation with Olivia, and they have continued their relationship. Olivia also maintains a relationship with her paternal and maternal relatives. Ms. Cottrell's family on her mother's side lives in the area although visits require 30 minutes to an hour of driving time.

On a more instrumental level, Ms. Cottrell meets her family's basic needs for housing and food through income from her employment as a bookkeeper and from child support. She has an automobile that is only occasionally out of commission because of repairs. However, the community in which they live has no public transportation system.

Parental System

Parental systems of antisocial youth are often characterized by high levels of marital conflict (Capaldi & Patterson, 1994; Krishnakumar & Buehler, 2000), low levels of acceptance and affection, social isolation, and lack of support (Henggeler, 1989). Although multisystemic treatment goes beyond the family system, the family is an important target for intervention; parents play a key element in many of the interventions. For example, parents will be responsible for supervision and monitoring to change the pattern of the teen's friendships (from consorting with antisocial peers to consorting with prosocial peers). Parents will also interface with the school system because involvement in a teen's school performance is associated with enhanced performance.

Ms. Cottrell has some difficulties balancing her own needs for companionship (achieved mainly through her current boyfriend) and the needs of her children for structure and supervision. Financially, she meets her children's basic needs but struggles with resources (for instance, they are only able to afford a two-bedroom apartment).

Assessment also involves the strengths of the parent system. Heng-geler et al. (1998) identify the following potential strengths at this level:

1. Social skills
2. Concern
3. Problem-solving ability
4. Attractiveness
5. Frustration tolerance
6. Patience
7. Altruism
8. Motivation

Ms. Cottrell is an attractive, youthful woman who supports her family on her earnings and child support. She possessed the strength to leave a violent marriage and to avoid further violence in relationships. She is a calm and patient woman and says she is motivated to participate in services because of concern for her daughter. She has some social support in the way of family and a boyfriend and is on friendly terms with her coworkers.

The Peer Group

Social skills to make prosocial friendships may be lacking with juvenile offenders. Early peer rejection has been associated with the development of antisocial behavior (Bierman, Miller, & Stabb, 1987). It is postulated that once rejected by "normal" peers, deviant youth form their own peer group and serve to enhance each other's antisocial behavior (e.g., McMahon, 1994).

In the afternoon, Olivia is unsupervised and spends that time with her boyfriend, Gilbert, her best friend, Misty, and other friends. Olivia identifies that this is when they often smoke marijuana. Olivia says that "everyone" smokes marijuana and that marijuana is "everywhere." She says she started smoking in middle school.

Olivia reveals that her boyfriend sometimes spends the night because he has family problems. She and her boyfriend are sexually active and rely on condoms and withdrawal as birth control methods.

Resources in the peer system are also examined and these may include the following (Henggeler et al., 1998):

1. Individual competencies and abilities of peers
2. Prosocial activities, hobbies, and interests
3. Family monitoring and involvement in peer activities

Olivia has some interest in athletics and modeling, which may increase her prosocial involvement.

The School System

Multisystemic treatment departs from more typical family interventions in that systems beyond the family are targeted. The school is a major ecological system for teens, and delinquency has been strongly associated with poor school performance, as well as dropping out (Loeber, 1990; Loeber et al., 1998). Lower IQ has been consistently associated with delinquent behavior (Moffitt, 1993).

Although Olivia's standardized test scores reveal average intelligence and no learning disabilities, she barely receives passing grades. Because of Olivia's fights at school, the principal conveyed to Ms. Cottrell the need to take a more active role in controlling Olivia's behavior, but Olivia's mother says, "What can I do? I'm not there."

The school system will also be assessed for the resources it offers the youth. Potential strengths include the following (Henggeler et al., 1998):

1. Appropriate and effective classroom management practices
2. Appropriate and effective schoolwide discipline procedures
3. Concerned school personnel
4. Teacher involvement in the community
5. Prosocial after-school activities (e.g., art, drama, athletics, interest clubs)
6. Cultural and community activities held at school
7. Efforts to engage families in their children's education

Olivia's school has managed to recruit many Hispanic and African American teachers to teach the mainly minority youth of the school. While class sizes are large and the school has few resources, the principal is committed to outreach efforts to involve parents. The school offers standard after-school activities, such as sports, cheerleading, yearbook, and so on, but does not offer after-school programs for enrichment and monitoring of teens.

◼️ Goal Setting and Assessment

After a multisystemic conceptualization of the causes of identified problems, intervention strategies targeting the different ecological levels are formulated. After implementation, the effectiveness of interventions and the barriers to change are assessed. Based on this feedback, new hypotheses may be generated about the causes of the problems and the potential solutions (Henggeler et al., 1998).

In this section, interventions will be described and illustrated with the case study. Goals from which interventions stem should not only be constructed for the immediate future (eliminate substance use and physical fighting, prevent pregnancy) but also be oriented toward an intermediary point (get off probation), and the more distant future (become a model). The purpose of developing goals in the distant future is to motivate the teenager to stop current behaviors that are incompatible with these goals. For instance, Olivia recognizes that a chronic juvenile record might prevent her from getting into a modeling agency.

Goals often involve complex behaviors and must be broken down into their separate tasks (for a more detailed discussion of the construction of well-formulated goals and tasks, see chapter 1). In multisystemic treatment, interventions to meet targeted goals must also be delineated by appropriate system level. These will be illustrated with the case study.

Individual System

Whenever possible, individual interventions with teenagers should be a last resort. More preferable, according to S. Henggeler (personal communication, August, 25, 2001), is for parents to be trained in the intervention they will then implement with their children. However, individual work was already occurring with the mother to bolster her parent position, and it was seen as necessary to address some of Olivia's high-risk behaviors immediately. Specifically, the cognitive-behavioral interventions of attribution training and problem solving were used to address Olivia's physical fighting and substance use. To prevent pregnancy, Olivia was educated about risk and the different options for birth control.

Attribution Training
Attribution training was enacted at the individual level to help Olivia with the goals of decreasing the substance use and physical aggression. Attribution training was used to address the threats and hostile intentions that Olivia attributed to her classmates. In attribution training, the practitioner asks the youth a series of perspective-taking questions.

Olivia was asked to consider what might be going on with the classmates who "instigated" her. She said maybe they were just jealous of her looks and of her having an attractive boyfriend. Rather than using this as a rationale for fighting, the possible motivations of her classmates were reframed as compliments for Olivia. When people looked at her or talked about her with others, she could see this as an indication that they admired her and her boyfriend's attractiveness. Perspective-taking questions also help Olivia to see the role she takes in interactions. For instance, when asked to describe her facial expression, she said that she might have a "mean look" on her face, but that she "couldn't help it." She was then asked to contrast her expression when she was with her boyfriend and her friends and saw that she could alter her facial expression, depending on the situation.

When Olivia was led through the steps of what occurred during her physical fights, she could also see how she escalated the arguments by making statements such as "What are you looking at?" "What's your problem?" and "You wanna fight?" She was then asked how people would tend to respond to these comments and could see that they were reciprocating some of her own hostility. The practitioner continued to deconstruct each incident in which Olivia felt that classmates were "trying to get on her nerves," so that she could understand and then change her role in the situation. Olivia was also taught problem-solving skills (described in a following section; also see chapter 4), and then she and the practitioner role played the different options.

Another example of attribution retraining drawn from Henggeler et al. (1998) involved Olivia's propensity to skip certain classes. For example, she described skipping her math class because the teacher, Ms. Silvana, was a "bitch." When asked to explain, Olivia further described that Ms. Silvana sometimes made sarcastic remarks when Olivia came into her class late, such as "I'm so glad you're here to grace us with your presence." Olivia said she'd rather skip her class than deal with that. Henggeler et al. (1998) propose that in such an instance, the therapist might ask the adolescent a number of questions, such as "What is the teacher's job?" "How do you think the teacher took your behavior?" "What choices did the teacher have in responding to you?" Olivia was asked, "How would you respond if you were the teacher and a student came in late all the time?" When Olivia was asked these questions, she said that she would probably end up hitting her students, which was probably worse than being sarcastic. In sum, the practitioner tries to help the adolescent understand that, in many situations, her negative attitude and behavior influence adult authorities to respond in a punitive fashion (Henggeler et al., 1998).

Henggeler et al. (1998) also suggest that practitioners work with teens by taking them on outings, such as the mall, and asking them to identify people's facial expressions and other physical cues and then identify their feelings and thoughts. When teens attribute hostile or aggressive motives, behaviors, or interactions to others, alternative possibilities are then suggested and elicited so that the teens learn how to more accurately interpret and respond to cues.

Problem Solving

The problem-solving process is another cognitive-behavioral method used to help juvenile offenders cope with situations that might trigger their illegal behaviors. In Olivia's case, the problem-solving process was applied to situations in which she was tempted to use marijuana or when she started to become angry at classmates. The problem-solving process involves defining the problem, brainstorming solutions, assessing the advantages and disadvantages of different options, deciding on an option, and implementing the option.

Education About Pregnancy Risk

In a discussion of pregnancy risk, Olivia revealed that she and her boyfriend were sexually active but they didn't have sex "that much." She further elaborated that it was "maybe once a week" after they had been smoking marijuana. She admitted that she didn't really like sex unless she was "high." She was asked about the possibility of abstaining from sexual activity since it was associated with marijuana use. Olivia worried that her boyfriend would be mad because he was already used to having sex with her. He might even break up with her, she said, to have sex with somebody else. When the practitioner reminded her of the priority of stopping marijuana use, Olivia said, "Yeah, I guess, and it would prove whether he cared about me or if he just wanted sex." Olivia agreed to consider the option of abstinence.

An ensuing discussion on different birth control methods and their rates of success revealed that Olivia underestimated her chances of pregnancy from the use of withdrawal as a birth control method. Because the young couple's use of condoms was intermittent, Olivia was trained in communication skills, which focused on how to respond to her boyfriend's attempts to get out of using condoms (i.e., "It doesn't feel as good" or "I want you to have my baby"). She recognized that when she had been smoking marijuana, her judgment was impaired regarding the viability of these excuses. The practitioner also suggested that she work with both Olivia and her boyfriend to facilitate this discussion.

The conversation with Olivia revealed that she was aware of some of the reliable methods, such as oral contraceptives and implant methods, but was afraid they would cause her to gain weight. She was given a handout on the various methods, their success and failure rates, their cost, and their side effects. Once she had decided on a more effective method, the practitioner would take her to a neighborhood health clinic to receive the procedure or prescription.

The tracks the practitioner took on pregnancy prevention with Olivia (exploration of the possibility of abstinence, skill training on effective contraceptive use, and linking her to a community-based clinic for the provision of contraceptives) were informed by a meta-analysis of programs to reduce pregnancy in keeping with the evidence basis in multisystemic treatment interventions. In the meta-analysis, abstinence-based programs were insufficient, however, training on contraceptive use and linking teens to clinics affected contraceptive use and childbearing more effectively (Franklin, Grant, Corcoran, O'Dell, & Bultman, 1997).

Parent-Child System

Parent discipline strategies are usually targeted for intervention in multisystemic therapy. In order for the supervision and discipline imposed to be effective, parental authority sometimes needs bolstering. Structural family techniques, as well as behavioral parent training, may be necessary.

Monitoring and Supervision

It was crucial for Ms. Cottrell to arrange for Olivia's monitoring and supervision after school. As Ms. Cottrell was unavailable because of her work schedule, the practitioner helped Ms. Cottrell and Olivia problem solve about how Olivia could be supervised. As part of the process, they were asked to brainstorm ideas that might use already existing support networks for supervision of Olivia (see chapter 4 for a more detailed illustration of the problem-solving process). In the end, several ideas became plausible. One day a week, Olivia could help Ms. Cottrell's sister-in-law, who is married with three children. Ms. Cottrell and her sister-in-law could chip in to pay Olivia to clean her house or watch the children so her aunt could run errands. In exchange, Olivia's aunt would pick her up from school that day. Olivia's paternal grandmother was available another day of the week for supervision of Olivia. The practitioner contributed the option of a school-initiated mentoring program for one afternoon a week. Other prosocial activities with which youth can become involved are after-school clubs, community-based sports and service organizations, church groups, recreation center activities, and after-school volunteer work.

Another school-related possibility involved Olivia joining the track team, given her interest in running. Olivia decided she would consider this option since she had some time before track season began. She was worried though that she wouldn't know anyone on the team and that she wasn't in good enough shape. In the meantime, the practitioner would work with her on building social skills so that she could more easily relate to prosocial peers (see also the section on the peer group, p. 197).

Another viable option involved Olivia seeking a job. As part of Olivia's goal of becoming a model, she wanted her head shots taken. Her mother couldn't afford this expense, so Olivia would have to earn the money herself. The practitioner agreed to shuttle Olivia around town to different fast-food restaurants and grocery stores to complete the application process.

Structural Family Therapy Techniques

Structural family therapy techniques were used to bolster Ms. Cottrell's parental authority. (Also see chapter 6 for a more in-depth discussion of structural family therapy.) First, the practitioner referred to Olivia's mother as Ms. Cottrell to clearly mark through the use of language the boundary between parent and child. However, Ms. Cottrell insisted the practitioner call her by her first name, Pearl, since she said Ms. Cottrell sounded "too old." Since the practitioner wished to avoid placing mother and child on the same level by the use of first names in conversation, the practitioner subsequently made reference to Ms. Cottrell's role of mother by calling her "Mom" in session.

Second, the practitioner was clear in placing final authority with Ms. Cottrell for decisions after hearing Olivia's input: "Mom, we have discussed the various options for Olivia, and you have heard from Olivia her feelings and opinions, so what would you like to put into place to make sure that Olivia is supervised in the afternoons?" Olivia resisted her mother's attempts to take charge, however, saying, "I don't care what she wants me to do, I'm going to do what I want" and "If my mom makes me do anything, I'll just take it out on her." When Ms. Cottrell seemed loath to exert her authority ("I don't really care if she yells at me. It doesn't bother me. I'd rather she got mad at me than took it out on her classmates or her boyfriend"), the practitioner said that, by allowing her daughter this control, she was teaching her little respect for authority and encouraging her inability to regulate herself. In other words, Ms. Cottrell needed to enforce the authority for Olivia's benefit.

The line between adults and children was also emphasized through asking Ms. Cottrell to list "the things that adults can do" and "the things that teens can do." This exercise conveyed the point that Ms. Cottrell allowed Olivia to have privileges that were commonly held by adults, such as having her boyfriend stay over.

Parent Training

Parents are taught skills through behavioral parent training. (For more details on parent training techniques, see chapters 2 and 4.) Specifically, parents learn to track the occurrence of concrete behaviors, such as class attendance, violating curfew, usage of drugs, association with deviant peers, and completion of homework. In addition to close monitoring of youth activities, parents are also trained to have close and frequent contact with the school to monitor homework and attendance. The effective use of praise and rewards is taught so that compliance is reinforced. Punishments should be both aversive and constructive (e.g., cleaning the toilet and bathtub, scrubbing the kitchen floor, cleaning the car).

Accordingly, Ms. Cottrell was taught how to reinforce compliance and punish disobedience. When a plan had been settled for how Olivia was to have supervision and monitoring after school, the rewards and punishments were established. If Olivia were to disobey and go off with her friends or bring her friends over, then she would have to clean the two bathrooms in the apartment that night. However, every afternoon of compliance would result in a visit to the gym with her mother that evening.

Communications skills training was also part of the work with the parent-child dyad. Both parties could benefit from learning how to be more assertive, since mother and child were coming from opposite communication styles (Olivia was aggressive while her mother was passive). The components of communication skills training include using "I" messages (talking about one's own position and feelings rather than making accusations about another person) and reflecting back the message of the speaker, empathizing with the speaker's position. Another component of the training involves teaching each person to make requests of the other by using "I" statements and being specific and polite. Once some mastery over techniques was established, one of the key topics for discussion was the use of birth control methods for Olivia and how Ms. Cottrell would help Olivia obtain regular health care services and access to birth control.

Parental System

Since parents may resist the practitioner's attempts to focus on their problems as they may find this focus irrelevant or intrusive, Henggeler et al. (1998) recommend that to engage parents, practitioners must make explicit the linkages between parents' presenting issues and their child's behavioral problems. For instance, the practitioner outlined the issue of assertiveness for Olivia's mother: "When you don't communicate to Olivia's father the necessity of removing Olivia's access to marijuana, Olivia continues to smoke marijuana when she is at her father's." Or, "When you allow Olivia to talk you out of enforcing rules, she gets in trouble, which will continue to hinder her progress in school and will prolong her involvement with the juvenile justice system."

Assertiveness Training

Since Olivia's father's smoking was continued modeling for Olivia and she also had access to his marijuana supply when she went for visits, Ms. Cottrell had to be empowered about initiating new visiting procedures with Olivia and her father. Subjecting Olivia to these conditions was only perpetuating her substance use. Mom responded that she didn't want to be held in contempt by the court for not allowing the visits but did not want to discuss the issue with him either.

Consistent with a multisystemic conceptualization, when a problem such as parental lack of assertiveness is identified, the ecological factors contributing to or maintaining the problem should be identified (Henggeler et al., 1998). For instance, Olivia's mother's lack of assertiveness might be attributed to several different factors: the possibility of violence and conflict, the trauma of long-term exposure to physical violence, loss from the divorce, lack of skills, irrational thought processes, and poor support networks. Since she clearly feared a violent response from her ex-husband, the practitioner assessed the safety issues involved. Olivia's mother reported there had been no violence since the divorce. She said her ex-husband didn't want to compromise his visitation with the children, although, she added, he was often not present during these visits.

To address her anxiety, the practitioner first educated Ms. Cottrell about the protections afforded by the criminal justice system. A safety plan was developed, which involved devising various escape routes and plans to alert the police in situations where violence might be likely to occur. She was also given information about filing a protective order with the county attorney's office if violence occurred.

The second strategy to address Ms. Cottrell's anxiety was to apply systematic desensitization to develop her assertiveness skills (Henggeler et al., 1998). Components of systematic desensitization included teaching progressive muscle relaxation and rank ordering situations in which she had difficulty being assertive, emphasizing those situations that affected her parenting. Education about assertive communication was also discussed and then role played for modeling and behavior rehearsal.

Problem-Solving

Another cognitive-behavioral intervention involved teaching Olivia's mother the problem-solving method. In this situation, her ex-husband might not change his behavior even after she talked to him, and she might have to recontact her lawyer to have the terms of visitation changed. Problem solving might involve ways she could afford lawyers' fees. In general, teaching the problem-solving model was important for Ms. Cottrell so that she could learn to generate options in stressful situations and, in this way, take a more active approach to problems that affected her children.

Assessing Support Networks

Henggeler et al. (1998) recommend, for the sake of ecological validity, that informal rather than formal support systems be identified and bolstered. Potential sources of support include neighbors, who may be particularly helpful for monitoring children's activities, and work-based relationships, which are sometimes the only opportunity for parents to share peer interactions. Neighborhood organizations, such as neighborhood watch groups, parent groups, tenant associations, local businesses, churches, the NAACP, the Urban League, 4-H clubs, Rotary clubs, labor unions, and advocacy groups, are other sources of support.

Henggeler et al. (1998) provide the following questions to ascertain the types of informal social support provided by friends, neighbors, coworkers, church members, and extended family:

1. Who would you go to for $100? (instrumental support)
2. If you couldn't pick your children up from school, how would you get them home? (instrumental support)
3. When troubles really get you down, who makes you feel better? (emotional)
4. Who do you go to for advice about your kids? (information)
5. What is the level of reciprocity in these relationships and to what extent are they equitable?
6. Who in the support network is a source of stress? What is the nature of that stress?

Although Ms. Cottrell said she had friends at work who shared their parenting challenges with each other, regarding other social support, her mother lives about an hour away in a rural area. She talks to her on the phone once a week and visits about once a month. Her brother, sister-in-law, and their children live about 30 minutes away. Ms. Cottrell's parents divorced when she was young. Her father moved to California and started another family. Sporadic telephone contact has marked Ms. Cottrell's relationship with her father. Their last conversation, she reports, was about 3 years ago. Most of Ms. Cottrell's social support stems from her boyfriend of 3 months.

When single parents of juvenile offenders are involved in partner relationships, Henggeler et al. (1998) offer the following assessment guidelines to determine their partner's role, the ecological factors contributing to the pattern of the relationship, and their impact on parenting:

1. Is the parent's struggle to make ends meet eased when a partner is found?
2. Does a single mother obtain relief from the stresses of monitoring and disciplining her children when the boyfriend steps in?
3. Does the parent have the requisite social skills to develop a support system?

Ms. Cottrell's boyfriend seemed to meet many of her companionship needs, although he wasn't involved in the care or disciplining of the children. Ms. Cottrell said she got married when she was 17 because she got pregnant with Olivia. Since her divorce, she has enjoyed dating men who are not violent to her.

Because she began parenting as an adolescent, her social development may have been compromised (Henggeler et al., 1998). To redress these deficits, assertiveness training and communication skills building would assist Ms. Cottrell in obtaining social support through the various avenues available to her.

One reason Olivia's mother did not seek out more support was because she "didn't want to be a bother." This attitude was reframed as a strength, that she wanted to engage with others as equals (Henggeler et al., 1998). An essential part of maintaining a social support network, the practitioner emphasized, is that individuals must not only receive from others but also reciprocate. For example, discussions about social support networks gleaned as a possible resource the large number of single-parent families that lived at the apartment complex. Ms. Cottrell decided she could possibly trade some supervision time of children with neighbors at times when she was home during the evenings and weekends.

Peer Group

A central intervention in multisystemic therapy involves helping parents to promote prosocial friendships and to discourage antisocial friendships. The success of this intervention is based on a number of factors (Henggeler et al., 1998). First, the adolescent must be convinced this is a worthy goal. When asked to name the advantages and disadvantages of associating with her current friends, Olivia stated the following advantages: she had known these friends since middle school; they had fun together; she and her boyfriend were "in love." When Olivia was asked to name the disadvantages, she admitted it would be difficult to quit marijuana since all of her friends smoked. Ms. Cottrell named another disadvantage. She said Olivia's friendship with her best friend, Misty, was very erratic. They would be best friends one day and then have an actual physical fight the next. The practitioner added another disadvantage: because marijuana was the commonality for her peer group, Olivia wasn't learning how to relate to people in a way that didn't rely on drugs.

Because Olivia was still so ambivalent, Ms. Cottrell was informed of the type of effort that would be necessary to loosen these ties. In large part, this effort involves monitoring, supervision, and creating opportunities for the teen to interact with more prosocial youth.

In order to achieve success, Ms. Cottrell would also have to elicit active and intensive support from friends, relatives, neighbors, and co-workers. The practitioner also offered assistance for the initial efforts. For example, she would be available late at night on call if Olivia violated curfew and would support Mom with her presence if Ms. Cottrell needed to implement an aversive consequence and no one else was available.

Since Olivia was unwilling to cut herself off from her friends, the practitioner spent time working on how Olivia could refuse marijuana if she were offered it. Olivia denied this would be useful: "It's not like anyone's going to force me." The practitioner responded, "No, they're not going to force you, but it's habit for you to accept. If you have the tools available to you, you will be more likely to resist the temptation."

The practitioner covered the principles of effective refusal: responding rapidly rather than stalling or hesitating, maintaining steady eye contact, and responding with a clear and firm "no," which does not leave the door open to future offers. Olivia wanted to add that she is on probation and is being tested regularly. The practitioner and Olivia then role played various situations.

In talking about breaking ties with her friends in the interest of stopping substance use, Olivia was particularly against the idea of splitting with her boyfriend. However, she understood the risks of continuing to see him when he was a habitual smoker. The practitioner, therefore, explored the extent to which exposure to marijuana could be renegotiated and limits set. A lot of effort was spent convincing Ms. Cottrell of the necessity of enforcing new limits. Ms. Cottrell said she pitied Gilbert his poor home environment. The practitioner was willing to talk to Gilbert about his situation and give him referrals for assistance. However, the practitioner stressed that Ms. Cottrell certainly didn't want her concern for Gilbert to override the effects on her daughter in terms of possible pregnancy and continued exposure to marijuana.

The practitioner facilitated a meeting with Ms. Cottrell, Olivia, and her boyfriend in which Gilbert was told he could no longer bring marijuana with him into the home. If Ms. Cottrell discovered that he had done so, he would be banned from the apartment. He was further requested to keep marijuana away from Olivia outside of the home and to refrain from bringing her to parties in which marijuana was present. Further, Gilbert would only be allowed to visit when Ms. Cottrell was in the home. In addition, while Olivia and Gilbert were allowed to spend time together in Olivia's bedroom because of the limited space of the apartment, they had to keep the door open.

Although Olivia initially bucked against the rules that restricted her contact with Gilbert, she admitted after only a short time period that she didn't "get so mad at him any more" (previously, her anger at him had resulted in physical outbursts). The practitioner explained to Olivia's mother that teenagers were often ill prepared for the demands of an intense emotional and sexual relationship. By setting limits on the time Olivia could spend with her boyfriend, Ms. Cottrell was helping her negotiate these demands at a more manageable level.

Part of the work for the peer system is to identity potential areas of competence and interest, such as Olivia participating in the track team or possibly modeling, and to figure out what pursuit of these prosocial activities would entail. Olivia will work out with her mother during the evenings to ensure that she is in good physical condition for the track team.

Mom has agreed to provide transportation to facilitate involvement in prosocial activities. For example, she will give rides to a job, to track practice, or to relatives' houses, but she will not provide rides for contacts with drug-using friends. Aversive consequences will be administered when Olivia consorts with antisocial peers, whereas positive consequences will follow prosocial contacts.

The practitioner will help Olivia develop social skills since teens whose commonality involves drug taking or who are used to interacting with others when under the influence may lack some of these basic skills. The following steps are involved in social skills training:

1. How to approach others, what to say to get a conversation going, how to join a group
2. Appropriate self-disclosure
3. Sharing and cooperation skills
4. Problem-solving and conflict resolution skills

Through such training, the adolescent is taught to respond appropriately to internal and external cues in order to enhance the likelihood of gaining and maintaining positive peer relationships (Henggeler & Borduin, 1990).

School System

Work with the school system involves the practitioner meeting with school personnel to understand the school's perception of the youth's performance, the cause of any problems, efforts made by the school to solve the problems, and the effectiveness of the attempts. In order to cultivate cooperation, the practitioner in multisystemic treatment is advised to take a "one down" position with school personnel rather than taking the role of an external authority who has come to tell personnel their jobs. This position assists the practitioner in developing interventions that have relevance and credibility for school personnel (Henggeler et al., 1998). The practitioner may help design behavior modification systems with the teacher, help a child get readmitted to school, connect the youth with a teacher who may serve as a role model, or link the child to extracurricular activities (Henggeler et al., 1996). School records are also examined, and relevant testing is advocated if it has not already been completed.

Testing on file for Olivia revealed average intelligence, and no learning disabilities were evident. This information indicated the need for psychosocial interventions rather than providing educational services for a youth with special requirements. In a meeting with the practitioner, Olivia's homeroom and math teacher said that Olivia was "smart enough, but doesn't try." The teacher said that Olivia was very sensitive about being corrected and, in general, tended to see "disrespect" from both other classmates and teachers. When asked how Olivia responded to praise, the teacher said, "She smiles. She has a pretty smile when she uses it," but that "Olivia needs to do more to earn praise." The teacher also complained about Olivia's mother's lack of involvement, that she didn't often respond to her attempts to talk about Olivia's behavior (skipping school, being tardy) or her grades (Olivia will probably have to take summer class in math unless she drastically alters her performance).

A couple of strategies were used with Olivia's teacher. The first was to empathize with the demands on the teacher in terms of conveying curriculum, managing behaviors, and working with many students of different needs and abilities. The second was to share some of the work the practitioner was doing with Olivia and her mother. She explained that she was working on an individual basis with Olivia on the negative way she interpreted neutral events. The promise of intense individual work on this issue seemed to make her teacher more amenable to taking the time to compliment Olivia each day, even for a behavior that may not seem particularly praiseworthy in the teacher's eyes, such as coming to class on time, making an effort toward solving problems, and asking for help. The practitioner shared another of Olivia's goals, which was to increase her involvement with prosocial peers. She said that Olivia's mother was to be a focal point of these efforts, but asked if the teacher had any ideas about how these prosocial relationships could be reinforced in the classroom. The teacher said she sometimes assigned her students into teams to work together to solve problems, which helped break them out of their usual cliques and groups.

Although the practitioner said she would work intensively with Olivia's mother to increase her school involvement, Henggeler et al. (1998) also suggest working at the school system level to enlist parental support for educational goals. Suggestions include briefing parents on their child's progress, perhaps by sending notes home with the youth, rather than only reporting problems, and personally extending invitations to parents for school conferences.

Work with Ms. Cottrell to increase her school involvement began by informing her that she, as Olivia's parent, had much more influence over Olivia's school performance than the school did (Henggeler et al., 1998). The following specific guidelines are offered for parents to increase their influence:

1. Monitor homework assignments. (Ask Olivia what homework she has for each day and ask to look over completed homework.)
2. Keep track of when quizzes and tests are scheduled and track their results. (Check in with Olivia about approaching quizzes and exams, coach her to prepare, and ask afterward about her performance and the grade.)
3. Set aside a specific time and a quiet place for study, like the kitchen table after dinner. (Olivia's mother agreed to leave the TV off until her children had finished their homework.)
4. Sit near the child while doing homework. (Ms. Cottrell would spend time going over mail, paying bills, and reading nearby to support their efforts.)
5. Support extracurricular school functions. (If Olivia decides to join the track team, Mom will pick her up after practice and, if possible, try to come to meets.)
6. Implement contingencies that are based on the child's efforts and

performance. (Allow Olivia telephone privileges when she finishes homework, buy her clothes when she performs well on tests.)

7. Support teachers' educational goals and standards for behavior. (Refrain from siding with Olivia when she "bad-mouths" her teachers, administer reinforcement contingencies and punishments based on school reports.)

8. Make frequent contact with the teacher. (See chapter 2 for how to help parents gain increased comfort with and confidence in their interactions with the school. Initial contacts may also involve the practitioner's presence so that a positive relationship is forged.)

▆▆▆▆ Conclusion

Multisystemic treatment offers intense interventions at the multiple system levels that interface with juvenile offending. The costs of applying multisystemic interventions to suit the individualized needs of youth and their families are offset by the costs saved in incarceration, institutionalization, and out-of-home placement. Despite its individualized and multiconceptual nature, however, treatment should be systematically applied and should adhere to the principles outlined by the creators of the model. Further, quality assurance should be aimed at promoting fidelity and achieving outcomes (S. Henggeler, personal communication, August 25, 2001).

PART III

Adulthood

 CLINICAL DISORDERS

8 Reinforcement Training with the Partners of Those Who Abuse Substances

■■■■ **Case Example**

Bobby Kelley, a 10-year-old white male, is brought in by his mother, Sheila, and his father, Robert. Mrs. Kelley stays home with Bobby while Mr. Kelley works in farm equipment sales. Bobby was referred from the school because of emotional outbursts in school (e.g., weeping when he was denied permission to do something) and not having friends. At home, Bobby calls his parents names, hits his mother, and has even tried to choke her when she was driving the car. Bobby is very angry at his father because "he doesn't do stuff with me." To his father's face, Bobby calls his dad "stupid." Mrs. Kelley claims her husband is more interested in drinking than spending time with his son.

In a meeting with the father alone, he says he drinks about a 6-pack every night. On the weekends, his intake goes up to a case of beer each day. Mr. Kelley claims he has no problems connected to drinking at work because it "loosens him up." His boss has no problem with his drinking as long as Mr. Kelley can perform his job. In fact, his boss does his own share of drinking at work. Mr. Kelley says his tolerance is very high, so he can drive "just fine." He says "maybe" he drinks too much but that anyone would drink with such a "bitch" of

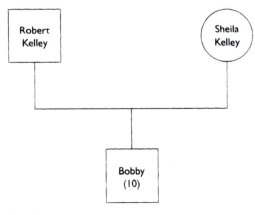

Race: Caucasian

Figure 8.1. Reinforcement Training Case Study: Bobby Kelley's Family

a wife. "You'd think she'd be grateful for being able to stay home," he says. "She should try getting a job and see how she likes it." He also says that a job would help get her focus off Bobby. He says his wife insists on driving their son the two blocks to school and home. He says Bobby needs to hang around kids his own age and get used to figuring out things for himself rather than running to his mother. Mr. Kelley reports that his wife and Bobby gang up on him; any limit he tries to set with Bobby is overruled by his wife and son. (See figure 8.1 for the genogram of this family.)

▰▰▰ Transtheoretical Stages of Change Framework

Although the presenting problem in this case involves a child problem, marital difficulties and substance abuse soon emerge as the underlying issues, and these need to be addressed before the child's situation can be altered in any significant way. This case points to the fact that chemical addiction often co-occurs with a wide variety of other problems, such as child problems, domestic violence, marital difficulties, and emotional and mental disorders, and these problems might be the initial reason for seeking treatment. Given that people often come in for other problems, they may not be willing to address substance abuse if it is present. However, it may be difficult to affect presenting problems if the alcohol or drug problem is not treated.

In acknowledgment of the reluctance of many substance abusers to change their patterns, Prochaska and colleagues (Connors, Donovan, & DiClemente, 2001; Prochaska & Norcross, 1994) developed the transtheoretical stages of change model. The model offers a novel conceptualization, which allows for many different theoretical approaches, each employed at the point where it will be most effective. Six stages of change have been formulated: (1) precontemplation, (2) contemplation, (3) determination, (4) action, (5) maintenance, and (6) relapse. In precontemplation, the individual believes there is no problem behavior and, therefore, is unwilling to do anything about it. In contemplation, the individual begins to consider that there might a problem and the feasibility and costs of changing the behavior. During this stage, the individual thinks about making change in the next 6 months. In determination (also called "preparation"), a decision is made to take action toward change in the next month. In action, the individual has started to modify the problem behavior in the previous 6 months. In maintenance, sustained change has occurred for at least 6 months. During relapse, the problem behavior has resumed and another cycle is begun. Particular techniques match the relevant stage of change with a primary focus on building motivation to get individuals to take action toward their goals and to maintain changes.

For those in the precontemplation stage, in which drinkers do not believe they have a problem and are unmotivated to seek help,[1] various researchers have developed a treatment option for the partners of these individuals, who, at least initially, are more distressed than the drinker is about the substance use. Called *reinforcement training* (Thomas, Santa, Bronson, & Oyserman, 1987), *unilateral treatment* (Sisson & Azrin, 1986), or the "pressures to change" model (Barber & Gilbertson, 1997), these approaches teach nondrinking partners to concentrate on their own well-being, to increase behaviors that will decrease their partners' substance use, and to ultimately induce their partners to enter treatment. Rather than suggesting that the spouse is responsible for the drinker's behavior, the family member is viewed as a source of leverage for change when other options have not yet worked. Change is enacted through the following components: an individual focus on the spouse, an interactional focus on the couple relationship, and a focus on the environment (Thomas & Ager, 1993; Thomas et al., 1987; Thomas, Yosh-

---

1. To avoid pejorative labels, the Barber & Gilbertson (1997) term, *drinker* will be used in this chapter.

ioka, & Ager, 1996). The individual focus includes venting feelings and scheduling outside activities for the nondrinking partner. The interactional focus includes communication, decision making, and conflict resolution skills training. The environmental focus includes supporting and reinforcing nondrinking behavior, removing environmental conditions that promote drinking behavior, scheduling activities that preclude alcohol use, and allowing the drinker to experience the negative consequences of alcohol use (Thomas et al., 1987).

In contrast to the Thomas et al. (1987) model, Sisson and Azrin's (1986) reinforcement training does not actually pursue the drinker into treatment; the drinker has to request treatment for himself (Edwards & Steinglass, 1995). The length of intervention for these approaches ranges in duration from one session (Barber & Gilbertson, 1998), to 5 (Barber & Gilbertson, 1996), or 7 weeks (Sisson & Azrin, 1986), or may last up to 6 months (Thomas et al., 1987).

Despite some of the differences among these approaches, they will be categorized together in this chapter. References will be made to *reinforcement training* as the term indicates the basis of behavioral theory underlying these approaches. The central premise of operant behavioral theory is the importance of reinforcement for increasing desirable behavior; in the case of substance abuse, the desirable behavior involves sobriety. Also central is the concept of antecedent conditions that cue certain behaviors to occur. Applied to substance abuse, nondrinking partners are trained to pay more positive attention to their partners when they are not using alcohol and to create opportunities for sobriety. Skills training in communication and conflict resolution are also offered as parts of a behavioral approach. Theoretically, positive reinforcement for non-drinking will then increase sobriety. (See box 8.1 for a brief overview of operant behavioral theory and additional resources for the interested reader.)

The traditional intervention approach for family members of substance users has been the 12-step model of Al-Anon. While Al-Anon has a similar focus to reinforcement training in its concern with the well-being of the family member and its espousal that drinkers should experience the consequences of their behavior, the Al-Anon philosophy is that partners should remain detached from the behaviors of the drinker and refrain from trying to change them.

It must be emphasized that while reinforcement training is oriented toward change of the drinker, this change is not viewed as enabling or codependent in which drinking behavior is allowed and per-

Box 8.1

**Key Assumptions of Operant Behavioral
Theory and Additional Resources**

Key Assumptions

- People are trained to attend to the *stimulus conditions*, or cues, that trigger a behavior and the consequences of a behavior, which determine its frequency.
- A focus is on *positive reinforcement*, increasing a response from another person by positively attending to it, and *extinguishing*, or ignoring, behavior that is unwanted.
- Emphasis is placed on training people in new skills, such as problem solving, relaxation, and communication skills.
- Methods to train individuals in applying conducive stimulus and reinforcement patterns include lecture, discussion, *modeling* by the practitioner, and *behavioral rehearsal* by the individual with *coaching* and *feedback* by the practitioner.

Additional Resources

J. G. Barber & R. Gilbertson. (1997). Unilateral interventions for women living with heavy drinkers. *Social Work, 42,* 69–78.

A. Kazdin. (2000). *Behavior modification in applied settings* (6th ed.). Pacific Grove, CA: Brooks/Cole.

haps even reinforced through the nondrinker's actions. Rather, in reinforcement training, nondrinking partners are trained to adjust their own behavior and to structure the environment to encourage sobriety.

Before presenting the application of the model, its empirical evidence will be briefly described, followed by a discussion of when reinforcement training is an option for treatment and when it is contraindicated.

Empirical Evidence

Reinforcement training programs have successfully motivated the drinker to enter treatment (Barber & Gilbertson, 1996; Barber & Gilbertson, 1998; Sisson & Azrin, 1986; Thomas et al., 1987) when compared to Al-Anon conditions (Barber & Gilbertson, 1996; Sisson & Azrin, 1986). Drinking rates have been reduced across studies (Barber & Gilbertson, 1996; Barber & Gilbertson, 1998; Sisson & Azrin, 1986; Thomas et al., 1987), typically by about half. In comparison, a slight increase in alcohol consumption occurred for drinkers in the delayed treatment condition (Thomas et al., 1987), and the Al-Anon condition failed to affect drinking patterns (Barber & Gilbertson, 1996; Sisson & Azrin, 1986).

Despite the impressive results of these programs on the drinker, the partner has not consistently fared as well in terms of marital satisfaction and personal adjustment. Longer-term treatment (6 months) might result in improved affectional expression and sexual satisfaction (Thomas et al., 1987) though these findings were not reflected in spouse well-being. Perhaps understandably, reinforcement training may not affect marital satisfaction since the drinker is not involved in changing interactional patterns. Barber and Gilbertson (1996) were the only researchers to show reductions in personal problems but only when partners of drinkers participated in an individual versus a group version of reinforcement training or when they attended Al-Anon groups. The results of these studies suggest that reinforcement training may benefit from an increased focus on partner well-being.

■■■■■ Screening for the Appropriateness of Reinforcement Training

Mrs. Kelley originally came in for a child problem. However, both she and her son continued to blame Mr. Kelley for Bobby's problems and were unwilling to try new strategies (parenting skills for Mrs. Kelley and cognitive-behavioral treatment for Bobby to teach Bobby feeling management, coping, and social skills). At the same time, Mr. Kelley refused to seek treatment for his alcohol use.

When reinforcement training was explained to Mrs. Kelley, she was amenable to the approach, mainly because of the ill effects of Mr. Kelley's drinking on her son. Secondarily, she did not wish to divorce Mr. Kelley, giving as the reason financial considerations. When the practitioner asked if she would like to pursue options for financial independence, Mrs. Kelley was adamantly against single-parenthood. Even though Mr. Kelley was not a good husband, "he was better than nothing." According to Mrs. Kelley, Mr. Kelley also did not wish to divorce mainly because he didn't want to "fork over" his income for child support. Mrs. Kelley said she would try reinforcement training as a last resort, and, if it did not work, then she would consider other options. The practitioner also assured her that, at any time during reinforcement training, she could decide to abandon her efforts toward getting her husband to change.

Part of the screening process involved discussing with Mrs. Kelley other options for partners of drinkers. As discussed, the traditional approach has been Al-Anon. Mrs. Kelley professed familiarity with the philosophy of Al-Anon from attending a couple of meetings and did not wish to go back. She didn't like the idea of "detachment" and was more amenable to trying an approach that more directly targeted her husband's drinking. While it did not sit well with her that she and not her husband was in counseling, she was willing to try for the sake of her son. Mrs. Kelley was unwilling, however, to come to counseling indefinitely and agreed to contract for six sessions.[2]

Along with a desire to stay with the drinker and a willingness to try the approach, to determine the appropriateness of such an approach, screening for family violence must further take place (Barber & Gilbertson, 1997). Mrs. Kelley recalled an incident in their early marriage when her husband had shoved her into a wall. She had not sought police involvement and no reoccurrence of the violence was mentioned. The practitioner said that, if she were to work with Mrs. Kelley, measures would have to be taken to ensure her safety in the event that he became violent. One of the conditions, therefore, was to agree to call the police and press charges if violence or threats occurred. A safety plan included putting money away to pay for a night in a hotel.

Other screening criteria for the approach include no severe mental illness and no substance abuse patterns by the partner of the drinker. Since none of these contraindications were present with Mrs. Kelley, the reinforcement training approach was deemed to be appropriate, and treatment proceeded.

▬▬▬ Application of Reinforcement Training

Different components of reinforcement training will be illustrated with Mrs. Kelley: venting feelings, delivery of positive consequences for nondrinking, effective communication, increasing positive activities, removing cues and reinforcers for intoxication, alternative activities for

2. As discussed, approaches vary as to time frame (one session to 6 months), but implicit is that the intervention lasts for a specified time period. If the intervention is not effective, then the practitioner's responsibility is to discuss other options, rather than continuing the approach indefinitely.

the partner, allowing the drinker to have consequences, leveraging the support of others, and motivating the drinker into treatment. Following will be a brief summary of the couples behavioral treatment Mr. and Mrs. Kelley eventually decided to pursue.

Venting Feelings

Part of the process of helping the partner cope with living with a substance-abusing spouse involves allowing for the ventilation of feelings of stress, anger, and depression in a supportive and empathic environment. Therefore, a certain amount of time each session was devoted to Mrs. Kelley giving vent to her anger and frustration. This does not require detailing here since the reader should get an ample picture of Mrs. Kelley's frustrations in the following descriptions.

Delivery of Positive Consequences for Non-Drinking

As discussed, reinforcement training is based on the principles of operant behavioral theory with the main premise being that reinforcement plays a key role in increasing behaviors. Applied to substance abuse, partners are trained to pay more positive attention to their partners when they are not drinking. Theoretically, positive reinforcement will then increase sobriety.

Conversely, Mrs. Kelley might inadvertently reinforce Mr. Kelley's drinking behavior by paying more attention to him then. She claimed he was always drinking, so she really couldn't tell. The practitioner explained that any type of attention, even negative attention, was very reinforcing. She was asked to be vigilant and to notice the small periods of time either when Mr. Kelley was not drinking or when he just had a small amount and pay more positive attention to him during these times.

To this explanation, Mrs. Kelley responded that it would be very difficult to give her husband positive consequences; during those rare times when he was relatively sober, they only argued about parenting. The practitioner said she would work with Mrs. Kelley on communicating more effectively her pleasure that he was at times sober and on making the discussions about parenting more productive.

Mrs. Kelley responded, "There is no communicating with him. He's either criticizing me, or he's drunk."

The practitioner empathized with the difficulty of the situation, but likened communication exchanges to dance steps: If one person changed his or her step, then the other person would be forced to dance differently. This analogy is used to help clients understand the reciprocal nature of interaction patterns.

Effective Communication

The practitioner began to teach Mrs. Kelley about assertive and effective communication, which involved the use of "I" statements about the self ("I want Bobby to go fishing with you, and I want him to be safe") rather than "you" statements ("You think I'm going to let him spend any time with a drunk like you? You're a bum, and your son already hates you!"). The practitioner role played with Mrs. Kelley, who acted her husband as belligerently as possible. The practitioner demonstrated that if Mrs. Kelley kept to the new skills, which might include stating she would leave the room if he raised his voice, she might be more successful in meeting her objectives. Mrs. Kelley admitted that Mr. Kelley did not tend to act as badly as she had played him; indeed, she raised her voice and made more disparaging remarks than he did to her.

After role plays of this conversation with her husband, Mrs. Kelley said, "Bobby probably won't go fishing anyway. He hates fishing." She recounted the one time Bobby had accompanied her father and his friends. They were at the lake for hours, and a lot of drinking was involved. Eventually, Bobby refused to fish any longer, demanding that his father take him home. When his father kept saying "in a few minutes" for more than an hour, Bobby ended up crying and "throwing a fit." His father, embarrassed in front of his friends, finally took Bobby home.

The practitioner counseled that Mrs. Kelley could negotiate the plans with her husband ahead of time: "Let's figure out how we can make this fishing trip work." The previous episode seemed to involve not only excessive drinking, but also the presence of adult men without other children and the length of time spent fishing. Mrs. Kelley role played negotiating these aspects with her husband. Then she said, "I just don't think my husband could go fishing without drinking. He might say he could do it, but I don't think he could stick to a promise. He never does." A safety plan was then formulated in which Bobby could call his mother and have her pick him up if drinking did occur. Mrs. Kelley ended this work by saying, "But it's up to Bobby if he doesn't want to go. I won't make him do anything he doesn't want to do." Mrs. Kelley was reminded of her original complaint, that her husband was uninvolved with their son. He should be reinforced rather than discouraged for wanting to spend time with his son.

Increasing Positive Activities

Part of reinforcement training involves planning family activities that are incompatible with drinking. Mrs. Kelley could not think initially of any activities since Mr. Kelley began drinking in the afternoons at work, came home with another 6-pack, and drank through the evening, watching TV, until he passed out on the couch. On the weekends, he would begin drinking in the morning as he did chores, and then he would either go fishing with his friends or watch sports on TV, drinking until he passed out.

With much difficulty in coming up with ideas, she finally decided that the family could go to the park on Sunday morning before Mr. Kelley began drinking. Mr. Kelley could play catch with Bobby, which would increase Mr. Kelley's potential positive influence over his son. Mrs. Kelley expressed trepidation, however, that her husband would make demeaning remarks about her son's lack of athletic abilities and then blame her for babying Bobby. She said, therefore, that she would stay on the sidelines, doing cross-stitch, so that she could intervene if her husband became critical.

The practitioner explained that concentrating on positives was more effective than being negative to get positive behavior. Mrs. Kelley was given the example of how her husband sometimes criticized her son for being a "baby." Did that make her son any better at playing ball? Mrs. Kelley quickly grasped the point: "Of course not. It'll just make Bobby feel bad about himself, and then he'll be sure to mess up even worse."

A discussion ensued about verbally reinforcing behavior that Mrs. Kelley wanted to continue to see in her husband. Since she was better able to apply this concept to her son, she was supplied with the example that she could say, "Good throw" or "Great catch" to her son rather than criticizing him when he dropped a ball or threw wild balls. Applied to her husband, she then said she could reinforce her husband for paying attention to their son: "I like you playing ball with Bobby" or "I like spending time together as a family." At first, Mrs. Kelley made faces as she said these statements but eventually sounded more convincing. The practitioner said that these new behaviors would probably feel artificial at first, but not to take the feeling of awkwardness as a sign to stop. As with any new skill, it would take some practice to feel comfortable praising her husband.

Removing Cues and Reinforcers for Intoxication

While the role of reinforcers is emphasized in behavioral theory, attention is also paid to stimulus conditions, those that trigger drinking. Mrs. Kelley was asked to examine the situations in which her husband was inclined to start drinking, so that they could study the cues for his drinking and how her behavior may unwittingly trigger him. The practitioner was quick to reassure Mrs. Kelley that she was not, however, responsible for his drinking, no matter how much her husband claimed she was.

Mrs. Kelley said it was difficult to come up with discrete drinking episodes since her husband drank almost continually. She was therefore asked to describe a typical day. According to Mrs. Kelley, the day would begin with her expressing disgust at his passing out on the couch, and an argument would begin. Bobby would join in, and Mr. Kelley would eventually slam out of the house. Mr. Kelley would return in the early evening in a better mood because he would have already been drinking, with another 6-pack in tow. She would make disparaging remarks. He would say, in turn, with a wife like this, a man needed to drink.

Mrs. Kelley justified this approach, saying she had to let him know how bad his drinking was for him and the family. The practitioner reminded Mrs. Kelley that criticizing rarely led to a change in behavior. "It's using negatives to get positives," the practitioner repeated. "Rather than discouraging his drinking, the remarks might cue him to begin drinking again."

"So I'm just not supposed to say anything? I'm just supposed to let him do what he wants?"

"Not at all. It is important to give him information about his behavior when drinking, especially if his behavior has been embarrassing or inappropriate."

Imagining a typical scenario, with some coaching, Mrs. Kelley was able to come up with, "Last night, you came home drinking and then had another 6-pack when you were home. You spent $12 on alcohol. You didn't talk to us, and you were too drunk to get off the couch to change, get ready for bed, and sleep in our bedroom."

She also had to ensure that her son refrained from calling Mr. Kelley a "stupid drunk" and so on when his dad was drunk, as this might serve the effect of cuing his father to begin drinking. (See the following discussion for leveraging Mrs. Kelley's son's behavior.)

Given the operant behavioral emphasis on the importance of reinforcement, behavior that is not reinforced should be decreased or extinguished. Therefore, Mrs. Kelley was directed to ignore Mr. Kelley when he became inebriated. Mrs. Kelley reacted negatively to this idea, thinking that he would just conclude that heavy drinking was acceptable; she wanted to get across to him that she found his behavior extremely distasteful and that it must stop. The practitioner repeated the information about reinforcement: "While this may seem surprising, any attention, even if it is negative, might be very reinforcing."

Returning to the pattern of intoxication Mrs. Kelley described, in which Mr. Kelley came home from work already inebriated, she was told to make sure he ate dinner and to supply him with nonalcoholic beverages. "I already do that," she said. "Long ago, I refused to bring him beers when he asked. I'd say, 'Get them yourself.' " She described that this would segue into his arguing about how he worked hard to support them all and the least she could do was bring him a beer. The argument would escalate, her son taking her side, saying Mr. Kelley didn't deserve anything because he was "a stupid drunk."

While Mrs. Kelley was praised for not enabling Mr. Kelley's drinking by bringing him alcohol or stocking it in the house, the practitioner worked with her on a less-coercive response: "I won't get you a beer since I don't support your drinking, but I will get you a glass of water or a cola, if you like."

If he continued to drink and was intoxicated in the evening, Mrs. Kelley was told to ignore him and partake in activities in another part of the house. Mrs. Kelley didn't particularly like this idea since the larger TV was in the living room, where Mr. Kelley drank in his recliner. She said she could always do cross-stitch in the bedroom, but if she ignored him, he would probably just pass out on the couch. She became very angry when he didn't sleep with her and would insult him about his "manhood." Mrs. Kelley could see, however, that insults would probably fail to increase his desire to sleep with her.

Alternative Activities

The practitioner spent some time discussing Mrs. Kelley's cross-stitch as a pleasant activity. Part of reinforcement training involves finding alternate activities for the spouse apart from the drinker. Mrs. Kelley said that she found working on cross-stitch in the evenings relaxing and the completion of wall hangings most satisfying. She described with some pride that her cross-stitches decorated every room in the house.

As for outside the home, she could not come up with any pleasant activities she pursued other than going to craft stores. She said she had no family living in the state and had lost contact with various friends through the years since her marriage to Mr. Kelley. She gave as the reason for these waning friendships her embarrassment over Mr. Kelley's drinking. When she used to plan couples events with her friends, she would often have to cancel, giving various excuses for Mr. Kelley's drinking. This information about Mrs. Kelley canceling led into a discussion about allowing the drinker to have his own consequences.

Allowing the Drinker to Have Consequences

When the consequences of drinking start to outweigh the benefits, a drinker might start to consider change. Therefore, a partner must allow the drinker to experience the full weight of his own consequences.

The practitioner explained to Mrs. Kelley that in no way should she make life easier for Mr. Kelley in terms of making excuses for him or letting him get away without the consequences of his behavior. If she made plans with friends, she could inform Mr. Kelley that if he were to get inebriated to the point of being unable to accompany her, she would go by herself. She said, "That wouldn't be any fun. I don't want to go to these affairs alone."

"I understand that it would be very difficult at first," said the practitioner. "But it's important that you don't let the drinker's behavior curtail your life. Sometimes the drinker has everything revolving around him, and you can't let that happen. And getting out with other people will help you break the isolation that is often associated with living with a drinker. Finally, protecting the drinker's habits from others doesn't allow him to suffer his own consequences."

Mrs. Kelley was asked to think about any other occasions in which she saved Mr. Kelley from his own consequences. The practitioner gave the common examples of calling in sick for work for the drinker, canceling important appointments, making excuses for inappropriate behavior, cleaning up after him, and providing rides at inconvenient hours. Mrs. Kelley said her husband occasionally did not go to work because of hangovers, but he would call in himself. No one much minded at his work setting if he didn't come in, but his earnings were dependent on his sales. If he wasn't at work, then he didn't make money. She couldn't think of any other ways to let him suffer more of the consequences but would be alert for opportunities.

Leveraging the Support of Others

Barber and Gilbertson (1997) discuss the need to train others who are important to the drinker about the reinforcement strategies so that pressure toward change of the drinker is maximized. Mrs. Kelley began this discussion by saying that she wanted her son to be able to express his feelings about his father's drinking. The practitioner agreed that feedback from family members was an important piece of influencing the drinker to change, but that "I" messages are more about expressing feelings than are "you" (accusation) messages. Mrs. Kelley said that it served her husband right to have his son against him. Mrs. Kelley's anger toward her husband was validated, but it was suggested that an appropriate place to ventilate these feelings was with the practitioner, rather than having her son express it for her.

Mrs. Kelley was also asked, "How successful have your and your son's efforts been to get him to change?" Mrs. Kelley admitted, "Not very." She was further asked to consider the effect on Bobby of taking this position with his mother against his father. Mrs. Kelley thought the only thing hurting Bobby was his father's drinking. The practitioner agreed that while his father's drinking was clearly deleterious, his mother was teaching Bobby to lack respect for authority. Bobby cried at school when he didn't get his way, and he tried to choke his mother and was otherwise violent to her. A more productive option, which might leverage his son's importance to Mr. Kelley, was to teach Bobby to communicate his feelings in the way she was learning through reinforcement training. Indeed, she could be a very effective model for him.

Motivating the Drinker into Treatment

Mrs. Kelley was asked whether there were times her husband had suffered particular remorse or negative consequences that made him question the amount he drank. She said that 3 years ago he was arrested on a Driving While Intoxicated charge, but a lawyer got him off. She added, "We're still paying for her fees." The practitioner said this was another way Mrs. Kelley could give her husband feedback about the cost of his drinking to the family, especially when he exhorted her to get a job.

Mrs. Kelley was given several numbers, including 24-hour hotlines for inpatient and outpatient treatment centers and a number for a central Alcoholics Anonymous group. If Mr. Kelley expressed concern about his drinking, she was told to provide him with this information.

█████ Subsequent Sessions

Mrs. Kelley initially experienced some difficulty in putting the principles of reinforcement training into practice. In sessions, she continued to express a great deal of anger at her husband for his drinking and claimed she was unable to stop herself from vituperative attacks on him. Although a part of reinforcement training is devoted to ventilation of feelings, Mrs. Kelley's anger about her husband's drinking and his lack of concern for Bobby consumed a great deal of time in session. Meanwhile, Bobby's teacher still reported Bobby's isolation from classmates, and Mrs. Kelley talked about Bobby's tantruming at home and calling his mother names.

The practitioner used two strategies to address Mrs. Kelley's continued ventilation without accompanying changes in behavior. The first was to enact a *decisional balance* (Miller & Rollnick, 1991) so that Mrs. Kelley could consider the advantages and disadvantages of allowing the situation to remain the same versus trying new behavioral patterns. As an example of a *decisional balance*, Mrs. Kelley produced the following list of advantages to making changes:

1. She would feel more in control of her family situation if she were doing something about it.
2. The counseling might help her son.

3. She might be able to stay married.
4. The relationship between her and her husband might improve.

The disadvantages involved:

1. Having to do the work and make changes when her husband refused to do so.
2. Having to make changes seemed to her to mean that her husband was right, that she was the cause of her son's problems.
3. Treatment cost money.

The helper's job is to address the disadvantages of changing so that they no longer exert such a powerful influence. As the first two disadvantages listed seemed a serious stumbling block for Mrs. Kelley, she was offered a reframe. Rather than treatment being an admission of her blame, the counseling was seen as an empowering move on her part to make changes in the family, despite her husband's refusal to do so. Mrs. Kelley was able to buy into this reframe, since it emphasized the concern she had for her son.

The second strategy to address Mrs. Kelley's continued ventilation about her husband's behavior was to discuss and then role play ways in which she could have handled a particular situation differently using the principles of reinforcement. In this way, the incidents were used as learning events rather than allowing her to simply complain about her husband's past behavior.

Reframing was also used to address Bobby's need for independence. Mrs. Kelley was defensive about allowing Bobby to do things for himself, such as allowing him to walk back and forth to school. If she made these changes, she thought it would prove her husband "right" about her being overprotective. The practitioner employed the following reframe: "You have been a very concerned parent for Bobby and very involved in taking care of him, which is good. It is important in a family where there is a parent who abuses substances for the child to know that one person, at least, will provide stability. Now that Bobby is entering a new stage of his development, the role of a concerned parent is to allow him to try things on his own. Of course, you will still be there for support, but in this phase, his world will increasingly involve the school and other children his age."

Mrs. Kelley took one small step by making her son walk himself home after school, but she gave in to his adamant demand that he be driven in the morning. Mrs. Kelley was encouraged to resume contact with some of her friends, meet them for coffee, and go to craft stores together. Some of these friends have children, so this had the added benefit of getting Bobby to socialize with other children.

The practitioner also referred Mrs. Kelley to a "craft circle," so that Mrs. Kelley could gather with other women with similar interests on a regular basis. Mrs. Kelley began researching craft shows in the area to display and sell her work. She found she was getting more cross-stitch completed now that she wasn't arguing so much with her husband. She was also surprised to find that he often now came to bed voluntarily, having had less to drink.

Mr. Kelley seemed pleased that she was pursuing some money-making ventures, Mrs. Kelley said, although he wasn't particularly supportive of the way she was going about it (her cross-stitch). She said he was also positive about her relinquishing some of her involvement with her son. But an outing to the park, she announced, was a disaster. Mr. Kelley criticized Bobby for being unable to catch balls. She, in turn, became angry with Mr. Kelley. Bobby refused to play any more, and the family was home within an hour. Mr. Kelley then drank heavily for the rest of the day.

The practitioner discussed with Mrs. Kelley some alternative ways to handle such a situation: talking with her husband beforehand about how she wanted Bobby to develop more coordination and how she and her husband could best encourage that; cheering father and son as a team when there was a successful throw or catch ("Way to go, guys!"); or joining in herself since she could lighten up the mood by laughing at her own lack of coordination. However, it was quite some time before Mrs. Kelley was willing to participate in another outing.

As she had predicted, Bobby didn't want to accompany his father fishing, but she sided with her husband on this one, to Mr. Kelley's great surprise, as long as Mr. Kelley did not drink. Bobby called her "stupid" and tried to attack her for "making him go" when he didn't want to. The positive side to this incident was that mother and father were united on the fact that Bobby should respect both his parents. Unfortunately, Mr. Kelley unexpectedly met some friends of his at the fishing site, and they offered him beer. As agreed, Bobby called his mother, triumphantly announcing that his father was drunk and could she please come and get him.

When Mr. Kelley later came home, inebriated, he was angry that his wife had humiliated him in front of his friends by arriving at the fishing site and taking his son away. Mrs. Kelley was pleased to report that she had remained calm in the face of his anger, simply repeating in "broken record" format their former agreement that she would support father-son fishing expeditions as long as no drinking and driving was involved. At this point, Mrs. Kelley expressed hopelessness about change in the family and seriously considered leaving Mr. Kelley. As the practitioner had assured Mrs. Kelley from the start, agreeing to try reinforcement training didn't mean that she couldn't leave her husband. However, Mrs. Kelley soon decided she couldn't afford a separation financially, but that she would redouble her efforts to sell her cross-stitch so that option could become more viable.

◼◼◼◼ Summary of Application of Reinforcement Training

Although Mrs. Kelley did not consistently implement the techniques, she experienced some success. Her husband's drinking was reduced somewhat, and the stalemate in their marriage seemed to be broken. For many years, neither would make changes until the other one did. For example, Mr. Kelley claimed to drink because she was a "bitch" and had turned their child against him. She said that she nagged Mr. Kelley and sided with her child because of her husband's drinking. When Mr. Kelley noted Mrs. Kelley's efforts to release her hold on Bobby and to be less unpleasant to him, Mr. Kelley felt more positive toward Mrs. Kelley and wanted to spend more time with her and his son. Mrs. Kelley was surprised to find that when she stopped insulting Mr. Kelley about his drinking and not sleeping with her, he came to bed more often rather than passing out on the couch. The couple unified a little more over Bobby's behavior, which had worsened toward Mrs. Kelley. When Mrs. Kelley asked if Mr. Kelley would join with her on couple-centered therapy to address his drinking, Mr. Kelley agreed to give it a try. He was more amenable to a treatment approach that took place in the context of the couple since he still saw a lot of his drinking as related to his marital problems. Behavioral couples therapy will be briefly summarized below. (For an application of the model, see McCrady, 2001.)

◼◼◼◼ Behavioral Couples Therapy

Common elements underlie both reinforcement training and behavioral couples therapy since they share as their basis behavioral theory. However, couples treatment targets the drinker at potentially more advanced stages of willingness to change drinking habits (Thomas & Corcoran, 2001). In the stages of change model, the individual may either be at the contemplation stage (considering change) or at the decision-making stage (decides to change).

Components in common to both behavioral couples therapy and reinforcement training include the delivery of positive consequences for nondrinking, effective communication, planning and implementing shared activities that do not involve drinking, removing reinforcers for intoxication, allowing the drinker to have consequences, and examining cues for drinking behavior (O'Farrell, 1993). Other components are initiating and acknowledging daily positive behaviors toward each other and learning negotiation and problem-solving skills (e.g., McCrady et al., 1986; O'Farrell, Choquette, Cutter, Brown, & McCourt, 1993).

Techniques to learn these skills include homework, role playing, and covert rehearsal. Treatment is generally brief, consisting of 10 (e.g., O'Farrell et al., 1993), 12 (Fals-Stewart, Birchler, & O'Farrell, 1996), or 15 weekly sessions (e.g., McCrady et al., 1986). Treatment is delivered in the context of either individual couples sessions (e.g., McCrady et al., 1986) or group couples sessions (e.g., O'Farrell et al., 1993).

Conclusion

For a variety of reasons, such as the presence of children, financial considerations, and religious commitment, some spouses who suffer distress due to their partners' drinking are unwilling to leave the relationship. Up until this time, few options have existed for intervention other than Al-Anon, which takes a strictly noninterventionist approach to changing the behavior of the drinker. With reinforcement training, spouses may be empowered to use behavioral skills to enact change.

9 Cognitive-Behavioral Marital Therapy with Depression

██████ **Case Example**

Annette (age 26) and Rob (age 30) Spears had been married a year when Annette came to treatment. She tearfully reported feeling depressed for about 11 months. She cried daily, had difficulty sleeping at night, and then slept late in the day. She tended to wear sweatpants all day, the same ones in which she had slept at night. Sweatpants were more comfortable now; Annette had gained 15 pounds since her wedding.

Annette said she had always wanted to be married, and she thought her dream came true when she met Rob. At the time, she was waiting tables instead of using the English degree she had just finished. Rob was an accountant and seemed very reliable compared to other men she had dated. Rob took Annette to nice restaurants, the movies, and the theater, which made her feel appreciated and cared about.

When Rob was offered a promotion in another state, he proposed after only 6 months of dating. Although Annette thought it premature, she became engaged anyway since everything seemed to be going so well.

Once married, moved, and settled into their new home, Annette claimed Rob had changed; he was so serious, didn't laugh with her any more, and they never had fun. Additionally, he worked such long hours—at least 70 per week. He was hardly ever home, and when he was, he claimed fatigue. She felt as if he had already turned into an old man, yet he was only 30. Annette was very disappointed. She had thought that married life would represent a vast improvement over being single, but she had never been like this, so depressed. She didn't even feel like he loved her any more.

Meanwhile, Annette didn't know what to do with herself. They were trying to start a family, but, so far, she had not become pregnant. They both had gone for medical appointments and were deemed physically able to have children, but their level of physical intimacy had decreased recently.

Annette now realized she wanted to do something with her life other than having children and staying home. She considered waitressing again, but Rob didn't want her doing so. That is how he had met her—he had come in for drinks one night at the restaurant where she worked—and he did not want her meeting other men at a restaurant job. She had looked for jobs in which she could use her English degree, but she was unable to find anything She had also considered going to graduate school, but the closest university was an hour away, and Rob did not want her driving that far. Plus, if she became pregnant, how would she continue?

Annette said that Rob had advised her to get counseling for depression and, possibly, medication; however, she told him she wanted marital rather than individual therapy because she had become so miserable since they got married. He agreed to go along with whatever the practitioner recommended, provided he could fit it into his work schedule. (See box 9.1 for information about the diagnosis of depression.)

■■■ Treatment of Depression Through Conjoint Therapy

Marital problems seem to be associated with depression. Reviews of this literature by Beach and colleagues (Banawan, O'Mahen, Beach, & Jackson, 2002; Beach, Fincham, & Katz, 1998; Beach & Jones, 2002) found several sources of empirical evidence to support this position. The first source involves cross-sectional research using epidemiological surveys. Weissman (1987), in a survey of 3,000 respondents, found a

Box 9.1

Diagnosis of Depression

The process of diagnosis first involves a physical examination. Annette had recently undergone a medical evaluation by her general physician for her depression and in preparation for becoming pregnant. No physical problems were noted. The practitioner understood Annette's reluctance to take antidepressants while trying to get pregnant but educated her on the process of how to obtain a psychiatric evaluation through her insurance company if the symptoms of her depression did not abate from their course of treatment or if the symptoms became too difficult to tolerate.

The assessment by the practitioner of Annette's diagnosis involved the following complete history of symptoms: when they started, how long they have lasted, severity of symptoms, alcohol and drug use, thoughts about death or suicide, whether family members have had a depressive illness, and whether she had suffered before from such symptoms, if treatment were received then, and how effective treatment was.

Following are symptoms of major depression, including examples of Annette's symptoms:

- Persistent sad, anxious, or "empty" mood. (Annette said she "felt bad and down" a great deal of the time and was tearful every day.)
- Feelings of hopelessness or pessimism. ("What's the point of getting dressed? I have nothing to get dressed for." "What's the use?")
- Feelings of guilt, worthlessness, or helplessness. (Annette wasn't empowered to take any action toward a career choice; she wanted Rob to solve her problems for her.)
- Loss of interest or pleasure in hobbies and activities that were once enjoyed, including sex. (The couple's sexual frequency had diminished.)
- Decreased energy, fatigue, or being "slowed down." (She slept late and didn't seem to have the energy to complete tasks, such as calling for home repairs or making dinner.)
- Difficulty concentrating, remembering, or making decisions. (Annette endlessly obsessed about what she was going to do with her life.)
- Insomnia, early morning awakening, or oversleeping. (Annette had difficulty getting to sleep at night and then slept late into the day.)
- Loss of appetite or weight loss or overeating and weight gain. (Annette had gained 15 pounds since she had gotten married.)
- Thoughts of death or suicide or suicide attempts. (Annette said she had only fleeting thoughts about "ending it" and had no specific plan.)
- Restlessness or irritability. (Annette was irritable and upset with Rob a lot of the time.)
- Persistent physical symptoms that do not respond to treatment, such as headaches, digestive disorders, or chronic pain. (Annette did not describe any physical symptoms.)

25 percent increased likelihood of depression when marital problems were present. Further evidence was provided by a sample of 4,933 married couples in Ontario. Whisman, Sheldon, and Goering (2000) found that marital functioning was related to the presence of depression. In a representative sample of 328 newlywed couples, a 10 percent increased likelihood of depression was found in the maritally distressed partners (O'Leary, Christian, & Mendell, 1994). In a review of 26 cross-sectional studies, Whisman (2000) reported that marital functioning was negatively correlated with depression in both wives ($r = -.42$) and husbands ($r = -.37$). Thus, it appeared that both men and women who were depressed suffered marital distress, though women had a slightly higher rate.

Prospective studies tracking couples over time are another source of evidence. An increased risk to women for depression was present when marital problems were reported one year (Beach et al., 1995, cited in Beach et al., 1998) and 18 months prior (Fincham, Beach, Harold, & Osborne, 1997). The same relationship between marital problems and depression did not exist for men. However, another longitudinal study of 198 newly-married couples did not find gender differences; for both the husbands and wives, depression levels were related to relationship quality (Kurdek, 1998). Similarly, Whisman and Bruce (1999), using data from the New Haven Epidemiologic Catchment Area program, discovered that poor marital quality predicted the diagnosis of Major Depressive Disorder for both men and women.

A third source of data involves clinical samples. Whisman (2001) reviewed 10 studies of this nature and reported a high negative correlation ($r = -.67$) between marital quality and depression.

It is clear from these studies that marital distress and depression are linked for both men and women. At the same time, the high rate of depression for women, twice that as for men, is widely known (see Nolen-Hoelsema, 2002). In a review of the literature, Kung (2000) reported that while marriage is a protective factor for men, it bestows less of a buffering effect for women in terms of depression. In general, the marital relationship imparts less support for women. Feminist explanations for these findings emphasize women's identity in relation to others and also their greater risk of depression in regard to disappointments in relationships (Chodorow, 1999; Gilligan, 1982). Therefore, marital distress may play a causative role for depression in women or it may maintain preexisting depression. The marital relationship may further affect response to treatment and may be an important factor in relapse (Hooley, Orley, & Teasdale, 1986; Hooley & Teasdale, 1989; Kung, 2000; Prince & Jacobson, 1995).

A small body of knowledge has accumulated on the use of cognitive-behavioral marital therapy with depression. Cognitive theorists discuss the cognitive errors that are experienced in both depression and couple distress (Wheeler, Christensen, & Jacobson, 2001).[1] These include an overfocus on the negative parts of partner behavior and a discounting of positive aspects, as well as attributing malicious motives to partners.

Behavioral marital therapy is a skill-building approach which follows the principles of social learning (box 2.1), cognitive therapy (box 4.1), and social exchange theory. Social exchange theory describes how individuals work to minimize costs, to maximize rewards, and to develop a relationship with another based on a perceived positive balance (i.e., the rewards should exceed the costs) (Thibaut & Kelley, 1959). Partners are taught specific skills to enhance marital support and intimacy and to reduce marital stress and negative expectancies.

In comparison-group designs in which conjoint therapy was contrasted with individual therapy, cognitive-behavioral marital therapy was as effective as individual cognitive therapy for alleviating depression and superior for improving marital adjustment (Emanuels-Zuurveen & Emmelkaump, 1996; Jacobson, Dobson, Fruzzetti, Schmaling, & Salusky, 1991; Beach & O'Leary, 1992.) A couples variant of interpersonal counseling was also effective for reducing both marital distress and depression (Foley, Rounsaville, Weissman, Sholomskas, & Chevron, 1989). Waring (1994) reported on three studies he and his colleagues conducted involving a cognitive marital treatment with the primary aim of enhancing intimacy through self-disclosure between partners (see Waring, 1988, for description of treatment model). Women in inpatient treatment for depression did not appear to benefit from the marital therapy in combination with antidepressant medication; however, in outpatient settings, marital therapy became a viable option for women diagnosed with depression.

Women's perspective on how marital distress is related to their depression seems to operate in a critical way. If women reported that marital problems preceded depression, when they received cognitive therapy, marital adjustment failed to improve (Beach & O'Leary, 1992;

1. The terms *couple* and *partner* will be used to broaden the scope of the discussion beyond marital relationships.

O'Leary, Risso, & Beach, 1990). However, if depression was viewed as preceding marital distress, then women showed improved mood, whether they attended cognitive therapy or marital therapy. Consistent with Beach and O'Leary (1992), Addis and Jacobsen (1991) discovered that women who saw their depression as caused by marital problems performed less well in cognitive therapy. Indeed, while individual therapy is often selected for individuals who are depressed, Beach and Whitman (1994) estimate that possibly 40% of those who have a diagnosis of major depression are suitable candidates for a conjoint intervention, with a review of the literature indicating that between 40 and 50% of individuals suffering with depression also present with significant marital discord (Prince & Jacobson, 1995).

▬▬ Types of Clients Appropriate for Behavioral Conjoint Therapy

In determining whether an individual who is depressed is a suitable candidate for conjoint therapy, certain considerations must be taken into account. These center on aspects of both the individual and the marital relationship and, therefore, should be assessed through both individual and conjoint interviews (Beach, Sandeen, & O'Leary, 1990). These factors will be discussed in the next sections. After the appropriate assessment of conjoint therapy, strategies to engage the partner will be explored.

Individual Considerations

Individual concerns involve, first, the gender of the client. Women, primarily, have been studied in relation to marital therapy for depression, although men should also benefit (Beach & Whitman, 1994). Second, the decision to select conjoint over individual therapy may depend on how individuals view the origins of their depression (Addis & Jacobson, 1991; Beach & O'Leary, 1992; O'Leary, Riso, & Beach, 1990). If an individual believes her depression is caused by relationship problems,[2] then marital therapy may be the treatment of choice. If the individual sees her depression as arising before relationship problems or

2. Female pronouns will be used here since, as discussed, studies mainly have involved women.

as unrelated to the relationship, then individual cognitive therapy may be indicated; however, O'Leary et al. (1990) have shown that marital treatment was just as effective as individual therapy when women saw their depression as preceding marital issues.

A third consideration when deciding between marital or individual treatment involves the practitioner's assessment of the client's suicidality (Beach et al., 1990). Actively suicidal clients may be better served by individual therapy prior to marital work. Further, if suicidal ideation emerges during conjoint work, then a brief switch to individual therapy may be necessary so that depressive symptoms receive full attention (Beach et al., 1990).

A fourth consideration related to the level of depressive symptomatology involves the amount of time needed to attend to individual issues. If couples therapy is initiated, and individual depression issues require a significant portion of the session time (more than half), the practitioner may need to take a break from the marital model until the individual concerns are more fully addressed, through either an individual course of cognitive or interpersonal therapy or through the administration of antidepressant medication (Beach et al., 1990).

In the case example, Annette saw her depression as prompted by her marriage and move with her husband to a new city. She was unwilling to take medication because she was trying to become pregnant.[3] Annette was not actively suicidal, and when she had her initial session with the practitioner alone, Annette talked a lot about her relationship issues. She also expressed her desire to have marital rather than individual treatment. Therefore, based on individual factors, conjoint therapy seemed to be the treatment of choice.

Marital Considerations

Marital considerations in deciding whether to pursue individual or conjoint therapy include, first, the level of discord present in the relationship. Beach et al. (1990) recommend at least a moderate level of marital discord. More specifically, they cite Jacobson (1989), who suggests the use of the Dyadic Adjustment Scale (Spanier, 1976) as a tool

3. The issue of combining medication and marital treatment and its differential effect over the separate components has not yet been explored in the literature (Beach et al., 1998).

to assess the necessary level of marital distress. (See Box 9.2.) The score on the DAS should be lower than 100 for the depressed individual and lower than 115 for the non-depressed partner.

An assessment of couple discord also includes finding out about the presence of physical violence, which should be assessed in individual interviews (Beach et al., 1990). Although women who are in violent relationships are at high risk for depression (Golding, 1999), couples counseling is generally avoided when physical violence is present in the relationship. For a discussion of this controversial issue, see Corcoran (2000). The current recommendation is that physical violence should be addressed with individual or group treatment prior to couples work.

The second consideration regarding the couple relationship involves the partners' level of commitment to the relationship, which should also be assessed in individual interviews (Beach et al., 1990). Depression tends to be associated with low frustration tolerance and feelings of futility in response to lack of success in treatment. Therefore, individuals with depression who lack commitment to the relationship are vulnerable to premature dropout if they experience initial failure in treatment. If one partner reveals a desire to exit the relationship, this must be assessed carefully. If the decision represents a solid, well-considered plan, then the individual is encouraged to reveal this intention to the partner in an appropriate manner, and the practitioner can offer individual therapy to the depressed partner.

On the other hand, if partners threaten each other with dissolution of the relationship with little intention of following through, then this maladaptive form of communication should be explored, and alternative skills should be presented in the course of treatment (Beach et al.,

---

Box 9.2

Dyadic Adjustment Scale

The Dyadic Adjustment Scale (Spanier, 1976) is a 32-item self-report inventory measuring marital adjustment. The Dyadic Adjustment Scale has established reliability and validity, and there are four subscales: Dyadic Consensus (agreement regarding marital issues), Dyadic Cohesion (extent to which partners are involved in joint activities), Dyadic Satisfaction (overall evaluation of the relationship and level of commitment), and Affectional Expression (extent of affection and sexual involvement).

1990). Level of commitment also involves an exploration of ongoing extramarital affairs, since conjoint treatment is incompatible with continuing affairs outside the relationship.

One issue unexplored by research involves the cooperation of the spouse in treatment, another obvious consideration in deciding the best course of treatment (Beach et al., 1998). In the case example, the Spearses revealed no physical violence or extramarital affairs. While Annette showed less commitment to the relationship than did Rob, she wanted to give marital therapy a chance to help the relationship work. While Rob had greater commitment, he wanted Annette to attend individual therapy since he believed the relationship would improve if her depression lifted. He also said he was so busy at work, it would be difficult to attend conjoint sessions. Possible strategies for engaging the spouse are discussed in the following section.

Engaging the Partner in Treatment

There are several ways in which the spouse can be engaged in marital treatment for a partner's depression. First, if the individual with depression initially attends treatment alone and it is determined that couples therapy is the best course of treatment, she is coached on how to invite her husband to attend in a way that will gain his help rather than invoke defensiveness.

If the husband then accompanies his wife, the practitioner must compliment him for caring about his wife's well-being and being willing to become actively involved in treatment. The practitioner might offer to share studies if the partner is convinced by empirical evidence that marital treatment is effective for depression.

The practitioner should also offer empathy about the difficulties of living with a person with depression. For instance, Rob was told that family members often find it difficult to understand why the person is unable to "snap out of it." They may be exhausted and frustrated by efforts to cheer the person up. To this aim, the practitioner provided education about depression and its widespread nature. The practitioner first shared information about the widespread nature of depression. According to the National Institute of Mental Health (2001), in any one-year period, 9.5% of the U.S. population, translating into 18.8 million adults, experiences depression.

Depression goes beyond a passing "blue" or "down" mood, the practitioner further explained. A depressive disorder is an illness that involves the body (eating and sleeping), mood (the way one feels), and thoughts. Thoughts typically fall into three categories of belief: thoughts about the self ("I'm no good," "I'm worthless"), thoughts about the world ("Nothing turns out well," "I can't trust anybody"), and thoughts about the future ("Nothing will turn out well," "Nothing will ever change") (Young, Weinberger, & Beck, 2001).

The cause of depression is considered to involve genetic, psychological, and environmental factors. A genetic vulnerability may be triggered by environmental stressors, such as the life changes Annette had experienced in the past year, and psychological factors, such as lack of problem-solving abilities. Depression cannot be solved by willpower or effort, but with appropriate treatment, suffering can be alleviated.

The NIMH report (2001) suggests the following do's and don't's for family members.

Do not

- accuse the person of "faking it" or of laziness;
- tell the person to "snap out of it";
- ignore remarks about suicide; or
- push for too many changes too soon as it is important for the person to experience success rather than failure.

Do

- help the person to get appropriate diagnosis and treatment;
- reassure the person that, with time and help, she will recover, as most people do;
- encourage the person to stay with treatment until symptoms improve, which may involve accompanying the person to treatment;
- offer emotional support in terms of understanding, patience, affection, and encouragement;
- listen carefully to the person's feelings;
- report suicidal feelings to the person's therapist; and
- engage the person in activities and outings, but do not push for too much too soon. While diversion and company are necessary, too many demands can increase feelings of failure.

After providing information, the practitioner said that the toll of living with a depressed partner may cause Rob's sense of marital satisfaction to also decline, and conjoint treatment would not only help Annette's depression but would also enhance marital adjustment for both partners. With the rationale for couples therapy presented in this way and with the practitioner arranging a Saturday morning session, Rob agreed to attend marital therapy.

■■■■■ Components of Marital Behavioral Therapy

While there are varying formats for conjoint therapy for the treatment of depression, Beach, O'Leary, and colleagues have done extensive research and writing on the topic, and therefore, their marital therapy format (Beach et al., 1990) will be selected for presentation here. They describe their treatment as cognitive-behavioral, although it shares many elements with behavioral marital therapy (Jacobson & Margolin, 1979) and integrative behavioral couple therapy (Christensen, Jacobson, & Babcock, 1995; Wheeler et al., 2001). The purposes of marital therapy include (Beach et al., 1990):

1. Increasing marital cohesion, defined as "the amount of positive time spent together engaging in joint, pleasant activities" (Gotlib & Beach, 1995, p. 419)
2. Increasing self-esteem support, including "behaviors such as expressing appreciation, complimenting, and noticing positive traits in the partner" (Gotlib & Beach, 1995, p. 423)
3. Enhancing marital satisfaction and support
4. Reducing or eliminating marital stressors or conflict

Three different stages are described with different strategies in each. In Stage 1, couple cohesion, caring, and companionship are enhanced, while stressors are reduced. The second stage is more flexible and individualized to the couple's needs, although structuring communication and teaching problem-solving skills is a major focus. The third stage is geared toward helping couples maintain their changes and preventing relapse of couple distress and depression (Beach et al., 1990).

The following sections will detail how to explain cognitive-behavioral treatment and how the practitioner should deal with depressive venting in the session. Then each stage will be illustrated through the treatment of the Spears couple.

■■■■ Introducing Couples to Treatment

Cognitive-behavioral treatment is explained as an action-oriented approach with the underlying premise that behaviors, feelings, and thoughts are mutually determined (Beach et al., 1990). Marital distress and depression share common elements in that a negative cycle is often generated. For example, when there are marital problems, one partner will make a derogatory remark to the other; in turn, the other partner will react defensively, causing both to feel negatively about the relationship and less likely to make caring gestures toward the partner. In contrast, cognitive-behavioral treatment works actively to generate positive cycles. If one partner acts in a caring way, then the other partner feels better about the relationship and reciprocates in a positive way.

Since cognitive-behavioral treatment is a skills-building approach, couples have to practice the new skills. A great deal of attention during session time is paid to explaining and assigning homework and evaluating its success. (Because of space limitations, the highlights of time spent on homework assignments will be illustrated in the case example, but the reader should understand that extensive session time is devoted to discussion of this topic.)

■■■■ Venting of Depressive Feelings

During marital therapy, the individual with depression may want to spend a lot of time discussing painful feelings. These complaints may be incorporated as useful material in the therapy process. By listening and offering empathy, the practitioner can model these skills since listening to depressive complaints is often very difficult for the partner. The practitioner can also encourage and reinforce the spouse to respond in a caring manner. If depressive concerns are not attended to, the individual may view the session material as irrelevant to her primary concerns and may not participate fully, which may, in turn, frustrate her partner. At the same time, after spending some time working therapeutically with depressive concerns, the practitioner should then look for opportunities to return to scheduled material, focusing on couple behaviors (Beach et al., 1990).

■ Stage I

Depending on the nature of the couple's relationship, treatment may initially need to focus on ameliorating negative patterns. The rationale involves Beach et al.'s (1990) claim that negative behavior is more deterministic of couple satisfaction level than is positive behavior. In addition, marital distress not only blocks marital support, it is also a direct form of stress. Negative patterns include verbal abuse, criticism and blaming, threats to terminate the relationship, behaviors that produce severe disruption of marital routines, and idiosyncratic major marital stressors (Gotlib & Beach, 1995). The Spears couple was guilty of all of these except for verbal abuse. For verbal abuse, Beach et al. (1990) recommend teaching partners how to take time out from each other. (See their excellent book for details of the procedure.) The other negative behaviors will be addressed and applied to the case example below.

Handling Negative Patterns

Criticism and Blaming

When criticism and blaming is present in the relationship, as it often was with the Spears couple, the practitioner offers feedback about the deleterious effects of criticizing, blaming, and derogating, especially the negative effects it may have for the partner with depression in terms of relapse (Hooley et al., 1986; Hooley & Teasdale, 1989). In couples with a partner experiencing depression, another way to reduce blame is to provide information related to the disorder. For instance, it is explained that fatigue, lack of concentration, sleep problems, irritability, and decreased sexual activity are all symptoms of depression. Rob was relieved that these characteristics were not necessarily who Annette was as a person and that these symptoms would lift as her depression improved. When partners see the behavior as attributable to depression rather than to dispositional qualities or characteristics under volitional control, then often the cycle of criticism and blaming is broken (Hooley & Licht, 1997).

Threats to Leave the Relationship

Rob reported that Annette sometimes said to him, "I was a lot happier when I was single. Maybe I shouldn't be married any more." When

Annette threatened to leave the relationship, the practitioner reminded her, "You do care about each other, you have both told me that, and you are invested in this relationship, otherwise you would not have come to marital therapy. I think, Annette, when you say that you don't want to be married, this reflects a feeling you have only in passing, rather than a deep conviction that it is the right thing for you to do" (Beach et al., 1990).

"That's true," she admitted. "Because at other times, I'm afraid I'm messing things up, and Rob's going to leave *me*. The thought of that really scares me."

"Since that is the case," said the practitioner. "You probably should not verbalize every time you have an impulse to leave the relationship since these thoughts sound like they're vacillating, depending on your mood, and inconsistent. Therefore, sharing these fleeting thoughts of leaving the relationship actually undermines the level of understanding between you two rather than clarifying your feelings regarding the relationship. However, if at any point, either of you are clear that you want to separate, then I can offer to help him or her with telling the other partner and will support you both through the decision" (Beach et al., 1990).

Disruption of Scripted Marital Behavior

Another source of stress identified by O'Leary and colleagues (1990) involves disruption of scripted spousal behavior, which means a breakdown in the routines of normal family life. O'Leary et al. (1990) refer to the specific type of disruption in which a spouse will have virtually no contact with the partner with depression. This lack of contact may be due to an undisclosed extramarital relationship, but more commonly results from a lack of resources in the family, which necessitates demanding work schedules, work stress, or workaholic patterns. Rob, for instance, worked late in the evenings and often was not home before 8 o'clock. That meant he missed eating dinner with Annette, and she spent considerable time alone without his company. After he ate and watched TV, he was then ready for bed. She did not go to bed with him at the same time because she had fallen into a pattern of staying up until the early morning hours and then sleeping late into the day. When Annette initially posed marital therapy, he said that he was too busy with work to attend sessions.

Therefore, the first priority was establishing a set routine so more prolonged interaction would take place. Beach et al. (1990) suggest mealtimes, telephone contact, notes left for each other, meeting during the day, evening routines, going to bed at the same time, and joint social activities. Only when some routine with reasonable frequency of interaction has been established can partners work on making their contact more enjoyable.

Rob wanted Annette to wake up early with him so they could drink coffee and eat breakfast together. However, she rebelled at this idea: "Great, so then I'm up at 6 o'clock, and now I have even more hours in the day with nothing to do until you come home more than 12 hours later. At least when I sleep in until 11, there's less time until you come home again." Rob said he would make more of an effort to come home in time for them to have dinner together. He agreed that if he went downtown to work on Saturdays, he would take Annette with him, and she could shop or go to the library. Then they could join each other for a snack or a meal. On Sundays, Rob usually brought work home, but he agreed to curtail the time he spent on projects, rather than working on them continuously throughout the day. He would make a concerted effort to work during a limited time frame and then spend more time on Sundays with Annette.

Idiosyncratic Major Marital Stressors

By *idiosyncratic major marital stressors*, Beach et al. (1990) refer to the specific type of situation in which women stay at home to take care of young children. Annette was in a similar situation since she stayed home all day, and she was trying to become pregnant. The practitioner educated Annette that her circumstances elevated the risk of depression. In order to counteract the risk, she would need to spend time with her partner and other adults, as well as have time alone to pursue meaningful and pleasurable activities.

Scheduling Pleasant Activities

Once the practitioner had addressed some of the couple's negative patterns, her attention turned toward increasing the positives in the relationship. One of these components is to schedule pleasant events, so that the relationship becomes associated with enjoyment and pleasure rather than coercion and dissatisfaction, and marital cohesion is built (Beach et al., 1990). In introducing the scheduling of pleasant events, the practitioner said this would help address one of Annette's complaints, that she and her husband no longer had any fun. The practitioner emphasized that, in terms of Annette's mood, it was a positive prognostic sign that Annette was actively seeking to engage in pleasurable activities; many times, people with depression have to be cajoled and pressured by their loved ones into more activities.

The practitioner further explained how the couple had evolved a negative pattern around activities together, which was mutually derived and symmetrical. Annette was bored because she had been in all day and complained to Rob. Already stressed from working, these complaints added to his stress level, and he felt like avoiding Annette rather than spending time in pleasant activities with her. She, in turn, became more resentful and more insistent on doing things together. The couple agreed they had been caught up in such a cycle. The practitioner used this as a rationale for scheduling time to spend together, without it being a constant source of argument.

The next concern the practitioner addressed was Annette's rebelling at the nonspontaneous nature of having to schedule events. When they were dating, Annette and Rob often did things on the spur of the moment, with no need to stick to a schedule. The practitioner referred back to the initial explanation about the cognitive-behavioral premise, in which feelings, thoughts, and behaviors are considered to be mutually determined. Therefore, if positive actions can be initiated, positive feelings will follow as both spouses reciprocate in a positive cycle of interaction. The case was further made that each one does care about the other. As evidence, they have chosen to remain married and to seek couples treatment. However, at the present time, these feelings of good will toward each other are blocked or are not expressed (Beach et al., 1990).

After working with them on these various concerns, the practitioner helped the couple to develop a plan of agreement: They would go out to dinner one weekday night and one weekend night and would go to the movies the other weekend night. They would also take a half-hour walk around the neighborhood on Sunday afternoons.

In the following session, the couple reported on their homework. Annette said she enjoyed their dinner together on Friday night. Rob talked a bit more about his work situation, and she enjoyed hearing about what it was like. Rob said in session, "Who wants to hear about the boring office?"

"I do," Annette said. "I want to hear what you do."

"How was it," the practitioner asked, "to talk to her about that stuff?"

"It was good, I guess," he said, "although I don't usually talk about work to anyone outside it."

"Did it help a bit with your work stress?" the practitioner asked.

"Maybe a little—it clarified some things. But she can't really help since she doesn't know the ins and outs of the business."

"I'm not stupid, Rob," Annette said.

"I didn't say you were," he said.

The practitioner interrupted the budding argument. "Actually, the best listening anyone can do is to reflect back your experiences. That helps you feel heard and clarifies your thoughts, so you can come up with your own answers. We'll be talking more about these kinds of skills in communication skills training." The practitioner then turned to complimenting, a basic building block of successful communication.

Complimenting

Self-esteem support is provided directly through training each partner how to positively track his partner's behaviors by communicating verbally that he appreciates the other's behaviors or qualities (Beach et al., 1990). In behavioral theory, the central operating principle is reinforcement, and in marital therapy, *complimenting* is the way partners reinforce each other for desired behaviors. Complimenting is introduced early in the process because it has more potential for success compared to other, more complex communication skills, such as reflective listening and problem solving. Although probably underused, complimenting is already within the response repertoire of most clients. Another reason complimenting may be more successful is because it is not dependent on the other partner changing, whereas the other skills require an interaction of new behaviors (Beach et al., 1990).

When people are courting, they tend to compliment each other freely, but over time, they may reduce their complimenting, for different possible reasons. First, they may take their partners' behaviors for granted, becoming habituated to the other person. For instance, Rob admitted that he was much more complimentary of Annette when they were dating. Second, partners may have unrealistic beliefs that their spouse should know what they are thinking without having to tell them. Rob often said, "She should know how I feel. I married her, didn't I? I want her to be the mother of my children. Why should I have to tell her?" A third, common response involves the idea that one's spouse should have been doing these things all along and, therefore, does not deserve complimenting. For instance, Annette said, "He used to say nice things about me when we were dating. He should be doing that now, too."

The practitioner provided the following rationale for complimenting: "If you don't tell each other what the other person is doing well, then your views of each other may become distorted in a negative way. That's why complimenting each other is essential for keeping the relationship on track" (Beach et al., 1990).

As a way to jog their thinking, the practitioner named types of behaviors and qualities that partners can acknowledge in each other, and asked the spouses to come up with examples. These included: tasks that the other partner does (Annette likes it when Rob fills her car up with gas; he likes it when she cooks him dinner), desired changes that the partner has made (Annette likes when Rob spends more time with her and less time working), and positive beliefs and feelings about the partner (Annette thinks Rob is a good provider; Rob says he finds Annette very attractive, although she looks a lot better when she isn't wearing the same pair of sweats she slept in).

If partners are reluctant to compliment each other or are unable to make a positive statement, either due to the way they say it or because of incongruent nonverbal behaviors (such as voice tone or posture), the practitioner models the appropriate response. In this instance, Rob paired his compliment of Annette (he was attracted to her) with criticism (she would look better if she didn't wear sweats so much). The practitioner explained this point and next modeled giving the compliment to Annette: "You look nice today, Annette." The practitioner then had Rob practice giving Annette a compliment as she role played Annette, which provided the opportunity to model a helpful response ("Thank you!"). This was contrasted with a punishing response ("Oh, yeah, right, like I haven't gained 15 pounds," "You're just saying that because the therapist told you to say it"). The practitioner then asked Rob to give the positive statement directly to Annette. Until the behavior is successfully performed in session, clients should not be assigned the homework of increasing the number of compliments paid to each other. Part of the homework also involves clients monitoring their own positive communications rather than focusing on what their spouse is not providing.

Behavior Exchange

Another way to build marital cohesion is through increasing the amount of day-to-day caring gestures, ameliorating partners' tendency to focus on the negative parts of the relationship (Wheeler et al., 2001; Beach et al., 1990). The practitioner provided the following rationale for behavior exchange (Beach et al., 1990): "Annette and Rob, you both care about each other and want to resolve problems and have a more satisfying relationship. But many of the day-to-day things that convey these feelings have disappeared from the relationship. Once these have been reestablished, they will begin to feel spontaneous and natural again. This is an important first step toward resolving problems."

Wheeler et al. (2001) suggest a step-by-step procedure for assigning behavior exchange. First, each partner is instructed to compile a list of activities that each can do to help improve the other person's satisfaction with the relationship. This is to be done independently as a homework assignment, and the lists are not to be shared until the next session. The activities on the list should have the following components:

1. Each item on the list should be a small and concrete unit of behavior that requires no new learning.
2. Items on the list should involve increased positive behavior rather than decreased negative behavior.
3. Behaviors should have the potential for frequent performance rather than special circumstances usually not present.
4. Behaviors should be under the giver's total control.
5. Activities should have no monetary expenditure attached to them.
6. Sexual activity can be a caring event, unless sexual problems are reported.[4]

The practitioner provided Rob and Annette with some examples of caring gestures: providing massages, leaving notes for each other, telephoning each other unexpectedly, preparing food, or taking care of a chore (Beach et al., 1990).

After client lists have been generated and are discussed in session,

4. At the same time, sexual problems are relatively common for both marital distress and depression. If sexual problems appear significant, sex therapy techniques may be implemented along with other treatment procedures, although it is expected that addressing depression and marital distress will also aid in ameliorating sexual problems (Beach et al., 1990).

each partner is assigned to do one of the activities on the list each day. (See table 9.1 for Annette's and Rob's lists.) Beach et al. (1990) suggest that this level of performance is necessary for a person who is depressed since anything below this frequency may not be observed or recalled. However, Addis and Jacobson (1991) caution that the functional level of the individual with depression must be taken into account when assigning homework tasks. Given Annette's low energy and Rob's busy work schedule, the practitioner settled for Wheeler et al.'s (2001) more general recommendation for maritally distressed clients to perform only one caring gesture per week.

The practitioner must warn the couple that one should not wait until the other has acted before implementing the spouse's desired activities, otherwise, a power struggle may result. When one partner acts in a positive manner, good will is generated, and the other person is likely to reciprocate in kind. When a caring gesture has been performed, the receiver should provide recognition in terms of complimenting, displaying a pleased facial expression, and attending physically to the partner simultaneously.

Wheeler et al. (2001) suggest that each person track her own caring gestures in a place the spouse can access. In this way, spouses are trained to notice the other partner's positive actions, which helps to emphasize individual responsibility for the change process. In the next session, partners are asked to evaluate the caring gestures they performed and what effect they had on their partner.

The following week, Annette said she had cooked dinner for Rob one night, but he ended up working late, and they ate separately. Rob said he had told Annette that she "looked nice" Friday night when

Table 9.1	
Behavior Exchange Lists	
Caring Gestures (Annette for Rob)	Caring Gestures (Rob for Annette)
Allowing Rob a period of 30 minutes to unwind when he gets home.	Taking Annette out to dinner.
Wearing something other than sweatpants when he comes home from work.	Talking about their days together. Walking around the neighborhood. Meeting neighbors together.
Doing a household task.	
Making dinner for him.	

they went out to dinner. Annette commented that she was willing to make an effort with her appearance if she were going somewhere, otherwise, "What is the point?" Other than the one compliment, Rob admitted he had not carried out any of the caring gestures. His claim was that he was "too busy" and "stressed out" with work. Annette was tearful and took his actions as evidence that he "didn't care" about her and that "it would always be this way, and nothing was going to change." As a result, she said she did not feel like doing anything for him, other than the one meal she prepared for him. She said that he could fix his "own damn dinner when he finally makes it home."

The practitioner stressed that each partner was responsible for carrying out tasks individually, no matter the behavior of the partner. Annette interjected, "This is very difficult to do when you get nothing back!" The practitioner acknowledged the challenge involved but urged both of them to complete tasks without overconcern about the other's actions.

In the conjoint session, the practitioner also worked with the partners, individually, on their schedules. For Rob, this meant taking some time to explain to Annette the specific job stressors he was up against, so she could gain more empathy for his position. It also meant helping him organize his time so he could prioritize tasks and not get derailed by office politics. For Annette, the practitioner spent some time assisting her in increasing her individual activities.

Increasing Individual Activities

A typical expectation of individuals with depression is that their partners should be the primary source of satisfaction in terms of companionship and activities; however, this places a significant burden of responsibility on spouses, decreasing couple cohesion. It also blocks the individual with depression from drawing on and developing her internal resources (Beach et al., 1990). A further problem with overfocus on the relationship is that it often leads to the other partner's appearing less invested in the relationship. Beach et al. (1990) recommend that increased commitment in the relationship sometimes results when the woman who is depressed is supported to engage in outside employment or more individual pleasant activities.

The practitioner also educated Annette that, for someone with depression, it is helpful to build structure into the day with activities—

ones from which she could derive accomplishment and enjoyment (Young et al., 2001). The practitioner advised that even an hour-to-hour scheduling of activities might need to be constructed so that Annette felt engaged in some meaningful activities. "That's what I keep telling her," Rob said, then, turning to Annette. "You just need to keep busy. That'll keep your mind off how miserable you are."

"It's not that easy," Annette snapped.

"No, it's not that easy," said the practitioner. "But for depression, it's important to have structure, otherwise it's easy to get overwhelmed.

The practitioner gave Annette a "mastery-pleasure" chart with the days divided into hour-long time slots (Young et al., 2001). Annette was to schedule as many activities as she wanted each day and then rate them according to the amount of either mastery or pleasure experienced. The reason for the ratings is because people with depression tend to misinterpret when they recall events and remember them as negative experiences. (See the problem-solving section for some of the individual activities that were formulated for Annette.)

In the following session, Annette said she had joined a gym. She wanted Rob to work out with her, but he said she needed to do it alone because he was too busy to go with her in the evenings. So far, she had not gone to the gym by herself during the day, although that was her plan for the next week. She had also called a plumber to fix the sink in the upstairs bathroom and had scheduled a time for him to come. However, he had not shown up. Annette said she didn't feel much pleasure at all the prior week except when she watched her favorite TV shows. She had a small sense of mastery for having joined the gym, but she felt guilty for not actually working out. She had gained very little mastery from calling the plumber since the bathroom sink had not been fixed. The practitioner complimented her for following through on some of these individual activities.

When the attention turned to Rob, he said that he had not been able to get much more done than the previous week in regard to the couple work (Annette confirmed this). Rob again gave the same excuses about his work stress. The practitioner followed up this information with a request to spend individual time with each partner.

When she was alone with Rob, she said, "I know you came here saying that you wanted to help your wife feel better, and you agreed that working on the marriage was a way to do that. You also wanted to make your marriage more solid as a couple and as a foundation for when you have children." He agreed this was so. The practitioner then went on to say that his actions regarding homework assignments were incongruent with his stated intentions.

He said, "Quite frankly, it's a lot that I'm even here at the session. I should be at work right now, I have so much to do. A lot of the partners are in on Saturday mornings, and it looked really good when I was able to do that, too. I try to tell Annette that, but she doesn't understand."

"So you're saying that Annette should be happy that you're even here and that she shouldn't expect any more from you?"

"That's not what I mean!" But when he tried to explain what he meant, he finally said ruefully, "I guess that is what I mean."

"Rob, if that's the case, then I think you should be honest with Annette that you don't plan on changing any of your behaviors and that you can't commit to the marital work."

"But then it makes me sound as if I'm not interested in this relationship working out."

"Other than following through with the marital treatment, what else do you think would let her know that you are interested in this relationship working out?"

"I'm here, aren't I? And I'm slaving away at this job. It's for both of us. It's for the family we're going to start."

"Does she see it that way?"

"No, I wish you could just convince her of that."

The practitioner then gently explained that her role did not involve trying to convince one partner that the other genuinely cared. She said the caring came through quite naturally when people performed actions that conveyed their commitment.

The practitioner said it was not fair to Annette and was a waste of Rob's time and energy if he just showed up to marital sessions when he had no intention of participating fully in the treatment. She told him to think about what he wanted to do and let her know at the next session.

For the next session, Annette tearfully came by herself. She expressed a lot of despair and said, "It would serve him right if I killed myself." This statement caused the practitioner to evaluate Annette's level of suicidality. Annette admitted to some recurring thoughts but without a definitive plan. She said she had also been thinking a lot about just leaving Rob and moving back to the city where she had lived when they met.

Concerned about Annette's depressive symptoms, which included thoughts of suicide, feelings of pain, and inability to follow through on structuring her days, the practitioner explored with her the options of placing her decision to have a child on hold and being evaluated for antidepressant medication. Annette said, "But we've been trying for a year. Why should we stop?"

The practitioner said, "If you become pregnant, Annette, it will be that much more difficult to leave the relationship."

"But maybe having a baby will make everything okay."

The practitioner explained that the stress of motherhood was often associated with increased levels of depression, as well as divorce. In addition, depression in mothers is a serious risk factor for children's emotional and behavior problems (Beck, 1999; Prince & Jacobson, 1995). For these reasons, it was critically important to treat her depression first and not begin childbearing before either she or the relationship was prepared.

After this session, Annette did not return for 3 weeks. When she did reschedule, Rob was with her. Annette had not seen the psychiatrist but had scheduled an appointment. Rob reported he had been taken aback that Annette no longer wanted to start a family. He had not realized the extent of their marital distress until then. He said he did not want to lose Annette and was willing to participate fully in therapy this time. The week following, he came home from work relatively early (6:30), and the couple was able to eat dinner together.

Summary of Stage 1

In the first phase of treatment, the interventions to increase the positives in the relationship had helped the couple's level of companionship and cohesion. Although these areas continued to need work, the time in sessions then turned to the second phase of treatment.

Stage 2

The next stage of the therapy process is more individualized, addressing the particular concerns of the couple, although it should contain communication and problem-solving training.

Communication Skills Training

A common communication pattern among women with depression is that, when they begin to talk about their feelings of distress, seeking understanding and comfort from their partners, they find themselves being "tuned out" or subject to advice. The nondepressed man tends to see his wife's talking about problems "as a sign of disaffiliation or rejection of the relationship, while she may see this behavior as a means of drawing closer" (Beach et al., 1990, p. 150). In addition, a typical fear of the nondepressed spouse is that listening empathically to complaints will only make matters worse ("It will only encourage her"). However, the opposite is true. When a person with depression feels heard, she usually feels a sense of relief that she is understood and experiences more closeness to her partner as a result.

The interactional pattern between women with depression and their nondepressed partners results in frustration on both sides. The speaker feels misunderstood, and the partner feels helpless and annoyed that the speaker will not do what he has suggested. To avoid these problems, couples are taught to request the type of communication they desire: problem solving (e.g., "Can you help me figure out my options about the situation in the office?") or sharing feelings (e.g., "I've been feeling bad. Can I talk about it with you?") (Beach et al., 1990). The other recommendation is that communicating may need to be scheduled for a specific time (as opposed to a vague "later"). A specific time is necessary so the person who wants to talk is reassured that she will be heard.

Communication and listening skills, including constructing "I" messages, reflective listening, validating the partner's experiences, and making behavioral change requests, will be covered in the next sections. Following will be an exploration of some negative communication patterns characteristic of depression and interventions to address these.

Constructing "I" Messages

In the first part of communication training, couples are taught the necessity of being vulnerable with their own feelings rather than accusing and blaming the other person (Wheeler et al., 2001). In order for them to gain perspective on the effect of these latter behaviors, the practitioner asked the Spears couple, "How do you feel when your spouse makes derogatory statements about your character?"

"I feel terrible when he calls me lazy," said Annette.

"Well, I don't feel so great either when you say I'm old before my time," Rob rejoined.

"So you don't feel good about yourselves," the practitioner summarized. "How do you feel about the other person?"

Both could see that these types of statements made them angry at each other. Annette said it made her want to lash out at him somehow. For Rob, it made him not want to spend time in Annette's company.

Like this couple, clients usually respond that they feel defensive and then counterattack in response to derogatory remarks. In contrast, if partners talk about their own feelings and reveal their vulnerabilities in the relationship, they can see that their partners are more likely to respond with understanding.

After building this rationale, the practitioner provided the basic format for giving "I" messages: "I feel (the reaction) to what happened (a specific activating event)." The practitioner then modeled this skill, role playing one partner (Annette wanting to talk to Rob about her depressive symptoms) and then the other (Rob relating his job stress).

The clients then practiced with the practitioner, who gave feedback, asking each to stop and practice again until the skill was performed satisfactorily. However, special care must be provided in giving feedback to individuals with depression because they will often interpret comments in both a personalized and globalized manner ("I'm worthless and stupid, even my therapist says so"). Beginning the training with the practitioner modeling and then acting as a surrogate partner is crucial so the possibility of unsuccessful rehearsal by the individual is reduced. The practitioner should give compliments, as well as providing correction (Beach et al., 1990).

Following is an example of Annette's attempt at communicating to her husband using "I" messages after she had role played with the practitioner.

ANNETTE: I feel . . . [searching for word] like you don't love me any more.

PRACTITIONER: Let me stop you for a moment, Annette. I know you're in a lot of pain, so what's the feeling?

ANNETTE: Sad, I guess. [Annette starts crying and can't speak for a few moments.]

[Rob, clearly uncomfortable, grabs the box of tissues and hands her one.]

PRACTITIONER [modeling empathy for Rob]: This is very painful to talk about . . .

[Annette's wave of emotion is spent.]

PRACTITIONER: Okay, Annette, are you ready to try again?

[Annette nods and blows her nose.]

ANNETTE: I feel sad [her voice trembles on the word] when you act like you don't love me any more.

ROB: I do love you, Annette. Would you stop saying that?

[The practitioner blocks him with her hand.]

PRACTITIONER: Okay, Rob, let Annette finish her part first, then you get a chance to talk. Annette, I want you to tell Rob about a specific behavior he does rather than your global comment, "You act like you don't love me any more."

[Annette struggles to think of something.]

ANNETTE: He doesn't seem to want to spend time with me any more. He acts sort of irritated.

PRACTITIONER: What does he do specifically that causes you to think he doesn't want to spend time with you any more?

ANNETTE: He comes home from work and when I start telling him about how bad I feel, he just watches TV, like he doesn't want to listen.

PRACTITIONER: Okay, so that's the behavior. You talk to him about your feelings when he comes home from work, and he watches TV. So start from the beginning. [prompting] "I feel sad . . ."

ANNETTE: I feel sad when you watch TV instead of listening to what I have to say.

PRACTITIONER: Okay, good.

The next part of the communication process involves listening to ensure that the speaker's message has been heard.

Listening Skills

Listening skills include both reflective listening and validation. The purpose of reflective listening is so that the speaker's perspective is understood by the partner. It also decreases the tendency of partners to draw conclusions about the intentions and meanings of a partner's statement (Wheeler et al., 2001). Reflective listening involves paraphrasing back the feelings and content of the speaker's message with the format: "What I hear you saying is . . ." or "You feel . . . (*feeling word*) when/because . . ." Other guidelines are offered as follows:

- Partners should put their partners' messages in their own words rather than using the exact words of the person.
- The partner does not have to share the same point of view in order to reflect back the message.
- If the speaker has talked for a long time, partners can stop the other person and reflect up to that point ("I think I know what you are saying," "So what I hear you saying so far is . . .").

Beyond reflection, validation is an advanced skill and involves conveying that, given the person's perspectives and assumptions, his experiences are legitimate and understandable ("I can see that if you were thinking I had done that, you would feel that way"). Beach et al. (1990) caution that many people are unable to learn this skill, but that it is worth teaching because the act of being validated can be a powerful and relationship-enhancing experience, particularly when depression plays a role in relationship difficulties. Different ways to express validation statements include the following (Beach et al., 1990):

- "I can understand that."
- "It makes sense to me."
- "I see how you felt that way."
- "I would have done the same thing in your position."

After the practitioner modeled these listening skills and then had each partner role play them, she had Rob attempt to use reflective listening with Annette in conversation, picking up on the "I" message Annette had conveyed to him earlier.

PRACTITIONER: Okay, Rob, why don't you give that a try?

ROB: It's not like I don't listen. It's just that she says the same thing every day, and she won't do anything about it.

PRACTITIONER: Rob, right now, rather than defending yourself, just try to reflect back what you heard Annette say.

ROB: But I do care about her, and I tell her all the time.

PRACTITIONER: You don't have to agree with what she's saying. You just have to paraphrase back to her what she said. [prompting] "What I hear you saying is . . ."

ROB: What I hear you saying is that you're sad because you don't think I'm listening to you.

PRACTITIONER: Annette, is that what you said?

ANNETTE [nodding tearfully]: Yes.

PRACTITIONER: Very good, Rob. Okay, Annette, how was that?

ANNETTE: That does feel pretty good.

PRACTITIONER: See, Rob, it's relatively easy. You just showed how
well you can do that, and the impact is surprisingly powerful.

ROB: Well, if that's all it takes . . .

Sometimes, communicating "I" messages and reflecting back feelings are all that is needed. When people's perspectives are validated,
they feel satisfied, supported, and do not need a behavior change by
their partners. However, sometimes it is necessary to request a change
in behavior.

Making Specific Behavioral Requests

People with depression often have difficulty with specifics and clarity,
often seeing others or life circumstances in absolutist terms ("Oh,
what's the use, he's always going to be selfish"). Several guidelines are
offered for making requests more effective:

- They should be specific ("making the bed") versus global ("being
  neater").
- They should be measurable ("If you're going to be 30 minutes
  late, I would like you to call," "I want you to make dinner three
  times a week").
- They should be stated as the presence of positive behaviors
  rather than the absence of negative behaviors ("pick up your
  clothes" rather than "don't be such a slob").

The practitioner followed the same format as before; she modeled the
skill with both partners, then had them rehearse with her as the surrogate partner. She then asked them to practice the skill with one another.

PRACTITIONER: Now, the next part of this is to make a specific behavioral request. What is it that you want him to do, Annette?

ANNETTE: I just want him to listen to me.

PRACTITIONER: Make it even more specific than that. You want him to
listen to you whenever or just when he comes home from work.
What do you want?

ANNETTE: Well, yeah.

PRACTITIONER: Do you think it's reasonable that at any time you want
to talk, he should be available to listen to you?

ROB: That's what you want, Annette.

ANNETTE: No, I don't, Rob. You're going to be busy sometimes, I know.

PRACTITIONER: A good rule of thumb is to make a request for time to talk. If he is not available for that, then he can let you know a specific time that he is. For instance, Rob may be tired when he first gets home from work and may need a little time to unwind.

ROB [relieved]: That's exactly what I need. I can't handle hearing about how bad she feels and how it's all my fault.

ANNETTE: I'm not saying it's all your fault, Rob. I never said that.

ROB: You pretty much imply it.

PRACTITIONER: Okay, Annette, so what is it that you're going to do?

ANNETTE: Ask him if he's available to talk.

PRACTITIONER: Very good. And Rob what are you going to do?

ROB: Turn off the TV and listen, but only after I've had a little time to unwind first. But how much time do I have to listen? I don't want it to last all night long.

ANNETTE [to the practitioner]: You see what I mean?

PRACTITIONER: That's what many people who live with a person with depression think. If they start listening to the feelings, they will go on forever. But actually, Rob, you will find that a short period of intense listening will reap you many more benefits than if you keep putting Annette off. She will probably feel at least a little better and closer to you, as a result.

The practitioner then led the couple through the exercise again, and Rob had a chance to talk about what was bothering him: He felt "frustrated" when he called from work to tell Annette he was running late as she would either start crying or become angry. He, in turn, would then become upset and was unable to concentrate on the work he needed to finish. Consequently, he would have to work even later. To avoid the upset, he would simply not call her. Of course, this resulted in even greater upset. His specific behavioral request was that she accept when he called to say he would be late. She agreed to this request as long as he tried to limit the number of nights he worked overtime.

Usually, a practitioner has to be quite directive when leading a couple through the communication skills, blocking partners when they make global statements about each other, asking them to focus on specific behaviors instead, and helping them make statements about their own feelings rather than making accusations. It is important that the other person also have a turn to give his or her perspective, allowing the other partner to reflect back the statement. In so doing, both people feel heard.

Similar to most couples, Rob and Annette had difficulty mastering the communication skills and admitted they did not practice much initially. Because their early attempts escalated into conflict, they concluded it was useless to try to implement them further. Therefore, when they returned for their next session, the practitioner role played for them the skills again, rehearsed with each couple, and then asked them to practice together once more in session before they were assigned the homework again.

Communication Patterns Characteristic of Depression

Problematic communication patterns particular to depression may also have to be addressed, in particular, reassurance seeking and negative verification. First, women with depression often request reassurance from their spouses. For instance, Annette asked Rob at least once a day, "Do you love me?" Unfortunately, reassurance-seeking patterns may result in rejection and dissatisfaction (Beach et al., 1998).

Negative verification is when the individual with depression makes negative remarks posed as questions for the spouse. For instance, Annette often said, "I'm fat, aren't I?" If the spouse agrees, the wife will obviously feel worse; if the spouse disagrees, the depressed individual may not feel reassured, and with repeated negative verification, the spouse may feel frustrated by these demands.

The practitioner brings these patterns to the couple's awareness, cautions the depressed individual against using these tactics, and trains the spouse in responses that provide support at a general level but do not encourage reassurance seeking or negative feedback seeking. The practitioner trained Rob, for instance, in the following type of response (S. Beach, personal communication, January 16, 2002): "I am very committed to making our relationship work well and to helping you feel better. I would answer your question if I didn't think it would work against both those goals. I think it will be better if I show you over time instead of answering this question. Is that okay?"

Just as important, the spouse with depression should also have an assignment, which is to notice that she had drifted into the reassurance-seeking pattern. Annette was encouraged to respond with the following: "Even though I really want to press you for an answer right now,

I won't. I know you are doing what you think will help our relationship the most in the long run."

Both partners would therefore be acting to help the couple exit from an unhelpful pattern. The overall goal in any particular case would be for the nondepressed partner to provide a supportive and nonpunitive answer, which also cues the partner to exit from the reassurance-seeking cycle (S. Beach, personal communication, January 16, 2002).

Problem-Solving Training

Problem-solving training instructs couples on strategies they can use for managing the problems of everyday life (Wheeler et al., 2001). Problem solving is called for when communicating concerns fails to resolve a disagreement (Beach et al., 1990). The format for problem solving involves the following steps: defining the problem, brainstorming, examining possible options, deciding on an option, implementing an option, and evaluating the implementation.

Defining the Problem

The first step of the problem-solving process involves defining the problem in clear and specific ways that both partners can understand. The behavior and the circumstances surrounding the problem should be delineated with only one targeted at a time (Wheeler et al., 2001). In addition, problems should be stated as the presence of positive behaviors, rather than the absence of negative behaviors. For example, rather than Annette saying that Rob never spends time with her, the problem could be stated as her wanting Rob to spend time with her on weekends. Solutions are easier to formulate when problems are clearly delineated. The problem on which both partners agreed was that Annette was bored and depressed with so much time on her hands. Rob agreed this was also a problem for him since, as a result, Annette called him a couple of times during the day and also wanted a lot of his energy and attention in the evenings.

Generating Alternatives

The next step for problem-solving training involves brainstorming with the purpose of producing all possible solutions. At this point, evaluative comments are not allowed so that an atmosphere of creativity is encouraged. All possibilities are written down, even those that seem impossible or silly. This phase of the problem-solving process will be illustrated with the Spears couple and the problem of Annette having nothing to do during the day.

ANNETTE: Well, maybe I could start waitressing again.
[The practitioner writes this on a dry erase board].
ROB: Annette, you know I don't want you waitressing.
ANNETTE: At least it would get me out of the house.
ROB: Waitressing was fine when you were single, Annette, but now—
PRACTITIONER: I'm going to stop you here because at this stage in the problem-solving process, you just want to brainstorm options. You don't want to shut down the creative process by arguing and criticizing ideas. The next stage is when you'll discuss the advantages and disadvantages of each plan.
ANNETTE: I've thought about graduate school, but I'm not sure. I don't think I'm interested enough in anything to dedicate 2 to 3 years of my life to it.
ROB: Do you think I had a particular *interest* in accounting? No, I just knew I could make a good living.
PRACTITIONER [writing down "graduate school" on the dry erase board]: I'm going to remind you again that, at this stage, you just want to come up with different alternatives.
ROB: Well, you could take classes at the community college or continuing education. Maybe in something creative—art classes, that sort of thing.
ANNETTE: I don't know—nothing sounds good.
PRACTITIONER: I'm writing this down anyway since it's another alternative to explore. [jots down on dry erase board] What else?
[The couple seems stuck at this point.]
PRACTITIONER: I wonder what else you could do, Annette, that would involve other people?
ANNETTE: That's just it—I don't know anyone.
ROB: How about volunteer work, maybe in an area you're thinking of taking classes? Then you could decide whether it interests you enough.
PRACTITIONER [writing it down]: Good. Annette, let's hear from you again. One of the problems with depression is that problem solving is sometimes impaired, so we'll have to work here on building that skill. At this point, you just want to come up with ideas.

They can be silly or outlandish; you don't want to restrict your creativity.

ANNETTE: Okay, if we could do anything, then maybe Rob could take a week off, and we could go on another cruise like we did on our honeymoon.

ROB: Annette, you know that's impossible right now.

ANNETTE: She said to just come up with ideas. It's not like I'd expect you to go, I'm just suggesting it.

PRACTITIONER: That's right—that's all we're doing at this point.

ROB: Well, then if we're getting totally crazy—how about doing more work around the house, doing some cleaning and calling about repairs?

ANNETTE: I told you when we got married, I didn't want to just be a housewife.

ROB: Well, then, you can't just stay home all day!

PRACTITIONER: Okay, you're still just trying to come up with ideas at this point. If you have strong feelings about some of this stuff, we'll go through the communication format, and you can express yourselves that way, or you can do it for homework. And I'm going to throw in another idea. Social support is very important for you to feel better, Annette. I know you're fairly new to the area and don't know many people yet. How well do you know your neighbors?

ANNETTE: They're just a bunch of middle-aged women. No one's my age.

PRACTITIONER: I understand that these women are older than you and that might feel a little uncomfortable, but what are they like? What do you know about them?

ANNETTE: I don't know them at all, but they don't look very friendly. They hardly ever say "hi" or anything when I drive by. One way I'd like to meet people is by going to church together. We've talked about this. Maybe we could even get involved in some activities with the church.

ROB: Annette, if you want to do stuff with a church, I'd say, "more power to you," but on Sunday mornings, you know I just like to relax, read the paper, and watch football.

PRACTITIONER: Remember, no criticizing ideas at this point, just brainstorming. Another suggestion on my part: Annette, you said you have an English degree. Does that mean you like reading?

ANNETTE: Yeah, but nothing too highbrow. Mysteries, bestsellers, romances—stuff like that.

PRACTITIONER: I was just thinking—a book group. There's a lot of them around now.

ANNETTE: I hadn't thought of that, but that's something I'd like to do as a couple.

PRACTITIONER: Okay, I'm going to write it down then.

Evaluating Alternatives

The third stage of the problem-solving process involves evaluating the alternatives. First, the couple marks out patently impossible items or ones irrelevant to the problem (Wheeler et al., 2001). However, both partners have to be in agreement before an item is crossed out. Then each viable alternative is discussed as to its advantages and disadvantages. In order to give a sense of this stage, this part of the problem-solving process will be illustrated with only one of the options: the possibility of Annette waitressing (see table 9.2).

Choosing and Implementing an Alternative

After the couple has been led through each of the viable alternatives, they select the one that emphasizes mutual satisfaction and maximizes benefits over costs (Beach et al., 1990). They also develop a plan for how the option will be implemented, along with a time frame. Annette committed to the task of calling for information from the university on some educational options, namely, attending business school or earning a teaching certificate. The couple agreed that driving one hour each way if classes were twice a week would be difficult but tolerable.

Evaluating the Implemented Option

During the following session, the practitioner followed up on how well the implementation of the choice had proceeded. Since individuals with depression tend to see situations in black-and-white terms, exploration of "failures" must be examined more closely for the elements that went well in addition to those still needing work (Beach et al., 1990).

When the couple returned for their next session, Annette said she had not made phone calls to the university. Rob expressed frustration that she had not done this and yet continued to complain about having nothing to do and feeling depressed. Annette said that, while she did not have the energy, she would force herself to do it. After all, if she

Table 9.2

**Illustration of the Process of Evaluating
Alternatives with the Spears Couple**

Advantages	Disadvantages
Annette: It would get me out of the house and would give me a chance to meet people my own age.	Annette: Working dinner shifts, you make more money, but that's when Rob comes home. Although sometimes I wonder why I should be at home in the evenings when all he wants to do is watch TV.
Rob: Maybe Annette would be happier if she had something to do, even if it is only waitressing.	Rob: We don't need her to be waitressing, for God's sake, when I earn a professional salary.
	Annette: Waitressing was fine as a transition after graduating from college, but now it's time for me to figure out what I really want to do.
	Rob: You're very attractive, Annette, and I wouldn't want you meeting somebody else who you think is more exciting than me.
	Rob: What would they think at my firm if they learned my wife was waitressing?

did not want to be a housewife, she needed to explore her career options. However, she said the more she thought about calling, the more distasteful the idea of further schooling became. She concluded that it just might be better if she looked for a job in the classifieds since she was not sure if she wanted to commit to a graduate program. Rob was a bit disgusted with this change of plan. "You keep trying this and then trying that, thinking of this, thinking of that, but you don't do anything. You just need to commit to one thing and then stick to it." The practitioner reminded him about the communication skills, so Rob constructed an "I" message: "I feel frustrated when I know you are feeling bad, and you don't take steps, like making some phone calls, that might make you feel better."

Annette reflected back his concern and then said, "I feel hurt when you get mad at me for not doing more. I feel so bad, and you don't understand what it's like. You picked out a career when you were 19 and just stuck to it. I've never known what I want to do. How do you think I ended up waitressing?"

After Rob was able to listen reflectively, the practitioner congratulated them on the use of these skills and then complimented Annette for finding out from this assignment what she did not want to do, at least at this stage of her life. In this way, noncompletion of the homework was reframed as a learning experience for Annette (Beach et al., 1990). The practitioner then spent some time helping Annette formulate a task she could commit to for the next week. Annette eventually agreed to find one job in the classifieds for which she had sufficient interest and to submit an application.

The practitioner also recommended a "5-minute plan" for managing procrastination since this seemed to represent a barrier to task completion. This plan entails asking clients to take action toward any part of the activity on which they are procrastinating for just 5 minutes. They can then give themselves permission to stop the activity; however, most people find that once they have started, it is easier to continue (Beach et al., 1990).

Ending Work of Stage 2

Annette called and said she could not make the following session because of her work schedule. She called the practitioner a couple of days later and said that the previous week she had seen advertisements in the paper for restaurants downtown. She had called the telephone numbers and had been invited down for a couple of job interviews. She said she did not tell Rob what she had done, because he had started coming home late in the evenings again, tired and impatient with her. She then began a lunch shift waitressing at an upscale restaurant downtown. She said she had met another young woman, and they had gone window shopping afterward. She had returned to suburbia feeling a little more cheered by the outing. When she told Rob what she had done, he was angry about her making this choice without his approval. Annette said, "I've got to do something while you go off to work every day and until I decide what type of career I really want."

With a few of the other young women from work, Annette went to a comedy club and out to dinner a couple of weeks after she had started working at the restaurant. When Rob came home from work, he was shocked that she was not there (even though she had told him she had plans that evening); indeed, she did not come home until he had gone to bed. She then decided after a few more weeks that the money at lunchtimes was not enough. A spot had opened up during the dinner shift, and she decided that she preferred "not waiting around for Rob at night," and took the opening. Meanwhile, she was putting the money away into her own bank account "in case she needed to leave."

Although the practitioner had not encouraged Annette to resume waitressing as it could potentially be a further source of argument between the spouses, it did have the result of pulling Rob back into the relationship. The couple began to attend couples counseling again. Rob started complimenting Annette more often, especially now that she seemed to have more energy and was more fun to be around. He wanted to spend time with her on the weekends, as well—going out to eat and taking walks. He found he was more willing to listen to her, but Annette found that she did not need him to as much since she now had a couple of other people she could call.

Annette's waitressing continued to be a bone of contention for Rob, but Annette was unwilling to stop until she thought the relationship was strong enough to support a change in her schedule. When both partners had attended and participated in counseling for some more sessions, Annette eventually found work through one of her restaurant customers at a travel agency with daytime hours.

Stage 3

The ending stage of therapy involves slowly fading out the role of the practitioner so she is less involved in directing the activity of the session. Gains are highlighted, and potential trouble spots are identified. For example, the practitioner asked the Spears couple, "If I were to call you up in a year and things were not going well between you, what would have happened?" Rob said he would have let his work take over his life, and begun taking Annette for granted. Annette said she would have stopped exercising and socializing, expecting Rob to be everything for her. Asked in this way, clients can usually say what it is they would have done to let the relationship deteriorate again. The couple can be directed to use their problem-solving skills to examine how best to avoid these probable pitfalls. The focus at this stage should be on how clients can identify problems early, before they are entrenched and hopelessness has set in.

The practitioner reinforces the skills the couple has developed to manage depressive moods or relationship conflicts as they emerge. Booster sessions can also be scheduled so couples are reassured that they can fall back on the practitioner if they are unable to extricate themselves from old patterns. Two booster sessions were scheduled for the Spears couple 2 months apart, but the couple canceled each time and said they were doing fine. Six months after that, the practitioner received a phone call from Annette. She was pregnant, and they were both excitedly awaiting the birth of their first child.

10 Multiple-Family Psychoeducational Group for the Parents of Persons with Schizophrenia

JOSEPH WALSH

◼ Presenting Problems

The Family Education and Support Group of Springfield Counseling Center is beginning a new 9-week course. The group, offered three times per year by a staff clinical practitioner, is open to all adult family members of agency clients who have schizophrenia. Twelve people are joining the group this week, and five of them, representing three families, are described below.

Linda Rudawski, 50, is the married mother of one daughter, Anne, age 25. Mrs. Rudawski, a Caucasian nurse, has been dealing with her daughter's disorganized schizophrenia for the past 10 years. Anne has been in and out of hospitals and mental health centers, receiving a variety of medications and therapies with little evident progress. Anne is chronically psychotic, expressing bizarre delusions and engaging in conversations filled with loose associations. She lives at home most of the time and is almost entirely dependent on her parents. Anne moves in for short periods with female friends or boyfriends who are either ill themselves or want to take advantage of her, sexually or financially. Mrs. Rudawski is exasperated. What can she do to help her daughter, find relief for herself, and save her marriage? Her husband, Guy, 51, has coped with the situation over the years by withdrawing. He will not attend the support group because he does not believe it will be helpful. (See figure 10.1 for a genogram of this family.)

Chuck and Kendra Fields are an African American couple in their late 30s. Kevin, their older son, is 19 and was diagnosed with undifferentiated schizophrenia, featuring grandiose delusions, less than 1 year ago. Kevin spent 3 months in a hospital before stabilizing and must take high doses of medicine to maintain a calm demeanor and eliminate his auditory hallucinations. Since leaving the hospital, Kevin has been abusing alcohol but has hidden the extent of his drinking from his parents. Mr. and Mrs. Fields are not concerned about Kevin's drinking because they see alcohol as a relatively harmless substance when used in moderation. Kevin now lives in a supervised apartment and works part time as a theater usher. His parents want him to go to college because he was a bright high school student and received a scholarship for his planned engineering studies. They expect Kevin to completely recover from his illness. They are concerned, however, about Kevin's inability to concentrate on any task for very long. He now can't solve even simple math problems. (See figure 10.2 for a genogram of this family.)

Nancy and Tom Nangle are Caucasian and in their late 60s. Their son Adam is 45 and has had paranoid schizophrenia since his 20s. The

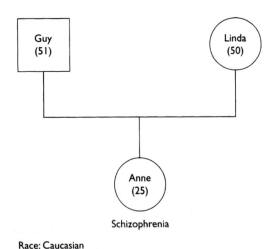

Schizophrenia

Race: Caucasian

Figure 10.1. Psychoeducation Case Study #1: Rudawski Family

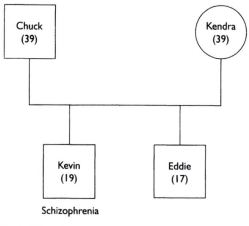

Schizophrenia

Race: African American

Figure 10.2. Psychoeducation Case Study #2: Fields Family

Nangles have learned much about the disorder over the years but still maintain hope that Adam will recover. Mrs. Nangle had recurrent major depression for many years and recovered in midlife. Adam lives in an apartment, which is paid for by his parents, where he tends to isolate. The Nangles are upset with their other three children for not making more of an effort to include Adam in their lives. Adam has been cruel to his siblings at times when agitated or delusional, and his behavior is generally erratic. The Nangles believe that if their other children knew more about schizophrenia they would be more empathic toward Adam. They want help in learning how to reach their children. (See figure 10.3 for a genogram of this family.)

This chapter will proceed with a brief overview of multiple-family psychoeducational group interventions and their rationale for use with the family members of persons who have schizophrenia, along with a review of the empirical studies in this area. This will be followed by an application of the intervention to the parents described above, who participated in the same group, along with other parents. Three sessions will be described with commentary on how the multiple-family group intervention was enacted. The chapter will conclude with a brief discussion of the other group sessions.

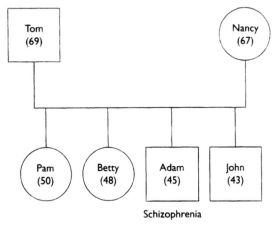

Schizophrenia

Race: Caucasian

Figure 10.3. Psychoeducation Case Study #3: Nangle Family

▆▆▆▆ Overview of Multiple-Family Groups

Clinical practitioners conduct multiple-family groups (MFGs) for the purposes of education and providing support to members. Common group topics include theories of schizophrenia, its course, the positive and adverse effects of medications, the relationship between stress and symptoms, available resources for persons with schizophrenia and their families, the nature of professional interventions, managing family emotional responses to the illness, and mobilizing strengths for improved family functioning (McFarlane, 2000). The group process is intended to help families experience less burden and stress, reduce their sense of stigma, assist each other with parenting, and normalize their communications.

While similar in general purpose, MFGs may take on a variety of formats related to size, duration, session length, content, and range of membership (such as nuclear families, extended families, and siblings) (McFarlane, 2000). Groups may be open or closed. Open groups attract a broad membership and can provide immediate support to members but also are less stable, require more time for trust to develop, and foster less personal disclosure. Closed groups require a longer-term commitment from members but are more stable, encourage a deeper exploration of relevant issues, and tend to be more cohesive. Multiple family groups should always serve as only one part of a comprehensive intervention plan. The person with schizophrenia and perhaps his family members should also participate in counseling, medication, and rehabilitation programs to maximize positive outcomes.

Change occurs in multiple-family groups as members help each other to alter their patterns of family interaction; increase their responsiveness to one another; reduce their social isolation, anxiety, and overinvolvement with the client member; positively reframe perspectives on their problem situations; and build new, healthy relationships inside and outside the family (Laqueur, 1976). Family members learn by analogy, indirect interpretation, modeling, identification, trial and error, and gaining insight into the subtleties of their communication styles. An underlying assumption is that systemic and individual growth is enhanced when outsiders other than professionals are included in family intervention. The presence of the other members represents the larger society in which new support systems can develop. (See box 10.1 for the key assumptions of the psychoeducational model and for additional resources.)

Box 10.1

Key Assumptions of the Psychoeducational Model and Additional Resources

Key Assumptions

- Rather than being seen as a cause of schizophrenia, the family is viewed as a potential resource for continued remission of the individual with schizophrenia.
- Education about schizophrenia, treatment strategies, and coping skills for the family members are provided to reduce *expressed emotion* (hostility, criticism, and overinvolvement), which has been associated with higher relapse rates in the individual with schizophrenia.

Additional Resources

C. M. Anderson, D. J. Reiss, & G. E. Hogarty. (1986). *Schizophrenia and the family: A practitioner's guide to psychoeducation and management.* New York: Guilford.

I. Falloon, J. Boyd, & C. McGill. (1984). *Family care of schizophrenia.* New York: Guilford.

■ Empirical Evidence of Effectiveness

Corcoran and Phillips (2000) conducted an extensive literature review that focused on outcomes for family members *and* individual clients in both multiple-family and single-family interventions (SFIs). Both types of family intervention produced many positive outcomes for participants. MFGs helped individual clients by reducing the frequency and intensity of symptom relapse, improving medication compliance, and enhancing participation in work-related activities. The groups were helpful to families in knowledge acquisition, reducing family conflict and *expressed emotion* (measures of critical comments, hostility, and emotional overinvolvement), and the adoption of improved coping behaviors. They had a positive impact on family member *self-efficacy*, defined as the ability to understand and cope with mental illness. It was not clear whether MFGs reduced family member subjective distress, burden, depression, or grief. There are five models of single-family intervention, which may focus on psychoeducation, behavior therapy, systemic therapy, interactional therapy, or solution-focused therapy. These are useful for individual clients in reducing rates of symptom relapse and improving medication compliance, social functioning, and adjustment. For families, they help to increase self-efficacy and the quality of family interactions, but results are mixed with regard to subjective distress, burden, depression, and received social support.

The authors concluded that, while both types of intervention are effective, MFGs are superior to SFIs in their provision of substantial support to members. Families identify support as a valuable outcome. The social supports of MFGs are artificial in the sense of being provided by new peers in a formal setting, but they are real for the duration of the group and possibly beyond. SFIs need to rely on the family securing support outside the treatment setting. MFGs are also cost-effective compared to individual family interventions.

Other, more recent reviews support the effectiveness of the modality. Bustillo, Lauriello, Horan, and Keith (2001) reviewed the randomized control literature on psychosocial treatments for schizophrenia since 1996. They concluded that family interventions combined with community-based treatment prevent client relapses into psychosis and rehospitalizations. The interventions did not show consistent impact on outcomes related to other client symptoms, social functioning, and employment. Pitschel-Walz, Leucht, Kissling, and Engel (2001) conducted a meta-analysis of 25 English and German studies conducted between 1977 and 1997 regarding the effects of including relatives in the treatment of persons with schizophrenia. They focused on programs designed to educate families and to help them cope with the client member's illness. The researchers noted a 20% reduction in relapse rates if relatives were included in treatment and stated further that family intervention programs continuing longer than 3 months showed particularly marked effects. Various types of family programs (such as single-family groups, multiple-family groups, mutual support groups, and intensive family management programs) yielded similar results.

Other recent experimental studies lend support to the effectiveness of the MFG modality. Mueser et al. (2001) compared two family intervention programs on measures of client social functioning, relatives' attitudes, and family burden. One program featured monthly support groups for 2 years, and the other included 1 year of behavioral family therapy with the support groups. The social functioning of clients in both groups improved, and there were no significant differences between them. The authors concluded that behavioral family therapy and MFG participation together improved family atmosphere. Tomaras et al. (2000) conducted an experiment to examine whether MFG intervention (13 sessions) combined with individual psychosocial treatment (featuring vocational and social skills training) was more effective than individual treatment alone in improving the clinical and social prognosis of 40 clients with schizophrenia from families with high levels of expressed emotion (EE). Measures were collected after 1 year of intervention and 2 years of follow-up. Results indicated a significant reduction in symptom relapse rates, but not in hospitalizations, for the experimental group. Shimodera et al. (2000) studied the relative benefits of SFIs following MFG sessions compared with MFG sessions alone in a randomized controlled study of 30 clients with schizophrenia who had at least one family member with high EE. After 9 months, there were no significant differences in symptom relapse rates. For clients living with a family high in emotional overinvolvement, however, relapse risks were lower in the experimental group.

Relatively little is known about the effectiveness of MFGs with first-episode psychosis and other subgroups of persons with schizophrenia (Fadden, 1998). For example, Linszen, Dingemans, Scholte, Lenior, and Goldstein (1998) did not discern additional benefits of combining an MFG program with individual intervention for families whose relatives with schizophrenia were hospitalized with an initial episode. They did find, perhaps surprisingly, that clients from low-EE families in the combination group had higher relapse rates than clients with families in individual treatment alone. The authors concluded that intervention needs to be tailored to family type.

Despite their demonstrated effectiveness, interventions with the family members of persons with schizophrenia and other serious mental illnesses are far from routine in hospitals and agencies. Data from the Schizophrenia Patient Outcomes Research team, for example, were examined to determine the extent to which families of adults with the illness receive services and whether training staff in the provision of these services increased their availability (Dixon et al., 1999). In a sample of 15,425 persons with schizophrenia, only 530 (3%) reported family contact. In four agencies where staff received didactic training on family intervention, there were no changes in the amount of family contact after 1 year.

Other small-scale studies support this finding. Dixon, Luckstead, Stewart, and Delahanty (2000) surveyed 36 therapists at an urban community mental health center about contacts with the family members of 214 clients with serious mental illness. Therapists reported at least one contact during the previous year with a family member for 61% of the clients. These contacts were typically by phone, however, and took place during a crisis. These results suggest that informal services to families are common and helpful but fall short of best practice standards. Fadden (1997) surveyed 86 behavioral family therapists in England and found that 70% had used the intervention, but the mean number of families seen was only 1.7. She found that obstacles to family intervention included the type of agency (community versus inpatient) and the number of therapists with family training in the setting. Factors related to nonadherence to this prescribed intervention among 87 persons with schizophrenia in one area of Spain included the client member's being older, having a higher number of previous hospital admissions, living in a small household, and having relatives with little knowledge about mental illness at the time of initial admission (Montero, Ascencio, Ruiz, & Hernandez, 1999). Goldstein (1996) summarized barriers to family intervention in the United States as the lack of an infrastructure for training professionals, the absence of funding mechanisms for incorporating these programs into the mental health system, and a lack of agreement on the most cost-effective models (such as single-versus multiple-family interventions and whether or not clients are included). The good news is that multiple-family group interventions are consistently shown to be effective for participants, so ongoing research is likely to promote their implementation.

◼ A Multiple-Family Group Application

The setting of the Family Education and Support Group is the Springfield Counseling Center's meeting room. It is located in an annex behind the main building, so participants do not need to enter the agency to get there. The 12 participants are seated comfortably around a large table. A chalkboard stands at the front of the room, which the leader occasionally uses during formal presentations. He will be directing a structured 9-week program (Walsh, 2000) in which presentations are interspersed with general discussions as follows:

Week #1: Orientation and Introductions
Week #2: Community Resources
Week #3: Presentation on Diagnosis
Week #4: Group Discussion of the Previous Week's Presentation
Week #5: Presentation on Psychotropic Medication
Week #6: Group Discussion of the Previous Week's Presentation
Week #7: Professional Roles and Intervention Strategies
Week #8: Group Discussion or Presentation
Week #9: Termination

The five goals of the program are

- for professionals and the families of persons with serious mental illness to determine together what may be realistically achieved in the social adjustment of impaired relatives;
- to educate families about current theories of those disorders that result in mental illness, including causes, course, degree of impairment, interventions, and prognosis;
- to educate families about the purposes and actions of the various medications used in the treatment of mental illness;
- for family members to act as an ongoing mutual support system in the day-to-day management of ill relatives, with special emphasis on reducing and controlling behaviors disruptive to the family; and

- to inform families of the various agencies locally available to provide services to clients and families, including vocational services, welfare agencies, housing providers, clubhouses, drop-in centers, and advocacy organizations.

Included below are excerpts from 3 sessions over the course of the 9 weeks, each of which tended to focus on a different family.

▆▆▆▆ Session I

The leader's task during the first group session is to help members interact and share concerns with each other so that a process of mutual education and support can begin. Most participants are reluctant to talk at first because they are with strangers and have little prior experience discussing mental illness in their family with an uncritical audience. Recognizing this fact, the leader is very active in the first few sessions, the first one in particular, modeling an empathy that he hopes others will follow. This transcript begins after the leader has taken a seat among the 12 members and oriented them to the group's purpose and format. He has placed fruit, cake, coffee, tea, and soft drinks on the table as snacks for the members, since these are early evening meetings. He hopes that the snacks will also add an element of informality to the setting.

This session's focus is on Chuck and Kendra Fields, who are beginning, this evening, to consider that their son's schizophrenia may be a more debilitating condition than they have assumed. As upsetting as this is, they acquire some ideas for maximizing his chances for a positive outcome. The leader also begins educating the group members about the nature of schizophrenia, even though this topic is formally scheduled for the third week. The leader must be flexible enough to address significant topics as they arise. Notice the "everyday" language he uses in talking about schizophrenia. Also, there is a theme evident in all three vignettes of the leader impressing the importance of members attending to their own well-being.

LEADER: At this time I'd like us to go around the room, not in any particular order, and introduce ourselves. Please add why you are here. Beyond that, you can say as much or as little as you wish about your family situation.

KENDRA [after several seconds of uncomfortable silence]: Well, my husband, Chuck, and I are here to learn how to help our son get back into the mainstream. He has schizophrenia. Last year was a nightmare! He went away to college and out of the blue we started getting phone calls from him about conspiracies. The professors were out to kill him. Then he claimed to have found the cure for lung cancer, a crazy idea. He was out all night and missing classes and was seen talking to himself. We were panicking, and then his dormitory manager called us one day to come and get him. He was in the hospital here for over a month, and he still wasn't coming around very well, settling down. We worried that he'd never get over his psychotic break. Thank God, he is doing better. He's still home, but he's working on getting back to college.

LINDA [matter of factly]: Is he taking medicine?

CHUCK: Yes. He takes one called, I think, Risperdal.

LINDA: And he's going back to college soon?

KENDRA: Well, he's been kind of lazy about that, but we think he should begin making plans to go back. He's always needed to be pushed to do things.

TOM [sounding suspicious]: Are you sure he has schizophrenia?

KENDRA [unsure of herself]: Well, yes. That's what the doctors have said all along. Why?

TOM: Well, I'm not sure he should be going back to college this soon if he has schizophrenia, if that's what he has. Are you sure he's up to it?

CHUCK [slightly perturbed]: He's a smart kid. And they've got his illness under control now. He seems to be in pretty good shape. He's still a little slow in his thinking, like he's tired or sedated. But he's doing better every day. And he wants to get out of the house.

LINDA [sympathetically]: It's great if he's ready to get out of the house. I get upset with my daughter because she usually wants to stay home, in her room. But I also know that life is tougher for her when she's away than when she's with my husband and me. I hope your son is ready for the stress of college. I'd be careful about that.

[The leader breaks in, recognizing an important point to be made to the group.]

LEADER: Let's remember that Kevin hasn't had schizophrenia for long. I've met him, and the diagnosis seems pretty accurate, but every client's response to the illness is different. Some people become stable and stay that way. Others need more support, and all people with schizophrenia should stay in regular contact with professionals. Chuck, have the doctors talked with you about their expectations for Kevin?

CHUCK: They've talked about keeping him on the medicine, and us giving him time to adjust, and us staying in touch with the therapist. It does bother me, though, that they talk about him like he's an invalid.

NANCY [smiling]: They always do that, don't they? They never seem to have much faith in recovery. Of course our son never really has recovered.

KENDRA [curious]: How long has he been ill?

NANCY: Twenty years.

KENDRA [shocked]: Really?

TOM: Oh sure. That's the way schizophrenia works. You never really get over it. Well, I mean, our son never has. Maybe yours will. But our son has never gotten very good care from the professionals. The thing they emphasize to us most is not making things worse for Adam, as if that's what we tend to do. And the medications weren't as good when he first got sick. They didn't have as many rehabilitation programs, either.

LEADER [interjecting]: I want to emphasize again that each case is different. I guess we don't know for sure how Kevin will do when he leaves home again. Hopefully, he will do well and succeed in school. You might consider enrolling Kevin for a single course at first, to see how he does.

LINDA [getting back to Tom's comment and laughing cynically]: Well, just because they have more programs now doesn't mean that they're very good. I really don't think half the professionals know what they're doing. They always get your hopes up about the next new program, and then it doesn't seem that helpful. Anne has been in job-training programs. Once they recommended that she take a job pasting labels on soup cans. Great job, huh?

CHUCK: Well, we could be wrong, but Kevin may not need a lot of special programs. He'll probably go back to college from home. We want to give him about 6 months to recuperate.

LINDA [emotionally]: Look, I don't want to discourage you. I've been sitting here trying to decide whether to say this. My daughter has been sick for 10 years. She's had a few stable periods, but not many. Maybe your son will be different. But Anne is still at home! You'd better find out what services are there for you in case you need any! I've heard promises from this nurse or that doctor over the years that some medication was going to make Anne better, or some program was going to help her be able to live alone. Nothing has worked! I'm sorry, but you should at least prepare yourselves for some more hard times with your son's illness. If it really is schizophrenia! Because maybe they don't know for sure. There's no test to verify the condition.

LEADER [very formally]: Linda is right about the fact that there is no test for schizophrenia. [pause] Before we go on, let me share with you what is known about the disorder.

Schizophrenia is a disorder of *thinking*. Other mental illnesses, like depression or bipolar disorder, are disorders of *mood*. Something happens in the brain of people with schizophrenia to prevent them from being able to process their thoughts. As much as an individual tries, he cannot take an idea and think it through to its conclusion. He may begin to have a normal thought, but it may be blocked, or stop for no apparent reason. There may be thought insertion, meaning that as the person moves from one idea to another, an unrelated idea suddenly appears and disrupts the logical sequence. A thought may abruptly "fly away," out of the person's control, taking him off on an unrelated tangent. The person may be unable to formulate a thought at all, even though he tries, seeming to lack access to necessary brain circuits. Or, irrelevant ideas may appear out of nowhere to occupy the person's thoughts. As you can imagine, all of these things cause the person to become very confused and frightened.

The diagnosis of schizophrenia is based on a number of symptoms—the delusions, hallucinations, odd speech, and odd behavior that you are all familiar with—that last for certain periods of time. The core of schizophrenia, though, is the thought disorder. Something in the brain short-circuits the normal process. The hallucinations and delusions are by-products of that process. A hallucination, for example, is hearing one's own thought but experiencing it as coming from someone else. Delusions often represent the person's effort to make sense out of the confusion that arises with disordered thinking.

We don't know exactly what schizophrenia is, but we do know that bad parenting does not cause it! Schizophrenia does tend to be chronic, however, meaning that it rarely goes away completely. The fact that we don't know what exactly is happening in the brain is one reason that it can't be treated more effectively. But it can often be controlled with medication and the person's participation in support and rehabilitation programs. Some of you have had bad luck with professionals and these programs, and you are disappointed with the course of the illness in your children. But I would recommend that you at least have regular involvement with a clinical practitioner as well as the doctor. That person's job is to know about all of the resources in this community for people with schizophrenia. And their families, too, because there are some advocacy organizations that you might decide to participate in.

CHUCK [seeming alarmed]: But I don't think Kevin is going to need any of this stuff. He's going to go back to college. Are you suggesting that he's never going to be able to get back to normal?

NANCY: No, we aren't saying that. We're saying that you need to be prepared, to keep your options open, in case things don't go as planned for your son. It seems that Linda's daughter has not done well, and that's too bad. Our son has never gotten back to his old self, either. But Tom and I have known some other families whose children recovered nicely. It's like the leader says, you just can't be sure until time passes. But if your son Kevin has schizophrenia, which I guess he does, you need to understand that it is serious. It may not go away. But even if it doesn't, he can be close to normal. If he goes to college, he may not be quite as good a student as he once was.

LINDA: And you have to think about how to take care of yourself.

LEADER: That's important, Linda. Say more about that.

LINDA: Well, I never took care of myself. I was too busy being upset with my daughter and my husband about the fact that nothing was going well. Everybody was treating me like I should be able to make it all better. They didn't say so, exactly, but they acted like it. My husband acted like that, too. So I felt guilty. My daughter, husband, and I were all miserable! It didn't seem that anyone was on our side. And when I tried to act like a parent, and Anne still didn't improve, I decided that they were right. At least they've stopped blaming parents as much in the past few years about this mental illness stuff.

TOM: So where is your husband?

LINDA [sadly]: At home. He's given up. He can't deal with it any more. He tries to ignore it and keeps to himself.

KENDRA [suddenly tearful]: Do you get along? Are you close?

LINDA: I don't know. Not really. Well, it's not too bad. We get along if we avoid certain topics. But our daughter is right there with us— she's a big topic for us to have to avoid! I don't know. Maybe our relationship would have become like this regardless of our daughter. He works, he's a good man.

NANCY: But don't you think the schizophrenia brought all this on? I mean, for long periods, it is all that Tom and I talk about. And it's all so unpleasant. It really has ruined our lives in some ways. It makes you feel lonely. Nobody in your neighborhood understands.

CHUCK [flustered]: I . . . think we'll be all right. We are now, and it's been a year.

KENDRA: I guess we need to be careful. Our families have been supportive so far.

LINDA: Just don't let schizophrenia and your son be the only things you relate around.

CHUCK: Yes. Right.

LEADER [attempting to affirm the families' experiences with references to the literature]: The research does show that schizophrenia is hard on all family members [Karp, 2001; Lefley, 1996]. That can't be avoided no matter no matter how hard you try. It tends to be a drain on your money and time. Again, Kendra and Chuck, we are only speculating about your family, but the message seems to be that you should be prepared in case Kevin's progress isn't quite as you hope.

The leader was surprised at the depth the group achieved in this first meeting. While this was positive in many ways, he was concerned that the Fieldses might be upset about what they had heard and not come back the following week. He spent the last 10 minutes summarizing the session. He reviewed what the families said that they wanted to get from their participation in the Family Education and Support Group and outlined ways that this could happen. He was careful not to be too encouraging or too discouraging of any of the families in an effort to keep their expectations realistic. He congratulated the Fieldses on how hard they had been working to get Kevin back to college and affirmed that their goals were reasonable but not guaranteed. He also echoed sentiments from others in the group that being aware of services and supports was good as a preventive measure.

■■■■■ Session 4

By this time, the group had met three times. The previous two sessions had featured the leader's presentation of content about community resources for treating mental illness and the process of diagnosing schizophrenia, including theories of its cause. This week's session is intentionally less structured so that members have an opportunity to process and react to what they have been learning. Linda Rudawski's concerns become the focus of this session. She carries much anger about the inability of the mental health professions to provide more effective treatment for her daughter, Anne, and she is quite emotional throughout the meeting.

The practitioner welcomes the group back and reviews the major topics addressed at the previous meeting. Participants had questions about the DSM and the symptoms associated with their family members' diagnoses. They also had questions about related diagnoses, such as schizoaffective and bipolar disorder. The members had tried to sort out the various causes of mental illness, uncomfortable with the psychiatric community's lack of certainty about them. Many members asked questions about prognosis, hoping to be able to determine what changes over time they could expect of their ill relatives. They were discouraged with the limited state of knowledge about all of these issues, but the tone of the conversation was initially lively. The group was becoming cohesive. Even the Fieldses, who were becoming aware by now of the long-term nature of their son's disabilities, had seemed energized by the exchange.

Much of the conversation this evening focuses on issues related to expressed emotion, although it is not labeled as such during the session.

LINDA: But don't you all see? This business of psychiatry is all guesswork. Nobody seems to know where mental illness comes from, or how long it is going to last, or what can be done about it. This is what I've been racking my brain about for 10 years, trying to get some solid answers to what I can do for my daughter! I don't mind so much that they don't know more about treating schizophrenia. Well, I do mind that, but what makes me so mad is that the doctors always get your hopes up, and then you get discouraged all over again. There's always some new drug, or some new diagnostic test, or some new research study that shows patients getting better. But nothing ever changes for Anne. Nothing changes for our family, except that we get more miserable. It drags us all down.

The leader says nothing but waits for the group to respond. He makes a point never to get defensive about mental health professionals. Any professional who leads a family support group must be sensitive to the fact that he (in this case) represents the mental health system to the families. Even if they like the leader, members may take their frustrations out on him, particularly in the early weeks of the group, when relationships are being established. This ventilation process should be encouraged, not discouraged by defensive reactions. Venting negative emotions frees members' energies from being channeled into negative interactions with others, including the client relative (Atwood, 1983). When supported, the full range of members' emotional reactions gradually moves away from what has been lost to what can be gained. Further, members acquire a sense of safety that reduces their own defensiveness. The early stage of criticizing the leader, not directly evident in these vignettes, invariably passes.

CHUCK [tentatively]: I know you're right, Linda. You've been dealing with this longer than we have. But it seems to me that they pretty much do know what schizophrenia is. Maybe it doesn't matter that they don't know where it comes from. But since they know what it is, they can focus on finding medications that help.

LINDA [agitated]: But that's just it! They don't help all that much! They don't do much for Anne! And face it, even when they do help, you have to worry about side effects. Anne used to almost get knocked out by some of them. Other times, she got so stiff, she couldn't even walk. What kind of a way to live is that?

NANCY [calmly]: Linda, our son has had schizophrenia even longer than your daughter. We learned a long time ago not to put that much hope into medications. Sometimes they help, but the person still has to take responsibility for himself. Schizophrenia seems to do something traumatic to the person's confidence. Our son has never been able to get motivated to do much for himself. The more time that goes by, the more afraid he is to take chances. This has been true even when he didn't have so many of the symptoms. Does Anne ever get motivated to do anything? She seems to have more energy than our son.

LINDA: Well, she is different from Adam. Not better, just different. She gets carried away with ideas that she can't follow through on. A lot of her ideas are crazy anyway, like the time she wanted to become a sex therapist. She's not manic, just disorganized, like we talked about last week. She gets motivated, I guess, but not for very long. If she could just keep her attention on something halfway constructive, halfway manageable, that would be good. [sighs] It's hard to be hopeful that it will happen after this long. My point is that the doctors shouldn't keep giving us false hope!

LEADER [who wants to make several points about symptoms and has been waiting for an appropriate moment to intervene]: I think what both of you are talking about are symptoms of schizophrenia. With schizophrenia, people usually think first about the bizarre symptoms, the strange ideas and voices, and the loose talk. But the lack of motivation you referred to, Nancy, is a symptom of the disorder, too. It's called a negative symptom. It's called *negative* because the effect is of something being extracted from the personality. The lack of ambition, the lack of desire to be around people, the passivity. Those behaviors may represent your son's need to limit the stimulation he experiences. Adam may need to limit his activity to protect himself from becoming overwhelmed. I admit that it gets hard to know where the symptoms end and the personality begins, meaning, his loss of confidence. And Linda, you know this, but I want to point out for the rest of the group that Anne's short attention span also is a symptom of her schizophrenia. Perhaps her concentration can't be any better, unless her symptoms remit.

KENDRA: But this creates a lot of problems for us as parents. I mean, our son Kevin was always kind of lazy and always needed to be pushed. Now you're saying that his laziness is a symptom of schizophrenia? I can't really buy that. I don't want to start giving him permission to do nothing because he has schizophrenia.

LEADER: Well, you've hit on a major dilemma there. No, you don't want to support passive behavior that is under your son's control. But some of it may be due to the illness. So how do you decide what is what? I'm not saying that you can never know, only that each family needs to work that out individually. But it might help your own sense of adequacy as a parent to know that the illness does include negative symptoms that are actually more persistent than the dramatic symptoms. Knowing this may help you avoid berating yourselves for not being more effective parents. You are all doing your best, and you don't always get the credit you deserve from other people in your family or from your friends.

NANCY: But I still think that our son—

LEADER [interrupting]: I'm sorry, Nancy. I want you to share your thought with us in just a moment. But I want to summarize one other point first. We seemed to stray from Linda's point about professionals giving false hopes to families. I know that it happens. Professionals want to be effective with their clients, and they sometimes become too excited about a brand-new medication or therapy program. Let's not forget that there are clients who do improve remarkably with each new development. But professionals can become almost delusional themselves about a client's progress, because they need to see progress to feel validated as helpers. And maybe families do something similar—create expectations that can be too high, because you want so badly for your children to do well. I don't want to be discouraging, but families do tend to overlook the negative symptoms and see their ill relative's withdrawal as a personality flaw that should be managed with discipline. And when it doesn't work, you feel inadequate. Well, it may not be your ineffectiveness at all. It may be the symptoms of the disorder.

NANCY: Linda, I forget what I was going to say a minute ago [group laughs], but I think he's right. You'll drive yourself crazy unless you can accept that you can't make Anne better by yourself, and the professionals can't either.

LEADER [jumping in again]: But that's not to say that you shouldn't look for professionals who can be honest with you and spend time with you and treat you with the highest respect.

TOM: If you're unhappy with your present providers, some of us can help you, because we have quite a bit of community experience in this group. [to the leader] I think we should take some time to share information with each other about the agencies and doctors we know and which ones provide good and bad service.

NANCY: And the reasons why we think so.

LEADER: That's a fine idea, Tom. [to the group] Do we want to do that now, or are there other topics we should finish up first?

LINDA [relaxing]: Yes, there is something I want to raise. How do I get my husband to be more interested in our daughter? I wish I didn't have to make decisions about her all by myself. [The question seems to strike a nerve with all of the members, and a period of tense silence ensues.]

KENDRA: Well, we don't know your husband. You said he's a good man, in general. One thing that Chuck and I do is to set aside a little bit of time to talk about Kevin and our other son every day. This is usually in the evening when they are away or in their rooms. We've always talked in the evening like that. One thing we decided a few months ago is not to talk about problems with our kids for more than 15 minutes. After 15 minutes, the conversation isn't productive. So we set this time limit. It helps us not get overwhelmed.

NANCY: That's not bad! I hadn't thought of that. Linda, if your husband feels hopeless and gets upset if he has to dwell on Anne, maybe he'll communicate more with you if he knows it will be brief.

LEADER: I don't know your husband either, Linda. But you obviously care about him, and I'm sure he cares about your daughter. Many people get so sad and frustrated about chronic mental illness that they withdraw. It's usually the men in the household, by the way, who do so. The research shows this [Milliken, 2001]. Men have a harder time dealing with their emotions. Now, that's not an excuse for their withdrawing!

LINDA [becoming tearful]: But some fathers do seem involved. Like Chuck and Tom, you fellows. Why can't Guy be more like you? It would be so much easier . . .

LEADER: It still wouldn't be easy, of course, but you would have more support in the family.

KENDRA: And a better marriage, too.

TOM: What do you think about telling your husband about Linda's suggestion? Ask him if he'll try it out. It's only 15 minutes a day.

CHUCK: I'd suggest making it only 5 minutes a day at first. He'll be more likely to agree, don't you think? And it would be better than what you have now. Five minutes a day about your daughter.

NANCY: At a time that's convenient for him.

KENDRA: Now wait, we don't want to cater too much to this one! [group laughs].

LINDA [again composed]: I'll try. Thank you all. You're good people. I hope Guy will agree to this.

NANCY [loudly, in partial jest]: Tell him the group says he has to! He has no options! [more laughter. The members are relieving their anxiety after the tense conversation].

LEADER: Very good! What I like about this idea is that it is modest. It might help, and it can't hurt.

During the last 20 minutes of this session, the group moved on to the topic of positive and negative experiences with agencies, programs, and treatment providers. The leader prefaced this conversation with some general information about area services.

LEADER: Before you begin sharing your experiences, let me fill you in on what services are available in this county. Since you are all involved with this agency, I know that your children are seeing a physician for medication and have an assigned case manager. Please understand that the case manager, not the physician, is responsible for figuring out what services might help your relatives and arranging for those linkages. Not all services will be available at the same agency. Things can get confusing and frustrating when it seems like your relative is inconveniently being referred to providers all over the county. But these services can be very helpful. Springfield County has several psychosocial centers, places where people with schizophrenia can go every day and learn basic life skills, such as housekeeping, budgeting, and work. These centers have professional staff, but they share a lot of responsibility for program activities with the members. There are also two clubhouses in this county where your relative can go to just relax and have fun with other people who are dealing with mental illness. There are no staff or programs in the clubhouses—they are entirely informal. There are several job-training programs in the area. The state Department of Rehabilitation is the best known of these, but some mental health agencies have their own job-training programs. Housing services are provided by several agencies. The state provides funds for this, and a few mental health agencies have put together their own housing programs. Depending on self-care skills, a person might qualify for a supervised apartment or independent living.

Finally, I would not underestimate the importance of a person with schizophrenia having a good counselor or therapist. Some case managers act as counselors and meet with their clients regularly to help them manage their various life challenges. But other case managers don't see themselves as serving in that role. The importance of counseling is a point on which agency directors may disagree. Some agencies have the philosophy that "doing" is more helpful than "talking" and that if you encourage case managers to be counselors they'll be distracted from providing the concrete services. But I think that anyone with mental illness can benefit from a long-term trusting relationship with a skilled professional. So I would encourage that.

LINDA: But the point remains that some services, or staff, are better than others are, at least in our experiences.

LEADER: I agree! So help each other evaluate the programs you've experienced.

All of the members took notes during this conversation. When the group ended, the members seemed to be in a positive mood, feeling that they had gotten some useful information. The leader was pleased, as he wanted to end each session on an upbeat note. If the members were upset near the end of this or any session, he would take time to summarize the constructive aspects of the meeting.

■■■■ Session 8

Near the end of the previous meeting, the leader had given the participants two options for this session. With only two meetings left, and no specific topic scheduled, members could select a topic for formal presentation or use the time less formally to talk about general concerns. They voted for the latter option almost unanimously. While this indicated that the participants were feeling comfortable with each other, choosing a special presentation would not have been construed as a negative sign regarding the support process. All groups are different, and sometimes participants develop a shared interest in certain topics, for example, legal or housing issues.

The vignette below focuses on two issues. The leader provides education to the families about several medications used to treat schizophrenia. The topic of medications, so central to the experiences of persons with schizophrenia and their families, arises in almost every session. The leader must acquire some expertise in this topic area so that he can competently educate families about matters related to their positive and adverse effects. Please see table 10.1, adapted from Bentley and Walsh (2001).

Also, the Nangles share their concerns about what their son's mental illness has done to the family. In addition to facilitating a discussion in which several members become quite emotional, the leader educates them about common dynamics in families with a relative who has schizophrenia. He differentiates the experiences of parents and siblings. This is intended to help them feel less guilty about troubling family dynamics and more understanding of their other children. Linda starts with a question about her daughter's medication.

LINDA: I'm having trouble again with Anne's doctor. I'd been complaining to him that Anne sleeps most afternoons, so he changed her medicine. He was sure that the drugs were making Anne tired. But now she's restless, and she's not sleeping well. She's not tired, but being restless and fidgety is no better.

LEADER: What is she taking now? I know she was on Clozapine earlier.

LINDA: Yes, she was. She took four hundred milligrams per day. Now she takes Risperidone, 4 milligrams per day.

CHUCK [surprised]: What? She went from four hundred to only 4 milligrams? That can't be right!

LEADER: Remember, Chuck, you can't compare dosages between medications. They're different chemical compounds. Those doses are actually equivalent. When you get home, look again at that sheet I passed out when we had the medication presentation.

LINDA: But you see, this supports the point I've made in the group before. The drugs don't work well enough. You get some relief from symptoms, but the side effects almost cancel out the benefits.

CHUCK [to the leader]: I'm sorry, but I'm still confused about why the drugs are so different.

LEADER: Linda, we'll get back to you in a minute. Let me review this for everyone. Ever since the 1950s, scientists have been trying to

Table 10.1

A Sample of Antipsychotic Medications

Drug	Trade Name	Preparation*	Usual Daily Dosage
Older Medications			
Chlorpromazine	Thorazine	T, C, S, I	300–800 mg
Fluphenazine	Prolixin	T, I	1–20 mg
Haloperidol	Haldol	T, S, I	6–20 mg
Newer Medications			
Clozapine	Clozaril	T	400–600 mg
Risperidone	Risperdal	T	4–6 mg
Olanzapine	Zyprexa	T	10–20 mg
Ziprasidone	Geodon	C	40–160 mg

Common Adverse Effects of Antipsychotic Medications

Akathisia: Restlessness with anxiety or agitation
Anticholinergic Effects: Blurred vision, confusion, constipation, dry skin, delayed urination, perspiration, gastrointestinal discomfort, sexual dysfunction, tachycardia, weight gain
Parkinsonism: Psychomotor slowing, rigidity, gait disturbance, tremor

Medications Used to Treat Extrapyramidal Symptoms (Stiffness)

Benztropine	Cogentin	T	.5–8 mg
Trihexiphenidyl	Artane	T, I	2–20 mg

*T = tablets, C = capsules, S = syrup, I = injectable

find drugs to eliminate the symptoms of schizophrenia. The first drugs were discovered by accident. It wasn't known why they worked, only that they did work for many people. Later, theories were developed about the drugs having effects on certain central nervous system brain chemicals. One chemical, for example, was called dopamine. Researchers began developing drugs that targeted limited areas of the brain and certain chemicals. Each new drug that comes along tries to target just one or two chemicals, perhaps in just one part of the brain. To the extent that it is successful at affecting that one target, the drug helps. But since the drugs aren't precise enough, they also hit other targets, or chemicals, and other parts of the brain. That's what causes the side effects.

As a general rule, Chuck, the drugs that come in higher milligram amounts tend to cause sedation, and the drugs that come in small milligram amounts can cause agitation. That's over-simplifying things, because there are other possible side effects. These are all listed on the handout you got earlier. But we all have unique brain chemistries, too, which is why some people with schizophrenia respond better to one medication than another, and why people experience side effects differently.

CHUCK: So the doctor thought Anne might respond well to the Risperidone, and he just hoped she wouldn't have the agitation and restlessness?

LEADER: That's it! Right, Linda?

LINDA: Yes, but I need, or Anne needs, to decide if she wants to keep taking it.

LEADER: Did you remember that there are additional drugs that can take care of the agitation?

LINDA: I did remember that. But I wasn't sure if it was something we should consider. We thought it might be dangerous to take an extra drug.

NANCY: Oh, you should do it, Linda. Our son took Haloperidol for years. By itself, it made him feel stiff. But he took a drug called Benztropine along with it. It worked well. He didn't have any trouble. I understand that it's common to take the two drugs together.

LEADER: Yes, it is. It seems that this might be worth Anne talking to her doctor about. You have some important observations to share about how it affects her, too, Linda. Perhaps you could join Anne for a discussion with the doctor.

LINDA: I think I will. Thanks, everyone.

CHUCK: I'll be darned. They've got medications to treat the side effects of other medications! [Soon, the group moves on to another issue.]

NANCY: Well, if you don't mind, I have something that I need help with. Tom and I both. You see, our other three children won't spend much time with our son Adam except when we have big family gatherings on holidays. I've mentioned this before. What can we do to get them more involved with Adam? He is their brother!

LEADER: How old are they, Nancy?

TOM: Adam is 45, John is 43, Betty is 48, and Pam is 50. They live nearby. Not here in town but within an hour's drive.

LEADER: Do they have families of their own?

NANCY [more emotionally]: Yes, they all do! John is divorced, but they all have kids. Some of their kids are grown. Adam hardly knows his nieces and nephews. He's never really had time to get to know them.

KENDRA: Did your other kids ever get along with Adam?

TOM [trying to be matter-of-fact, as his wife is becoming upset]: They were never close, but they got along okay while they all lived at home. Pam and Betty are close, but John is more distant, I guess. They see each other now much more than they see Adam. What Nancy means is that it wouldn't hurt them to reach out to their brother more often. He's sick, and he needs them. He doesn't have other people in their lives, besides us, like they do.

LINDA: But you did say that Adam could be irritable and even hostile. How does he behave toward them?

TOM: Not very well. But he's hurting, and he takes it out on them. I think he's probably jealous or angry with them.

NANCY: We tell the other kids that, but they won't listen. Don't you all think they should try harder to be considerate? Chuck, your other son gets along with Kevin since he's had schizophrenia, doesn't he?

CHUCK: Well, yes, but things have changed some. Eddie seems less comfortable since he saw Kevin psychotic in the hospital. They are both at home, so they are obviously around each other a lot. I'm assuming they'll continue to spend time together, but I guess I can't be sure.

NANCY: We try and try to get the children to spend more time with Adam, and they wind up getting angry with us!

LEADER: Nancy, and this is for the whole group, really. I wonder if you know how much the other children are affected when a sibling develops schizophrenia?

LINDA: Well, I don't have other kids, but I suppose they would be affected terribly. Look at what it did to my husband.

LEADER: Yes, it affects everyone in the family, but the other kids have reactions different from what parents experience. I'm talking now about what the research shows [Carlisle, 1984; Greenberg, Kim, & Greenley, 1997; Lefley, 1996]. Brothers and sisters often feel ostracized, or they may intentionally distance themselves from friends and classmates. Forgive me for putting it this way, but it's like everyone in the neighborhood knows that someone crazy is living at the house. It may not be talked about openly. The other kids think there is something wrong with the family, so they tend to stay away from the sibling. At home, brothers and sisters can feel jealous and angry about the attention that the ill sibling gets. This is nobody's fault, of course. We all know that a person with schizophrenia requires a great deal of time and energy. You all do your best to be fair to the other kids, but sometimes they don't see this. I think you can understand that they might get angry about the imbalance in the parents' attention. On top of that, they often feel guilty for being angry, because they know that their brother or sister has a terrible problem, or because the brother got the illness instead of them. They wonder why they were "spared," so to speak. And there's one other thing I want to mention. Siblings might feel like they have to be extra good or at least hide their problems and feelings so that they don't stress out the family any more. The research shows that siblings tend to develop a narrow range of emotional expressiveness. This can make them into tense people. In fact, they sometimes leave the household early, partly to save their parents the trouble of having them around. Of course, their parents want them around, but kids at certain ages have a hard time accepting this.

LINDA [upset]: This is all so unfair! Why do we have to put up with all of this? Why can't we have good family lives?

LEADER: You are absolutely right. It is unfair! You all deserve better for your efforts. But there can also be some positive effects of having a person with schizophrenia in the family [Mannion, 1997; Marsh et al., 1997].

CHUCK [laughing]: Oh really? Do they make it all worthwhile?

LEADER: Well, no. But think about this for a minute. Can anyone share any positive family experiences related to the schizophrenia?

KENDRA: Actually, our other son, Eddie, has a better relationship with all of us since Kevin got sick. He was always the social one of our boys, always away with his friends and not very involved with the family. I'd been worried that we might lose touch with him when he left for college. But he's spending more time with us. I think he's learned that he has an important role in the family, that he has the ability to help us all cope.

LINDA [shaking her head]: I'm sorry, but I don't see anything good at all that's come out of this.

TOM: I can see some good outcomes, as hard as it's been on us. Most of the time we've gotten along well with our son. Counselors have tried to tell us we were too involved, but to hell with that. I used to be a strict father—way too much so. Adam helped me learn to be patient. He helped me get my priorities straight. I'm very pleased that I got diverted from being a workaholic. That's where I was headed.

LEADER [after a pause]: Of course, it is not a good thing to have a child with schizophrenia. But sometimes family members can be brought together by the problem. Siblings can feel good about their caregiving abilities. It can be a maturing experience for them.

The conversation continued for 10 more minutes until the session ended. The leader felt uncomfortable with the tone of the group as it ended. There was more tension than usual among the members in reaction to the sensitive topic. But he heard Chuck Fields joking with the Nangles on his way out, saying, "I need to call my sister more often," trying to lighten the atmosphere.

Summary of the Three Sessions

The above vignettes took place during a series of meetings in which other topics were also covered. What should be apparent from these excerpts is the major role that the clinical practitioner sometimes assumes in the meetings, primarily as a facilitator and information provider. The leader is *most* active during the first few weeks as the group develops cohesion, and he brings a structured teaching agenda for the first hour of the second, third, fifth, and seventh sessions. The leader may, of course, choose to invite an expert presenter to cover some of the topics, for example, medications.

The vignettes also illustrate how the process of support unfolds throughout the program. Each family has unique concerns, and a major purpose of the group is to provide a forum for sharing them. Corcoran and Phillips (2000) noted that MFGs are superior to SFIs in that they offer mutual support, a quality that is important to family functioning. During session 1, one couple was helped to consider that their son's schizophrenia might be more chronic and debilitating than they first assumed. While this fact would be difficult for any parents to face, they were helped to consider this possibility with kindness and empathy, which allowed for the possibility that their son might be capable of successfully returning to college. There was nothing harsh about the input they received, and this enabled them to hear the information without feeling upset. In session 4, Mrs. Rudawski was helped to channel her long-term frustrations with her husband and with her daughter's professional providers into constructive actions. It seemed that she did not have opportunities to share her concerns with other people in her life, and she was helped by her peers to reflect on new options. Likewise, in session 8, the Nangles received new suggestions from the group members about how they could interact with their other children to improve those relationships. They were shown how their high expectations for family harmony might be unrealistic. The other group members seemed surprised that the Nangles were holding on to hopes of their children's reconciliation after so many years and with so little progress. This demonstrates how families with a mentally ill member can develop rigid patterns of problem solving and that input from peers can help them see things differently.

The most important elements in the process were how constructively the practical suggestions were delivered and received. This was an excellent group in that there was a sense of connection among the members featured in these vignettes. Not all groups unfold this way. Some groups contain members who can at times be rude and insensitive or who monopolize the group's time. The leader must be active in those situations to set limits on any behaviors that might disrupt a constructive process and to foster equitable, shared interactions.

The Final Session

The leader must bring all group themes to closure during the final session. In preparing for this meeting, he should review his notes about the group's evolution and identify any topics that may require additional or summary attention. The leader becomes more directive in this session toward the goal of moving the members toward termination. He also schedules a short presentation by a member of a local family advocacy organization to provide information about ongoing support opportunities for interested members.

The practitioner's responsibilities in the final session include facilitating member sharing, introducing the speaker, directing a termination process, and collecting evaluation forms. The meeting begins with the leader encouraging members to address any unfinished business from previous sessions. He asks them if there are any topics from the previous 8 weeks that merit more discussion. Following this, the consumer group representative makes a presentation of about 30 minutes. The guest provides an overview of the organization's mission and activities and highlights ways in which family members may participate. The practitioner could provide basic information about these organizations himself, but a participating representative does a much better job of describing the range of experiences open to members.

The leader of the Family Education and Support Group always selects speakers from one of two organizations that are active in the Springfield area. The local chapters of the national Mental Health Association (MHA) and the national Alliance for the Mentally Ill (AMI) are composed of consumers, families, and friends of people with mental illness. They invite members to assist in developing advocacy, education, and program activities related to the needs of persons with mental illness and their families. Their activities include support groups, public education and advocacy campaigns, and participation in the development of rehabilitation, socialization, and housing services. While affiliated with state and national organizations, the local units have the flexibility to develop programs tailored to the Springfield community. They are different from each other in that the MHA is concerned with broad issues of mental health and illness, while the AMI is more focused on severe mental illnesses, like schizophrenia and bipolar disorder. In the recent past, the local MHA helped a group of consumers organize a Schizophrenics Anonymous self-help group and sponsored a workshop on Understanding and Preventing Youth Violence. The Springfield AMI affiliate held regular monthly membership meetings that featured guest speakers on various topics relevant to serious mental illness and its treatment.

In the second half of the meeting, the practitioner asks members to share their impressions of the overall group experience. A useful strategy for initiating this process is his review of the goals of the course, significant themes that developed, relevant information that was presented, and what members shared with each other. The practitioner then asks members to respond to the following questions:

- What did they learn that was important to them?
- How comfortable did they feel about sharing personal concerns with the group?

- How can they apply their learning to situations outside the group?
- How can they generate support systems for themselves outside the group?
- Is there anything they would like to say to the other members?

Finally, members are asked to complete and return the evaluation forms. The leader reserves 30 minutes of socialization time at the end of the meeting, so the members have ample time to say good-bye to each other and can speak privately with some of their peers.

Conclusion

The above illustration from the Family Education and Support Group, which focused on the concerns of three sets of parents, provides one example of how a multiple-family group intervention might proceed. It should be evident that the manner in which the practitioner leads the group, and the direction that each session takes, is unpredictable. The specific content and process of each session depend on the members' particular concerns, personalities, and experience and knowledge levels and the severity of the ill member's schizophrenia. What should also be evident are the important functions that mutual support and interaction play in the members' processes of learning and problem solving. Members often value input from their peers more than that of the professional, who, in some ways, is an outsider. The practitioner can best prepare for the MFG by organizing a useful sequence of topics and developing expertise about them, perhaps including contributions from several outside presenters. The intervention requires much effort from the practitioner but can produce great rewards as family members benefit from the experience.

PART IV

Older Adulthood

 SOCIAL PROBLEMS

11 Psychoeducation with Caregivers of Older Adults

PATRICIA GLEASON-WYNN

▬▬ Case Presentation

Mrs. Betty Jackson, Caucasian, age 53, was referred to the clinical social worker by a psychiatrist for counseling. She is the primary caregiver for her 75-year-old mother, Mrs. Catherine Lee. Mrs. Lee has been a widow since 1986. Mrs. Lee, who suffers from dementia, probably of the Alzheimer's type, is a patient of the psychiatrist. Mrs. Jackson is an only child. She has two children: a 27-year-old daughter, Kate, who is married with a child of her own, and a 19-year-old son, Mike, who is still living at home while attending a local junior college. Mrs. Jackson has been married for 30 years to Frank Jackson. Mrs. Jackson resigned from her job as an administrative assistant shortly after Mrs. Lee moved in so she could care for her mother. She reports feeling very sad about leaving her job and has not gotten over the loss of responsibility nor the loss of the daily contact with her friends at the workplace.

Mrs. Lee was living independently until 5 months ago, when Mrs. Jackson decided to move her mother in with the Jackson household. After a series of examinations and tests, Mrs. Lee was diagnosed with dementia, possibly Alzheimer's disease. She is also under the care of a geriatrician, who monitors the progression of the disease. Mrs. Jackson was concerned about her mother's safety because Mrs. Lee's confusion was getting progressively worse. Mrs. Lee has wandered outside, getting down to the corner at least two times before Mrs. Jackson realized her mother was gone. She is up all night, out in the kitchen, wandering around the house. Mrs. Jackson states that at times, "I just want to shake her to get her to stop doing these things."

According to Mrs. Jackson, her husband, Frank, was very supportive of Mrs. Lee moving in at the time, but for the past two months, he and his wife have been arguing and getting on each other's nerves. Mrs. Jackson also reports more conflict with her son, who will not help with his grandmother's care. Mrs. Jackson states that she is frequently crying, hardly eating, and has difficulty falling asleep. (See figure 11.1 for the genogram of this family.)

▄▄▄▄ Overview of Aging Demographics and Caregivers

The population in the United States is aging. In 2000, the Administration on Aging reported that 1 in every 8 Americans is 65 years of age or older, nearly 13% of the population. The fastest growing segment of the population is in the 85 years of age and older group. This phenomenon is expected to continue. By the year 2030, an estimated 20% of the U.S. population will be 65 years of age or older (Administration on Aging, 2000). Approximately 31% of noninstitutionalized older persons live alone. A small percentage (4.3%) reside in nursing facilities. The majority (67%) of older persons live in a family setting; about 13% of older persons are living with children, siblings, or other relatives (Administration on Aging, 2000). Family living arrangements usually occur because the older adult is too infirm mentally or physically to live independently.

A National Family Caregiver survey, sponsored by the National Alliance for Caregiving and the American Association of Retired Persons (AARP), documented the prevalence of informal caregiving in the United States (National Alliance for Caregiving & AARP, 1997). The study found that nearly 1 in 4 (23%) U.S. households had been involved in helping care for an individual 50 years old or older at some point during the previous 12 months. The typical caregiver is a married woman in her mid-40s, who provides an average of 18 hours per week

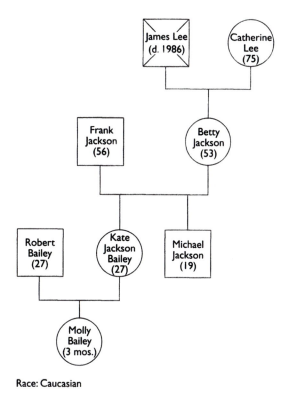

Race: Caucasian

Figure 11.1. Psychoeducation Case Study: Betty Jackson's Family

of caregiving, lives near the care recipient, and works full time. Informal caregivers provide much assistance to older adults who wish to remain at home but who need help with activities of daily living, such as personal care, medication management, transportation, and shopping (Pandya & Coleman, 2000).

The demands of caregiving can affect the emotional, mental and physical well-being of caregivers (Gallagher-Thompson & DeVries, 1994; Pandya & Coleman, 2000). Caring involves such tasks as managing medications, preparing meals, keeping the person safe from wandering, and handling personal care, including bathing, dressing, and toileting. According to the study conducted by the National Alliance for Caregiving and the AARP (1997), more than half of those who provide major care for their parents (and 1 in 4 who provide any care) experience stresses and strains. Caregivers are often torn among career, family, and caregiving. Often, caregivers experience decreased leisure time, decreased time with the family, and, most critically, decreased attention toward their own physical, mental, and emotional needs.

One of the serious disorders affecting older adults and affecting caregivers is dementia. *Dementia* is a deterioration of intellectual function and other cognitive skills, leading to a decline in the ability to perform the activities of daily living (Merck, 2000). In the United States, approximately 4–5 million people are affected (Merck, 2000). The most common kind is dementia of the Alzheimer's type. More than 80% of Alzheimer caregivers report that they frequently experience high levels of stress (Alzheimer's Association, 2000). It is common for caregivers to feel burdened or distressed by the demands of caregiving as well as to experience symptoms of depression and anxiety (Biegel & Schulz, 1999). Most caregivers fail to seek help because they don't recognize their needs, or if they do recognize a need, they don't know where to turn for help (Alzheimer's Association, 2000).

In this chapter, the use of psychoeducation with caregivers of older adults with dementia will be described. An overview of the psychoeducational model will be provided, including the empirical support for use with caregivers.

▰▰▰▰ Use of Psychoeducation with Caregivers

The psychoeducational model first emerged for work with individuals with schizophrenia and their families (Anderson, Reiss, & Hogarty, 1986). Psychoeducational interventions seek to support and empower family members to cope with an ill member. The goal of psychoeducational therapy is to maximize the adaptation of ill or disabled persons and their families (Anderson et al., 1986). (See also chapters 1 and 10 for descriptions of psychoeducational approaches.) Though this model was initially used for the treatment of schizophrenia, Anderson et al. (1986) suggest that psychoeducation is applicable to any chronic illness or problem, such as that presented by caregiving for an elderly relative with dementia.

Psychoeducation uses educational techniques and methods to help caregivers understand the process of the disease (in this case, dementia) and acknowledge and cope with their emotions and reactions. Ongoing education is important for family members who are caring for relatives with dementia. It is an endless job to care for a person with dementia and especially demanding as the person's mental condition deteriorates (Alzheimer's Association, 2000).

Caregivers need planned respite care, information about dementia, services, and benefits, and recognition for their hard work. In addition, they need to recognize and deal with the warning signs of caregiver stress: denial, anger, social withdrawal, anxiety, depression, exhaustion, sleeplessness, irritability, and lack of concentration (Alzheimer's Association, 2000). In combination with education, cognitive-behavioral strategies are used to assist caregivers in coping with the stressful situations encountered in caregiving (Gallagher-Thompson & DeVries, 1994).

Psychoeducation is used with groups of families, with individual families, with the patient present, or in the patient's absence (Anderson et al., 1986). In their review of the research on family treatment with the elderly, Corcoran, Fairchild-Kienlen, and Phillips (2000) found that interventions tended to be individual in format, structured, and relatively short term. Length of time for treatment varied from 4 (Schmidt, Bonjean, Widem, Schefft, & Steele, 1988) to 20 sessions (Gallagher-Thompson & Steffen, 1994). (Also see box 11.1 for a brief summary of the psychoeducational framework and additional resources for the interested reader.)

Psychoeducational interventions have been found to be very effective for affecting the stress of caregivers and improving their coping skills (Gallagher Thompson & DeVries, 1994; Gallagher-Thompson et al., 2000; Haupt, Karger, & Jaenner, 2000; Rivera, 2000). Campbell and Patterson (1995) reported that family psychoeducational interventions are more effective than support groups or respite care for influencing family members' interactions and improving the mental health of the caregivers. Further, Toseland, Rossiter, Peak, and Smith (1990) found that individual interventions produced more positive effects on caregivers' psychological functioning and well-being than group intervention. This finding was also supported by a meta-analytic review of interventions for caregiver distress conducted by Knight, Lutzky, and Macofsky-Urban (1993). Given the efficacy of the psychoeducational approach with individual caregivers, the remainder of the chapter will focus on its application with the Lee/Jackson family.

**Key Assumptions of the Psychoeducational
Framework and Additional Resources**

Key Assumptions

- Originally psychoeducation was developed for families with a member with schizophrenia, but the framework has been expanded to other disorders and illnesses that are biologically based and chronic in nature.
- Education about dementia and other progressive illnesses is supplied to family members who are caring for an older person. Available treatments for the older person and coping strategies for the caregiver are provided.
- Psychoeducation allows for cognitive-behavioral interventions integrated within the model, as a shared assumption is that information and knowledge mediates distress.

Additional Resources

C. M. Anderson, D. J. Reiss, & G. E. Hogarty. (1986). *Schizophrenia and the family: A practitioner's guide to psychoeducation and management.* New York: Guilford.
A. Robinson, B. Spencer, & L. White. (1991). *Understanding difficult behaviors.* Eastern Michigan University, Alzheimer's Care and Training Center.

Application of Theory and Technique

In the psychoeducational model, collaboration exists between the practitioner and the caregiver with a focus on the strengths of the caregiver. In order for the intervention to be effective, the practitioner needs to develop a rapport with the client and establish an atmosphere of support and trust. The practitioner seeks to find out the caregiver's knowledge about the dementia process and what the caregiver perceives as relevant to her situation, and then places this information into a framework that the caregiver can understand without feeling blame (Anderson et al., 1986).

Regardless of the format (individual or group) or length of time, the psychoeducational approach with caregivers of older adults includes the following components (Anderson et al., 1986; Haupt et al., 2000), which will be discussed with the case study:

1. Joining with the family, developing rapport and empathy
2. Providing an explanation of the psychoeducational approach
3. Education on dementia and management of behavioral symptoms

4. Information on caregiver stress and coping strategies
5. Education on depression and cognitive-behavioral strategies
6. Information on community resources for in-home and long-term care including nursing home placement

The application of the psychoeducational intervention to Mrs. Jackson will first involve joining with Mrs. Jackson, recognizing her stress, and helping her cope with it. Education about dementia of the Alzheimer's type follows, which includes a description of the disease, its prevalence, and its progression. Information on caregiver stress, including an explanation of depression and an application of cognitive-behavioral techniques is included. Finally, education on behavior management techniques and accessing the various community resources is provided.

At the start of the first session, Mrs. Jackson looked apprehensive and stated, "I am not sure why I am here. I don't know how you can help me with my mother, but I am willing to give it a try. Her doctor seems to think it will help me."

The practitioner responded, "I am glad that you were able to come in today to talk with me. I know you are caring for your mother in your home. Is that right?" When Mrs. Jackson nodded, the practitioner continued, "Though it can be rewarding to be a caregiver, it can also be very overwhelming at times. Tell me how your life has been over the past 5 months."

As she began talking, Mrs. Jackson appeared to become more comfortable and relaxed in her chair. "You know, I thought I was doing the right thing, having my mother move in with us. She couldn't live alone any more. She was going to burn the house down. She got lost one time coming home from the grocery store—at least one time that I know about. Her neighbors were calling me because she was seen outside at midnight, just walking around her yard, like she was looking for something. She would forget to pay her bills." She paused and looked directly at the practitioner. "I am exhausted! Don't get me wrong, I love my mother, but it is getting to be too much. I promised her I wouldn't put her in a nursing home. I don't know why I can't do it all like I used to. I must be losing it!"

At this point, she became teary-eyed and ceased talking. The practitioner validated Mrs. Jackson's concerns and praised her for her dedication over the past months. The practitioner also sought to clarify the client's emotions: confusion, sadness, guilt, and uncertainty. The practitioner reassured Mrs. Jackson that these feelings are quite usual for caregivers to experience. It was also explained that it is important for caregivers to get help for themselves in the way of support, information, and coping strategies, as well as help for the care receiver. The practitioner commented, "You need to take care of yourself, otherwise there will be two patients at home—you and your mother."

"Now that you mention it, I was wondering if I should have brought my mother today. I thought this might upset her, and I really don't want to do that."

The practitioner assured Mrs. Jackson that the psychoeducational sessions could be conducted without Mrs. Lee being present; especially due to her cognitive impairment, it was not practical. The practitioner suggested that in future sessions over the next 2 to 3 months, Mr. Jackson and the son living at home could be included.

"I am glad that my mother doesn't need to be here with me. I don't think I could tell you how I feel in front of her. Sometimes she just drives me crazy, and I just want to shake her!"

Elder abuse is a growing social and medical problem in the United States (Merck, 2000). Wolf (1998) reports that two caregiver factors were found to predict the risk of abuse: the perceived stress of caring for a mobile but demented older adult and the need to provide social and emotional support for that person. In addition, caregiver depression and living arrangements, specifically an older adult residing with immediate family rather than a spouse, predicted abuse (Paveza et al., 1992).

Because it appeared that Mrs. Jackson was experiencing all of these factors, the practitioner explored for the presence of elder abuse. "Have you ever done that—'shaken' her?"

"No, oh no!" Mrs. Jackson appeared embarrassed when responding to the question. "I just feel like it—like I could shake some sense into her. But I know better, it isn't going to help."

"It is very common for caregivers to become frustrated with the care receiver. When you are frustrated with her or just want to 'shake her,' what do you do?"

"I just throw up my hands, and walk away . . . muttering a prayer to give me strength. Sometimes, though, when I see her later, she is ready to do what needed to be done but didn't want to do before."

The practitioner complimented Mrs. Jackson on this strength—to be able to take a time out when caregiving gets to be too much. Additionally, the practitioner responded, "It sounds like you call on your faith in God to help you get through the rough times."

"Oh, yes. If I didn't have my faith, I don't know how I would handle all of this. When I pray, it gives me a chance to collect my thoughts and remind myself that Mother is not doing this just to bug me."

When Mrs. Jackson was asked about her knowledge of the dementia process and effective behavioral interventions, she replied, "I don't know a whole lot. I know she is going to get worse. I have some pamphlets at home about Alzheimer's disease that Mother's doctor gave me, but I haven't looked at them. I just don't want to think of my mother having Alzheimer's, and I don't want to put her in a nursing home."

"Mrs. Jackson, I have heard you say a couple of times that you do not want to place your mother in a nursing home, and I want you to know that I am not here to convince you to place your mother in a nursing home."

"Oh, what a relief! I figured you would tell me I had to place her in one. Everyone else keeps telling me I should do that."

The practitioner continued, "As we continue to work together, I want to explore and discuss with you the various options, including nursing facilities, that are available in the community to help care for Mrs. Lee. I think it is important to point out to you that, eventually, as the individual requires more intensive care, families often opt for nursing home placement. What else did the doctor suggest?"

Mrs. Jackson stated that the doctor suggested that she contact the local Alzheimer's Association for more information on support groups and services in the community. Though she did call the Alzheimer's Association, Mrs. Jackson had not attended any support groups nor had she had any contact with other caregivers.

The practitioner pointed out to Mrs. Jackson that her willingness to come to the counseling sessions, to talk openly about her feelings, and to care for Mrs. Lee at home were considered strengths; otherwise, it was probable that Mrs. Lee would be institutionalized. Thus, she played an important role as the caregiver in Mrs. Lee's life.

"I feel better talking to you. I have felt very alone. I am not sure that Frank really understands what I am going through. Mother is always nice to him."

Mrs. Jackson was receptive to continuing the counseling, so the practitioner described a tentative plan for intervention using a psychoeducational approach.

"The approach that I have found to be very helpful for caregivers includes giving you some information on dementia of the Alzheimer's type—prevalence, causes, and treatment—and providing information about stress related to caregiving and symptoms related to caregiver stress: depression, anxiety, and how to take care of yourself. I will also discuss with you community resources, including long-term care options. I assure you that many of your questions and concerns will be addressed. How does that sound to you?"

"Sounds like a lot of information. I hope I can keep up."

"I know this probably seems like a great deal of information, and we won't discuss all of it today, but the more you know and understand about the disease process, the more realistic and better prepared you will be to deal with your mother's illness as it develops. I thought we would start with some education on dementia. If you have any questions along the way, just stop me."

██████ Education on Dementia of the Alzheimer's Type

The practitioner proceeded to present information to Mrs. Jackson on dementia of the Alzheimer's type. She informed Mrs. Jackson that 1 in 10 persons over 65 and nearly half of those over 85 have Alzheimer's disease (Alzheimer's Association, 2001). The practitioner explained that Alzheimer's disease is a degenerative brain disease.

"Scientists are not sure what causes Alzheimer's disease, and they continue to explore for probable causes. There is not even a test to determine if someone has Alzheimer's disease. As you know with your mother, the doctor took a thorough medical history and conducted physical, psychological, and neurological exams in order to rule out any other cause for the dementia. The only way to confirm a diagnosis of Alzheimer's disease is after the person has died and an autopsy is performed."

Researchers also know that the rate of progression varies from person to person, beginning gradually, causing a person to forget recent events or familiar tasks, and eventually resulting in confusion, personality and behavior changes, and impaired judgment. The person struggles to find words, finish thoughts, or follow directions. Changes in behavior can include agitation, anxiety, delusions, depression, hallucinations, insomnia, and wandering. Most people with Alzheimer's disease become unable to care for themselves (Alzheimer's Association, 2001).

"I've heard that before, but it's so hard to accept when it is your mother. I don't know how long I can continue to care for her."

"Yes, it is difficult when it happens to someone you love," the practitioner said. "Do you recall what made you take your mother to the doctor to have her evaluated?"

"Well, she was calling me a lot and asking where her keys were, or where her checkbook was. Of course, I hadn't been to visit her in a few days, so I would have no idea. She would get mad and blame me for taking them or hiding them. Then, one day, her neighbor called and told me that she had seen Mother out in the yard at midnight a couple of times, just walking around in the snow without a coat. When I asked Mother about it, she had no idea what I was talking about and said her neighbor was just nosy. But it really alarmed me when I received a call from the electric company stating the electricity to Mother's house was going to be cut off for nonpayment. Something just wasn't right."

"It sounds like she was experiencing some of the common warning signs, such as misplacing items or putting them in inappropriate places and then not recalling how they got there. Another one was showing poor judgment by being outside in the middle of winter without a coat. Other signs include difficulty performing familiar tasks, forgetting simple words or substituting inappropriate words, and being disoriented to time and place. People with Alzheimer's disease can become lost on their own street, not know where they are, or how to get back home. They can experience rapid mood swings for no apparent reason, changes in personality, and loss of initiative" (Alzheimer's Association, 2001).

"Mother is showing a bunch of those symptoms now. I think that's why I get so frustrated. I just don't understand how she can be that way."

The practitioner continued, "Alzheimer's dementia affects people in different ways, making it difficult for medical professionals to predict how the individual's disease will progress. Sometimes, you will hear people refer to the disease by stages—early, middle, and late." The practitioner gave Mrs. Jackson a handout describing the disease by these stages, correlating behaviors and functional deterioration with the various stages (Reisberg, Ferris, Leon & Crook, 1982). (See table 11.1.)

Table 11.1

Deficits Associated with the Early, Middle, and Late Stages of Alzheimer's Disease

Early Stage	Deficits are displayed in the following areas of cognitive and physical functioning: • Subjective complaints of memory deficit • Forgets where a familiar item was placed • Forgets names of familiar people • Continuation of word- and name-finding deficit, which becomes evident to others • Inability to retain much material that was read • Inability to remember names when introduced to new people • Gets lost when traveling to an unfamiliar location • Loses or misplaces an object of value • Decreased performance in demanding employment and social settings Mild to moderate anxiety may accompany symptoms.
Middle Stage	Deficits are displayed in the following areas of cognitive and physical functioning: • Decreased knowledge of current and recent events • Some difficulty remembering personal history, though able to recognize familiar persons and faces; maintains knowledge of own names and generally knows spouse's and children's names • Unable to recall when asked a major relevant aspect of current lives, e.g., an address or telephone number of many years, names of close family members (such as grandchildren) • Some disorientation to time (date, day of week, season) or to place • Decreased ability to travel and to handle finances • Inability to perform complex tasks • May have some difficulty choosing the proper clothing to wear, but requires no assistance with toileting or eating • Withdrawal from challenging situations; can no longer survive without some assistance
Late Stage	Deficits are displayed in the following areas of cognitive and physical functioning: • Forgets the name of the spouse or person upon whom they are dependent • Unaware of all recent events and experiences in their lives • Unaware of their surroundings, the year, the season and so on • Almost always recalls their name • Frequently continues to be able to distinguish familiar from unfamiliar persons in their environment • Requires assistance with activities of daily living, including toileting and feeding • Eventually, becomes incontinent of bowel and bladder • Unable to perform psychomotor skills, e.g., walking, feeding self • At the end, all verbal abilities are lost; frequently there is no speech at all. Personality and emotional changes occur.

"Yes, I remember the doctor telling me that Mother was in the early part of the middle stage. At the time, it didn't mean much to me."

"Do you recall the doctor suggesting any treatment for your mother at that time?"

"No, not that I remember. I don't think Alzheimer's can be cured."

The practitioner nodded. "That's right. Currently, there is no medical treatment available to cure or stop the progression of Alzheimer's disease. However, four FDA-approved drugs—Cognex®, Aricept®, Exelon®, and Reminyl®—may temporarily relieve some symptoms of the disease, such as cognitive loss, agitation, anxiety, unpredictable behavior, disrupted sleeping patterns, and depression. There are also strategies you can use to reduce some of the behavioral symptoms. In your case, you told me your mother wanders at night. Have you mentioned this to her doctor?"

"No, I wasn't sure what he would do."

"I encourage you to call his office and talk to the nurse. Perhaps they can prescribe something to help her sleep, so you can get some sleep."

Mrs. Jackson smiled and said, "That would be great!"

"Are there other behaviors that concern you? Does your mother become anxious or irritated when she is trying to express herself or when you are helping her get ready for the day?"

"Well, she doesn't want me to help her get dressed, but if I don't help, who knows what she would put on, or in what order she would put her clothes on? One time, she came out of her room with her bra over her blouse. I should have cried but I was so tickled, I couldn't help but laugh."

"You know, humor is a strength and is recognized as a great coping strategy. Many caregivers have reported that humor has helped them get through the rough times. In addition to the humor, you have your faith and prayers to help you get through the bad days."

Mrs. Jackson responded thoughtfully, "I never thought of them as coping strategies. I just knew that it helped to laugh, and when that didn't work, then I prayed for strength. I just think though that I need something more to help me. Mother's behavior just gets the best of me some days."

"You're right, there are additional strategies. I thought that in one of our sessions we could discuss some ways you might address and manage the behavioral changes that your mother experiences, if that is okay with you?"

"Yes, that would be helpful. I need to know how to get her to do things, like take a bath, when she doesn't want to. She just gets more agitated with me, and I get more frustrated with her."

"I am going to give you a copy of a book, *The 36-Hour Day* [Mace & Rabins, 1991], which you can take home and look over during the week. This book is a guide to caring for a person with Alzheimer's dementia, and many caregivers think of it as their bible. I think you will find it enlightening and helpful. We can review the information next week."

▄▄▄▄ Dealing with Caregiver Stress

The practitioner moved on to the next educational topic—caregiver stress. "As you know, caring for your mother can be difficult at times, especially with her mood swings and confusion. It is important that you know the symptoms of stress to be able to monitor your own symptoms and know when to ask for help. Some of the symptoms are denial, anger, social withdrawal, anxiety, depression, exhaustion, sleeplessness, irritability, and lack of concentration."

"I have a lot of those symptoms, don't I? What can I do about it?"

"Great question. You have already started by making the decision to come in and talk with me today. I have some other recommendations that caregivers have shared with me, which they have found helpful. Here are a few."

In keeping with the psychoeducational framework, the practitioner gave a handout to Mrs. Jackson on how to deal with the stress she is experiencing as a caregiver. The recommendations included:

1. Talk with family and friends about what you are feeling; don't keep everything inside.
2. Educate yourself: The more you know about the disease and what to expect, the better prepared you will be.
3. Set reasonable expectations: Don't get angry with yourself for failing to be superwoman.
4. Most important, take care of yourself physically: Eat regular, balanced meals and exercise. Use relaxation techniques: meditation, deep breathing, massage, and humor.
5. Avoid destructive ways of coping, such as overeating, alcohol or

drug misuse, and neglecting or taking out your stress on the care receiver.
6. Maintain activities and social contacts that you enjoy. Ask a family member or a friend to give you a break, contact visiting nurses or the Alzheimer's Association to set up respite services. Accept the fact that you need and deserve time for yourself.
7. Don't try to handle it all yourself. Ask other family members and friends to participate in caregiving.
8. Join a support group for caregivers of people with Alzheimer's disease; share experiences and coping strategies with other caregivers.

"How do these recommendations look to you? Can you pick one to work on before we meet next week?"

"I am going to get out and go to the bridge club this week. I haven't been in a while, and I really miss my friends."

"Great. What needs to happen so you will be able to go?"

"I need to make sure that Frank or my son, Mike, will be home to watch Mother. I will call the girls and tell them to count me in this week." As she spoke, she looked as though a burden had been lifted.

The practitioner briefly summarized the content discussed in the session and reminded Mrs. Jackson to review the handouts and book provided. "When we meet next week, let's discuss any questions that came up while you were reading the materials and talk some more about caregiving stress and taking care of your mental health. Also, I recommend that your husband attend the counseling sessions with you. I suggest that you talk with him this week about coming to counseling, and I look forward to hearing how your bridge club outing went."

▮▮▮▮▮ Education About Depression

Major depressive disorder is characterized by a depressed mood or loss of interest or pleasure for at least 2 weeks along with at least four additional symptoms of depression. These symptoms include sleep disturbance, diminished interest or pleasure, appetite changes, feelings of worthlessness or excessive guilt, loss of energy, diminished ability to think or concentrate, psychomotor agitation or retardation, and recurrent thoughts of death or suicidal ideation (American Psychiatric Association, 2000).

It is important that caregivers recognize and deal with the warning signs of caregiver stress. Among these warning signs are the symptoms of depression. To address this concern, the practitioner can combine other theoretical approaches with psychoeducation such as cognitive-behavioral strategies (Gallagher-Thompson & DeVries, 1994).

When applied to depression, the goals of cognitive-behavioral therapy are to alleviate depression and to prevent its reoccurrence by helping the client to identify and test negative cognitions, to develop alternative and more flexible schemas, and to rehearse new cognitive and behavioral responses (Beck, Rush, Shaw, & Emery, 1979). The approach has three components: a didactic aspect, cognitive techniques, and behavioral techniques (Kaplan & Sadock, 1997).

The didactic aspect includes explaining to the client the cognitive triad (thoughts, affect, behavior), the interactions of thinking and feeling, and the relationship to depression. The goal is to help the client identify and change cognitive distortions that maintain the depressive symptoms.

Mrs. Jackson came back 1 week later to continue counseling. She reported that she attended the bridge club as planned, and she enjoyed visiting with her friends. She had also started to read *The 36-Hour Day*. "The book has a lot of information on dementia, which I find helpful. But," Mrs. Jackson paused, and then continued, "I am feeling very stressed today."

"You say you are feeling very stressed today. Can you tell me a little more?" the practitioner asked.

"My son almost didn't make it home from classes in time for me to get here, so I had to rush. But it's more than that. All this week, I have felt terrible."

"What are you experiencing?"

Mrs. Jackson responded, "Any time someone asks me how I am doing, I start crying. I don't feel like eating, and I have lost a few pounds. I have trouble falling asleep because I lay there in bed listening for Mother to get up and begin her nightly rummaging. The thing that worries me the most is that my husband and I seem to be arguing all the time, and I am impatient with my son. I wasn't like this before Mother came to live with us." Mrs. Jackson went on to explain that she had given up a job she enjoyed very much and was good at.

"How long have you been feeling the way you described to me?"

"I have been feeling like this for about 3 months, since shortly after Mother came to live with me and I realized how bad her condition was."

"I have heard you say that you are exhausted, and you have listed a number of symptoms that are indicative of depression—sleep disturbance, loss of interest in previous activities, sadness, lack of energy, loss of appetite and weight loss, and agitation with your husband and son. Do you think you could be depressed?"

"You know, one of the women in my bridge club asked me that this week. I told her I was fine, but I am not too sure, now that you mention it."

The practitioner further explained that depression is an illness that involves the body, mood, and thoughts. "It affects the way you eat and sleep, how you feel about yourself, and the way you think about things. People with a depressive illness cannot just 'pull themselves together' and get better. Without treatment, symptoms can last for weeks, months, or years. Appropriate treatment can help most people who suffer from depression. What have you tried to do to make it better?"

"I haven't done anything really to make it better. I guess I didn't realize how bad it had become. Every once in a while, I would have a glass of wine to help me relax, but that didn't help."

"I know that Mrs. Lee has been in to see Dr. Brown [psychiatrist] recently. Did you mention to him how you were feeling?"

"No, he is Mother's doctor. I didn't want to burden him."

"Would you feel comfortable going to see Dr. Brown yourself? To explore treatment options for depression?"

"I don't know. What will he do for me?"

The practitioner explained that treatment options include the use of antidepressant medication alone, medication combined with psychotherapy, or just psychotherapy. "Some people may do well with psychotherapy alone. Others with moderate to severe depression most often benefit from antidepressants. Most do best with combined treatment: medication to gain relatively quick symptom relief and psychotherapy to learn more effective ways to deal with life's problems, including depression."

The practitioner continued, "We can work on some strategies together while you decide if you want to go to Dr. Brown. How does that sound?" Mrs. Jackson agreed.

The practitioner began to integrate cognitive-behavioral principles and techniques into the psychoeducational framework to address the emotional issues Mrs. Jackson was experiencing.

"I am wondering if some of the depression you are experiencing is related to your thoughts about your caregiving for your mother and how consuming that is for you. Let me explain. There is a school of thought that believes that our moods are created by our thoughts. When we are feeling depressed, our thoughts and the way we see the world are predominantly negative in nature. The negative thoughts that cause this emotional disturbance usually contain distorted conceptions or beliefs about some event or person."

"This is a little confusing."

"Let me give you an example. In the last session you stated, 'I don't know why I can't do it all like I used to.' " Mrs. Jackson nodded with recognition. "Tell me what you meant by that."

"Well, I used to be able to juggle a lot: the housework, my job, running over to Mother's house to check on her after work, making sure my son has what he needs for school and that he gets to work on time, spending time with Frank so he won't feel neglected, teaching Sunday school, and going to the bridge club. Then, when Mother moved in, making sure she was safe. I don't want to let anyone down, but it just keeps piling up. Now I don't feel like doing any of it."

"When you think that you don't want to let anyone down, and it just keeps piling up, how do you feel?"

"I feel terrible, and I am so disappointed in myself. And when I say that, it makes me feel sad."

"So, when you think that everything is piling up and you can't get to it, you feel disappointment and sadness. Does that sound about right?"

Mrs. Jackson nodded her head.

The practitioner continued, "This is an example of what I was explaining to you earlier. The way we think is connected with the way we feel. If you believe you are letting someone down and everything is piling up, you feel terrible. Negative thinking causes negative emotions, such as those related to depression."

"Okay. I think I understand what you are saying."

The second aspect of the cognitive-behavioral approach involves cognitive techniques. The practitioner introduces the cognitive aspects by eliciting automatic thoughts from the client. *Automatic thoughts* are those that come between the external event and the person's emotional reaction to the event. The approach continues with the practitioner exploring and testing cognitive distortions by discussing the validity of the thoughts. The practitioner seeks to generate alternative explanations for the events, to identify maladaptive assumptions, and to test the validity of these assumptions (Beck et al., 1979).

"Let's go a bit further with this technique. It sounds like you are concerned or afraid you will let someone down if you don't do 'it all.' Has anyone ever said anything to you about wanting you to be a superwoman?"

"No, I just think it is expected of me. Maybe that's why I don't ask for help."

"When you see that you're not able to do it all, how do you feel?"

"Like I am a failure."

The practitioner identified the maladaptive assumption for the client. "I hear you saying that, if you can't do it all and you have to ask for help, then you are a failure. Does that sound about right?"

"Yes, but it sounds a little silly when I hear it put that way. No one has ever said I'm doing a bad job. I don't know why I would think that. I've always done good work with things I take on. I just have high expectations of myself, I guess, and I don't think I am living up to them with the care I am providing Mother."

"Is there something you would do differently? What more do you believe that you could be doing for your mother, that you are not doing now?"

Mrs. Jackson paused, deep in thought. "I don't know. I think I am doing what needs to be done. I just wish she didn't have this dementia."

The practitioner continued, "It sounds to me that you are doing all you can for your mother, and no one is criticizing you. As far as her care is concerned, you're not a failure, you are keeping her safe and providing her shelter. You just wish the dementia would go away, and because you can't change that, it makes you feel helpless and sad. Does that sound right?"

"Yes, that's pretty much it."

"Let's go back to the original thought, which was 'you are a failure if you ask for help.' What do you think now?"

Mrs. Jackson smiled and said, "I can see that it's not a sign of failure and that I am not a failure. I just need to stop thinking that it is. Though I'm not sure who will help."

The third part of the cognitive-behavioral approach involves the use of behavioral techniques that help the individual test maladaptive cognitions or inaccurate assumptions and that improve the individual's level of functioning. Techniques include recording the degree of mastery and pleasure associated with an activity, activity scheduling, assertiveness training and role playing, diversion techniques, and cognitive rehearsal. The therapeutic approach chosen is dependent upon the specific needs of the client (Beck et al., 1979).

"Mrs. Jackson, over the past several months you have not been attending your bridge club because you didn't want to leave your mother alone at home, and you didn't want to ask anyone for help. Yet, after attending last week, you found that you really enjoyed the outing and being back with your friends. Is this something you would like to resume?"

"I think so, but I have to ask someone to watch Mother. I don't know if I can do that again."

"What do you mean? Ask for help?"

"Yes."

The practitioner asked Mrs. Jackson to list the people who might be available to help. Mrs. Jackson hesitantly responded by listing her husband, her son, and maybe the neighbor who has been staying with Mrs. Lee so Mrs. Jackson could attend therapy sessions. The practitioner wondered if Mrs. Jackson were receptive to utilizing community resources, such as respite services offered by the Visiting Nurses Association (VNA) or adult day care.

"Mrs. Jackson, what would you think about contacting the VNA and asking for respite help? The respite program allows a caregiver up to 3 hours to leave the home and take a break from caregiving. They provide a professionally trained sitter to stay with the individual at little or no cost."

"I hadn't heard of that program before. I don't know how Mother would handle a stranger." The practitioner gave Mrs. Jackson the local phone number for the VNA, but because Mrs. Jackson was hesitant to leave her mother with a stranger, the practitioner decided to work with Mrs. Jackson on accessing the informal support people she had named. She suggested that they start with a role play so Mrs. Jackson could practice her skills.

Mrs. Jackson laughed, "This sounds like something I did once with my son when he was afraid to talk to his teacher."

The practitioner asked, "Did it work?" Mrs. Jackson nodded yes.

The practitioner asked, "Who do you want to ask for help?"

Mrs. Jackson responded, "Well, my neighbor is already helping me out so I can come here, and I don't want to ask her for more help right now. My son has too much going on. I guess Frank would be the one."

The practitioner assumed the role of Mr. Jackson, and Mrs. Jackson role played herself asking Frank to stay with Mrs. Lee so Mrs. Jackson could attend the bridge club each week. After the completion of the role-playing activity, the practitioner processed with Mrs. Jackson her thoughts and feelings.

Mrs. Jackson responded, "I think I can tell Frank that I need some help with Mother and that I need a break once in a while. I feel more comfortable, but still—" She paused and then said aloud to herself, "No, I am not failing Mother if I ask for help!" Then, to the practitioner, she stated, "I feel a little unsure, but I am going to do it!"

The practitioner complimented Mrs. Jackson on her ability to recognize and stop the negative cognitions that lead to negative emotions and assert a positive thought, which would lead to an enhanced level of functioning. The session concluded by assigning homework for Mrs. Jackson. She was to sit down with Frank and tell him that she needed a break from caregiving and ask for his help so she could attend her bridge club. Mrs. Jackson was also asked to record her feelings and thoughts prior to the conversation and then after its completion. Mrs. Jackson set an appointment to return to see the practitioner in 1 week.

Summary of Subsequent Sessions

Mr. Jackson attended the next session because he had questions about his mother-in-law's condition. He also wanted to know about community resources that could provide care for Mrs. Lee. He was very attentive and concerned about his wife. Throughout the session, he held his wife's hand and smiled at her. He told the practitioner that he had not been aware of the stress his wife was experiencing until she told him and asked for his help so she could go to the bridge club.

Community Resources

The practitioner presented the Jacksons with a list of various resources available in the community, including the Visiting Nurses Association respite program, the Alzheimer's Association education and support groups, the adult day care program at the local church, and assisted living facilities and nursing facilities that provide specialized care for persons with dementia.

Utilizing cognitive-behavioral approaches, the practitioner worked with Mrs. Jackson on her thoughts and beliefs about getting help. Mrs. Jackson remained steadfast that her mother was not going into a nursing home, although she talked with the practitioner about the possibility of placement in an assisted living apartment.

In a later session, the practitioner and Mrs. Jackson rehearsed a visit to a nearby facility so that Mrs. Jackson could assert her questions and expectations. Mrs. Jackson discussed with the practitioner her thoughts and feelings after the visit with the practitioner but stated she wasn't yet ready to move her mother.

Legal Aspects

The practitioner encouraged Mrs. Jackson to meet with an attorney who specializes in elder law to ensure that Mrs. Lee's advance directives, such as her living will, medical power of attorney, business power of attorney, and finances were complete and in order (Merck, 2000). (See table 11.2 for definitions of these terms.)

Behavior Management

Mrs. Jackson reported that Mrs. Lee continued to exhibit behaviors that her family had difficulty dealing with, such as wandering all night and resisting assistance with care. The practitioner suggested that Mrs. Jackson obtain from the local Alzheimer's Association a book entitled *Understanding Difficult Behaviors* by Anne Robinson, Beth Spencer and Laurie White, (1991). As noted by the authors, there are many reasons for the occurrence of difficult behaviors. It is helpful for caregivers to try to understand why the person is behaving in a particular way and, in doing so, determine what may be causing or triggering the behavior and then figure out ways to prevent it from occurring again.

These problem-solving strategies include exploring some of the common physical problems with which caregivers need to be familiar. These include the effects of medication, dehydration, constipation, fatigue, and physical discomfort. Environmental problems for the elderly include clutter, overstimulation, a lack of orientation cues, and an un-

Table 11.2	
Definition of Legal Documents	
Advance Directives	Documents that allow a person to state treatment preferences to be honored in the future when the person's capacity to make decisions has lapsed.
Durable Power of Attorney	Document that addresses decision making concerning financial matters or property rights and allows the person to appoint an agent to handle such affairs in the event that the person becomes temporarily or permanently incapacitated or legally declared incompetent.
Living Will/Directive to Physician	Document that lists the medical interventions that the patient would request, accept, or reject in the future, which is often used to document the patient's decision to refuse life-sustaining care when such care would merely prolong the dying process or support the vegetative state.
Medical Power of Attorney/Durable Power of Attorney for Health Care	Document that allows the patient to appoint an agent to make health care decisions for the patient in the event that the patient becomes temporarily or permanently incapacitated or legally declared incompetent.

Note: From Merck, 2000.

familiar environment. Using many of the suggestions provided in the book, the practitioner worked with Mrs. Jackson and encouraged her to take the information home to her husband and son.

In summary, Mrs. Jackson met with the practitioner for a total of eight sessions over 3 months. Mr. Jackson was able to attend only one session. To allow Mrs. Jackson's continued attendance at the sessions, it was decided that Mr. Jackson would remain home and care for Mrs. Lee as the neighbor was no longer available.

Mrs. Jackson was very receptive to recommendations. She continued to attend the bridge club regularly, and she enjoyed being with her friends. After working on her belief systems about help seeking, she was able to receive more assistance, and her mood improved. She reported that the depressive symptoms, such as frequent crying and agitation at her husband and son, had subsided. Though she continued to worry about her mother's future, she reported less stress.

■ Conclusion

As the population continues to age, and the biopsychosocial needs of the older adult increase due to various impairments, informal caregiving provided by family members and friends is likely to rise. As noted in this chapter, the demands of caregiving for older adults can affect the emotional, mental, and physical well-being of caregivers.

This case study demonstrated the application of psychoeducational techniques and cognitive-behavioral strategies and illustrated how caregiver stress can be reduced, while improving coping skills and psychological well-being. It is important that practitioners focus on interventions that are effective and efficient in working with caregivers of older adults. The intervention techniques presented in this chapter are strongly recommended toward this effort.

Introduction

Abikoff, H., & Klein, R. G. (1992). Attention-deficit hyperactivity and conduct disorder: Comorbidity and implications for treatment. *Journal of Consulting and Clinical Psychology, 60,* 881–892.

Alexander, J., & Parsons, B. (1982). *Functional family therapy.* Monterey, CA: Brooks/Cole.

American Psychiatric Association. (2000). *Diagnostic and statistical manual of mental disorders* (4th ed., text revision). Washington, DC: Author.

Bateson, G., Jackson, D., Haley, J., & Weakland, J. (1956). Toward a theory of schizophrenia. *Behavioral Science, 1,* 251–264.

Brannen, S. J., & Rubin, A. (1996). Comparing the effectiveness of gender-specific and couples groups in a court-mandated spouse abuse treatment program. *Research on Social Work Practice, 6,* 405–424.

Brent, D., Holder, D., Kolko, D., Birmaher, B., Baugher, M., Roth, C., Iyengar, S., & Johnson, B. (1997). A clinical psychotherapy trial for adolescent depression comparing cognitive, family, and supportive therapy. *Archives of General Psychiatry, 54,* 877–884.

Chambless, D. L., & Hollon, S. D. (1998). Defining empirically supported therapies. *Journal of Consulting and Clinical Psychology, 66,* 7–18.

Corcoran, J. (2000). *Evidence-based social work practice with families: A lifespan approach.* New York: Springer.

Cournoyer, B., & Powers, G. (2002). Evidence-based social work practice: The quiet revolution continues. In A. R. Roberts & G. Greene (Eds.),

Social workers' desk reference (pp. 798–807). New York: Oxford University Press.

Foreyt, J., Poston, W., Winebarger, A., & McGavin, J. (1998). Anorexia and bulimia nervosa. In E. J. Mash & R. A. Barkley (Eds.), *Treatment of childhood disorders* (2nd ed., pp. 647–691). New York: Guilford.

Franklin, C., & Jordan, C. (1999). *Family practice: Brief systems methods for social work.* Pacific Grove, CA: Brooks/Cole.

Gambrill, E. (1999). Evidence-based practice: An alternative to authority-based practice. *Families in Society, 80,* 341–350.

George, E., Friedman, J., & Miklowitz, D. (2000). Integrated family and individual therapy for bipolar disorder. In S. Johnson, A. Hayes, T. Field, N. Schneiderman, & P. McCabe (Eds.), *Stress, coping, and depression* (pp. 307–323). Mahwah, NJ: Erlbaum.

Gibelman, M. (2002). Social work in an era of managed care. In A. R. Roberts & G. J. Greene (Eds.), *Social workers' desk reference* (pp. 16–23). New York: Oxford University Press.

Glick, I., Clarkin, J., Haas, G., Spencer, J., & Chen, C. (1991). A randomized clinical trial of inpatient family intervention: VI. Mediating variables and outcome. *Family Process, 30,* 85–99.

Goldenberg, I., & Goldenberg, H. (2000). *Family therapy: An overview* (5th ed.). Belmont, CA: Brooks/Cole.

Kazdin, A. E. (1995). *Conduct disorders in childhood and adolescence* (2nd ed.). Thousand Oaks, CA: Sage.

Kazdin, A. E., Bass, D., Ayers, W. A., & Rodgers, A. (1990). Empirical and clinical focus of child and adolescent psychotherapy research. *Journal of Consulting and Clinical Psychology, 58,* 729–740.

Kutchins, H., & Kirk, S. A. (1997). *Making us crazy: DSM: The psychiatric bible and the creation of mental disorders.* New York: Free Press.

McGoldrick, M., & Gerson, R. (1985). *Genograms in family assessment.* New York: Norton.

Miklowitz, D., & Goldstein, M. (1997). *Bipolar disorder: A family-focused treatment approach.* New York: Guilford.

Miklowitz, D., Simoneau, T., George, E., Richards, J., Kalbag, A., Sachs-Ericsson, N., & Suddath, R. (2000). Family-focused treatment of bipolar disorder: One-year effects of a psychoeducational program in conjunction with pharmacotherapy. *Biological Psychiatry, 48,* 582–592.

Minuchin, S., Baker, L., Rosman, B., Liebman, R., Milman, L., & Todd, T. (1975). A conceptual model of psychosomatic illness in children. *Archives of General Psychiatry, 32,* 1031–1038.

Minuchin, S., Rosman, B. L., & Baker, L. (1978). *Psychosomatic families: Anorexia nervosa in context.* Cambridge, MA: Harvard University Press.

Nichols, M., & Schwartz, R. (2001). *Family therapy: Concepts and method* (5th ed.). Needham Heights, MA: Allyn & Bacon.

Sackett, D., Robinson, W., Rosenberg, W., & Haynes, R. (1997). *Evidence-based medicine: How to practice and teach EBM.* New York: Churchill Livingston.

Thyer, B. (2002). Principles of evidence-based practice and treatment development. In A. R. Roberts & G. J. Greene (Eds.), *Social workers' desk reference* (pp. 739–742). New York: Oxford University Press.

Chapter I

Abikoff, H., & Klein, R. G. (1992). Attention-deficit hyperactivity and conduct disorder: Comorbidity and implications for treatment. *Journal of Consulting and Clinical Psychology, 60,* 881–892.

American Psychiatric Association. (2000). *Diagnostic and statistical manual of mental disorders* (4th ed., text revision). Washington, DC: Author.

Anastopoulos, A. D., Shelton, T. L., DuPaul, G., & Guevremont, D. C. (1993). Parent training for attention-deficit hyperactivity disorder: Its impact on parent functioning. *Journal of Abnormal Child Psychology, 21,* 581–596.

Anderson, C. M., Reiss, D. J., & Hogarty, G. E. (1986). *Schizophrenia and the family: A practitioner's guide to psychoeducation and management.* New York: Guilford.

Bandura, A., & Walters, R. (1963). *Social learning and personality development.* New York: Holt, Rinehart & Winston.

Barkley, R. A. (1998). Attention-deficit/hyperactivity disorder. In E. J. Mash & R. A. Barkley (Eds.), *Treatment of childhood disorders* (pp. 55–110). New York: Guilford.

Barkley, R. A. (2000). *Taking charge of ADHD* (rev. ed.). New York: Guilford.

Barkley, R. A., Fischer, M., Edelbrock, C., & Smallish, L. (1990). The adolescent outcome of hyperactive children diagnosed by research criteria: I. An 8-year prospective follow-up study. *Journal of the American Academy of Child and Adolescent Psychiatry, 29,* 546–557.

Basu, S., & Aniruddha, D. (1996). Parent training in children with attention deficit hyperactivity disorder: An integrated approach for greater effectiveness. *Indian Journal of Clinical Psychology, 23*(2), 184–191.

Bateson, G., Jackson, D., Haley, J., & Weakland, J. (1956). Toward a theory of schizophrenia. *Behavioral Science, 1,* 251–264.

Bentley, K. J., & Walsh, J. (2001). *The social worker and psychotropic medication.* Belmont, CA: Brooks/Cole.

Bienert, H., & Schneider, B. H. (1995). Deficit-specific social skills training with peer-nominated aggressive-disruptive and sensitive-isolated preadolescents. *Journal of Clinical Child Psychology, 24,* 287–299.

Briere, J. (1996). *Trauma symptom checklist for children: Professional manual.* Lutz, FL: Psychological Assessment Resources.

Brown, G. W., Monck, E. M., Carstairs, G. M., & Wing, J. K. (1962). Influence of family life on the course of schizophrenic illness. *British Journal of Preventive Social Medicine, 16,* 55–68.

Cantwell, D. (1996). Attention deficit disorder: A review of the past 10 years. *Journal of the American Academy of Child and Adolescent Psychiatry, 35*(8), 978–987.

Cohen, S., & Wills, T. (1985). Stress, social support, and the buffering hypothesis. *Psychological Bulletin, 98,* 310–357.

Dodge, K. A., Price, J. M., Bachorowski, J., & Newman, J. P. (1990). Hostile attributional biases in severely aggressive adolescents. *Journal of Abnormal Psychology, 99,* 385–392.

Ervin, R. A., Bankert, C. L., & DuPaul, G. J. (1996). Treatment of attention-deficit/hyperactivity disorder. In M. Reinecke, F. Dattlio, & A. Freeman (Eds.), *Cognitive therapy with children and adolescents: A casebook for clinical practice* (pp. 38–61). New York: Guilford.

Frankel, F., Myatt, R., Cantwell, D., and Feinberg, D. (1997). Parent-assisted transfer of children's social skills training: Effects on children with and without attention-deficit hyperactivity disorder. *Journal of the American Academy of Child and Adolescent Psychiatry, 36*(8), 1056–1064.

Franklin, C., & Jordan, C. (1999). *Family practice: Brief systems methods for social work.* Pacific Grove, CA: Brooks/Cole.

Hoza, B., Waschbusch, D. A., Pelham, W. E., Molina, S. G., & Milich, R. (2000). Attention-deficit/hyperactivity disordered and control boys' responses to social success and failure. *Society for Research in Child Development, 71*(2), 432–446.

Jacobvitz, D., Sroufe, L. A., Stewart, M., & Leffert, N. (1990). Treatment of attentional and hyperactivity problems in children with sympathomimetic drugs: A comprehensive review. *Journal of the American Academy of Child and Adolescent Psychiatry, 29,* 492–518.

Johnston, C., Fine, S., Weiss, M., Weiss, J., Weiss, G., & Freeman, W. (2000). Effects of stimulant medication treatment on mothers' and children's attributions for the behavior of children with attention deficit hyperactivity disorder. *Journal of Abnormal Child Psychology, 28,* 371–382.

Kazdin, A. E. (1985). *Treatment of antisocial behavior in children and adolescents.* Homewood, IL: Dorsey.

Kazdin, A. E. (1987). Treatment of antisocial behavior in children: Current status and future directions. *Psychological Bulletin, 102,* 187–203.

Kazdin, A. E. (2000). *Behavior modification in applied settings* (6th ed.). Pacific Grove, CA: Brooks/Cole.

Klein, R. G., & Mannuzza, S. (1991). Long-term outcome of hyperactive children: A review. *Journal of the American Academy of Child and Adolescent Psychiatry, 30,* 383–387.

Lincoln, K. D. (2000). Social support, negative social interactions, and psychological well-being. *Social Service Review, 74*(2), 231–252.

McCormick, L. (2000). Improving social adjustment in children with attention-deficit/hyperactivity disorder. *Archives of Family Medicine, 9,* 191–194.

McMahon, R. J. (1994). Diagnosis, assessment, and treatment of externalizing problems in children: The role of longitudinal data. *Journal of Consulting and Clinical Psychology, 62,* 901–917.

Morrissey-Kane, E., & Prinz, R. J. (1999). Engagement in child and adolescent treatment: The role of parental cognitions and attributions. *Clinical Child and Family Psychology Review, 2*(3), 183–198.

MTA (Multimodal Treatment Study of Children with Attention-Deficit/

Hyperactivity Disorder) Cooperative Group. (1999). A 14-month randomized clinical trial of treatment strategies for attention-deficit/hyperactivity disorder. *Archives of General Psychiatry, 56,* 1073–1086.

Nichols, M., & Schwartz, R. (2001). *Family therapy: Concepts and methods* (5th ed.). Needham Heights, MA: Allyn & Bacon.

Ohan, J., & Johnston, C. (1999). Attributions in adolescents medicated for attention-deficit/hyperactivity disorder. *Journal of Attention Disorders, 3,* 49–60.

Patterson, G. R., Reid, J. B., & Dishion, T. J. (1997). *Antisocial boys: A social interactional approach* (Vol. 4). Eugene, OR: Castilia.

Pelham, W., Wheeler, T., & Chronis, A. (1998). Empirically supported psychosocial treatments for attention deficit hyperactivity disorder. *Journal of Clinical Child Psychology, 27*(2), 190–205.

Pfiffner, L., & McBurnett, K. (1997). Social skills training with parent generalization: Treatment effects for children with attention deficit disorder. *Journal of Consulting Clinical Psychology, 65,* 749–757.

Reid, J. B. (1993). Prevention of conduct disorder before and after school entry: Relating interventions to development findings. *Development and Psychopathology, 5,* 243–262.

Satterfield, J. H., Satterfield, B. T., & Schell, A. M. (1987). Therapeutic interventions to prevent delinquency in hyperactive boys. *Journal of the American Academy of Child and Adolescent Psychiatry, 26,* 56–64.

Shelton, T., Barkley, R., Crosswait, C., Moorehouse, M., Fletcher, K., Barrett, S., Jenkins, L., & Metevia, L. (2000). Multimethod psychoeducational intervention for preschool children with disruptive behavior: Two-year post-treatment follow-up. *Journal of Abnormal Child Psychology, 28*(3), 253–266.

Sheridan, S., Dee, C., Morgan, J., McCormick, M., & Walker, D. (1996). A multimethod intervention for social skills deficits in children with ADHD and their parents. *School Psychology Review, 25*(1), 57–76.

Simeon, J. G., & Wiggins, D. M. (1993). Pharmacotherapy of attention-deficit hyperactivity disorder. *Canadian Journal of Psychiatry, 38,* 443–448.

Swanson J., Lerner, M., March, J., & Gresham, F. (1999). Assessment and intervention for attention-deficit/hyperactivity disorder in the schools: Lessons from the MTA study. *Pediatric Clinics of North America, 46,* 993–1009.

Webster-Stratton, C., & Herbert, M. (1993). What really happens in parent training? *Behavior Modification, 17,* 407–457.

Weinstein, D., Staffelbach, D., & Biaggio, M. (2000). Attention-deficit hyperactivity disorder and posttraumatic stress disorder: Differential diagnosis in childhood sexual abuse. *Clinical Psychology Review, 20,* 359–378.

Chapter 2

American Psychiatric Association. (2000). *Diagnostic and statistical manual of mental disorders* (4th ed., text revision). Washington, DC: Author.

Anastopoulos, A. D., Shelton, T. L., DuPaul, G. T., & Guevremont, D. C. (1993). Parent training for attention-deficit hyperactivity disorder: Its impact on parent functioning. *Journal of Abnormal Child Psychology, 21,* 581–596.

Barkley, R. A. (1998). Attention-deficit/hyperactivity disorder. In E. J. Mash & R. A. Barkley (Eds.), *Treatment of childhood disorders* (pp. 55–110). New York: Guilford.

Barkley, R. A. (2000). *Taking charge of ADHD* (Rev. ed.). New York: Guilford.

Barkley, R., Edwards, G., Laneri, M., Fletcher, K., & Metevia, L. (2001). The efficacy of problem-solving communication training alone, behavior management training alone, and their combination for parent-adolescent conflict in teenagers with ADHD and ODD. *Journal of Consulting & Clinical Psychology, 69,* 926–941.

Blakemore, B., Shindler, S., & Conte, R. (1993). A problem-solving training program for parents of children with attention deficit hyperactivity disorder. *Canadian Journal of School Psychology, 9,* 66–85.

Brestan, E. V., & Eyberg, S. M. (1998). Effective Psychosocial treatments of conduct-disordered children and adolescents: 29 years, 82 studies, and 5,272 kids. *Journal of Clinical Child Psychology, 27*(2), 180–189.

Conduct Problems Prevention Research Group. (1992). A developmental and clinical model for the prevention of conduct disorder: The FAST Track program. *Development and Psychopathology, 4,* 509–527.

Dinkmeyer, D., McKay, G., & Dinkmeyer, J. (1990). *Parenting young children: Helpful strategies based on systematic training for effective parenting.* New York: Random House.

Firestone, P., Crowe, D., Goodman, J. T., & McGrath, P. (1986). Vicissitudes of follow-up studies: Differential effects of parent training and stimulant medication with hyperactives. *American Journal of Orthopsychiatry, 56,* 184–194.

Forehand, R., & Wierson, M. (1993). The role of developmental factors in planning behavioral interventions for children: Disruptive behavior as an example. *Behavior Therapy, 24,* 117–141.

Kazdin, A. (2000). *Behavior modification in applied settings* (6th ed.). Pacific Grove, CA: Brooks/Cole.

McMahon, R. J. (1994). Diagnosis, assessment, and treatment of externalizing problems in children: The role of longitudinal data. *Journal of Consulting and Clinical Psychology, 62,* 901–917.

McNeil, C., Eyberg, S., Eisenstadt, T., Newcomb, K., & Funderburk, B. (1991). Parent-child interaction therapy with behavior problem children: Generalization of treatment effects to the school setting. *Journal of Clinical Child Psychology, 20*(2), 140–151.

Miller, G., & Prinz, R. (1990). Enhancement of social learning family interventions for childhood conduct disorder. *Psychological Bulletin, 108,* 291–307.

MTA (Multimodal Treatment Study of Children with Attention-Deficit/Hyperactivity Disorder) Cooperative Group. (1999). A 14-month randomized clinical trial of treatment strategies for attention-deficit/ hyperactivity disorder. *Archives of General Psychiatry, 56,* 1073–1086.

Odom, S. (1996). Effects of an educational intervention on mothers of male children with attention deficit hyperactivity disorder. *Journal of Community Health Nursing, 13*(4), 207–220.

Patterson, G. R. (1982). *Coercive family process: A social learning approach.* Eugene, OR: Castalia.

Patterson, G. R. (1986). Performance models for antisocial boys. *American Psychologist, 41,* 432–444.

Patterson, G. R., & Fisher, P. A. (2002). Recent developments in our understanding of parenting: Bidirectional effects, causal models, and the search for parsimony. In M. H. Bornstein (Ed.), *Handbook of parenting: Vol. 5. Practical issues in parenting* (2nd ed.). (pp. 59–88). Mahwah, NJ: Erlbaum.

Patterson, G. R., Reid, J., & Dishion, T. (1998). Antisocial boys. In J. Jenkins & K. Oatley (Eds.), *Human emotions: A reader* (pp. 330–336). Malden, MA: Blackwell.

Reid, J. B. (1993). Prevention of conduct disorder before and after school entry: Relating interventions to development findings. *Development and Psychopathology, 5,* 243–262.

Serketich, W. J., & Dumas, J. E. (1996). The effectiveness of behavioral parent training to modify antisocial behavior in children: A meta-analysis. *Behavior Therapy, 27,* 171–186.

Sonuga-Barke, E., Daley, D., Thompson, M., Laver-Bradbury, C., & Weeks, A. (2001). Parent-based therapies for preschool attention-deficit/hyperactivity disorder: A randomized, controlled trial with a community sample. *Journal of the American Academy of Child & Adolescent Psychiatry, 40,* 402–408.

Webster-Stratton, C. (1981; revised 2001). *Incredible years parents and children training series.* Available from Incredible Years, Seattle, WA (www.incredibleyears.com).

Webster-Stratton, C., & Herbert, M. (1993). What really happens in parent training? *Behavior Modification, 17,* 407–457.

Weinberg, H. (1999). Parent training for attention-deficit hyperactivity disorder: Parental and child outcome. *Journal of Clinical Psychology, 55*(7), 907–913.

Chapter 3

Berg, I. K. (1994). *Family-based services: A solution-focused approach.* New York: Norton.

Berg, I., & Kelly, S. (2000). *Building solutions in child protective services.* New York: Norton.

Bertolino, B., & O'Hanlon, B. (2002). *Collaborative, competency-based counseling and therapy.* Boston: Allyn & Bacon.

Cade, B., & O'Hanlon, W. H. (1993). *A brief guide to brief therapy.* New York: Norton.

Corcoran, J. (2002). *A comparison group study of solution-focused therapy versus "treatment-as-usual" for behavior problems in children.* Manuscript submitted for publication.

Corcoran, J., & Stephenson, M. (2000). The effectiveness of solution-focused therapy with child behavior problems: A preliminary report. *Families in Society, 81,* 468–474.

deJong, P., & Berg, I. K. (2001). *Interviewing for solutions* (2nd ed.). Pacific Grove, CA: Brooks/Cole.

de Shazer, S. (1988). *Clues: Investigating solutions in brief therapy.* New York: Norton.

de Shazer, S., Berg, I. K., Lipchick, E., Nunnally, E., Molnar, A., Gingerich, W., & Weiner-Davis, M. (1986). Brief therapy: Focused solution development. *Family Process, 25,* 207–221.

Franklin, C., Biever, J., Moore, K., Clemons, D., & Scamardo, M. (2001). The effectiveness of solution-focused therapy with children in a school setting. *Research on Social Work Practice, 11,* 411–434.

LaFountain, R., & Garner, N. (1996). Solution-focused counseling groups: The results are in. *Journal for Specialists in Group Work, 21,* 128–143.

Lee, M. Y. (1997). A study of solution-focused brief family therapy: Outcomes and issues. *American Journal of Family Therapy, 25,* 3–17.

Littrell, J., Malia, J., & Vanderwood, M. (1995). Single-session brief counseling in a high school. *Journal of Counseling and Development, 73,* 451–458.

O'Hanlon, W. H., & Weiner-Davis, M. (1989). *In search of solutions: A new direction in psychotherapy.* New York: Norton.

Selekman, M. (1993). *Pathways to change.* New York: Guilford.

Selekman, M. (1997). *Solution-focused therapy with children.* New York: Guilford.

Thompson, R., & Litrell, J. (1998). Brief counseling for students with learning disabilities. *Professional School Counseling, 2,* 60–67.

Wheeler, J. (1995). Believing in miracles: The implications and possibilities of using solution-focused therapy in a child mental health setting. *ACPP Reviews and Newsletter, 17,* 250–261.

White, M., & Epston, D. (1990). *Narrative means to therapeutic ends.* New York: Norton.

Zimmerman, T., Jacobsen, R., MacIntyre, M., & Watson, C. (1996). Solution--focused parenting groups: An empirical study. *Journal of Systemic Therapies, 15,* 12–25.

Chapter 4

Acton, R. G., & During, S. M. (1992). Preliminary results of aggression management training for aggressive parents. *Journal of Interpersonal Violence, 7,* 410–417.

Azar, S. T., Barnes, K. T., & Twentyman, C. T. (1988). Developmental outcomes in physically abused children: Consequences of parental abuse or the effects of a more general breakdown in caregiving behaviors? *Behavior Therapist, 11,* 27–32.

Azar, S. T., & Wolfe, D. A. (1998). Child abuse and neglect. In E. J. Mash

& R. A. Barkley (Eds.), *Treatment of childhood disorders* (2nd ed., pp. 501–544). New York: Guilford.

Barkley, R. A. (2000). *Taking charge of ADHD* (Rev. ed.). New York: Guilford.

Barth, R. (1990). Theories guiding home-based intensive family preservation services. In J. Wittaker, J. Kinney, E. Tracey, & C. Booth (Eds.), *Improving practice technology for work with high risk families: Lessons from the "Homebuilders" social work education project* (pp. 91–113). Seattle, WA: Center for Social Welfare Research.

Beck, J. (1995). *Cognitive therapy: Basics and beyond.* New York: Guilford.

Brunk, M., Henggeler, S. W., & Whelan, J. P. (1987). Comparison of multisystemic therapy and parent training in the brief treatment of child abuse and neglect. *Journal of Consulting and Clinical Psychology, 55,* 171–178.

Carroll, K. (1998). A cognitive-behavioral approach: Treating cocaine addiction. Retrieved August 28, 2001, from http://www.drugabuse.gov/TXManuals/CBT/CBT1.html

Conaway, L. P., & Hansen, D. J. (1989). Social behavior of physically abused and neglected children: A critical review. *Clinical Psychology Review, 9,* 627–652.

Conduct Problems Prevention Research Group. (1992). A developmental and clinical model for the prevention of conduct disorder: The FAST Track program. *Development and Psychopathology, 4,* 509–527.

D'Zurilla, T., & Nezu, A. (2001). Problem-solving therapies. In K. Dobson & S. Keith (Eds.), *Handbook of cognitive-behavioral therapies* (2nd ed., pp. 211–245). New York: Guilford.

Ellis, A., & McLaren, C. (1998). Rational emotive behavior therapy: A therapist's guide (Vol. 2). Atascadero, CA: Impact.

Famularo, R., Kinscherff, R., Bunshaft, D., Spivak, G., & Fenton, T. (1989). Parental compliance to court-ordered treatment interventions in cases of child maltreatment. *Child Abuse & Neglect, 13,* 507–514.

Forehand, R., & Kotchick, B. (1996). Cultural diversity: A wake-up call for parent training. *Behavior Therapy, 27,* 187–206.

Forehand, R., & Long, N. (1988). Outpatient treatment of the acting out child: Procedures, long term follow-up data, and clinical problems. *Advances in Behavioral Research and Therapy, 10,* 129–177.

Gelardo, M. S., & Sanford, E. E. (1987). Child abuse and neglect: A review of the literature. *School Psychology Review, 16,* 137–155.

Graziano, A. M., & Mills, J. R. (1992). Treatment for abused children: When is a partial solution acceptable? *Child Abuse & Neglect, 16,* 217–228.

Hansen, D. J., Pallotta, G. M., Tishelman, A. C., Conaway, L. P., & MacMillan, V. M. (1989). Parental problem-solving skills and child behavior problems: A comparison of physically abusive, neglectful, clinic, and community families. *Journal of Family Violence, 4,* 353–368.

Hembree-Kigin, T., & McNeil, C. B. (1995). *Parent-child interaction therapy.* New York: Plenum.

Hepworth, D. H., Rooney, R. & Larsen, J. (2002). *Direct social work practice: Theory and skills* (5th ed.). Belmont, CA: Brooks/Cole.

Kaufman, K. L., & Rudy, L. (1991). Future directions in the treatment of physical child abuse. *Criminal Justice and Behavior, 18*, 82–97.

Kazdin, A. (1989). *Behavior modification in applied settings* (4th ed.). Pacific Grove, CA: Brooks/Cole.

Kazdin, A. E., Hayes, S. C., Henry, W. P., Schacht, T. E., & Strupp, H. H. (1992). Case study and small sample research. In A. E. Kazdin (Ed.), *Methodological issues and strategies in clinical research* (pp. 235–242). Washington, DC: American Psychological Association.

Kolko, D. J. (1996). Clinical monitoring of treatment course in child physical abuse: Psychometric characteristics and treatment comparisons. *Child Abuse & Neglect, 20*, 23–43.

Kolko, D. J., & Swenson, C. C. (2002). *Assessing and treating physically abused children and their families: A cognitive-behavioral approach.* Thousand Oaks, CA: Sage.

Malinosky-Rummell, R., & Hansen, D. J. (1993). Long-term consequences of childhood physical abuse. *Psychological Bulletin, 114*, 68–79.

McKay, M., Davis, M., & Fanning, P. (1997). *Thoughts and feelings: Taking control of your moods and your life.* Oakland, CA: New Harbinger.

Meichenbaum, D. (1999). *Cognitive-behavior modification: An integrative approach.* Cambridge, MA: Perseus.

Morrissey-Kane, E., & Prinz, R. (1999). Engagement in child and adolescent treatment: The role of parental cognitions and attributions. *Clinical Child and Family Psychology Review, 2*, 183–198.

Mueller, E., & Silverman, N. (1989). Peer relations in maltreated children. In D. Cicchetti & V. Carlson (Eds.), *Child maltreatment: Theory and research on the causes and consequences of child abuse and neglect* (pp. 529–578). Cambridge: Cambridge University Press.

Nelson, K., & Landsman, M. (1992). *Alternative models of family preservation: Family-based services in context.* Springfield, IL: Thomas.

Nicol, A. R., Smith, J., Kay, B., Hall, D., Barlow, J., & Williams, B. (1988). A focused casework approach to the treatment of child abuse: A controlled comparison. *Journal of Child Psychology and Psychiatry, 29*, 703–711.

Patterson, G. R. (1982). *Coercive family process: A social learning approach.* Eugene, OR: Castalia.

Patterson, G. R. (1986). Performance models for antisocial boys. *American Psychologist, 41*, 432–444.

Patterson, G. R., & Fisher, P. A. (2002). Recent developments in our understanding of parenting: Bidirectional effects, causal models, and the search for parsimony. In M. H. Bornstein (Ed.), *Handbook of parenting: Vol. 5. Practical issues in parenting* (2nd ed.). (pp. 59–88). Mahwah, NJ: Erlbaum.

Patterson, G. R., Reid, J., & Dishion, T. (1998). Antisocial boys. In J. Jenkins & K. Oatley (Eds.), *Human emotions: A reader* (pp. 330–336). Malden, MA: Blackwell.

Rivara, F. P. (1985). Physical abuse in children under two: A study of therapeutic outcomes. *Child Abuse & Neglect, 9*, 81–87.

Sayger, T. V., Horne, A. M., Walter, J. M., & Passmore, J. L. (1988). Social learning family therapy with aggressive children: Treatment outcome and maintenance. *Journal of Family Psychology, 1,* 261–285.

Schinke, S., Schilling, R., Kirkham, M., Gilchrist, L., et al. (1986). Stress management skills for parents. *Journal of Child & Adolescent Psychotherapy, 3,* 293–298.

Serketich, W. J., & Dumas, J. E. (1996). The effectiveness of behavioral parent training to modify antisocial behavior in children: A meta-analysis. *Behavior Therapy, 27,* 171–186.

Steinberg, L. (2000, April 1). We know some things: Parent-adolescent relations in retrospect and prospect. Presidential address, Society for Research on Adolescence, Chicago, IL. Retrieved June 18, 2001, from http://astro.temple.edu/lds/sra.htm

Szykula, S. A., & Fleischman, M. J. (1985). Reducing out-of-home placements of abused children: Two controlled field studies. *Child Abuse & Neglect, 9,* 277–283.

Toth, S. L., Manly, J. T., & Cicchetti, D. (1992). Child maltreatment and vulnerability to depression. *Development and Psychopathology, 4,* 97–112.

Webster-Stratton, C. (1981; revised 2001). *Incredible years parents and children training series.* Available from Incredible Years, Seattle, WA (www.incredibleyears.com).

Webster-Stratton, C., & Herbert, M. (1993). What really happens in parent training? *Behavior Modification, 17,* 407–457.

Webster-Stratton, C., Hollinsworth, T., & Kolpacoff, M. (1989). The long-term effectiveness and clinical significance of three cost-effective training programs for families with conduct-problem children. *Journal of Consulting and Clinical Psychology, 57,* 550–553.

Webster-Stratton, C., Kolpacoff, M., & Hollinsworth, T. (1988). Self-administered videotape therapy for families with conduct-problem children: Comparison with two cost-effective treatments and a control group. *Journal of Consulting and Clinical Psychology, 56,* 558–566.

Wells, K. (1994). A reorientation to knowledge development in family preservation services: A proposal. *Child Welfare, 73,* 475–488.

Whiteman, M., Fanshel, D., & Grundy, J. F. (1987). Cognitive-behavioral interventions aimed at anger of parents at risk of child abuse. *Social Work, 32,* 469–474.

Wolfe, D. A., Edwards, B., Manion, I., & Koverola, C. (1988). Early intervention for parents at risk of child abuse and neglect. *Journal of Consulting and Clinical Psychology, 56,* 40–47.

Wolfe, D. A., Jaffe, P., Wilson, S., & Zak, L. (1985). Children of battered women: The relation of child behavior to family violence and maternal stress. *Journal of Consulting and Clinical Psychology, 53,* 657–664.

Chapter 5

Cohen, J. A., & Mannarino, A. P. (1993). *A treatment model for sexually abused children and their nonoffending parents: A cognitive-behavioral approach.* Thousand Oaks, CA: Sage.

Cohen, J. A., & Mannarino, A. P. (1996a). A treatment outcome study for sexually abused preschool children: Initial findings. *Journal of the American Academy of Child and Adolescent Psychiatry, 35,* 42–50.

Cohen, J. A., & Mannarino, A. P. (1996b). Factors that mediate treatment outcome of sexually abused preschool children. *Journal of the American Academy of Child and Adolescent Psychiatry, 34,* 1402–1410.

Cohen, J. A., & Mannarino, A. P. (1997). A treatment study for sexually abused preschool children: Outcome during a 1-year follow-up. *Journal of the American Academy of Child and Adolescent Psychiatry, 36,* 1228–1235.

Cohen, J. A., & Mannarino, A. P. (1998). Factors that mediate treatment outcome of sexually abused preschool children: Six and 12-month follow-up. *Journal of the American Academy of Child and Adolescent Psychiatry, 37,* 44–51.

Cole, J. (1988). *Asking about sex and growing up.* New York: Morrow.

Corcoran, J. (1998). In defense of mothers of sexual abuse victims. *Families in Society, 79,* 358–369.

Deblinger, E., & Heflin, A. H. (1996). *Treating sexually abused children and their nonoffending parents: A cognitive-behavioral approach.* Thousand Oaks, CA: Sage.

Deblinger, E., Lippmann, J., & Steer, R. (1996). Sexually abused children suffering posttraumatic stress symptoms: Initial treatment outcome findings. *Child Maltreatment, 1,* 310–321.

Deblinger, E., McLeer, S., & Henry, D. (1990). Cognitive-behavioral treatment for sexually abused children suffering post-traumatic stress: Preliminary findings. *Journal of the American Academy of Child and Adolescent Psychiatry, 29,* 747–752.

Deblinger, E., Stauffer, L., & Landsberg, C. (1994). The impact of a history of child sexual abuse on maternal response to allegations of sexual abuse concerning her child. *Journal of Child Sexual Abuse, 3,* 67–75.

Deblinger, E., Stauffer, L., & Steer, R. (2001). Comparative efficacies of supportive and cognitive behavioral group therapies for young children who have been sexually abused and their nonoffending mothers. *Child Maltreatment, 6,* 332–343.

Deblinger, E., Steer, R., & Lippmann, J. (1999a). Maternal factors associated with sexually abused children's psychosocial adjustment. *Child Maltreatment, 4,* 13–20.

Deblinger, E., Steer, R., & Lippmann, J. (1999b). Two-year follow-up study of cognitive behavioral therapy for sexually abused children suffering post-traumatic stress symptoms. *Child Abuse and Neglect, 23*(12), 1371–1378.

Deblinger, E., Taub, B., Maedel, A., Lippmann, J., & Stauffer, L. (1997). Psychosocial factors predicting parent reported symptomatology in sexually abused children. *Journal of Child Sexual Abuse, 6,* 35–49.

DeJong, A. (1988). Maternal responses to the sexual abuse of their children. *Pediatrics, 81,* 14–21.

Faller, K. (1989). Why sexual abuse? An exploration of the intergenerational hypothesis. *Child Abuse & Neglect, 13,* 543–548.

Goodwin, J., McCarthy, T., & DiVasto, P. (1981). Prior incest in mothers of abused children. *Child Abuse & Neglect, 5,* 87–95.

James, B. (1989). *Treating traumatized children: New insights and creative interventions.* New York: Free Press.

Kendall-Tackett, K. A., Williams, L. M., & Finkelhor, D. (1993). Impact of sexual abuse on children: A review and synthesis of recent empirical studies. *Psychological Bulletin, 113,* 164–180.

King, N., Tonge, B., Mullen, P., Myerson, N., Heyne, D., Rollings, S., Martin, R., & Ollendick, T. (2000). Treating sexually abused children with posttraumatic stress symptoms: A randomized clinical trial. *Journal of the American Academy of Child and Adolescent Psychiatry, 39,* 1347–1355.

Lazarus, R., & Folkman, S. (1984). *Stress, appraisal, and coping.* New York: Springer.

Mayle, P. (1990). *Where did I come from?* New York: Carol.

McKay, M., Davis, M., & Fanning, P. (1997). *Thoughts and feelings: Taking control of your moods and your life.* Oakland, CA: New Harbinger.

Myer, M. (1985). A new look at mothers of incest victims. *Journal of Social Work and Human Sexuality, 3,* 47–58.

Newberger, C., Gremy, I., Waternaux, C., & Newberger, E. (1993). Mothers of sexually abused children: Trauma and repair in longitudinal perspective. *American Journal of Orthopsychiatry, 63,* 92–102.

Parad, H., & Caplan, G. (1960). A framework for studying families in crisis. *Social Work, 5,* 1–15.

Peterson, R., Basta, S., & Dykstra, T. (1993). Mothers of molested children: Some comparisons of personality characteristics. *Child Abuse & Neglect, 17,* 409–418.

Planned Parenthood. (1986). *How to talk with your child about sexuality.* New York: Doubleday.

Sanford, D. (1986). *I can't talk about it.* Sisters, OR: Multnomah.

Sanford, D. (1993). *Something must be wrong with me.* Sisters, OR: Multnomah.

Sirles, E. A., & Franke, P. J. (1989). Factors influencing mothers' reactions to intra-family sexual abuse. *Child Abuse & Neglect, 13,* 131–139.

Spivack, G., Platt, J., & Shure, M. (1976). *The problem-solving approach to adjustment: A guide to research and intervention.* San Francisco: Jossey-Bass.

Stauffer, L. B., & Deblinger, E. (1996). Cognitive behavioral groups for nonoffending mothers and their young sexually abused children: A preliminary treatment outcome study. *Child Maltreatment, 1,* 65–76.

Toseland, R., & Rivas, R. (2001). *An introduction to group work practice.* Boston: Allyn & Bacon.

Tufts New England Medical Center, Division of Child Psychiatry. (1984). *Sexually exploited children: Service and research project.* Final report for the Office of Juvenile Justice and Delinquency Prevention, U.S. Department of Justice. Unpublished manuscript, Tufts New England Medical Center Library, Boston.

Wachter, O. (1983). *No more secrets for me*. New York: Little, Brown.

Wolfe, V. V. (1998). Child sexual abuse. In E. J. Mash & R. A. Barkley (Eds.), *Treatment of childhood disorders* (2nd ed., pp. 545–597). New York: Guilford.

Chapter 6

Alexander, J., & Parsons, B. V. (1982). *Functional family therapy*. Monterey, CA: Brooks/Cole.

American Psychiatric Association (2000). *Diagnostic and statistical manual of mental disorders* (4th ed., text revision). Washington, DC: Author.

Aponte, H. (2002). Structural family therapy. In A. R. Roberts & G. J. Greene (Eds.), *Social workers' desk reference* (pp. 263–267). New York: Oxford University Press.

Barkley, R. A., Guevremont, D. C., Anastopoulos, A. D., & Fletcher, K. E. (1992). A comparison of three family therapy programs for treating family conflicts in adolescents with attention-deficit hyperactivity disorder. *Journal of Consulting and Clinical Psychology, 60,* 450–462.

Barton, C., Alexander, J. F., Waldron, H., Turner, C. W., & Warburton, J. (1985). Generalizing treatment effects of functional family therapy: Three replications. *American Journal of Family Therapy, 13,* 16–26.

Borduin, C. M., Mann, B. J., Cone, L. T., Henggeler, S. W., Fucci, B. R., Blaske, D. M., & Williams, R. A. (1995). Multisystemic treatment of serious juvenile offenders: Long term prevention of criminality and violence. *Journal of Consulting and Clinical Psychology, 63,* 569–578.

Corcoran, J. (2000). *Evidence-based social work practice with families: A life-span approach*. New York: Springer.

Friedman, A., Tomko, L., & Utada, A. (1991). Client and family characteristics that predict better family therapy outcome for adolescent drug abusers. *Family Dynamics of Addiction Quarterly, 1,* 77–93.

Goldenberg, I., & Goldenberg, H. (2000). *Family therapy: An overview* (5th ed.). Belmont, CA: Wadsworth/Thomson Learning.

Gordon, D. A., Arbuthnot, J., Gustafson, K. E., & McGreen, P. (1988). Home-based behavioral-systems family therapy with disadvantaged juvenile delinquents. *American Journal of Family Therapy, 16,* 243–255.

Gordon, D. A., Graves, K., & Arbuthnot, J. (1995). The effect of functional family therapy for delinquents on adult criminal behavior. *Criminal Justice and Behavior, 22,* 60–73.

Henggeler, S. W. (1989). *Delinquency in adolescence*. Newbury Park, CA: Sage.

Henggeler, S. W., & Borduin, C. M. (1990). *Family therapy and beyond: A multisystemic approach to treating the behavioral problems of children and adolescents*. Pacific Grove, CA: Brooks/Cole.

Henggeler, S. W., Cunningham, P. B., Pickrel, S. G., Schoenwald, S. K., & Brondino, M. J. (1996). Multisystemic therapy: An effective violence prevention approach for serious juvenile offenders. *Journal of Adolescence, 19*, 47–61.

Joanning, H., Thomas, F., Quinn, W., & Mullen, R. (1992). Treating adolescent drug abuse: A comparison of family systems therapy, group therapy, and family drug education. *Journal of Marital and Family Therapy, 18*, 345–356.

Lewis, R. A., Piercy, F. P., Sprenkle, D. H., & Trepper, T. S. (1990). Family-based interventions for helping drug-abusing adolescents. *Journal of Adolescent Research, 5*, 82–95.

Lewis, R. A., Piercy, F. P., Sprenkle, D. H., & Trepper, T. S. (1991). The Purdue brief family therapy model for adolescent substance abusers. In T. C. Todd & M. D. Selekman (Eds.), *Family therapy approaches with adolescent substance abusers* (pp. 29–48). Boston: Allyn & Bacon.

Minuchin, S. (1974). *Families and family therapy.* Cambridge, MA: Harvard University Press.

Minuchin, S., & Fishman, H. C. (1981). *Family therapy techniques.* Cambridge, MA: Harvard University Press.

Minuchin, S., Montalvo, B., Guerney, B. G., Jr., Rosman, B. L., & Schumer, F. (1967). *Families of the slums: An exploration of their structure and treatment.* New York: Basic.

Minuchin, S., & Nichols, M. P. (1993). *Family healing: Tales of hope and renewal from family therapy.* New York: Free Press.

Minuchin, S., Rosman, B. L., & Baker, L. (1978). *Psychosomatic families: Anorexia nervosa in context.* Cambridge, MA: Harvard University Press.

Nichols, M., & Schwartz, R. (2001). *Family therapy: Concepts and methods* (5th ed.). Boston: Allyn & Bacon.

Szapocznik, J., Perez-Vidal, A., Brickman, A. L., Foote, F. H., Santisteban, D., & Hervis, O. (1988). Engaging adolescent drug abusers and their families in treatment: A strategic structural systems approach. *Journal of Consulting and Clinical Psychology, 56*, 552–557.

Szapocznik, J., Rio, A., Murray, L., Cohen, R., Scopetta, M., Ribas-Vasquez, A., Nervis, O., Posada, V., & Kurtines, W. (1989). Assessing change in child psychodynamic functioning in treatment outcome studies: The psychodynamic child ratings. Revista Interamericana de Psicologia/Interamerican. *Journal of Psychology, 27*, 147–162.

Chapter 7

Bateson, G. (1972). *Steps to an ecology of the mind.* New York: Ballantine.

Bateson, G., Jackson, D., Haley, J., & Weakland, J. (1956). Toward a theory of schizophrenia. *Behavioral Science, 1*, 251–264.

Bienert, H., & Schneider, B. H. (1995). Deficit-specific social skills training with peer-nominated aggressive-disruptive and sensitive-isolated preadolescents. *Journal of Clinical Child Psychology, 24*, 287–299.

Bierman, K. L., Miller, C. L., & Stabb, S. D. (1987). Improving the social behavior and peer acceptance of rejected boys: Effects of social skill training with instructions and prohibitions. *Journal of Consulting and Clinical Psychology, 55*, 194–200.

Borduin, C. M., Mann, B. J., Cone, L. T., Henggeler, S. W., Fucci, B. R., Blaske, D. M., & Williams, R. A. (1995). Multisystemic treatment of serious juvenile offenders: Long term prevention of criminality and violence. *Journal of Consulting and Clinical Psychology, 63,* 569–578.

Brofenbrenner, U. (1979). *The ecology of human development: Experiments by nature and design.* Cambridge, MA: Harvard University Press.

Brown, T., Henggeler, S., Schoenwald, S., Brondino, M., & Pickrel, S. (1999). Multisystemic treatment of substance abusing and dependent juvenile delinquents: Effects on school attendance at posttreatment and 6-month follow-up. *Children's Services: Social Policy, Research, and Practice, 2,* 81–93.

Capaldi, D. M., & Patterson, G. R. (1994). Interrelated influences of contextual factors on antisocial behavior in childhood and adolescence for males. In D. C. Fowles, P. Sutker, & S. H. Goodman (Eds.), *Progress in experimental personality and psychopathology research* (pp. 165–198). New York: Springer.

Dodge, K. A., Price, J. M., Bachorowski, J., & Newman, J. P. (1990). Hostile attributional biases in severely aggressive adolescents. *Journal of Abnormal Psychology, 99,* 385–392.

Franklin, C., Grant, D., Corcoran, J., O'Dell, P., & Bultman, L. (1997). Effectiveness of prevention programs for adolescent pregnancy: A meta-analysis. *Journal of Marriage and the Family, 59,* 551–567.

Henggeler, S. W. (1989). *Delinquency in adolescence.* Newbury Park, CA: Sage.

Henggeler, S. W. (1991). Multidimensional causal models of delinquent behavior and their implications for treatment. In R. Cohen & A. W. Siegel (Eds.), *Context and development.* Hillside, NJ: Erlbaum.

Henggeler, S. W., & Borduin, C. M. (1990). *Family therapy and beyond: A multisystemic approach to treating the behavioral problems of children and adolescents.* Pacific Grove, CA: Brooks/Cole.

Henggeler, S., Borduin, C., Melton, G., Mann, B., et al. (1991). Effects of multisystemic therapy on drug use and abuse in serious juvenile offenders: A progress report from two outcome studies. *Family Dynamics of Addiction Quarterly, 1,* 40–51.

Henggeler, S. W., Cunningham, P. B., Pickrel, S. G., Schoenwald, S. K., & Brondino, M. J. (1996). Multisystemic therapy: An effective violence prevention approach for serious juvenile offenders. *Journal of Adolescence, 19,* 47–61.

Henggeler, S. W., Melton, G. G., Brondino, M. J., Scherer, D. G., & Hanley, J. H. (1997). Multisystemic therapy with violent and chronic juvenile offenders and their families: The role of treatment fidelity in successful dissemination. *Journal of Consulting and Clinical Psychology, 65,* 821–833.

Henggeler, S. W., Melton, G. B., & Smith, L. A. (1992). Family preservation using multisystemic therapy: An effective alternative to incarcerating serious juvenile offenders. *Journal of Consulting and Clinical Psychology, 60,* 953–961.

Henggeler, S., Pickrel, S., & Brondino, M. (1999). Multisystemic treatment of substance abusing and dependent delinquents: Outcomes, treatment fidelity, and transportability. *Mental Health Services Research, 1,* 171–184.

Henggeler, S. Pickrel, S., Brondino, M., & Crouch, J. (1996). Eliminating (almost) treatment dropout of substance abusing or dependent delinquents through home-based multisystemic therapy. *American Journal of Psychiatry, 153,* 427–428.

Henggeler, S. W., Rodick, J. D., Borduin, C. M., Hanson, C. L., Watson, S. M., & Urey, J. R. (1986). Multisystemic treatment of juvenile offenders: Effects on adolescent behavior and family interaction. *Developmental Psychology, 22,* 132–141.

Henggeler, S. W., Schoenwald, S. K., Borduin, C., Rowland, M., & Cunningham, P. B. (1998). *Multisystemic treatment of antisocial behavior in children and adolescents.* New York: Guilford.

Henggeler, S. W., Schoenwald, S. K., Rowland, M. D., & Cunningham, P. B. (2002). *Serious emotional disturbance in children and adolescence: Multisystemic therapy.* New York: Guilford.

Krishnakumar, A., & Buehler, C. (2000). Interparental conflict and parenting behaviors: A meta-analytic review. *Family Relations, 49,* 25–44.

Loeber, R. (1990). Development and risk factors of juvenile antisocial behavior and delinquency. *Clinical Psychology Review, 10,* 1–41.

Loeber, R., Farrington, D., Stouthamer-Loeber, M., & Van Kammen, W. (1998). *Antisocial behavior and mental health problems: Explanatory factors in childhood and adolescence.* Mahwah, NJ: Erlbaum.

McMahon, R. J. (1994). Diagnosis, assessment, and treatment of externalizing problems in children: The role of longitudinal data. *Journal of Consulting & Clinical Psychology, 62,* 901–917.

Moffitt, T. E. (1993). Adolescence-limited and life-course-persistent antisocial behavior: A developmental taxonomy. *Psychological Review, 100,* 674–701.

Patterson, G. R. (1986). Performance models for antisocial boys. *American Psychologist, 1,* 432–444.

Scherer, D. G., Brondino, M. J., Henggeler, S. W., Melton, G. B., & Hanley, J. H. (1994). Multisystemic family preservation therapy: Preliminary findings from a study of rural and minority serious adolescent offenders. *Journal of Emotional and Behavioral Disorders, 2,* 198–206.

Chapter 8

Barber, J. G., & Gilbertson, R. (1996). An experimental study of brief unilateral intervention for the partners of heavy drinkers. *Research on Social Work Practice, 6,* 325–336.

Barber, J. G., & Gilbertson, R. (1997). Unilateral interventions for women living with heavy drinkers. *Social Work, 42,* 69–78.

Barber, J. G., & Gilbertson, R. (1998). Evaluation of a self-help manual for the female partners of heavy drinkers. *Research on Social Work Practice, 8,* 141–151.

Connors, G., Donovan, D., & DiClemente, C. (2001). *Substance abuse treatment and the stages of change: Selecting and planning interventions.* New York: Guilford.

Edwards, M. E., & Steinglass, P. (1995). Family therapy treatment outcomes for alcoholism. *Journal of Marital and Family Therapy, 21,* 475–509.

Fals-Stewart, W., Birchler, G. R., & O'Farrell, T. J. (1996). Behavioral couples therapy for male substance-abusing patients: Effects on relationship adjustment and drug-using behavior. *Journal of Consulting and Clinical Psychology, 64,* 959–972.

McCrady, B. S. (2001). Alcohol use disorders. In D. H. Barlow (Ed.), *Clinical handbook of psychological disorders* (3rd ed., pp. 376–433). New York: Guilford.

McCrady, B. S., Noel, N. E., Abrams, D. B., Stout, R. L., Nelson, H. F., & Hay, W. M. (1986). Comparative effectiveness of three types of spouse involvement in outpatient behavioral alcoholism treatment. *Journal of Studies on Alcohol, 47,* 459–467.

Miller, W., & Rollnick, S. (1991). *Motivational interviewing: Preparing people to change addictive behavior.* New York: Guilford.

O'Farrell, T. J. (1993). *Treating alcohol problems: Marital and family interventions.* New York: Guilford.

O'Farrell, T. J., Choquette, K. A., Cutter, H. S., Brown, E. D., & McCourt, W. F. (1993). Behavioral marital therapy with and without additional couples relapse prevention sessions for alcoholics and their wives. *Journal of Studies on Alcohol, 54,* 652–666.

Prochaska, J., & Norcross, J. (1994). *Systems of psychotherapy: A transtheoretical analysis* (3rd ed.). Pacific Grove, CA: Brooks/Cole.

Sisson, R. W., & Azrin, N. H. (1986). Family-member involvement to initiate and promote treatment of problem drinkers. *Journal of Behavioral Therapy and Experiential Psychiatry, 17,* 15–21.

Thomas, C., & Corcoran, J. (2001). Empirically based marital and family interventions for alcohol abuse: A review. *Research on Social Work Practice, 11,* 549–575.

Thomas, E. J., & Ager, R. D. (1993). Unilateral family therapy with spouses of uncooperative alcohol abusers. In T. J. O'Farrell (Ed.), *Treating alcohol problems: Marital and family interventions* (pp. 3–33). New York: Guilford.

Thomas, E. J., Santa, C., Bronson, D., & Oyserman, D. (1987). Unilateral family therapy with the spouses of alcoholics. *Journal of Social Service Research, 10,* 145–162.

Thomas, E. J., Yoshioka, M., & Ager, R. D. (1996). Spouse enabling of alcohol abuse: Conception, assessment, and modification. *Journal of Substance Abuse, 8(1),* 61–80.

Chapter 9

Addis, M., & Jacobson, N. (1991). Integration of cognitive therapy and behavioral marital therapy for depression. *Journal of Psychology Integration, 1,* 249–264.

Banawan, S., O'Mahen, H., Beach, S., & Jackson, M. (2002). The empirical underpinnings of marital therapy for depression. In J. Harvey & A. Wenzel (Eds.), *A clinician's guide to maintaining and enhancing close relationships* (pp. 133–155). Mahwah, NJ: Erlbaum.

Beach, S., Fincham, F., & Katz, J. (1998). Marital therapy in the treatment of depression: Toward a third generation of therapy and research. *Clinical Psychological Review, 18*, 635–661.

Beach, S., & Jones, D. (2002). Marital and family therapy for depression in adults. In I. Gotlib & C. Hammen (Eds.), *Handbook of depression* (pp. 422–440). New York: Guilford.

Beach, S., & O'Leary, K. (1992). Treating depression in the context of marital discord: Outcome and predictors of response of marital therapy versus cognitive therapy. *Behavior Therapy, 22*, 507–528.

Beach, S., Sandeen, E., & O'Leary, K. (1990). *Depression in marriage: A model for etiology and treatment.* New York: Guilford.

Beach, S., Whitman, M., & O'Leary, K. D. (1994). Marital therapy for depression: Theoretical foundation, current status, and future directions. *Behavior Therapy, 25*, 345–371.

Beck, C. T. (1999). Maternal depression and child behaviour problems: A meta-analysis. *Journal of Advanced Nursing, 29*, 623–629.

Chodorow, N. (1999). *The power of feelings: Personal meaning in psychoanalysis, gender, and culture.* New Haven, CT: Yale University Press.

Christensen, A., Jacobson, N., & Babcock, J. (1995). Integrative behavioral couple therapy. In N. S. Jacobson & A. S. Gurman (Eds.), *Clinical handbook of couple therapy* (pp. 31–64). New York: Guilford.

Corcoran, J. (2000). *Evidence-based social work practice with families: A life-span approach.* New York: Springer.

Emanuels-Zuurveen, L., & Emmelkamp, P. (1996). Individual behavioural-cognitive therapy v. marital therapy for depression in maritally distressed couples. *British Journal of Psychiatry, 169*, 181–188.

Fincham, F., Beach, S., Harold, G., & Osborne, L. (1997). Marital satisfaction and depression. *American Psychological Society, 8*, 351–357.

Foley, S., Rounsaville, B., Weissman, M., Sholomaskas, D., & Chevron, E. (1989). Individual versus conjoint interpersonal psychotherapy for depressed patients with marital disputes. *International Journal of Family Psychiatry, 10*, 29–42.

Gilligan, C. (1982). *In a different voice: Psychological theory and women's development.* Cambridge, MA: Harvard University Press.

Golding, J. M. (1999). Intimate partner violence as a risk factor for mental disorders: A meta-analysis. *Journal of Family Violence, 14*(2), 99–132.

Gotlib, I., & Beach, S. (1995). A marital/family discord model of depression: Implications for therapeutic intervention. In N. S. Jacobson & A. S. Gurman (Eds.), *Clinical handbook of couple therapy* (pp. 411–436). New York: Guilford.

Hooley, J., & Licht, D. (1997). Expressed emotion and causal attributions in the spouses of depressed patients. *Journal of Abnormal Psychology, 106*, 298–306.

Hooley, J., Orley, J., & Teasdale, J. (1986). Levels of expressed emotion and relapse in depressed patients. *British Journal of Psychiatry, 148*, 642–647.

Hooley, J., & Teasdale, J. (1989). Predictors of relapse in unipolar depressives: Expressed emotion, marital distress, and perceived criticism. *Journal of Abnormal Psychology, 98*, 229–235.

Jacobson, N. S., Dobson, K., Fruzzetti, A., Schmaling, K. B., & Salusky, S. (1991). Marital therapy as a treatment for depression. *Journal of Consulting and Clinical Psychology, 59*, 547–557.

Jacobson, N., & Margolin, G. (1979). *Marital therapy: Strategies based on social learning and behavior exchange principles.* New York: Brunner/Mazel.

Kung, W. (2000). The intertwined relationship between depression and marital distress: Elements of marital therapy conducive to effective treatment outcome. *Journal of Marital and Family Therapy, 26*, 51–63.

Kurdek, L. (1998). The nature of predictors of the trajectory of change in marital quality over the first 4 years of marriage for first-married husbands and wives. *Journal of Family Psychology, 12*, 494–510.

National Institute of Mental Health. (2001). Depression. NIH Publication No. 00-3561. Retrieved January 16, 2002, from http://www.nimh.nih.gov/

Nolen-Hoeksema, S. (2002). Gender differences in depression. In I. Gotlib & C. Hammen (Eds.), *Handbook of depression* (pp. 492–509). New York: Guilford.

O'Leary, K. D., Christian, J., & Mendell, N. (1994). A closer look at the link between marital discord and depressive symptomatology. *Journal of Social & Clinical Psychology, 13*, 33–41.

O'Leary, K. D., Riso, L., & Beach, S. (1990). Attributions about the marital discord/depression link and therapy outcome. *Behavior Therapy, 21*, 413–422.

Prince, S., & Jacobson, N. (1995). A review and evaluation of marital and family therapies for affective disorders. *Journal of Marital and Family Therapy, 21*, 377–401.

Spanier, G. (1976). Measuring dyadic adjustment: New scales for assessing the quality of marriage and similar dyads. *Journal of Marriage and the Family, 38*, 15–28.

Thibaut, J., & Kelley, H. (1959). *The social psychology of groups.* New York: Wiley.

Waring, E. (1988). *Enhancing marital therapy through cognitive self-disclosure.* New York: Brunner/Mazel.

Waring, E. (1994). The role of marital therapy in the treatment of depressed married women. *Canadian Journal of Psychiatry, 39*, 568–571.

Weissman, M. (1987). Advances in psychiatric epidemiology: Rates and risks for major depression. *American Journal of Public Health, 77*, 445–451.

Weissman, M., & Klerman, G. (1985). Sex differences in the epidemiology of depression. *Archives of General Psychiatry, 34*, 98–111.

Wheeler, J., Christensen, A., & Jacobson, N. (2001). Couple distress. In D.

Barlow (Ed.), *Clinical handbook of psychological disorders: A step-by-step treatment manual* (3rd ed., pp. 609–630). New York: Guilford.

Whisman, M. (2001). The association between depression and marital dissatisfaction. In S. Beach (Ed.), *Marital and family processes in depression: A scientific foundation for clinical practice* (pp. 3–24). Washington, DC: American Psychological Association.

Whisman, M., & Bruce, M. (1999). Marital distress and incidence of major depressive episode in a community sample. *Journal of Abnormal Psychology, 108,* 674–678.

Whisman, M., Sheldon, C., & Goering, P. (2000). Psychiatric disorders and dissatisfaction with social relationships: Does type of relationship matter? *Journal of Abnormal Psychology, 109,* 803–808.

Young, J., Weinberger, A., & Beck, A. (2001). Depression. In D. Barlow (Ed.), *Clinical handbook of psychological disorders: A step-by-step treatment manual* (3rd ed.). New York: Guilford.

Chapter 10

Anderson, C. M., Reiss, D. J., & Hogarty, G. E. (1986). *Schizophrenia and the family: A practitioner's guide to psychoeducation and management.* New York: Guilford.

Atwood, N. (1983). Supportive group counseling for the relatives of schizophrenic patients. In W. R. McFarlane (Ed.), *Family therapy in schizophrenia* (pp. 189–205). New York: Guilford.

Bentley, K. J., & Walsh, J. (2001). *The social worker and psychotropic medication.* Belmont, CA: Brooks/Cole.

Bustillo, J. R., Lauriello, J., Horan, W. P., & Keith, S. J. (2001). The psychosocial treatment of schizophrenia: An update. *American Journal of Psychiatry, 158*(2), 163–175.

Carlisle, W. (1984). *Siblings of the mentally ill.* Saratoga, CA: R & E.

Corcoran, J. & Harakal Phillips, J. (2000). Family treatment with schizophrenia. In J. Corcoran, *Evidence-based social work practice with families: A lifespan approach* (pp. 428–501). New York: Springer.

Dixon, L., Luckstead, A., Stewart, B., & Delahanty, J. (2000). Therapists' contacts with family members of persons with severe mental illness in a community treatment program. *Psychiatric Services, 51*(11), 1449–1451.

Dixon, L., Lyles, A., Scott, J., Lehman, A., Postrado, L., Goldman, H., & McGlynn, E. (1999). Services to families of adults with schizophrenia: From treatment recommendations to dissemination. *Psychiatric Services, 50*(2), 233–238.

Fadden, G. (1997). Implementation of family intervention in routine clinical practice following staff training programs: A major cause for concern. *Journal of Mental Health, 6*(6), 599–612.

Fadden, G. (1998). Family intervention in psychosis. *Journal of Mental Health, 7*(2), 115–122.

Falloon, I., Boyd, J., & McGill, C. (1984). *Family care of schizophrenia.* New York: Guilford.

Goldstein, M. (1996). Psychoeducational family programs in the United States. In M. Moscarelli & A. Rupp (Eds.), *Handbook of mental health economics and health policy: Vol. 1. Schizophrenia* (pp. 287–293). Chichester, UK: Wiley.

Greenberg, J. S., Kim, H. W., & Greenley, J. R. (1997). Factors associated with subjective burden in siblings of adults with severe mental illness. *American Journal of Orthopsychiatry, 67*(2), 231–241.

Karp, D. P. (2001). *The burden of sympathy: How families cope with mental illness.* New York: Oxford University Press.

Laqueur, H. P. (1976). Multiple family therapy. In P. J. Guerin (Ed.), *Family therapy: Theory and practice.* New York: Gardner.

Lefley, H. P. (1996). *Family caregiving in mental illness.* Thousand Oaks, CA: Sage.

Linszen, D. H., Dingemans, P. M. A., Scholte, W. F., Lenior, M. E., & Goldstein, M. (1998). Early recognition, intensive intervention and other protective and risk factors for psychotic relapse in patients with first psychotic episodes in schizophrenia. *International Clinical Psychopharmacology, 13*(Suppl. 1), S7–S12.

Mannion, E. (1997). Resilience and burden in spouses of people with mental illness. *Psychiatric Rehabilitation Journal, 20*(2), 13–23.

Marsh, D. T., Lefley, H. P., Evans-Rhodes, D., Ansell, V. I., Doerzbacher, B. M., LaBarbera, L., & Paluzzi, J. E. (1997). The family experience of mental illness: Evidence for resilience. *Psychiatric Rehabilitation Journal, 20*(2), 3–12.

McFarlane, W. R. (2000). Psychoeducational multi-family groups: Adaptations and outcomes. In B. Chuckdale & A. Bateman (Eds.), *Psychosis: Psychological approaches and their effectiveness* (pp. 68–95). London: Gaskell/Royal.

Milliken, P. J. (2001). Disenfranchised mothers: Caring for an adult child with schizophrenia. *Health Care for Women International, 22*(1–2), 149–166.

Montero, I., Ascencio, A. P., Ruiz, I., & Hernandez, I. (1999). Family interventions in schizophrenia: An analysis of non-adherence. *Acta Psychiatrica Scandinavia, 100*(2), 136–141.

Mueser, K. T., Sengupta, A., Schooler, N. R., Bellack, A. S., Xie, H., Glick, I. D., & Keith, S. J. (2001). Family treatment and medication dosage reduction in schizophrenia: Effects on patient social functioning, family attitudes, and burden. *Journal of Consulting and Clinical Psychology, 69*(1), 2–12.

Pitschel-Walz, G., Leucht, S., Kissling, W., & Engel, R. R. (2001). The effect of family interventions on relapse and rehospitalization in schizophrenia: A meta-analysis. *Schizophrenia Bulletin, 27*(1), 73–92.

Shimodera, S., Inoue, S., Mino, Y., Tanaka, S., Kii, M., & Motoki, Y. (2000). Expressed emotion and psychoeducational intervention for relatives of patients with schizophrenia: A randomized control study in Japan. *Psychiatry Research, 96*(2), 141–148.

Tomaras, V., Mavreas, V., Economou, M., Ioannovich, E., Karydi, V., &

Stefanis, C. (2000). The effect of family intervention on chronic schizophrenics under individual psychosocial treatment: A 3-year study. *Social Psychiatry and Psychiatric Epidemiology, 35*(11), 487–493.

Walsh, J. (2000). *Clinical case management with persons having serious mental illness: A relationship-based perspective.* Pacific Grove, CA: Wadsworth-Brooks/Cole.

Chapter 11

Administration on Aging. (2000). A profile of older Americans: 2000. Washington, DC: Author.

Alzheimer's Association. (2000). *Caregiver stress.* Chicago: Author.

Alzheimer's Association. (2001). *People with Alzheimer's: Frequently asked questions.* Chicago: Author.

American Psychiatric Association. (2000). *Diagnostic and statistical manual of mental disorders* (4th ed., text revision). Washington, DC: Author.

Anderson, C. M., Reiss, D., & Hogarty, G. E. (1986). *Schizophrenia and the family: A practitioner's guide to psychoeducation and management.* New York: Guilford.

Beck, A. T., Rush, A. J., Shaw, B. F., & Emery, G. (1979). *Cognitive therapy of depression.* New York: Guilford.

Biegel, D. E., & Schulz, R. (1999). Caregiving and caregiver interventions in aging and mental illness. *Family Relations, 48*(4), 345–354.

Campbell, T., & Patterson, J. (1995). The effectiveness of family interventions in the treatment of physical illness. *Journal of Marital & Family Therapy, 21,* 545–583.

Corcoran, J., Fairchild-Kienlen, S., & Phillips, J. H. (2000). Family treatment in caregivers of the elderly. In J. Corcoran, *Evidence-based social work practice with families* (pp. 505–559). New York: Springer.

Gallagher-Thompson, D., & DeVries, H. M. (1994). "Coping with frustration" classes: Development and preliminary outcomes with women who care for relatives with dementia. *Gerontologist, 34*(4), 548–552.

Gallagher-Thompson, D., Lovett, S., Rose, J., McKibbin, C., Coon, D., Futterman, A., & Thompson, L. W. (2000). Impact of psychoeducational interventions on distressed family caregivers. *Journal of Clinical Geropsychology, 6*(2), 91–110.

Gallagher-Thompson, D., & Steffen, A. M. (1994). Comparative effects of cognitive-behavioral and brief psychodynamic psychotherapies for depressed family caregivers. *Journal of Consulting and Clinical Psychology, 62,* 543–549.

Haupt, M., Karger, A., & Jaenner, M. (2000). Improvement of agitation and anxiety in demented patients after psychoeducative group intervention with their caregivers. *International Journal of Geriatric Psychiatry, 15*(12), 1125–1129.

Kaplan, H. I., & Sadock, B. J. (1997). *Synopsis of psychiatry* (8th ed.). Baltimore, MD: Williams and Wilkins.

Knight, B. G., Lutzky, S. M., & Macofsky-Urban, F. (1993). A meta-analytic review of interventions for caregiver distress: Recommendations for future research. *Gerontologist, 33*(2), 240–248.

Mace, N., & Rabins, P. (1991). *The 36-hour day.* Baltimore, MD: John Hopkins University Press.

Merck. (2000). *The Merck manual of geriatrics.* Whitehouse Station, NJ: Author.

National Alliance for Caregiving & American Association of Retired Persons. (1997). *Family caregiving in the U.S.: Findings from a national survey.* Washington, DC: Author.

Pandya, S. M., & Coleman, B. (2000). *Caregiving and long-term care.* Washington, DC: American Association of Retired Persons.

Paveza, G. J., Cohen, D., Eisdorfer, C., Freels, S., Semla, T., Ashford, W. J., Gorelick, P., Hirschman, R., Luchins, D., & Levy, P. (1992). Severe family violence and Alzheimer's disease: Prevalence and risk factors. *Gerontologist, 32*(4), 493–497.

Rivera, P. A. (2000). Effectiveness of psychoeducational intervention for the reduction of distress in Mexican-American caregivers of dementia patients. *Dissertation Abstracts International, 60*(8-B), 4248.

Robinson, A., Spencer, B., & White, L. (1991). *Understanding difficult behaviors: Some practical suggestions for coping with Alzheimer's disease and related illnesses.* Ypsilanti, MI: Eastern Michigan University, Alzheimer's Care and Training Center.

Schmidt, G. L., Bonjean, M. J., Widem, A. C., Schefft, B. K., & Steele, D. J. (1988). Brief psychotherapy for caregivers of demented relatives: Comparison of two therapeutic strategies. *Clinical Gerontologist, 7,* 109–125.

Toseland, R. W., Rossiter, C. M., Peak, T., & Smith, G. C. (1990). Comparative effectiveness of individual and group interventions to support family caregivers. *Social Work, 35,* 209–217.

Wolf, R. S. (1998, March-April). Caregiver stress, Alzheimer's disease, and elder abuse. *American Journal of Alzheimer's Disease, 13,* 81–83.